FEMINIST
RESEARCH
PRACTICE

Sharlene wishes to honor her husband, Michael Peter Biber, MD, and their daughters, Sarah Alexandra Biber and Julia Ariel Biber.

Patricia dedicates this book to her father, Bob Leavy.

FEMINIST RESEARCH PRACTICE

A Primer

Sharlene Nagy Hesse-Biber
Boston College

Patricia Lina Leavy
Stonehill College

SAGE Publications
Thousand Oaks ▪ London ▪ New Delhi

Cover: *Galactic Storms,* by Lucy Arnold. Used by permission. For more information about Ms. Arnold's art, please go to www.lucyarnold.com.

For information:

Sage Publications, Inc.
2455 Teller Road
Thousand Oaks, California 91320
E-mail: order@sagepub.com

Sage Publications Ltd.
1 Oliver's Yard
55 City Road
London, EC1Y 1SP
United Kingdom

Sage Publications India Pvt. Ltd.
B-42, Panchsheel Enclave
Post Box 4109
New Delhi 110 017 India

Printed in the United States of America.

This book is printed on acid-free paper.

Library of Congress Cataloging-in-Publication Data

Hesse-Biber, Sharlene Nagy.
Feminist research practice : a primer / Sharlene Nagy Hesse-Biber and Patricia Lina Leavy.
     p. cm.
Includes bibliographical references and index.
ISBN 0-7619-2891-X or 978-0-7619-2891-1 (cloth)
ISBN 0-7619-2892-8 or 978-0-7619-2892-8 (pbk.)
   1. Women's studies. 2. Feminism—Research. I. Title.
HQ1180.H47 2007
305.4207—dc22   2006018378

10   11   12   13   14   7   6   5   4   3

Acquisitions Editor:	Lisa Cuevas Shaw
Editorial Assistant:	Karen Greene
Production Editor:	Laureen A. Shea
Copy Editor:	Quads and Linda Gray
Typesetter:	C&M Digitals (P) Ltd.
Proofreader:	J. G. Robinson
Indexer:	Molly Hall
Cover Designer:	Michelle Kenny

CONTENTS

————•◆•————

Part III: Feminist Praxis

ACKNOWLEDGMENTS

————•◆•————

We appreciate the help of a number of people who supported the work toward this book. We thank the many feminist scholars who let us go "behind-the-scenes" with them and shared their personal stories and insight about feminist research as well as the scholars who took the lead writing chapters for this book.

We are very grateful to our students for their inspiration and support. We want to acknowledge the research assistance we received from so many. Several research assistants from Boston College, Cooley Horner, Melissa Ricker, and Faith Kirkpatrick, were invaluable in their energy and effort to make our manuscript sparkle, and we extend our appreciation to them for their editorial and library research! Thanks as well to the Boston College undergraduate research fellowship grants office.

Our heartfelt thanks to Stonehill graduate Paul Sacco for his tireless help with literature reviews, proofing, and day to day operations. We thank Stonehill students Kim Foley and Kristina Nicastro for formatting the final manuscript and for general research assistance. We also thank Stonehill student Kathryn Maloney for helping with the literature review for the postmodern feminism chapter, Stonehill graduates Lauren Sardi and Leandra Smollin for their help with the literature reviews for the chapters on feminist oral history and content analysis, and Stonehill graduate Laura MacFee for her assistance. We are also grateful to Bonnie Troupe and Kathy Conroy, who run the Summer Undergraduate Research Experience program (SURE) at Stonehill through which we obtained first-rate assistance for this project. Also, Patricia thanks Stonehill College Academic Vice President Katie Conboy, Dean of Faculty Karen Talentino, and Sociology Chairperson Sue Guarino for their mentorship, for supporting a course release to facilitate the completion of this book, and for their unfailing support of faculty research goals. We are also grateful to our friend C. Deborah Laughton for her help with the book proposal. We want to acknowledge the enthusiastic support we received from the staff at Sage Publications. In particular, we extend a spirited thank you to Alison Mudditt, Lisa Cuevas Shaw, Laureen Shea, and Karen Greene.

Sharlene: I want to expresses my love and deepest appreciation to my family, in particular my daughters, Julia Ariel and Sarah Alexandra, for their patience, love, and forbearance. I especially value the friendship, love, and support of my husband, Michael Peter Biber, MD. In addition, I want to thank Jodi Wigren for providing me with encouragement and advice and Kira Stokes, my personal trainer, who reminds me how important it is that we keep our mind in balance with our body and spirit.

Patricia: I dedicate my work on this book to my father, Bob Leavy, who always supports me in all possible ways, and always from a loving and unselfish spirit. Dad, when people ask me about you, I always say the same thing: "My dad is simply a goodness." You are a person of remarkable integrity, reliability, generosity, kindness, goodness-of-spirit, and humor and this does not go unnoticed or unappreciated. Above all, you have a truly remarkable ability to love people exactly as they are, with all of their own interests, oddities, and mistakes, and to celebrate those you love for their own uniqueness. This makes you very special. I love you like crazy! Mom, thanks for being my other best friend, I adore and appreciate you too! As always, to my magnificent daughter, Madeline Claire, who benefits from the sacrifices of pioneering feminists and who will no doubt make her own beautiful contributions on our collective journey. Finally, to the strong women who have helped shape my life, in particular, Aina Smiltens, Mollie Leavy, Helen Leavy, Lydia Vizbulis, Peggy Evangelakos, Liz Loughery, Tara D'Errico, Linda Leavy, Ally Field, Patricia Arend, Janet Landau, and again, my talented, amazing mother, Sylvia Leavy.

PREFACE

---•·◆·•---

THE PEDAGOGY OF THE BOOK

Feminist research is not something that can simply be learned through written explanations. As all feminist researchers and professors know, there is much more to understanding the practice of feminist research than can be gleamed from a laundry list of methods alone. Feminist research is a complex process that intimately links theory, epistemology, and method. To make this book user-friendly for students and scholars alike, and to get inside the practice of feminist inquiry, we have included a distinct feature in this book. We introduce exciting "Behind-the-Scenes" vignettes that relate the experiences of sociologists who are navigating and exploring new levels of inquiry.

When thinking about the complexity of writing about feminist research, we quickly realized two things. First, feminism is not one thing, nor is there a feminist methodology per se. Feminism is a window onto the social reality and encompasses a wide range of perspectives and practices. As such, feminism is multivocal. With this in mind, we wanted to make sure that multiple feminist voices come through this text. One of the ways of accomplishing this was to invite contributing authors for some of the chapters of this book. We invited authors to take the lead by writing chapters where we felt they offered a special level of knowledge, insight, and experience on the particular subject.

We also wanted to make sure that multiple voices were offered in all the chapters of the book. In this vein, and inspired by Erving Goffman's notion of "front stage" and "back stage," we began to realize that the information available in many books on research methods represents the "front stage" of the research process. In other words, most books on research methods present definitions of key terms and concepts followed by descriptions of research methods and models for how to design a research project. What this kind of approach fails to get at is the complexity of the *practice* of social research. What guides researchers' topic selection? How do epistemological beliefs and theoretical commitments come to bear on the research process? What values, issues, and motivations do researchers bring to their projects? How do ethics play out in practice? What are the emotional aspects of a research project *really like*? Why do some researchers select particular methods and how do those methods enable their research? These are critical questions and considerations in the practice of feminist research that explicitly require a synergy between the various components of the research process. In an attempt to get at some of these issues, we have invited well-known feminist researchers to contribute pieces about a range of epistemological and methodological concerns as well as "tales from the field," so to speak—experiences feminists have had employing some of the methodological options reviewed in this text. The rich texts they have generously shared with us are included throughout the book in what we call "Behind-the-Scenes" boxes. These boxes offer a glimpse behind the curtain of feminist research—a window into the feminist researcher's vantage point.

ABOUT THE AUTHORS

Sharlene Nagy Hesse-Biber, PhD, is Professor of Sociology at Boston College in Chestnut Hill, Massachusetts. She has published widely on the impact of sociocultural factors on women's body image, including her book *Am I Thin Enough Yet? The Cult of Thinness and the Commercialization of Identity* (1996), which was selected as one of *Choice* magazine's best academic books for 1996. She is coauthor of *Working Women in America: Split Dreams* (2005). She is coeditor of *Feminist Approaches to Theory and Methodology: An Interdisciplinary Reader* (1999), *Approaches to Qualitative Research: A Reader on Theory and Practice* (2004), and *Emergent Methods in Social Research* (Sage, 2006). She is also coauthor of *The Practice of Qualitative Research* (Sage, 2006). She is editor of the *Handbook of Feminist Research: Theory and Praxis* (Sage, 2006) and author of two upcoming books, *The Cult of Thinness* and a primer on mixed methods (forthcoming). She is codeveloper of the software program HyperRESEARCH, a computer-assisted program for analyzing qualitative data, and the new transcription tool Hyper-TRANSCRIBE (www.researchware.com).

Patricia Lina Leavy, PhD, is Assistant Professor of Sociology at Stonehill College in Easton, Massachusetts. She is also the Founder and Director of the Gender Studies Program at Stonehill College. She has published articles in the areas of collective memory, mass media, popular culture, body image, feminism, and qualitative research methods and is regularly quoted in newspapers for her expertise on popular culture, current events, and gender. She is coauthor of *The Practice of Qualitative Research* (Sage, 2006) and coeditor of *Approaches to Qualitative Research: A Reader on Theory and Practice* (2004) and *Emergent*

Methods in Social Research (Sage, 2006). She is also the author of *Iconic Events: Media, Power and Politics in Retelling History* (forthcoming). She wrote much of this book while listening to the music of Tori Amos.

ABOUT THE
CHAPTER CONTRIBUTORS

Abigail Brooks is a PhD candidate in Sociology at Boston College. Her areas of interest include feminist theory, sociology of gender, critical gerontology and feminist age studies, sociology of the body, science and technology studies, and social theory. Her dissertation investigates women's lived experiences and interpretations of growing older against the contextual backdrop of growing prevalence, acceptance, and approval of cosmetic surgery. She has recently published an article titled "'Under the Knife and Proud of It': An Analysis of the Normalization of Cosmetic Surgery" in *Critical Sociology.*

Elana D. Buch is a PhD candidate in the Joint Program in Social Work and Anthropology at the University of Michigan. She is broadly interested in studying the relationships between social policy, kinship practices, and women's paid and unpaid labor. Her dissertation research focuses on how differences in kinship ideologies and care experiences influence practices of paid home care of elders in the United States. She holds an MSW from the University of Michigan School of Social Work and an MA in Anthropology from the University of Michigan.

Toby Epstein Jayaratne is a research psychologist at the University of Michigan. She currently directs a national study exploring Americans' beliefs about possible genetic influences on perceived gender, class, and race differences and on sexual orientation. Her academic interests focus on the use of genetic explanations to justify and support various social and political ideologies. She has written and presented several papers on the topic of feminist methodology. She received her PhD in Developmental Psychology from the University of Michigan.

Denise Leckenby is a PhD student of Sociology at Boston College. Her areas of interest include qualitative methodology, feminist methodology, feminist theory, and sexuality. She is coeditor of *Women in Catholic Higher Education: Border Work, Living Experiences and Social Justice* (2003).

Kathi Miner-Rubino is Assistant Professor of Psychology at Western Kentucky University. She has published several papers in the areas of gender, social class, and psychological well-being. Her most recent publications focus on vicarious exposure to the mistreatment (i.e., incivility and harassment) of women in work settings. She teaches courses in social psychology, psychology of women, and research methods. She received her PhD in Psychology and Women's Studies from the University of Michigan.

Karen M. Staller is Assistant Professor at the University of Michigan School of Social Work. Her research interests include the study of runaway and homeless youth, child sexual abuse, and the intersection of law and social work. She has conducted community-based, interdisciplinary research as well as historical projects. She teaches in the areas of social welfare policy, qualitative research methods, and social work and the law. She holds a PhD from Columbia University and a JD from the Cornell University School of Law.

ABOUT THE BEHIND-THE-SCENES CONTRIBUTORS

Kristin L. Anderson is Associate Professor of Sociology at Western Washington University. Her recent publications on gender and partner violence include "Theorizing Gender in Intimate Partner Violence Research," in *Sex Roles* (2005) and "Perpetrator or Victim? Relationships Between Intimate Partner Violence and Well-Being," in *Journal of Marriage and Family* (2002).

Maxine Birch is Lecturer in Mental Health at the Faculty of Health and Social Care at the Open University. Her PhD research established her interest in looking at narratives and stories to make sense of lived experiences. Her discussion of alternative psychotherapies, self-identity stories, and expressions of spirituality is published in *Post-Modernity, Sociology & Religion* (1996). She has also written about several aspects of the research process encouraged and supported by her involvement in a feminist network of academic researchers. She discusses the autobiographical approach in *Feminist Dilemmas in Qualitative Research* (Sage, 1998) and the research relationship when engaged in interviews for researching private and personal experiences (*International Journal of Social Research*, 2000). She was one of the editors for *Ethics in Qualitative Research* and contributed a chapter to examine participation in research ("Encouraging Participation: Ethics and Responsibilities," Sage, 2002).

Lisa Cosgrove, PhD, is Clinical and Research Psychologist in the Graduate College of Education in the Department of Counseling and School Psychology at the University of Massachusetts at Boston. She is coeditor, with Paula Caplan, of *Bias in Psychiatric Diagnosis* (2004) and author of several of its chapters. She has published articles and book chapters on critical psychology, social policy issues, research methods, and theoretical and philosophical issues related to clinical practice. Her research has been supported through grants from NIMH (to the Murray Center, Radcliffe Institute, Harvard University) and from the University of Massachusetts. She was a Fellow in the William Joiner Center for the Study of War and Social Consequences (2002–2003), and she has conducted research on the intergenerational impact of war-related PTSD.

Lisa Dodson is Research Professor of Sociology at Boston College. For over two decades she has been conducting research, teaching, and contributing to public policy about low-income America.

Antoinette Errante is Associate Professor of Comparative Education and History of Education at The Ohio State University. Her research in the United States and Southern Africa has focused on the role of schooling in social movements and identity formation. She has also conducted comparative research on violence, reconciliation, and healing as cultural practices.

Sandra Harding teaches Philosophy of Social Science and Postcolonial and Feminist Studies at the University of California at Los Angeles. She has written or edited 14 books and special issues of journals that focus on feminist and postcolonial epistemology, methodology, and philosophy of science. *The Feminist Standpoint Theory Reader: Intellectual and Political Controversies* was published in 2004 and *Science and Social Inequality: Feminist and Postcolonial Issues* in April 2006. She coedited *Signs: Journal of Women in Culture and Society* from 2000 to 2005, and she is currently working on a manuscript titled *Women, Science, and Modernity*.

Shirley A. Hill is Professor of Sociology at the University of Kansas, where she teaches classes on the family, medical sociology, qualitative research, and social inequality. Her research has focused on health policies, especially as they affect families, and how race, class, and gender inequalities shape families. The latter is the focus of her most recent book, *Black Intimacies: A Gender Perspective on Families* (2005). She is also the author of *African American Children: Socialization and Development in Families* (Sage, 1999) and *Managing Sickle Cell Disease in Low-Income Families* (1994), both based on qualitative research. She is Deputy Editor for the *Journal of Marriage and Families* and has served on many committees for the American Sociological Association and Sociologists for Women in Society.

Dana Crowley Jack holds an EdD in Human Development and Psychology. She is Professor at Fairhaven College of Interdisciplinary Studies/Western Washington University and the author of *Behind the Mask: Destruction and Creativity in Women's Aggression* (1999), *Silencing the Self: Women and Depression* (1991), and *Moral Vision and Professional Decisions* (1989), as well as articles and chapters on women's psychology. The Silencing the Self scale, designed to test her theory of women's vulnerability to depression, as well as the book, has been translated into numerous different languages. She was a Fulbright Senior Scholar to Nepal in 2001, teaching in the graduate Women Studies program of Tribhuvan University and conducting research on gender and depression in Nepal. She is currently editing a book on international perspectives on women's self-silencing and depression.

David Karp is Professor of Sociology at Boston College. He is the author of *The Burden of Sympathy* (2002); *Speaking of Sadness: Depression, Disconnection, and the Meanings of Illness* (1997); *Being Urban: A Sociology of City Life* (1994); *Sociology in Everyday Life* (1993); *Experiencing the Life Cycle: A Social Psychology of Aging* (1993); and *The Research Craft: An Introduction to Social Research Methods* (1992). He received his PhD from New York University in 1971.

Süheyla Kirca Schroeder is working at Bahcesehir University, Faculty of Communications. She has published a variety of articles on the issues of gender, identity and representation, feminist cultural studies, popular culture and media, globalization of culture, music, and youth. In addition to her academic work, she took part in the "Women's Leadership and Democracy Building" project (2004–2005), and she is working on a project titled "Violence Against Women in Turkey." She completed her PhD in British Cultural Studies at the University of Warwick, England, her MA in Media and Culture at the University of Strathclyde, Scotland, and she has a BA in Social Anthropology, Istanbul University, Turkey.

Patti Lather is Professor in the Cultural Studies in Education Program, School of Educational Policy and Leadership, at Ohio State University, where she teaches qualitative research in education, feminist methodology, and gender and education. She began her career as a faculty member at Mankato State University in Women's Studies. She has held visiting positions at the University of British Columbia, Göteborg University, and the Danish

Pedagogy University as well as a 1995 sabbatical appointment, Humanities Research Institute, University of California-Irvine, seminar on feminist research methodology. She was the recipient of a 1989 Fulbright to New Zealand. She is the author of two books, *Getting Smart: Feminist Research and Pedagogy With/In The Postmodern* (1991 Critics Choice Award) and *Troubling the Angels: Women Living with HIV/AIDS*, coauthored with Chris Smithies (One of CHOICE's Outstanding Academic Titles for 1998). Her articles have appeared in *Harvard Educational Review, Qualitative Studies in Education, Educational Theory*, and *Signs: Journal of Women in Culture and Society*. Her most recent publications include "Scientific Research in Education: A Critical Perspective," a joint publication in the *British Educational Research Journal* and the *Journal of Curriculum and Supervision* and "This IS Your Father's Paradigm: Governmental Intrusion and the Case of Qualitative Research" in *Qualitative Inquiry*. She has chapters in the *Handbook of Research on Teaching* (edited by V. Richardson, 2001), *Working the Ruins: Feminist Theory and Methods in Education* (edited by E. St. Pierre and W. Pillow, 2000), and *The Handbook of Ethnography* (edited by P. Atkinson et al., 2001). She is working on a manuscript, *Getting Lost: Feminist Efforts Toward a Double(d) Science,* under contract with SUNY Press. Her hobby aspirations include learning to play the accordion and bridge.

Deborah Piatelli is an activist and PhD student of Sociology at Boston College, where she is writing her dissertation on the challenges contemporary mobilizations for peace and social justice face as they work across race, class, and gender.

Judith Preissle is the 2001 Distinguished Aderhold Professor in the qualitative research program at the College of Education, University of Georgia (UGA), and an affiliated faculty member of UGA's Institute for Women's Studies. She began her career teaching middle grades in 1965, and she has worked at UGA since 1975, where she teaches, researches, and writes in educational anthropology, qualitative research, gender studies, and ethics. Her spouse, a computer network manager at UGA, and their two miniature schnauzers and two Chinese pugs share her interest in philosophical quandaries.

Diana E. H. Russell is Professor Emerita of Sociology at Mills College, Oakland, California. She is the author, coauthor, editor, or coeditor of 17 books, most of which are on sexual abuse and/or sexual violence against women and girls. She was corecipient of the 1986 C. Wright Mills Award for the outstanding social science research exemplified in her book *The Secret Trauma: Incest in the Lives of Girls and Women.* Her other groundbreaking books include *The Politics of Rape*; *Rape in Marriage*; and *Sexual Exploitation: Rape, Child Sexual Abuse, and Workplace Harassment.* She has also been a pioneer in activism. Her dream of an International Tribunal on Crimes Against Women was implemented in Brussels, Belgium, in 1976, when more than 2,000 women from 40 countries met to participate and testify against patriarchal crimes against us. Simone de Beauvoir saluted the International Tribunal as being "the beginning of a radical decolonization of women."

Leah Schmalzbauer is Assistant Professor of Sociology at Montana State University and member of the executive board of Proyecto Hondureño in Chelsea, Massachusetts. She researches and writes on the daily life strategies of poor transnational families. She continues to pursue participatory research in the United States and Central America.

ONE

AN INVITATION TO FEMINIST RESEARCH

Abigail Brooks

Sharlene Nagy Hesse-Biber

———◆◆◆———

RIDING THE TRAIN WITH ALICE AND MARIE

On a recent train ride between New York City and Boston, Sharlene was struck by a conversation between two college-aged women sitting nearby. Because these young women were talking about feminists and their ideas, Sharlene couldn't help being interested in what they had to say. In the course of their talk, it became clear that these young women, whom we'll call Alice and Marie, were attending an Ivy League university and had gone to private schools most of their lives. Here is a short excerpt from their conversation as Sharlene recollects it:

Alice: I really think feminists have gone too far, they think that women are treated unfairly all the time. Just the other day, I ran across one of my high school friends and she's really changed—she wasn't wearing any makeup and she'd cut off all her hair and it was really short and her clothes, you know, she didn't look feminine at all! Anyway, she was ranting and raving about how women are underpaid and they are harassed in the workplace. I couldn't even listen to her. You know?

Marie: These women are so ideological; they are so radical and have no facts to back them up! My friend Sally is just the same, she goes on and on about inequality. I have never been discriminated against and I feel like the women's movement is something passé. These girls just can't get over it. You know?

As we embark on the journey of this book, we can't help thinking about this train ride conversation and want to share it with you. In many ways, Alice and Marie's ideas about feminist identity and what feminism means are framed by their everyday experiences. As white middle- to upper-middle-class females who attend a highly esteemed Ivy League school, they may not have bumped up against gender discrimination in their own daily lives. Feminism does not appear to be a central aspect of Alice and Marie's world, nor does it inform the lives of individuals in their personal and familial networks. For both Alice and Marie, the issues feminists advocate are a thing of the past— feminist concerns with issues of social justice and social change for women are primarily ideological in nature and don't really exist. Alice and Marie also hold stereotypical ideas and views about feminists (no makeup, short hair, and a lack of femininity), and they view them as a single, unified category that implies all feminists come with the same political ideas as well as body image.

What would we say to Marie and Alice about feminists and feminism if we had the opportunity to engage in a conversation? We would begin by say-ing that feminists come in all sizes, shapes, and colors. Some dress up in high-fashion clothing from Neiman Marcus and have long hair. Some don't have enough money to buy makeup or fashionable clothing; some do not buy into these ideas of beauty and fashion. Some are married and partnered with or without children, others are single, some are straight, some are transgendered, and some are gay. Some are religious and some are not. The notion that there is a proper way to look, act, and behave in the world as a feminist is to rein-force the stereotype that distances both Alice and Marie from feminist con-cerns and issues.

Feminists hail from different classes, races, and cultures and have lived through different life experiences. While many share some common goals, such as gender equality, social justice for women, and an emphasis on the concerns and issues of women and other oppressed groups, not all feminists are cut from the same cloth, nor do they share the same values, perspectives, and interests. Alice knows a feminist who has short hair, doesn't wear makeup, holds strong convictions, and is an activist. While Alice views these characteristics negatively, they can easily be understood as positive attributes, and conjure up positive associations with feminism, for another. But where Alice and Marie's conclusion really goes wrong—and requires an impossible leap of logic—is in the assumption that all feminists have short hair, wear no makeup, and hold the same views and perspectives.

Alice and Marie may not have encountered any gender-related bias, discrimination, oppression, or struggle in their own daily lives. It is imperative, however, to recognize that most feminist views and perspectives are not simply ideas, or ideologies, but *rooted in the very real lives, struggles, and experiences of women.* In fact, Alice and Marie's apparent lack of gender-related discrimination and bias in their own daily lives can be attributed, in large part, to the ongoing hard work and activism on the part of women throughout the last several decades. The gains and contributions that feminist researchers and activists have made toward overcoming widespread gender stereotypes and improving women's rights and equality across the globe are significant and should not be taken for granted. It is only in the last 25 to 35 years that many colleges and institutions of higher learning have opened their doors to women. Laws protecting women against sexual harassment in the workplace did not come to fruition until the early 1990s. Women are entering the workforce and joining previously male-dominated professions such as law, business, and medicine in increasing numbers, and gender-based discrimination in hiring and promotions has declined. On the other hand, women continue to earn only 70% of the salary men earn in equivalent positions, and they are underrepresented in the fields of science and engineering and in upper-level positions in law, business, and medicine. A lack of affordable child care and inflexible corporate environments can make balancing work and family difficult for many working women. The feminization of poverty is increasing—women and girls make up a large and growing percentage of the world's poor—and violence against women and girls continues to expand globally in new and particularly virulent forms (Hesse-Biber & Carter, 2005).

Thousands of women from all points on the globe face a diverse array of challenges on a daily basis, and there are many different struggles and actions that we, as women, engage with and participate in. Those described above are only a few of the many women-centered issues and concerns that continue to motivate feminist activists and underscore the need for feminist, women-centered research. It is probably safe to say, however, that most feminists, whether activists, researchers, or both, continue to share some central concerns, goals, and commitments, including giving voice to women's lives and experiences, improving the quality and life chances and choices for women and girls, and overcoming gender inequality and the oppression of women.

WHAT IS FEMINIST RESEARCH?

Feminist research is primarily "connected in principle to feminist struggle" (Sprague & Zimmerman, 1993, p. 266). By documenting women's lives, experiences, and concerns, illuminating gender-based stereotypes and biases, and unearthing women's subjugated knowledge, feminist research challenges the basic structures and ideologies that oppress women. Feminist research goals foster empowerment and emancipation for women and other marginalized groups, and feminist researchers often apply their findings in the service of promoting social change and social justice for women.

Just as we cannot reduce all women to one group with a uniform experience, race, class, or culture, there is no one single method, methodology, or epistemology that informs feminist research. Feminist researchers hold different perspectives, ask different questions, draw from a wide array of methods and methodologies, and apply multiple lenses that heighten our awareness of sexist, racist, homophobic, and colonialist ideologies and practices. Some feminists use traditional methodologies but ask new sets of questions that include women's issues and concerns, while others rework, or even radically upset, traditional epistemologies and methodologies. In fact, to unearth hidden aspects of women's lives and those of other oppressed groups, and to reclaim subjugated knowledge, some feminist researchers continue to develop new epistemologies, methodologies, and methods of knowledge building altogether.

Feminist research is a holistic endeavor that incorporates all stages of the research process, from the theoretical to the practical, from the formulation of research questions to the write-up of research findings. Feminist researchers emphasize the synergy and interlinkages between epistemology, methodology, and method and are interested in the different ways that a researcher's perspective on reality interacts with, and influences, how she goes about collecting and analyzing her data (Charmaz, 2006; Hesse-Biber & Leavy, 2006). An *epistemology* is "a theory of knowledge" that delineates a set of assumptions about the social world and about who can be a knower and what can be known (Harding, 1987, p. 3). The researcher makes decisions rooted in these assumptions that influences what is studied (based on what *can* be studied) and how the study is conducted. A *methodology* is a theory of how research is done or should proceed (p. 3). Finally, a *method* is a "technique for (or way of proceeding in) gathering evidence" (p. 2).

It is the primary task of this book to provide you with a hands-on under-standing of how feminists build knowledge through the practice of research. This means introducing you not only to the theories developed by feminist researchers that inform feminist research, but also to *how feminist researchers actually go about applying these theories in their research projects.* What is the relationship between a particular theory of knowledge building, or episte-mological framework, the questions a feminist researcher asks, and the methods she uses to collect her data? And how might the questions a feminist researcher asks influence her choice of research methods and shape her epis-temological framework? In this book, we hope to expose you to the diverse range of theoretical and epistemological frameworks, methodologies, methods, and research questions that make up feminist research. Finally, we cannot underestimate the interconnection between feminist research and activism. In this book, you will learn about the different ways that activism forms an integral component and motivation for feminists at all stages of the research process: from questions, to methods, to findings.

THE ORIGINS OF FEMINIST RESEARCH

To discuss feminist research without any mention of feminist activism would be nonsensical, even impossible, because feminist research *originated within the context of the second wave feminist movement.*[1] As female scholars and students participated in feminist consciousness-raising groups throughout the late 1960s and 1970s, they became increasingly aware of glaring contradic-tions between their lived experiences as women and mainstream research models, studies, and findings. In the words of feminist sociologist Dorothy Smith, the theories and methods being taught did not apply to "what was hap-pening" as the female students "experienced it" (Smith, 1987, p. 86). These contradictions led early feminist scholars to illuminate a shortcoming within a range of academic disciplines and in mainstream social science research, namely the omission of women and the lack of accurate representation of women's experiences. Women were often left out of scholarship and research samples all together, and research topics consistently failed to take women's activities and experiences into account. Furthermore, mainstream theoretical and methodological frameworks often proved ineffective, falling short of fully reflecting women's perspectives. The failure of academic scholarship and mainstream research to "give voice" to women's activities, experiences, and perspectives provoked early feminist scholars and researchers to seek remedies for these omissions. These remedies included the reworking of traditional theoretical and methodological techniques and the creation of new research models altogether.

THE FEMINIST CRITIQUE OF POSITIVISM

By calling attention to the invisibility of their experiences in social science research and to the contradictions between their lived experiences as women and mainstream social science findings, feminists launched a powerful critique of one of the most broad-reaching paradigms in social science—positivism.[2] Positivism originated in the late 1800s and evolved out of the European rationalist and empiricist movements. Rationalist thought, characterized by the Cartesian mind-body split and the privileging of the mind over the bodily, subjective, and emotional realms, and empiricism, with its emphasis on objective observation and its origins in the scientific revolution, combined to form the basis for the positivist paradigm in sociology. Positivist social scientists, like rationalists and empiricists, assert the existence of an objective reality, or truth, lying out there to be discovered. They also advocate the application of particular methods for the accurate illumination of that objective reality.

Within the positivist paradigm, it is the external or objective reality that serves as the basis of "fact" and "truth" and it is within this objective reality that pure, invariable, and universal knowledge must be sought after and potentially realized. The classic sociologist Émile Durkheim (1938/1965), following within the positivist tradition, distinguishes facts from values: values stem from individual consciousness and thus are mere interpretation, riddled with variability, whereas facts lie "outside of the human mind," have an "independent existence outside of the individual consciousness," and are therefore objective, unchanging, and free from contamination. In other words, facts, "far from being a product of the will . . . determine it from without" (p. 20).

In promoting the discovery of "facts" to increase knowledge of objective reality and universal, unchanging truth, positivists advocate the use of objective and neutral instruments of measurement as applied by the objective and value-free researcher. John W. Murphy states, "Positivism implies that methodological techniques are value-free. . . . By following certain techniques, interpretation can be overcome and facts revealed" (Murphy, 1989, p. 38). In *The Rules of Sociological Method*, Durkheim (1938/1965) provides us with a set of guidelines, or methods, that must necessarily be applied to conduct objective, value-free research and will ultimately lead to the discovery of universal truth, absolute knowledge, or in Durkheim's words, "social facts." The methods advocated by Durkheim are largely quantitative in nature, and positivism continues to provide an epistemological grounding for quantitative research. Quantitative researchers often use survey data and statistical analysis to test hypotheses and causal relationships, to measure and predict large-scale patterns, and to produce findings that are considered generalizable.

By starting from women's previously invisible experiences, exposing the underrepresentation of these experiences within the positivist research paradigm, and finally, highlighting the ways in which women's experiences often contradicted mainstream research findings, feminists posed a serious challenge to the so-called value neutrality of positivistic social science. Feminist scholars and researchers' illumination of women's experiences disrupted the positivist claim to universal knowledge, and the so-called objective methodologies that accompanied and justified that claim. Indeed, feminists exposed the dominance of the positivist paradigm as stemming not from its objectivity or its universality, but from its privileged location within a historical, material, and social set of patriarchal power relations. In short, despite all claims to the contrary, knowledge building was never value-free, social reality was not static, and positivism or social scientific inquiry in general did not exist outside of the social world.

The following Behind-the-Scenes piece consists of an excerpt from an interview with renowned feminist scholar and philosopher Sandra Harding, titled "Starting from Marginalized Lives: A Conversation with Sandra Harding" and conducted by Elizabeth Hirsch and Gary A. Olson (1995). In it,

Harding challenges positivist claims to objectivity and value neutrality and critiques the traditional standards and methods that accompany these claims. She illuminates the various ways that women have been excluded and marginalized from dominant Western knowledge canons throughout the course of history. However, unlike some feminist researchers and scholars, Harding does not reject the concept of "objectivity" altogether. Instead, she reclaims, redefines, and renames it "strong objectivity," such that the experiences and voices of marginalized others, including women, are not only incorporated but serve as the starting point for building knowledge. Researchers and scholars who practice "strong objectivity" do not begin from a position of so-called value neutrality. They have a clear political and social commitment to strengthening the truthfulness and objectivity of knowledge claims—in other words, to taking the voices and experiences of the silenced and marginalized into account.

Behind-the-Scenes With Sandra Harding

Q. In many of your works you have argued that "maximizing objectivity in social research requires not total value neutrality, but instead, a commitment by the researcher to certain social values." You then demonstrate that "social research directed *by certain* social values can be more objective than research in which these values play no role." Would you elaborate on this notion of "strong objectivity"?

A. For one thing, there's a certain range of social values (if you want to talk about it that way) and interests that the conventional standards for objectivity have no way of getting at—namely, the values or interests that are shared by an entire, let me put it in these terms, "scientific community." This is not a problem that feminism or, certainly, that I have invented. It's one that Kuhn is talking about when he's discussing paradigm shifts; it's the problem of the episteme. There's a long history by now, three decades or more, of suspicion in the West that the objectivity that the West prizes so highly has been flawed and that the standard ways of trying to maximize it in fact have not been effective. Again, I'm trying to indicate it's not just the "radical" groups that have raised this; it's somebody like Richard Bernstein, for instance. In his *Beyond Objectivism and Relativism,* he reviews the problems in a variety of different social science and philosophic tendencies that are associated with a notion of objectivity, and in each case it seems to come down to pretty much the same thing: the paradigms, the conceptual frameworks, within which methods are defined. Those methods can't then turn around their lens and look at the conceptual framework that generated them in the first place, right? And that, of course, has been the kind of argument that's been so powerfully mounted in feminism and antiracism and so on. The issue is not the sexism of individuals; it's the androcentric assumptions of the conceptual schemes of philosophy, of sociology, of economics.

Let me give some pointed examples from my own discipline. Look at the dominant conceptions of human nature in philosophic traditions. Aristotle says that man is a rational animal, and yet women have been persistently described, by him and everybody else all the way up, as emotional, as concerned with their passions, as irrational. So we would say that you can't add "women as rational animals" to a conceptual scheme that in the first place has been defined *against* the feminine. It ends up that a rational woman is in a certain sense a contradiction in terms of that conceptual scheme. But that's an assumption that escapes notice until you try to bring into that category a group that's been excluded from it. Aristotle also says that what's distinctive about man is that he's a political animal—he constructs his way of life through public discourse, public meetings—and yet women have been excluded from participation in the public realm. We could pretty much go through every definition of what's distinctively human and notice that women have been excluded from it. The "worker" that Marx is particularly concerned with: women have been excluded from positions in wage labor of the sort that Marx had in mind when he was looking at the nineteenth-century proletariat. Then we could come to "humans as language users," and yet a good woman is like a child: seen but not heard. Women have not been permitted public speech. We could look at sociology's ways of defining community as constructed by public and visible and dramatic actors rather than the informal and less-visible and less-dramatic ways in which women and other minority groups have in fact contributed to community organization. We could look at any discipline and see that the standard methods for maximizing objectivity are unable to get at these large widely shared assumptions and interests that in fact define the conceptual framework of the field. Another way to put the issue is that the way scientific method in any discipline tries to identify and eliminate social factors is by repeating observations across individuals— you repeat the experiment, having somebody else test out the validity of your claims—but if all the people who are repeating the experiment share

(Continued)

(Continued)

the same values, as members of any culture would do, then that method is flawed. So, a strong objectivity is an attempt to develop stronger standards. Feminists and antiracists and other members of the new social movements have certainly criticized the notion of objectivity in a variety of ways, but for the most part they want *more* objective accounts. We need more objective accounts of how our bodies work, how the international political economy works, what causes environmental destruction, what effects industrialization is going to have on the environment and on the social structure, and so forth. We don't need *less* objective accounts, and we don't need subjective accounts. The problem is that we've *had* subjective accounts—or ethnocentric accounts, I guess we could call them. So, strong objectivity is an issue, to put it in an extremely simplistic way, of learning to see ourselves as others see us. (What's that Robert Burns said, "Oh, would some power the gift give us/To see ourselves as others see us!"?) It's an argument for stepping outside of the conceptual framework, starting off research projects, starting off our thought about any particular phenomenon, from outside the dominant conceptual framework. Marginal lives are at least one good place, one good strategy for doing that. Starting off thinking about Western conceptions of rationality from the lives of people who have been excluded and who are claimed to be constitutionally unable to exhibit that rationality—racial minorities, the working class, lesbians and gays, women of ethnic groups of various sorts—is a good way to be able to identify those widely shared values and interests that have framed the dominant ways of thinking about the notion of rationality.

SOURCE: Reprinted with permission from Hirsch and Olson (1995).

In many respects, feminist empiricism (discussed in the next section) embodies the practice of "strong objectivity." Most feminist empiricists remain committed to the achievability of objective research findings. However, they critique the claims to objectivity and value neutrality within traditional, positivist research methods and findings because such methods and findings fail to take women's lives and experiences into account. Feminist empiricists seek to produce stronger, more objective, more truthful results through including women in their research studies and by documenting women's lives and experiences that have been previously marginalized or left out of dominant knowledge canons altogether.

FEMINIST MODIFICATIONS TO
THE POSITIVIST PARADIGM

Some feminist researchers continue to find affinity with the basic epistemo-logical and methodological characteristics of positivist research (that objec-tive, value-free knowledge exists and is attainable through the application of neutral, value-free instruments of measurement) but advocate reworking tradi-tional positivist approaches to include women's experiences. Other feminist researchers discard positivism altogether and focus on the development of alternative epistemological and methodological frameworks, and they may favor qualitative research as more consistent with their research objectives and guiding epistemological beliefs.

Feminist researchers who remain committed to the basic tenets of posi-tivism, such as the potential application of value-free research methods and the attainment of objective research findings, are often termed *feminist empiri-cists.*[3] However, feminist empiricists have sought to improve the accuracy and objectivity of positivist research by modifying traditional positivist methods to take women's activities and experiences into account. They have also pushed for the inclusion of women in research samples, guided research toward top-ics and issues that hold relevance for women, and remodeled some traditional, positivist methods to ensure greater reflection of women's experiences. Some feminist empiricists assert that these new positivist research techniques, inclu-sive of women's activities and experiences, increase the potential for neutral, objective, and generalizable research findings.

New empirical data gathered by feminist researchers have contributed to "setting the record straight" by revealing the previously silenced or forgotten experiences of many women. Feminist researchers have also drawn on the strengths of empiricism to document the social construction of gender roles and to garner new empirical evidence that challenges dominant norms of femininity. For example, the archival research conducted by Laurel Thatcher Ulrich (1991) teaches us about the courage and skill of an American midwife practicing in the late 18th and early 19th centuries. Joan M. Jensen (1977) uses archival data to document the political power and control wielded by the Native American women of the Seneca tribe in the 18th and early 19th centuries. Ruth Milkman's (1987) archival content analysis documents the American media's radical reconstruction and deconstruction of women's roles during and immediately after WWII, while Emily Martin's (1991) narrative analysis reveals a prevalence of gender stereotypes and biases imbedded in the descriptions of reproduction in mainstream medical and biology textbooks. These are just a few examples of the wealth of empirical data collected by feminist researchers that expose previously unknown and/or repressed experiences of women and disrupt traditional, essentialist beliefs pertaining to women's capacities and behaviors. By collecting new empirical data, feminist researchers continue to remedy the shortcomings and omissions, and even to improve the objectivity and empirical accuracy, of mainstream research studies, models, and findings. The vast contributions of feminist empiricists are reviewed in Chapter 2 of this book.

FEMINIST ALTERNATIVES TO THE POSITIVIST PARADIGM

As noted above, many feminist researchers, feminist empiricists among them, continue to rework and modify aspects of the positivist paradigm such that women's experiences are included *while adhering to* the basic positivist principles and goals of objective, value-free research methods and the potential for neutral, generalizable research findings. Other feminist scholars and researchers (including, more recently, some feminist empiricists) have embarked on a more fundamental critique of the positivist paradigm, challenging the methodological techniques that accompany it and the epistemological assumptions that inform it. Instead of modifying positivist methods to improve the potential for conducting value-free research that yields objective, universal findings, many feminists openly question the viability and utility of neutral, value-free research methods and the positivist concept of objectivity itself. They ask, Can so-called value-free research give full voice to women's knowledge and experiences? Finally, the methodologies that flow from positivism often rely on a strict separation between the knower and that which is conceptualized as knowable. Put differently, there is a sharp divide between the subject and object, the researcher and the researched. In positivist research models, the researcher may be privileged as the knowing party and placed on a higher plane than the researched. Many feminists question the utility and ethics of such a design.

These feminist researchers and scholars argue that to more fully illuminate women's knowledge and experiences, we must engage in what Dorothy

Smith terms an "alternative way of thinking" (Smith, 1990, p. 20) about research and knowledge building.[4] This alternative way of thinking refutes the positivist notion that there exists a fixed and unchanging social reality, or some truth lying "out there" to be discovered, and the viability of the objective researcher and neutral, value-free tools of empirical observation. Most important, however, this approach incorporates interpretation, subjectivity, emotion, and embodiment into the knowledge-building process, elements historically associated with women and excluded from mainstream, positivist research. Indeed, many feminist researches and scholars have begun to illuminate potential new sources of knowledge and understanding precisely *within* the lived experiences, interpretations, subjectivities, and emotions of women. Instead of viewing these aspects as contaminants or barriers to uncovering *the objective truth*, feminist researchers explain how paying attention to the specific experiences and situated perspectives of human beings, both researchers and respondents alike, may actually become a *tool* for knowledge building and rich understanding.

Joyce McCarl Nielsen (1990), Donna Haraway (1991), Alison Jaggar (1997), and Helen Longino (1999) are just a few of the feminist scholars and researchers who continue to expand the potential for new and meaningful forms of inquiry outside the positivist, empirical framework. Joyce McCarl Nielsen calls our attention to the fact that all researchers carry their particular worldviews, histories, and biographies with them into their research projects, while Donna Haraway explores the situated aspects of knowledge building. According to Nielson, worldviews are not necessarily corrupters of knowledge or truth, but instead can be understood as "maps" that guide researchers to particular research topics with which they find affinity, or to particular respondents with whom they share rapport. Similarly, Haraway argues that our situated location—our particular biography, history, and positionality—does not have to be perceived as a barrier to achieving knowledge or truth but instead can offer each of us a unique way of seeing the world, a "focusing device" so to speak, through which we may be able to catch, see, and/or understand phenomena in ways that others cannot.

Helen Longino and Alison Jaggar illuminate the interconnections between knowledge and the body and knowledge and emotion. By reclaiming the bodily and emotional realms as sources of knowledge, Longino and Jaggar actively refute the rationalist, Cartesian mind-body split (for Descartes, the body was associated with irrationality, emotion, and deception—it was only the mind, or the "disembodied self," that could perform acts of pure reason) *and* the positivist, empirical tradition of the detached, objective, value-free observer. Longino (1999) argues that knowledge *is* "possible for the embodied subject" and that our bodies are situated in "particular places, in particular times, oriented in a particular way to their environments" (p. 133). The situated locations of our bodies serve not as contaminants to building knowledge but instead as potential "cognitive resources" that direct our attention to "features . . . that we would *otherwise overlook* [italics added]" (p. 335). On a similar note, Jaggar urges us not to cleanse ourselves of our emotions to achieve some notion of objective truth or knowledge but instead to pay closer attention to our emotions and listen to them more carefully. For Jaggar, emotions are a "necessary feature of all knowledge and conceptions of knowledge" (Jaggar, 1997, p. 190). Emotions give our lives meaning and contribute to our survival—they prompt us when to "caress or cuddle," when to "fight or flee" (p. 191).

These feminist scholars and researchers profess that by discarding positivist assumptions of the value-free researcher, the actuality of an objective reality, and the realizability of universal, fixed, and objective truth, we do not lose the ability to build knowledge. In fact, rather than dismissing human emotions and subjectivities, unique lived experiences, and worldviews as contaminants or barriers to the quest for knowledge, we might embrace these elements to gain new insights and understandings, or in other words, *new knowledge.* After all, why do researchers who could study any number of topics, from any number of angles, end up selecting a particular topic? A researcher's personal experience, emotions, and worldview may serve as the impetus for the creation of a research project or guide the choice of a research topic. For example, if domestic violence or disordered eating has touched your life in some way or you feel compelled to work toward the equality and safety of women or girls, this may be an area you are particularly interested in studying. Rather than being removed from your passions, your research project may be derived from them, or at least from your interests, which have been shaped by many things.

This feminist epistemological framework offers a *new* form and application of inquiry that is necessarily inclusive of, and pays close attention to, elements such as personal experience, subjectivity, positionality, worldview, and emotion. As Helen Longino explains, this new form of feminist inquiry is at once *"honest and value laden"* (Longino, 1999, p. 349). But how do feminist researchers actually go about collecting their data within this new feminist epistemological framework? And how do issues of experience, positionality, subjectivity, emotionality, and embodiment interact with the feminist research process and influence the kinds of questions feminists ask and the methods they use? Here we can draw from Dorothy Smith's (1990) statement about sociology—"If sociology cannot avoid being situated then sociology should take that as its beginning and build it into its methodological strategies" (p. 22)—and apply it to the multiple disciplines within which feminists are conducting research. In this book you will be introduced to feminists' new and innovative use of interviewing, oral history, and ethnography techniques. For instance, we will explore collaborative interviewing styles whereby the "interaction" between researcher and respondent "produces the data" (Anderson & Jack, 1991; Charmaz, 1995, p. 9) and the researcher draws from her own lived experience to "co-construct" new words that more accurately reflect her respondents feelings and experiences (DeVault, 1990). Indeed, feminist researchers are increasingly open about their own positionalities, perspectives, and worldviews and engage in collaboration with their respondents throughout *all phases* of the research process, from data gathering and analysis (Borland, 1991) to writing and authorship (Horne & McBeth, 1998).

Most of the feminist scholarship and research discussed in this section indicates a shift away from goals of value neutrality and claims to objectivity in the research process. The researcher is encouraged to openly acknowledge, and even to draw from, her situated perspective in the course of her research project. In the following Behind-the-Scenes piece (also excerpted from the interview conducted by Hirsch & Olson 1995), Sandra Harding revisits the concept of strong objectivity. Many feminist scholars and researchers challenge the viability and utility of objectivity for the feminist research project. However, Harding illuminates another aspect of strong objectivity—called "strong reflexivity"—that resonates with the feminist emphasis on situated knowledge described above. Strong reflexivity is the manifestation of strong objectivity through method. It requires the researcher to be cognizant and critically reflective about the different ways her positionality can serve as both a hindrance and a resource toward achieving knowledge throughout the research process.

Behind-the-Scenes With Sandra Harding

Some people are coming to understand that maximizing objectivity requires a stronger method, a more expansive notion of method, and what that is is a production of strong reflexivity. That is, it's coming to see that the fact that the observer changes, interacts with the object of observation, with what he or she's looking at, is not necessarily a negative, having a negative influence on the results of research, but can be used in a positive way. That is, it's understanding that we can use the resources of the particular place from which we speak in order to gain stronger method and stronger objectivity; strong reflexivity requires that.

Now, what does it mean to have socially situated knowledge, to use the place from which we speak as a resource, a part of the method, a part of the instruments of inquiry? Let me take myself as an example. Everybody writes about reflexivity in all kinds of different ways, but it's hardly ever seen as a resource. It's seen as a problem or a dilemma or something to be gotten around, or it's seen stoically: "Alas, there's nothing you can do about it." Consequently, the way it's enacted frequently is as a confessional: "I, a white woman from Newark, Delaware. . . ." You do the confession, and then you do the analysis as if your confession takes care of it. . . . That doesn't even begin to get at the problem. It leaves all the analysis up to the reader. It leaves the reader to ask, "Well, what is the relationship between the fact that Sandra Harding is a white woman, an academic from Delaware, and her analysis? And she's a philosopher, and a feminist, and so forth; what effect does *that* have on her analysis?" The point is for the author, the observer, to make that analysis, to do that work. It's lazy and irresponsible to leave that work up to the audience. It pretends that it doesn't matter at all. The feminist standpoint theory which I've been a part of developing enables us to see the value of that. Strong objectivity asks us to take a critical look at the conceptual schemes, the frameworks, that *comprise* our social location. What are the assumptions I'm making as somebody who comes from Anglo-American analytic philosophy at this moment in history and who's trained in logical positivism? How does that lead me to frame questions and projects that are actually less than maximally objective, that are constrained by my particular social location? So the first set of questions to enable one to strengthen reflexivity, to use reflexivity as a resource, is to do that analysis, to look at a field's conceptual frameworks. It's not so much, "I, Sandra Harding, white woman. . . ," but that's an issue.

The question is, "How have the conceptual frameworks that I'm using been shaped to fit the problems of white women in the West more generally?"

So the first step is to do the kind of critique the various new social movements in fact are doing of the conceptual frameworks of the West and its disciplines, its political policy, and its philosophy. But there's a step beyond that, and that's to try and rethink how one's social location can nevertheless be used as a resource in spite of the fact that we're members of dominant groups. There's been a tendency to think that only the dominated, only the marginalized can use their social location as an instrument of the production of knowledge. They certainly *can* use it and *do* use it, but it's also the case that the people in the dominant groups can learn how to use their position (as a white woman in my case; for another, say, as a white man) to ask the kinds of questions and think the kinds of thoughts that would make use of the resources of that particular position. For example, I'm very familiar with Western philosophy; insofar as I don't ask questions about those assumptions, that's an obstacle to my gaining a less Eurocentric perspective on the world and on philosophy. But I also know that tradition fairly well, so if I *do* turn the critical lens on it, I can learn; I'm in the place to be able to do that. And it's something that I have an obligation to do. I'm using my position in a way that somebody who comes from another tradition might not. Why should they spend all *their* time criticizing Western philosophy? I don't think we should leave to the victims of the West the burden of having to do the whole critique of the West. That's a resource that we have an obligation to use; we're familiar with it so we should learn to do that critique ourselves. Those of us who are in these dominant positions *are* in dominant positions: our voices have a lot of power, and that's a resource. It's unfortunate that the world is hierarchically organized, that we do have power relations; but given that we do, I think that those people who do have classrooms to teach in, and whose papers do get accepted in journals read all over the world, and whose publishers do publish their books, are a local resource that we can use in scientifically and politically progressive ways.

SOURCE: Reprinted with permission from Hirsch and Olson (1995).

Sandra Harding urges all individuals, including women, in the dominant groups to be self-critical and to use their power in "politically progressive ways." In the next section, we hear from women in the less-dominant groups. We are reminded to be mindful and respectful of differences between women, to be aware of the multitude of ways that race, class, and gender intersect in an individual woman's lived experience, and to be cognizant and watchful of power dynamics and differentials throughout the research process.

THE TURN TOWARD DIFFERENCE
IN FEMINIST THEORY AND PRACTICE

Early feminist scholars and researchers called attention to the invisibility and misrepresentation of women in academic scholarship across many disciplines and in mainstream social science research. Revealing and correcting this widespread androcentric bias became the primary work of many feminist researchers. Other feminist researchers and scholars began to ask new questions and develop new epistemological frameworks and research methods that took women's lives and experiences into account and that valued women's life stories as knowledge. But which women's stories were being told? Whose experiences were included and whose were left out? Without denying the importance and significance of these early feminist contributions, it is also important to note that many pioneering feminists focused on women as a universal category and overlooked the diversity among and between women's lives and experiences. In this way, much of this early feminist research focused on the issues of importance to white, middle- and upper-class women and neglected the issues of import to women of color and working-class women.

Feminists of color exposed the shortcomings of early feminist research and prompted white feminists to examine white privilege as a form of oppression (McIntosh, 1995). As Hirsch and Keller (1990) put it, "Feminists of color have revealed to white middle-class feminists the extent of their own racism" (p. 379). Feminists of privilege have come to realize that by listening to the experiences of the "other," and engaging in dialogue with poor women and women of color, they gain a more complete, accurate, and nuanced understanding of social reality. Black feminist sociologist Patricia Hill Collins (1990) argues, for example, that to survive and flourish in an overwhelmingly white society, black women must navigate the rules of a privileged white world while negotiating their own marginalized social position—a position that reflects race, class, and gender. Through understanding these aspects of black women's lives, it becomes abundantly clear that the privileged, academic positionality of sociological insiders places them "in no position to notice the specific anomalies apparent to Afro-American women, because these same sociological insiders produced them" (Collins, 1990, p. 53).

Feminist researchers and scholars of color also illuminate vast interconnections among categories of difference concerning gender, ethnicity, race, and class (Anzaldúa, 1987; Collins, 1990; hooks, 1984, 1990; Mohanty, 1988). Patricia Hill Collins (1990) stresses the complex interlinkages between race, class, and gender—or what she terms the *matrix of domination*. Collins's matrix of domination can be applied to conceptualize difference along a range of interlocking inequalities of race, class, and gender. These socially constructed factors inflect each other, and it is only through collectively examining the intricate connections between them that we can fully understand a given individual's life experience.

By asking the questions "which women?" and "whose experiences?" feminists of color have broadened the scope of feminist research. Feminist researchers and scholars of color continue to develop new theoretical frameworks and methodological strategies that take a diverse range of women's lives, experiences, and cultures into account. In the chapter on feminist standpoint epistemology in this book (Chapter 3), you will learn about how feminist scholars of color have problematized the concept of the standpoint of women, arguing instead that women hold multiple standpoints across a diversity of classes and cultures. For example, Patricia Hill Collins illuminates a standpoint of and for black women and emphasizes the interrelations between race, class, and gender that contribute to the construction of that standpoint (Collins, 1990). In the chapter on interviewing techniques (Chapter 5), you will learn about some of the issues and dilemmas, the possibilities and the dangers, that confront feminist researchers in the context of studying across difference. What can we learn, for example, from the research and scholarship of feminists of color about studying difference? Are there particular interviewing strategies that are more respectful and work better at building connections across difference than others?

THE CHALLENGE AND POSSIBILITIES OF THE POSTMODERN PERSPECTIVE FOR FEMINIST RESEARCH

In many respects, feminist research goals and pursuits find affinity with postmodern and poststructural perspectives. Due in large part to the scholarship and research of feminists of color, but also to feminism's interaction with post-colonial, poststructural, and postmodern perspectives, most feminists have discarded the notion of one essential experience of women in favor of a plurality of women's lived experiences. The postmodernist emphasis on bringing the "other" into the research process also "meshes well with the general currents within the feminist project itself," as feminists from all traditions have always been "concerned with including women in their research in order to rectify the historic reliance on men as research subjects" (Hesse-Biber, Leavy, & Yaiser, 2004, p. 18). Like many feminists, postmodernists challenge social science research paradigms such as positivism and reject notions of universality, objectivity, and truth with a capital "T" in favor of multiple, situated, and constructed interpretations of social reality. Finally, the postmodernist emphasis on empowering oppressed groups finds resonance with the feminist commitment to "political cultural resistance to hierarchical modes of structuring social life" and with feminists' attention to "the dynamics of power and knowledge" (p. 18).

Postmodern and poststructural perspectives can invigorate feminist theories and praxis. However, some feminists worry that the postmodern emphasis on social construction, interpretation, multiplicity, plurality, and difference may dilute and diffuse the feminist commitment to social change and social justice for women. Some feminists ask, "With so much attention being placed on multiple interpretations of social reality, and difference between and among women, do women lose the capacity to identify commonalities, to engage in dialogue, and to come together as an organized force for social change?" Other feminists wonder, "Can we take seriously, and fight, women's very real, material experiences of oppression if we adhere to the postmodern privileging of interpretation and social construction?" As Sharlene Hesse-Biber, Christina Gilmartin, and Robin Lydenberg (1999) point out, there are some potential risks, dangers, and losses that come with an increasing fragmentation and polarization among and between feminist theorists, researchers, and activists. According to Michelle Barrett and Ann Phillips, the fear now expressed by some feminists is that with the "changing theoretical fashions [postmodernism among them] . . . we may stray too far from feminism's original project" (Barrett & Phillips, 1992, p. 6). The utility and affinity of the postmodern perspective for feminist research, and the struggles and debates among and between feminists about the advantages and limitations of postmodernism and poststructuralism will be thoroughly reviewed in Chapter 4 of this book.

ORGANIZATION OF THE BOOK

Our primary goal in writing this book is to provide you with a grounded understanding of the principle epistemological, theoretical, and methodological approaches that inform feminist research. The organization of the book reflects feminist holistic practice and highlights the synergy between the epistemological and methodological strands of the research process. Part I of the book focuses on the major epistemological and theoretical groundings that guide many feminists in their research and includes chapters on feminist empiricism, feminist standpoint theory, and feminist postmodernism. In Part II, we review a diverse array of research methods employed by feminist researchers and address the linkages between particular methods and feminist epistemological frameworks and perspectives. You will learn about how particular methods have been used to serve feminist research agendas and how different methods and methodologies are useful at different times and in different contexts. We even include a chapter on multimethod designs to illustrate how feminists sometimes merge qualitative and quantitative paradigms in the service of feminist research goals. Examples of empirical research will be provided. Part III of the book examines the feminist practice of analysis and interpretation of research findings.

We hope that in reading this book, you will come to realize the many different ways that feminist research can serve as a vehicle for women's empowerment. Data collected by feminist empiricists challenge gender biases and "set the record straight." Feminist archival, content, and narrative analyses document the social and historical construction of gender roles. Feminist ethnographers illuminate the links between dominant, constrictive notions of femininity, women's everyday experience, and larger systems/structures of power. Formally silenced and disenfranchised women speak out through the forum of feminist oral history and intensive interviews. These are just a few examples of the many ways that feminist research empowers women.

We extend to you our personal invitation to make this exciting journey with us!

NOTES

1. This is not to dismiss the work of the many courageous and talented women who contributed to knowledge building before the 1960s. However, our point here is

that feminist research—as a new branch of theories, methodologies, and methods—was consciously named and constructed as part of, and resulting from, the women's movement of the 1960s and 1970s.

2. A *paradigm* implies a particular worldview, model, or approach to knowledge building. The positivist paradigm includes an epistemological set of assumptions, in other words an approach to knowledge building or inquiry, and the theoretical and methodological models that accompany that approach. (See Kuhn, 1962; Nielsen, 1990, for a more detailed explanation of our application of the term *paradigm*.)

3. *Empiricist* implies an empirical approach to knowledge building, one based on the traditional scientific method of objective, neutral (sensory-based) observation.

4. While Dorothy Smith uses this phrase, or concept, in the context of discussing the discipline of sociology, we find it useful to apply this concept to social science research and knowledge building more generally. Please see Dorothy Smith (1990, pp. 19–24), *The Conceptual Practices of Power: A Feminist Sociology of Knowledge,* for more explanation and analysis.

REFERENCES

Anderson, Kathyrn, & Jack, Dana C. (1991). Learning to listen: Interview techniques and analyses. In Sherna Berger Gluck & Daphne Patai (Eds.), *Women's words: The feminist practice of oral history* (pp. 11–26). New York: Routledge.

Anzaldúa, Gloria. (1987). *Borderlands/la frontera: The new mestiza.* San Francisco: Spinsters/Aunt Lute.

Barrett, Michele, & Phillips, Anne. (1992). *Destabilizing theory: Contemporary feminist debates.* Stanford, CA: Stanford University Press.

Borland, Katherine. (1991). "That's not what I said": Interpretive conflict in oral narrative research. In Sherna Berger Gluck & Daphne Patai (Eds.), *Women's words: The feminist practice of oral history* (pp. 63–75). London: Routledge.

Charmaz, Kathy. (1995). Grounded theory. In Jonathan A. Smith, Rom Harre, & Luk van Langenhove (Eds.), *Rethinking methods in psychology* (pp. 27–49). Thousand Oaks, CA: Sage.

Charmaz, Kathy. (2006). What's good writing in feminist research? What can feminist researchers learn about good writing? In Sharlene Nagy Hesse-Biber (Ed.), *Handbook of feminist research: Theory and praxis.* Thousand Oaks, CA: Sage.

Collins, Patricia Hill. (1990). *Black feminist thought: Knowledge, consciousness, and the politics of empowerment.* Boston: Unwin Hyman.

DeVault, Marjorie. (1990). Talking and listening from women's standpoint: Feminist strategies for interviewing and analysis. *Social Problems, 37*(1), 96–116.

Durkheim, Émile. (1965). *The rules of sociological method* (8th ed.; S. A. Solovay & J. H. Mueller, Trans.). New York: Free Press. (Original work published 1938)

Haraway, Donna J. (1991). *Simians, cyborgs, and women: The reinvention of nature.* New York: Routledge.

Harding, Sandra. (1987). Introduction: Is there a feminist method? In S. Harding (Ed.), *Feminism and methodology* (pp. 1–14). Bloomington: Indiana University Press.

Hesse-Biber, Sharlene, & Carter, Gregg Lee. (2005). *Working women in America: Split dreams*. New York: Oxford University Press.

Hesse-Biber, Sharlene, Gilmartin, Christina, & Lydenberg, Robin (Eds.). (1999). *Feminist approaches to theory and methodology: An interdisciplinary reader*. New York: Oxford University Press.

Hesse-Biber, Sharlene Nagy, & Leavy, Patricia. (2006). *The practice of qualitative research*. Thousand Oaks, CA: Sage.

Hesse-Biber, Sharlene Nagy, Leavy, Patricia, & Yaiser, Michelle, L. (2004). Feminist approaches to research as a *process*: Reconceptualizing epistemology, methodology, and method. In Sharlene Nagy Hesse-Biber & Michelle L. Yaiser (Eds.), *Feminist perspectives on social research* (pp. 3–26). New York: Oxford University Press.

Hirsch, Elizabeth, & Olson, Gary A. (1995). Starting from marginalized lives: A conversation with Sandra Harding. *JAC: A Journal of Composition Theory, 15*(2), 193–225. Retrieved July 7, 2006, from http://Jac.gsu.edu/jac/15.2/Articles/1.htm

Hirsch, Marianne, & Keller, Evelyn Fox. (1990). Practicing conflict in feminist theory. In Marianne Hirsh & Evelyn Fox Keller (Eds.), *Conflicts in feminism* (pp. 370–385). New York: Routledge.

hooks, bell. (1984). *Feminist theory: From margin to center.* Boston: South End Press.

hooks, bell. (1990). *Yearning: Race, gender, and cultural politics*. Boston: South End Press.

Horne, Esther Burnett, & McBeth, Sally. (1998). *Essie's story. The life and legacy of a Shoshone teacher*. Lincoln: University of Nebraska Press.

Jaggar, Alison M. (1997). Love and knowledge: Emotion in feminist epistemology. In Sandra Kemp & Judith Squires (Eds.), *Feminisms* (pp. 188–193). Oxford: Oxford University Press.

Jensen, Joan M. (1977). Native American women and agriculture: A Seneca case study. *Sex Roles: A Journal of Research, 3*, 70–83.

Kuhn, Thomas. (1962). *The structure of scientific revolutions*. Chicago: University of Chicago Press.

Longino, Helen E. (1999). Feminist epistemology. In John Grecco & Ernest Sosa (Eds.), *The Blackwell guide to epistemology* (pp. 327–353). Malden, MA: Blackwell.

Martin, Emily. (1991). The egg and the sperm: How science has constructed a romance based on stereotypical male-female roles. *Signs, 16*(3), 485–501.

McIntosh, Peggy. (1995). White privilege and male privilege: A personal account of coming to see correspondences through work in women's studies. In Margaret L. Andersen & Patricia Hill Collins (Eds.), *Race, class, and gender: An anthology* (pp. 76–86). Belmont, CA: Wadsworth.

Milkman, Ruth. (1987). *Gender at work: The dynamics of job segregation by sex during World War II*. Urbana: University of Illinois Press.

Mohanty, Chandra. (1988). Under Western eyes: Feminist scholarship and colonial discourses. *Feminist Review, 30*, 61–88.

Murphy, John W. (1989). *Postmodern social analysis and criticism.* New York: Greenwood Press.

Nielsen, Joyce McCarl. (1990). Introduction. In Joyce McCarl Nielsen (Ed.), *Feminist research methods: Exemplary readings in the social sciences* (pp. 1–37). Boulder, CO: Westview Press.

Smith, Dorothy E. (1987). Women's perspective as a radical critique of sociology. In Sandra Harding (Ed.), *Feminism and methodology* (pp. 84–96). Bloomington: Indiana University Press.

Smith, Dorothy E. (1990). *The conceptual practices of power: A feminist sociology of knowledge.* Boston: Northeastern University Press.

Sprague, Joey, & Zimmerman, Mary K. (1993). Overcoming dualisms: A feminist agenda for sociological methodology. In Paula England (Ed.), *Theory on gender/ feminism on theory* (pp. 255–280). New York: Aldine de Gruyter.

Ulrich, Laurel Thatcher. (1991). *A midwife's tale. The life of Martha Ballard based on her diary 1785–1812.* New York: Vintage Books.

PART I

FEMINIST APPROACHES TO
EPISTEMOLOGY AND THEORY

TWO

FEMINIST EMPIRICISM

Challenging Gender Bias and "Setting the Record Straight"

Denise Leckenby

———•◆•———

T here is a common misconception that feminism and empiricism are incompatible. However, important research that has combined the tenets of feminism and empiricism has contributed and continues to contribute significantly to our understanding of gender and inequality.

- What makes feminist research empiricist?
- What makes empiricist research feminist?

The process of answering these two grounding questions draws us in from two distinct directions—into the terrain of feminist empiricist approaches to epistemology and their uses of methodology and method. Feminist empiricists ask many types of questions within many types of research disciplines. Unlike other feminist researchers, their work is not limited to either the natural sciences or the social sciences. Grounded in their empiricist epistemologies, they work across many methods and many research questions, affecting traditional paradigms of knowledge building in important ways. *Empiricism* refers to the position and belief that the only knowledge source available to us is that which can be experienced and measured by our senses. For Richmond Campbell (1994), empiricism relies on "the norms of predictive success, observation independence, and explanatory power" (p. 90). Campbell uses this delineation of empiricist standards to argue against Sandra Harding's (1986, cited in Campbell, 1994) critique of feminist empiricism, stating that "if feminism were internal to empiricism, then wouldn't it contain the very contradiction that critics attribute to the concept of feminist science? For if empiricist norms by their nature demand that a researcher be apolitical in testing hypotheses, how can there be a methodology for constructing and evaluating scientific tests that is at once both empiricist and feminist?" (Campbell, 1994, p. 93). Campbell argues for an internalization of feminist political goals within empiricist research, a different tactic from arguing that empiricism research methods should be internal to feminist political goals.

Embedded in this long tradition of research inquiry, feminist empiricists seek to understand the world around them, grounding their methodologies in what their senses can know and what their methods can measure. With other empiricists, feminist empiricists are located firmly in the positivistic belief that the social and natural world at large is accessible and understandable. As positivists, feminist empiricists want to develop knowledge that is objective and truthful; they believe strongly that such knowledge is obtainable. They are remarkable in their commitment to the positivist tools of research where their work takes place within already established structures of epistemology and methodology.[1] Their work is powerful in its assertions, commanding attention because it speaks from within the establishment of positivist science.

Although located resolutely in positivism, feminist empiricists also critique the practices and products of the traditional scientific establishment. Feminist empiricist research is connected to its feminist perspective as strongly as it is engaged with positivistic approaches. In her introduction to a special issue of *Signs* on gender and science, historian of science Londa Schiebinger (2003) notes that this

> research embodies many core feminist values . . . eliminating research that leads to exploitation of nature or other humans, resisting explanations stripped of social and political context . . . acknowledging our values and beliefs, being honest in our assumptions, being responsible in our language. (p. 861)[2]

Such goals are resolutely feminist in their perspective, shaping the research in various ways yet open to effort made by feminist empiricists to maintain their location within the positivist paradigm. Helen Longino (1990) states that "feminism is many things to many people, but at its core it is about the expansion of human potentiality" (p. 190). Such an expansion of human potentiality was impossible while women were not included in both the subject matter and the processes of knowledge building. Early on in the 20th century, women researchers began to realize and fight against the sometimes systematic and always pervasive exclusion of women and women's experiences from research questions and samples. Armed with their feminist perspective and positivist tools, they sought to create a "better" and more objective science. They have shown how traditional positivism's androcentric biases were and are built into positivism, leaving us with subjective rather than objective knowledge about our world. Committed to developing knowledge that is inclusive of women, feminist empiricists have sought knowledge that benefits the lives of women, accurately represents their experiences, and sheds light on the truth of human realities. They argue that science as a whole should aim for and achieve a better, more objective study, where the research process is more complex and factual when the political, social, and cultural implications of the research are taken into consideration.

COUNTING WOMEN IN:
SEEKING IGNORED AND OBSCURED TRUTHS

Feminist empiricists, through their politically steeped epistemology, aim to include women in the questions that the social sciences and natural sciences have traditionally asked. Both part of and influenced by second-wave feminist movements, an initial task at hand for feminist empiricists was aimed at changing the face of traditional, androcentric science. Androcentric science takes into account only the masculine or the male perspective and unit of analysis in research. Such research extrapolates knowledge gained from such questions to account for the entire human population, leaving out women's voices, their experiences, and the feminine altogether. Feminist empiricists approach this problem not by radically altering traditional modes of inquiry and traditional epistemological and ontological perspectives about the nature of reality or by throwing out established methods of research. Rather, they seek to push their empirical questions and empiricist methods to address and remedy the biases that lead the traditional positivist paradigm to produce less than objective results. They have sought to show, and prove, how women, when included in traditional research samples, often change the outcome of the research answers. Inclusion of women and gender in the research endeavor produces more truthful and less androcentric knowledge. Feminist empiricists sought and fought to show that neglecting to account for women's experiences took away from any objective goals that the sciences were trying to obtain. Positivistic science, the traditional paradigm for the social science research endeavor, built itself on the foundations of objectivity, reason, and truth seeking. As feminist empiricists began to draw women into the empirical pursuits, they began to show that traditional positivism was not objective at all.

Seeking the Truth of the Unnamed: Sexual Harassment

What does androcentric bias look or feel like? Imagine for a moment that nowhere in literature revolving around issues of sexuality and violence can you find any discussion of the realities of a particular woman's daily experiences with her male supervisor who continues to proposition her for sex. Imagine in fact that there is no name for this particular woman's problem, no term to describe this event. She cannot look for examples of her issue in legal texts. Her human resource manager does not have any policy standards by which to address her problem. This woman's experience is not studied in sociological research about the workplace. In fact those texts speak very little about her role in this company as a woman, let alone talk about what to do when sexual advances are made by male superiors or colleagues. This ongoing event in this particular woman's life is not known. Until the 1970s, sexual harassment remained unquestioned in the academic and public spheres because, "from men's perspective, sexual harassment, was neither salient nor a problem. Unhampered by sexual harassment, men had no compelling reason to distinguish it from the flux of ordinary life by naming it" (Bingham, 1994, p. 19). Imagine that a destructive and disruptive part of your work life is not even mentioned as an issue. Androcentric science begins and ends with men's experiences. In this case, androcentric science's assessment and understanding of the workplace held the nonobjective view that sexual harassment was a nonissue.

With other feminist researchers and activists, feminist empiricists identified that there was a problem that needed to be examined and understood in order to expand women's potentiality within the workplace. Uniting feminist political pursuits with a quest for empirical knowledge, feminist empiricists began to survey populations of women in the workplace to gain a more objective understanding of what was going on. Lynn Farley (1978) was the first feminist to conceptualize and theorize sexual harassment in the workplace. She built her research and theoretical concepts around consciousness-raising groups among working women, all of whom had experiences similar to our particular woman's. "The male behavior eventually required a name, and sexual harassment seemed to come about as close to symbolizing the problem as language would permit" (Farley, 1978, p. xi). Once the concept of sexual harassment had begun to be formulated, the question quickly became one of what was happening and to how many women. The absence of sexual harassment as an actual, knowable event, hidden by androcentric bias within the realm of knowledge building, was quickly being remedied in the late 1970s. The next step for researchers was to understand the who, what, when, where, and how of sexual harassment. Feminists were not the only researchers working on sexual harassment, nor were empiricists the only feminists in the field. But the contribution of feminist empiricists in the realm of sexual harassment research and policy added important and critical dimensions that grounded the knowledge we have about sexual harassment in its social and political context.

Androcentric science serves to eliminate perspectives, issues, and context that are central to producing knowledge that should accomplish positivist demands for truth and objectivity and could achieve feminist goals for expanding human potentiality. "Feminist empiricists maintain that sexism and androcentrism are identifiable biases of knowers that can be eliminated by stricter application of scientific and philosophical methodologies" (Goldman, 1999, p. 34). Feminist empiricists believe that everything that we need to gain knowledge about the objective reality of our lives is already at hand—it just needs to be used better. Imagine how a feminist empiricist would aim to gain insight into the general issue of sexual harassment. Her positivistic perspective would likely lead her down a path of deductive reasoning, whereby her knowledge and reading of the field of research already conducted concerning sexual harassment would help her formulate a hypothesis. She might notice through her literature review that androcentric biases seem to be at play in much of the research already conducted. For example, she notices that no one is thinking about or researching sexual harassment from a perspective that takes into account the inequality of the genders. No one is working on testing how power inequality might be related to incidences and responses to sexual harassment.

Within a field of knowledge, androcentric bias does not facilitate acknowledgment of the complex context of political and social situations to be part of the research endeavor. The feminist lens through which this particular researcher views the world and the research context enables her to produce research and knowledge that is more objective. By taking into account the context of power relations and inequality between the genders in the work environment, this feminist empiricist opens up new questions concerning the objective reality of sexual harassment. Her empiricist perspective might lead her to test her newly formed hypothesis with a sociological experiment, a statistical survey, or even a series of qualitative interviews, always in pursuit of the empirical data that measure and represent reality. Androcentric biases build an environment where research and knowledge about the world at large do not objectively test or measure reality and do nothing to expand human potentiality. Feminist empiricists seek better and more objective science by doing away with androcentric science.

Seeking the Truth Quantitatively

Counting women into empirical pursuits for knowledge not only refers to elimination of the androcentric bias of science, as seen in the example of sexual harassment, but it also refers to the quantitative inclusion of women in research samples and populations. Unlike other feminist researchers, feminist empiricists have tended to be the most accepting of traditional methods of inquiry such as quantitative research methods.[3] Many feminist empiricists use quantitative methodologies and survey tools to examine questions at hand. Quantitative research methods, although only one of the tools available for research endeavors, lend themselves particularly well to empirical pursuits. Quantitative research for many feminists requires a location in a positivistic paradigm, seeking knowledge that lends itself to generalizable and quantifiably significant statements.

Many feminist empiricists have argued and demonstrated that using quantitative methods does not have to be mutually exclusive from feminist political pursuits (Jayaratne, 1983). Although feminist empiricists were eager to maintain and work with the power of statistical research design, they also brought their feminist lens and critical perspective to bear on the method to make it better. Early feminist empiricist researchers were interested in critiquing survey research biases that were built with gendered and cultural assumptions that went unnoticed by traditional positivistic science. These researchers located these biases as one problem that reduced the objectivity of the research tool (Unger, 1979). During the 1980s, feminist empiricists aimed to theorize and use methodologies and methods that were nonsexist and develop research that would not discriminate against one gender (Griffin & Phoenix, 1994).[4] By drawing gender, culture, and context into quantitative survey methods, feminist empiricists highlighted the profoundly subjective and patriarchal assumptions that were built into the tools researchers employed.

Traditional positivist survey research methods tended to make women invisible. Quantitatively including gender as a variable in survey research served to illuminate and complicate research findings in a variety of research disciplines. Conducting survey research as a feminist implies a political engagement to look at the world with attention to gender dimensions and differences. Gender and women become the visible part of the story told by the statistical truths examined by feminist empiricists. Returning to our example of sexual harassment, one can certainly imagine what a quantitative research design employed by a traditional nonfeminist positivist might look for and find. Such research would see that sexual harassment is a real, knowable occurrence affecting significant numbers of women in a variety of workplaces. Such research would likely seek to find answers and solutions to the problem of sexual harassment.

But imagine what is left out when a feminist lens is not applied to the quantitative survey questions, the data analysis, and the text produced. Without a feminist lens to this particular empirical question, it is likely that an understanding of sexual harassment as an impediment to women's advancement within the workplace would be unexamined. For example, a feminist empiricist analysis would require questions and variables in the survey's design that measure the salary and promotion rates of men and women. Such measurement and analysis would require attention to women's equality. Gender difference and questions of power would likely go unexamined within a quantitative research design that was lacking a feminist perspective.

Just because research is conducted on women's lives does not mean that it is for women. Feminist values aim to resist explanations that are devoid of their social and political context. Feminist empiricists believe that the social and political context of the research question is measurable and observable. They also believe that the context is a pivotal piece of good research. Without the context, research produced is less than objective. Quantitative survey research may engage matters of great importance to women (such as sexual harassment), but counting women in from a feminist perspective requires that the social and political contexts of gender and power be a part of the truths told. Feminist empiricists who use quantitative research methods argue that they are particularly well positioned to create social change for women in meaningful ways.[5] They insist that statistics speak volumes to those in power. Roberta Spalter-Roth and Heidi Hartmann (1999) argue for a vision that attempts to "synthesize the views of two generations—to create research that meets both the standards of positivist social science and feminist goals of doing research 'for' rather than 'on' women" (p. 333). Feminist empiricists often begin their research from a position within the scientific and political establishment.

Counting women in refers to not only women and their concerns being reflected as part of research but also women making space for themselves in academic research settings, medical community research, or public policy debates, to name just a few. As Marjorie DeVault (1996) notes, "attention to sexism in research procedure probably often depends on the presence of feminists within research teams, where they are usually more likely than others to call attention to those biases" (p. 36). Combining their epistemological perspectives and feminist political goals, many feminist empiricists, like Spalter-Roth and Hartmann (1999), find themselves with a "dual vision of . . . research" (p. 337). Concerning their statistical public policy research on the situation for women at work and on welfare, Spalter-Roth and Hartmann (1999) remark:

> Our research reflects both dominant methodological and critical oppositional views because we employ mainstream social science techniques but filter these techniques through a feminist prism that critically examines how these techniques are likely to reproduce and legitimate relations of domination and inequality within genders, races, and classes. (p. 337)

Working within the established system of research methods, public policy demands, and traditional arenas of research criterion is a compromise that some feminists find necessary, practical, and prudent when working for social change. Such a compromise is too high of a price to pay for many other feminists, whose politics and epistemological perspective require that their research step out of the bounds of the positivist paradigm. However, feminist empiricists see that there is a need for women and feminists at all levels of epistemological inquiry, within all arenas where work for social change is going on, and in every discipline that seeks the betterment and well-being of humanity.

Exposing Untruths and Watching for Stereotypes

The empirical destruction of stereotypes, patriarchal ideologies, and untruths has been one major arena in which feminist empiricists have tended to work. Eliminating androcentric bias and including women in research in recent years has begun to transition itself from direct inclusion of women's lives and experiences toward a more complex questioning by feminist empiricists about how women are represented within the research itself. When feminism provides the political grounding through which an empiricist works, the researcher "must also consider the ways in which the discourse of science serves to reinforce prevailing social and cultural stereotypes, making them appear 'natural'" (Weasel, 2001, p. 30).

Drawing us into a different, real-world example, imagine again for a moment that every medical study about the experiences and effective treatments for heart disease has been conducted on male research subjects. Imagine that there is no single study that includes the question: How do women experience heart disease? Is it different from men's experience? How should women's treatment progress for the best possible outcome? Kim M. McCormick and Sheila M. Bunting (2002) examine the impact of feminist theory on nursing research. They examine recent research that has shown women's experience of heart disease as very distinct from that of men. Such research included women in the research design, questioning whether or not women's symptoms, experience, recovery, and treatment were adequate and successful when based on the universal model developed from research of men. Women were shown to have different symptoms, distinct experiences, and recovery requiring different treatments from those for men.

Yet McCormick and Bunting (2002) do not stop their discussion of feminist empiricists with the inclusion of women patients in the studies and the illustration of androcentric bias in this body of research. For McCormick and Bunting, it is not enough to "add women and stir." They continue to comment on the difficulties of communicating and representing differences between men and women in research texts that do not further harm women's status or health care. Efforts to eliminate research that exploits women have pushed some feminist empiricists to go beyond efforts to reduce androcentric bias and into a deep questioning of the political and social implications of the research produced. They show that "the challenge for researchers has been to discuss women in a manner that allows their differences to emerge but does not depict them as inferior to men" (p. 820). McCormick and Bunting quantitatively analyze the types of representations of women in nursing literature about heart disease. Again, they are trying to provide the most objective and contextually full picture of women's representation while at the same time critiquing knowledge that does harm to women and the feminine. Seeking the truth by adding women into the research design and questions does not go far enough.

Empirical examination and problematization of concepts has become a formidable part of feminist empiricist work. Similarly, feminist archeologist Margaret W. Conkey (2003) remarks, "Yes, there are now women, but in roles, activities, and significances that are unproblematized" (p. 876). Feminist empiricists are challenging their fields of research and disciplines to attend to their representation of women. Yet feminist empiricists offer their fields and disciplines as many questions as answers.

Further elaborating on the work by feminist empiricist scholars, we might think about how representation of women in research on sexual harassment might further exploit women. Empirical research not conducted with feminist values against exploitation might tend to represent women as victims. Such research might also tend to work within specific patriarchal assumptions leading to analysis and arguments representing women as "asking for it" by dressing provocatively in the workplace or engaging in flirtatious communication styles. Conducting empirical research as a feminist requires that the representation of women in the research analysis and research text be responsible and ethical. Some feminist empiricists would argue that research findings that position the woman as a victim or "asking for it" require assumptions made by the researcher that are imbued with patriarchy, androcentric, and soundly less than objective.

In spite of such political intentions by some feminist empiricists to attend to and remedy exploitative research, many other feminist researchers from different epistemological perspectives argue that their rigorous attachment to positivism and the establishment within which it resides has to be shaken. They argue that feminist empiricists continue to "add women and stir" in spite of their good intentions, relying on the dulled patriarchal tools of the scientific establishment such that the knowledge produced can still be used to exploit women. Such critiques are usually met by feminist empiricists with the resolve and belief that with care, political perspective, and objective standards for knowledge building, feminist empiricist pursuits can overcome such issues.

The content of stereotypes about women and men is varied, vibrant, and sometimes humorous. Take, for example, the case of the anthropologist Emily Martin's (1999) groundbreaking exposure of the androcentric bias in the natural sciences. She examined textbooks that dealt with human reproduction and found that these texts tended to construct a story where romantic and gendered stereotypes about the egg and sperm were created, re-created, and enforced. She found that typically the egg was spoken about with the terms that depicted its passivity, where it "is transported," "is swept," or even "drifts." The sperms, in contrast, were typically spoken about in active, aggressive, and energetic terms, such as "velocity" and "propelling," where they can "burrow through the egg coat" and "penetrate" it (p. 17). Martin shows that so-called truthful and objective medical textbooks were infused with nonobjective stereotypes, shaping both the medical and the cultural understanding of natural events. Martin's feminist empiricist stance argues that an understandable, objective reality is out there to be known about the processes of the egg and the sperm. She argues that medical textbooks were depicting gender stereotypes through scientific language that had little basis in reality.

Martin stands with many feminist empiricists who believe that when such stereotypes are brought to light, the implications they have in society begin to lessen. The goal of exposure of stereotypes and androcentric biases is a politically charged one. Feminist empiricists reach below the surfaces of unquestioned traditional research to look at the dark spaces where women and the feminine are cast in a negative and oppressive light. Returning again to our example of our particular woman's experience with sexual harassment, imagine that her experience is examined through the positivistic lens of a researcher who holds that the stereotypical view of women as nurturing and emotional is based in fact. Regarding gender roles, this researcher also holds the stereotypical view of men as aggressive, dominant, and unable to control their sex drives. Imagine for a moment how these untested, nonobjective stereo-types might imbue the research findings. Without the feminist intention to look beyond such stereotypes, which are themselves part of the larger social and political context in which sexual harassment resides, research findings would lean toward a cyclical reproduction of the said stereotypes. With Martin, fem-inist empiricists observe, examine, and test these stereotypes to differing degrees. For example, concerning sexual harassment, Jean Stockard and Miriam Johnson (1992) looked beyond the stereotypes that re-inscribe themselves into the research question and findings. They argue that women's socialization encourages them to avoid conflict (as opposed to the stereotype that women are naturally passive in the face of conflict) and affects women's patterns of reporting of sexual harassment. The empiricist intention to test and observe the answers to this feminist question leads researchers like Stockard and Johnson to provide a more objective basis for knowledge building.

Shaping new questions grounded in empirical analysis represents one strength of feminist empiricism.[6] To better understand the true impact of com-bining the tenets of feminism with empiricism, let's turn to an example. In the following in-depth Behind-the-Scenes piece, the renowned feminist scholar Diana E. H. Russell takes us into her quantitative rape study and the earned feminist position that guided it.

Behind-the-Scenes With Diana E. H. Russell

The Contribution of Feminism to My Research on Rape

"You have not made it clear that rape is an important problem or just the concern of a bunch of looney women."

—Gladys Handy,
National Science Foundation, 1971

My personal experiences of child sexual abuse and my feminism both played major roles in my decision to conduct research on rape and other forms of misogynist sexual abuse and violence against females—starting in 1971 and continuing up until today. A rape trial that occurred in San Francisco in 1971 served as a catalyst for my feminist outrage at the sexist double standard that was manifested by the portrayal of the victim as the one on trial for her active sex life. In contrast, the promiscuity of her rapist, Jerry Plotkin, was used as a defense against her charge of rape. "Why would he rape a woman if he had no trouble finding consenting female partners?" his attorney asked the jury in a skeptical tone.

My anger at such discriminatory "reasoning" resulted in my joining a feminist protest outside the courthouse with women who shared my feelings about the sexist character of the trial. We handed out leaflets denouncing the "Rape in the Courtroom." Informally, several of the protesters remarked about the many women they knew who had been raped, suggesting that rape is a common male practice. I was astounded by this claim and unaware that any of the women I knew had been raped.

This experience made it clear to me how little I knew about rape from the victim's perspective, and I decided to investigate what the scholarly literature had to say about it. Once again, my feminist perspective enabled me to recognize, with shock, how sexist and victim blaming the literature was. Later, my feminist perspective enabled me to recognize the role of misogyny in the many other forms of sexual exploitation, sexual coercion, and violence against women and girls—in addition to rape.

However, I believe that a traumatic experience of sexual abuse when I was 15 years old was by far the most potent motivator for my lifelong investigation of males' sexual abuse and sexual violence against women and girls. I wasn't aware of this source of my motivation at the time. It was an insight that developed much later.

I was enraged by Plotkin being found "not guilty" by the jurors. Realizing that the jurors had been forced to listen to highly prejudicial testimony, I was determined that my study would present the *victims'* perspectives (the term *survivor* came into use much later), which I predicted would be entirely different from the way they appeared in court records and newspaper accounts.

The ignorant, disrespectful, unprofessional, and sexist response to my grant proposal on rape by Gladys Handy, a staff member at the National Science Foundation whose task it was to evaluate my proposal, is cited in the opening epigram. Dismayed by Handy's hostile reaction, I embarked on an exploratory study of survivors' experiences of rape in Berkeley and Oakland, California, without benefit of funding. I and three student volunteers conducted face-to-face interviews with more than 80 volunteer rape survivors. This study resulted in my book *The Politics of Rape: The Victims' Perspective* (Russell, 1975), in which I argued that rape was not a deviant male act but one that conformed to typical notions of masculinity in our patriarchal society.

(Continued)

(Continued)

Because the publisher (Stein & Day) demanded the deletion of the main theoretical chapter in my manuscript, its publication was delayed for over a year. Nevertheless, it was the third feminist book to contribute to the revolutionizing of the social scientific literature on rape—and subsequently of large portions of the United States' population (Connell & Wilson, 1974, and Medea & Thompson, 1974, were the first two books published on rape; I was unaware of both these volumes when writing my book).

Having heard several feminists claim that rape was a common crime against women, in contrast to the assumption of most nonfeminists who considered it a relatively infrequent crime, I decided that it was vitally important that I try to get funding to conduct a relatively large scale scientific study of the prevalence of rape in nearby San Francisco to evaluate which of these diametrically opposed views was correct. By this time, the National Institute of Mental Health had provided funding especially for rape research. My proposed survey research project was among their first proposals to be funded in 1977.

In addition to wanting to ascertain the prevalence of rape in a probability sample of women residents who were 18 years and older in San Francisco, I also endeavored to determine the prevalence of incest, extrafamilial child sexual abuse, sexual abuse by authority figures, and the effects on the victims/survivors of all these forms of sexual violation and violence. However, this article will focus on the impact of my feminist perspective on my methodology for estimating the prevalence of rape.

Methodology

I considered subcontracting with the University of California at Berkeley's Survey Research Center to conduct the field work phase of my project. However, I learned that they would not allow me to have any input into the training of the interviewers. This was the major reason for my abandoning this idea. Here's why: one of the most basic tenets of survey research is that it is unnecessary to inform the interviewers about the subject under investigation or to select them on the basis of their attitudes to the topic—even if the topic is considered taboo in society. However, I decided that this standard survey research rule was inappropriate for my study because of the taboo nature of the topics I wanted to inquire about and the victim-blaming attitudes most people had about rape and other forms of sexual assault at that time. Many women are likely to remain silent when an unknown interviewer asks them about their experience(s) of rape because of their feelings of shame, self-blame, and anxiety about being blamed by the interviewer, especially if the interviewer conveys, even if subtly, that victims are responsible for their victimization. Sending *supposedly* unbiased interviewers into the field without first educating them about the issues involved would have severely undermined my attempt to obtain high disclosure of rape, incest, and other forms of sexual assaults.

Hence, I decided to subcontract only the drawing of my survey sample. I hired Field Research Corporation, a well-known and highly reputable marketing and public opinion research firm in San Francisco, for this task. I ended up with a probability sample of 930 women residents of San Francisco aged 18 years and older. A team of 33 interviewers with different ethnic and class identities interviewed this sample of women during the summer of 1978 (for further information about the methodology of this study, see Russell, 1984).

The 65 hours of intensive training for the 33 interviewers included at least 10 hours of education about rape and incest. This included listening to personal rape and incest testimony volunteered by some of the interviewers and other staff, viewing a feminist movie about rape, and receiving direct instruction about rape—for example, that many women are the victims of multiple rapes. Therefore interviewers were instructed not to be surprised when they found themselves interviewing such women.

However, 10 hours of training cannot transform a bigot into an unprejudiced person. Therefore, interviewers were selected for their nonblaming attitudes toward sexual assault victims as well as for their interviewing skills. In addition, since the survey was limited to female respondents, I did not even contemplate hiring male interviewers.

I also considered it vitally important to construct an interview schedule that would avoid any hint of victim blaming. So, for example, the respondents were asked to indicate their agreement or disagreement with a number of statements that were intended to achieve this goal before they were asked any questions about their experiences, if any, of rape, sexual abuse by relatives and/or nonrelatives, and so on: for example, "Any woman could be a victim of rape or sexual assault"; "Most women experience some kind of sexual assault at least once in their lives"; "Given the

(Continued)

(Continued)

right situation, most men are capable of committing rape"; and "Rape victims are not responsible for having been raped." Another statement was designed to encourage respondents to disclose their experiences: "It is usually helpful to talk about painful experiences." Conveying bias in this fashion is contrary to a basic tenet of questionnaire design requiring that researchers *avoid* showing any such bias by alternating such questions to convey "objectivity" about the topic under investigation.

My knowledge about rape caused me to avoid using this term unless there was an important reason to do so. For example, one of 38 questions on sexual assault and abuse in my interview schedule used the word *rape* to illuminate how many women conceptualized their experiences as rape—which I defined as forced intercourse, intercourse obtained by threat of force, or intercourse completed when a woman was drugged, unconscious, or physically incapacitated in some way, or attempts at such acts (this was the legal definition of rape in California at that time—except that my study included cases of wife rape). I excluded taboo terms because I anticipated that many respondents would not apply such value-laden terms to their experiences. My expectation was confirmed, as is evident in the next section.

Findings on Prevalence Rates

The wisdom of my feminist understanding of women's experiences of rape was confirmed by the unprecedentedly high disclosure rate obtained by my survey methodology. For example, 22% of the 930 respondents disclosed experiences of completed and/or attempted rape in answer to the one question that used the word *rape*.[1] When completed rape and attempted rape were combined, the standard practice of the official FBI's statistics, 44% of the sample disclosed at least one completed or attempted rape. Hence, the direct question about rape yielded only half the actual rape experiences reported by the respondents.

Conclusion

I believe that the high disclosure rates obtained by my methodology were due to my feminist understanding about rape. Following is a summary of some of the main methodological features that I believe explain how my survey obtained such relatively high prevalence rates for rape—substantially higher than any comparable study thereafter (see Russell & Bolen, 2000):

- The use of a large range of questions in the interview schedule that helped to tap women's memories of rape experiences
- The inclusion of questions that conveyed a non-victim-blaming attitude or bias on the part of the study
- Avoidance of the word *rape* in all but one of the questions in the interview schedule
- The exclusive use of female interviewers
- Careful selection of interviewers who did not subscribe to the usual myths about rape
- Rigorous training of interviewers in both administration of the interview schedule and education about rape
- Matching the ethnicity of interviewers and respondents, as far as this was possible

For reasons unknown, no researcher in the United States has replicated some of the important methodological features of my prevalence study, except for the use of female interviewers. Is it any wonder, then, that no other survey has even approached finding the prevalence rates for rape obtained in my survey? (This statement is substantiated in Russell & Bolen, 2000.) I believe my survey demonstrates the crucial importance of employing feminist research methodology to estimate the prevalence of rape and other forms of sexual abuse and violence. Only space prevented me from including a similar description of my feminist methodology and findings on the prevalence of incestuous and extrafamilial child sexual abuse. I believe a feminist perspective will be found to be equally important when conducting research on numerous other topics.

Feminist research and analysis of rape has revolutionized the understanding of rape in Western nations and others. I am proud to be one of the initiators with a few other researchers and many courageous rape survivors who were willing to speak up about their experiences.

Note

1. Two coders and I evaluated whether or not each of the experiences respondents described as rape met the study's definitions of rape and attempted rape.

EPISTEMOLOGICAL CHASMS: OBJECTIVITY

Feminist empiricists aim to address issues that are neglected and thereby made invisible by the traditional positivist paradigm of research. These include women and their experiences and perspectives as the direct research subject to be questioned, examined, and known through the research process. Feminist empiricists also aim to redress problems found within the traditional positivist paradigm, including androcentric biases and reconstruction of stereotypes. Informing each of these two broad intentions of feminist empiricists are the overarching goals of feminist values. In the end, the most significant movement of the feminist empiricist that sets her apart from other types of feminist researchers is the quest for objectivity. Efforts made by feminist empiricists to address the issues laid out above are all undertaken with the aim of pursuing, defining, and using a better form of objectivity than that engaged by traditional positivists. Ignoring and obscuring women and women's experiences, for feminist empiricists, limits the objectivity of research. Similarly, androcentric biases and research filtered through stereotypes debilitate objective quests for knowledge. Feminist empiricists seek to remedy this problem within the positivist paradigm, which distinguishes them from other feminist researchers while also exposing them to critique.

How feminist empiricists approach objectivity marks them as distinct from other kinds of feminist researchers. The location of empiricism within the positivist paradigm draws us into a more abstract understanding of their grounding as thinkers and knowers. Epistemologically and methodologically, the subject/object distinction forms the root of positivist social science formulation, positioning the researcher as a detached subject. Positivism holds that there is a "real" reality to be known that is understandable and obtainable through objectivist scientific practices. This real reality to be understood is built on the distinction and separation of the knowable object of study and the subject— namely, that of the knowing researcher. Through a subject/object dichotomy the position of the knowing researcher is inconsequential and inherently dislocated from the knowable object. The influence of the researcher is denied, and the voice rising out of a knowledge-building script is one of a "'disinterested scientist' as informer of decision makers, policy makers, and change agents" (Guba & Lincoln, 1994, p. 112). Empiricism approaches knowledge building with a particular form of positivism that holds that the subject/object divide can be understood and known only through the senses.

The subject/object distinction forms a basic dualism on which a great deal of the positivist paradigm is built. Feminist empiricists have particular ways of negotiating the critique of this epistemological and methodological stance. The feminist empiricist and philosopher of science Evelyn Fox Keller argues that positivist formulations of objectivity are static, requiring that the subject of the research, namely, the researcher, be utterly separate from the object of the research, namely, the object of the study. Keller (1985) posits that feminist researchers should move toward a form of dynamic objectivity that "aims at a form of knowledge that grants to the world around us its independent integrity but does so in a way that remains cognizant of, indeed, relies on, our connectivity with that world" (p. 117). For Keller, object relations that require an ideology of domination over the object (nature and women) form the basis for the empirical sciences.

Traditional definitions of objectivity imply a separation of ideology and science, an observation of the world at large without the trappings of political and individual beliefs. This normative valuation of science over ideology, and its expression of either/or but not both, is what is presented on the surface of objective social science research. Feminist empiricists negotiate the tight rope of the ideological and scientific divide, arguing that acknowledging and working on the boundaries of subject/object and ideology/science distinctions is what makes their approach the most objective. Caroline Ramazanoglu (2002) remarks that feminists have long grappled with Enlightenment notions of reason and objectivity as outlined by Decartes and Kant. They have had a difficult time trying "to decide whether they can or should be 'soaring in thought' so that women can stride around the universe and dive into the nature of wo/man" (pp. 25–26).

By interrogating the boundaries between science and ideology, feminist empiricists show how biased objective science has become. As feminist empiricists look deeper below the surface of traditional positivism, they find that ideological and personal beliefs muddy the transparent waters of knowledge production. Feminist empiricists aim to negotiate the traverse between ideology and science, shaping a better science in which knowledge about women can be built. Many critiques of feminist empiricism remark that such attempts are still not knowledge for women, however. Ramazanoglu (2002) states that "feminists can be reasonable, logical and systematic in their research, without treating reason as a neutralizing force. They can (problematically) pursue truth in the sense of claiming a 'better story,' but they cannot claim to be objective" (p. 49). In spite of such criticisms, feminist empiricists remain committed to and content with their compromises.

With feminist empiricists, the philosopher Sandra Harding (1992) critiques objectivity while not desiring to do away with the word altogether. She finds that objectivity is simply not objective enough, that it blocks and limits the representation of less distorted and less destructive accounts of the world. These accounts destroy the possibility of shaping and creating the resources that objective knowledge can bring, "such as fairness, honesty, detachment, and . . . advancing democracy" (p. 574). The hands that wield the power of the word *objective* used it from their own position and for their own gain, in structural and personal terms. Harding (1993) states that "the methods and norms in the disciplines are too weak to permit researchers systematically to identify and eliminate from the results of research those social values, interests, and agendas that are shared by the entire scientific community" (p. 52). Adding to already established methods and strengthening their power to access objective knowledge is the goal of feminist empiricists.

Where most feminist researchers from all epistemological perspectives come to critique and grapple with issues of subject/object distinction, the answers and tools they employ to deal with this issue form one distinction among them. On their path to engage, encourage, and employ the feminist goals for research, feminist empiricists are epistemologically rooted in objectivity. Their vision of objectivity, however, aims to pursue a richer, more detailed, and more vibrant reality than that of a "detached, objective reflection of a singular 'natural' reality" (Weasel, 2001, p. 27).[7] Value-free objectivity implies the efforts of traditional positivistic paradigms that seek to hold up a mirror to the world and view it for what it is.

> Value-free objectivity requires also a faulty theory of the ideal agent—the subject—of science, knowledge and history. It requires a notion of the self as a fortress that must be defended against polluting influences from its social surroundings. (Harding, 1991, p. 158)

By positioning the influences of the social surroundings as polluting, including those residing within the researcher herself, positivistic science ignores vast amounts of information, affecting processes, and valuable insights that could otherwise make research findings more objective.[8] Illusions of the detached, unemotional researcher hinder objective pursuits of truth. Such value-free objectivity is not objective enough because it seeks to be blind to important contexts that make the knowledge gained full of intensity, clarity, and commitment.

The union of feminist political goals and empiricist approaches to objectivity can be seen in the research of Zuleyma Tang Halpin (1989), who brings her disciplinary lenses of both biology and women's studies to bear on the scientific establishment's uses of scientific objectivity at its worst. She outlines two problems with scientific objectivity that serve to reconstruct systems of oppression, subjugation, and violence toward all those who constitute the other. The first issue she addresses concerns the emotional detachment necessitated by the practice and aim of scientific objectivity. The second issue Halpin cites as reproducing systems of oppression is the epistemological separation of the object, or the one who is studied, from the subject, or the one who is producing knowledge. These two issues bring about the core dimension of feminist empiricist approaches to scientific knowledge building. Yet Halpin still advocates the maintenance of objectivity as the standard, stating:

> While true objectivity is undeniably necessary for the rational pursuit of science, the concept of scientific objectivity as commonly understood and practiced by scientists, often has been formulated in ways that are actually antithetical to truly objective and unbiased scientific inquiry. (p. 285)

The antithetical employment of scientific methods to pursue objective knowledge has required a gentle and subtle epistemological shift for feminist empiricists. This shift has drawn them not away from earlier notions of objectivity but rather in pursuit of their inherent and most basic elaborations. The practice of science, the use of positivist methods, and the aim toward truly objective scientific inquiry have empowered feminist researchers across disciplines.

What happens when awareness of and sensitivity to ideological and value-laden underpinnings are explored? To ground us back in our example, the traditional paradigms of knowledge about sexual harassment were argued to be lacking a great deal of nuance and objectivity according to feminist researchers. Nonfeminist researchers continued to hold assumptions and biases that, from a feminist empiricist's perspective, were less than objective. An assumption that carried a great deal of weight at the time of our sexual harassment example, in the 1980s, in spite of a lack of empirical data to support its claim, held that perpetrators of sexual harassment were psychologically disturbed (Hotelling & Zuber, 1997, p. 100). Extending from such individual and psychological arguments, we find ourselves in a morass of assumptions about men's high sex drives that cause them to be incapable of controlling themselves. Boundless other assumptions permeated traditional positivist paradigmatic research, limiting the human potentiality, the possibilities for social change, and the potentiality of the research. Feminist empiricists weighed in on such assumptions, aiming to provide empirical evidence of the social context of sexual harassment.

CONCLUSION

The varied and vibrant contributions of feminist empiricists have created an environment where paradigm shifts are already taking place. These contributions are leading to better and more objective science and are often subsumed into the establishment's notions of good science, frequently leaving their feminist label behind. Feminist empiricists are hardly monolithic in their epistemology, methodology, and uses of method. But they have had a cumulative impact on the positivist paradigm. Along the many dimensions that provide the web of grounding for looking at feminist researchers, feminist empiricists tend to stay the closest to their positivistic forefathers. They critique positivist science from within, arguing and pushing for a stronger, better, more objective knowledge that can be gained when rigorous examination of the political and discursive context of knowledge building is part of the research process. They argue that the world is knowable, that truth can be found, and that much of science has built blinders that obscure the rich and colorful context of knowledge processes and reality, serving to uphold and strengthen the positivist paradigm and patriarchal constructions of the status quo. They use their dual vision of political goals and empiricist means, arguing that they have found a balanced way to access the best of both worlds.

Despite the contributions of empiricism to the larger project of feminism, as Chapters 3 and 4 of this volume show, there are many who view feminist empiricism as a case of adding women to preexisting models, stirring, and assuming things are "better." These feminists have pioneered new epistemological and methodological approaches to knowledge building, unraveling some of the "foundations" of empiricism. If we are to look at epistemological positions as existing on a continuum, empiricism might be on one end, followed by standpoint epistemology and then postmodernism, which entirely rejects the essentialism necessary to empiricism and standpoint. In the next chapter we review standpoint epistemology as the first powerful critique of feminist empiricism, and an alternative to it.

NOTES

1. Richmond Campbell (1994) argues that in fact positivism

> concedes that political concerns could influence the "discovery" of a certain hypothesis or certain data, but insists that the question of whether this hypothesis "h" is supported by this evidence "e" is another matter. The positivist says that whether "e" confirms "h," no matter where either came from is a matter of logic, and this at least is beyond politics. (p. 90)

Campbell argues that epistemologically and methodologically we must be careful about specifying whether we are talking about politics influencing the context of discovery or the context of justification. Campbell agrees with Sandra Harding (1986, cited in Campbell, 1994), who argues that politics and social biases guide a researcher's entrance into the context of discovery, and he believes that "what ends up being confirmed, if 'e' confirms 'h', reflect[s] these biases" (Campbell, 1994, p. 95). But Campbell (1994) argues that Harding's critique of feminist empiricism goes too far, implying that "the confirmation relation taken just in itself is untouched by political concerns." Campbell argues that "the very logic of confirmation . . . depends on the context of discovery. That is, whether a given 'e' confirms a given 'h' cannot be determined independently of the context of discovery" (p. 95).

2. This edition of *Signs* provides many useful and thoughtful examples of feminist research within both the natural and the social sciences. Particularly notable are the contributors' reflexive assessments of their roles as researchers aiming to produce empirical knowledge and as feminists with political values and perspectives. Some of these contributors are discussed in this chapter.

3. In spite of the frequently debated quantitative/qualitative divide within feminist methodology literature, Dunn and Waller (2000) found that of the 1,826 gender-content articles published between 1984 and 1993, 93% were based on quantitative data. Of the 544 articles that were feminist-oriented gender content articles, 83% were based on quantitative data. Quantitative methodologies are still a dominant forum in which gender- and feminist-oriented knowledge is being built and disseminated. Interestingly, men were first authors of more gender-content articles than women.

4. For example, in *On the Treatment of the Sexes in Research*, Margrit Eichler and Jeanne Lapointe (1985) outlined specific and thorough guidelines in which survey research parameters that include gender and avoid androcentrism are laid out.

5. Marjorie DeVault (1996) notes that "one common approach to feminist quantitative work involves correcting gender and other cultural biases in standard procedure." Such approaches serve feminist objectives, for example, by pointing out "the

many ways that standard survey techniques build in unnoticed assumptions about gender and culture. Those working with survey data have begun to alter survey design and analytic procedures to lessen or eliminate these sources of bias" (p. 36).

6. Janet Saltzman Chafetz (1990) cites the many questions that all feminists have contributed to their fields by way of critiquing traditional scientific endeavors as one space that feminist empiricists must address. She argues that it is not sufficient to critique, building new theories, concepts, and variables, but rather feminist researchers must work to answer the questions that they pose to their fields. Remarking on concepts such as patriarchy, sexism, and race/class/gender, she notes: "To my knowledge, no one has begun the difficult but fundamentally important job of empirically examining which of these clusters of variables is more important in maintaining (or changing) systems of gender inequity; which constitute independent and which intervening constructs?" (p. 13).

7. Although she is not a feminist empiricist in her current writings, Helen Longino (1990) elaborates on the potential richness and complexity of knowledge produced through a more objective science whereby the researcher takes into account the political context of the researcher self. She states:

> I am suggesting that a feminist scientific practice admits political considerations as relevant constraints on reasoning, which through their influence on reasoning and interpretation shape content. In this specific case those considerations in combination with the phenomena support an explanatory model that is highly interactionist, highly complex. (p. 193)

This consideration of the complex context of the research process is not the responsibility of the researcher alone. Longino goes on to require that the readers of knowledge take some responsibility in the process of scientific communication and learning, whereby

> the first step however, is to abandon the idea that scrutiny of the data yields a seamless web of knowledge. The second is to think through a particular field and try to understand just what its unstated and fundamental assumptions are and how they influence the course of inquiry. Knowing something of the history of a field is necessary to this process, as is continued conversation with other feminists. (p. 193)

8. Marianne Janack (2002) remarks:

> The connection between objectivity and truth has been an important tool for feminist and other libratory projects, but failures of objectivity are not always or only epistemic failures. The claim that there is still sexism in the world can only be denied by someone who fails to be objective. This is a failure that has two different and separable aspects to it. It is an epistemic failure, in so far as it seems to involve a willful avoidance of evidence that is all too clear. . . . It is also an instance of a theory or claim that fails to correspond to the facts. (p. 268)

REFERENCES

Bingham, Shereen G. (Ed.). (1994). *Conceptualizing sexual harassment as discursive practice.* Westport, CT: Praeger.

Campbell, Richmond. (1994). The virtues of feminist empiricism. *Hypatia, 9*(1), 90–115.

Chafetz, Janet Saltzman. (1990, August). *Some thoughts by an "unrepentant positivist" who considers herself a feminist nonetheless.* Paper presented at the 85th Annual Meeting of the American Sociological Association, Washington, DC.

Conkey, Margaret. (2003). Has feminism changed archaeology? *Signs, 28*(3), 867–880.

Connell, Noreen, & Wilson, Cassandra (Eds.). (1974). *Rape: The first sourcebook for women.* New York: New American Library.

DeVault, Marjorie. (1996). Talking back to sociology: Distinctive contributions of feminist methodology. *Annual Review of Sociology, 22,* 29–50.

Dunn, Dana, & Waller, David V. (2000). The methodological inclinations of gender scholarship in mainstream sociology journals. *Sociological Spectrum, 20*(2), 239–257.

Eichler, Margrit, & Lapointe, Jeanne. (1985). *On the treatment of the sexes in research.* Ottawa, Ontario, Canada: Social Sciences and Humanities Research Council of Canada.

Farley, Lin. (1978). *Sexual shakedown: The sexual harassment of women on the job.* New York: McGraw-Hill.

Goldman, Alvin. (1999). *Knowledge in a social world.* Oxford, UK: Oxford University Press.

Griffin, Christine, & Phoenix, Ann. (1994). The relationship between qualitative and quantitative research: Lessons from feminist psychology. *Journal of Community & Applied Social Psychology, 4*(4), 287–298.

Guba, Egon G., & Lincoln, Yvonna S. (1994). Competing paradigms in qualitative research. In Norman Denzin & Yvonna S. Lincoln (Eds.), *Handbook of qualitative research* (pp. 105–117). Thousand Oaks, CA: Sage.

Halpin, Zuleyma Tang. (1989). Scientific objectivity and the concept of "the other." *Women's Studies International Forum, 12*(3), 285–294.

Harding, Sandra. (1991). *Whose science? Whose knowledge? Thinking from women's lives.* Ithaca, NY: Cornell University Press.

Harding, Sandra. (1992). After the neutrality ideal: Science, politics, and "strong objectivity. *Social Research, 59*(3), 567–587.

Harding, Sandra. (1993). Rethinking standpoint epistemology: What is "strong objectivity"? In Linda Alcoff & Elizabeth Potter (Eds.), *Feminist epistemologies* (pp. 49–82). New York: Routledge.

Hotelling, Kathy, & Zuber, Barbara A. (1997). Feminist issues in sexual harassment. In William O'Donohue (Ed.), *Sexual harassment: Theory, research and treatment* (pp. 99–111). Boston: Allyn & Bacon.

Janack, Marianne. (2002). Dilemmas of objectivity. *Social Epistemology, 16*(3), 267–281.

Jayaratne, Toby Epstein. (1983). The value of quantitative methodology for feminist research. In Gloria Bowles & Renate Duelli Klein (Eds.), *Theories of Women's Studies* (pp. 140–161). Boston: Routledge & Kegan Paul.

Keller, Evelyn Fox. (1985). *Reflections on gender and science.* New Haven, CT: Yale University Press.

Longino, Helen E. (1990). *Science as social knowledge: Values and objectivity in scientific inquiry.* Princeton, NJ: Princeton University Press.

Martin, Emily. (1999). The egg and the sperm: How science has constructed a romance based on stereotypical male-female roles. In Sharlene Hesse-Biber et al. (Eds.), *Feminist approaches to theory and methodology: An interdisciplinary reader* (pp. 15–28). Oxford, UK: Oxford University Press.

McCormick, Kim M., & Bunting, Sheila M. (2002). Application of feminist theory in nursing research: The case of women and cardiovascular disease. *Health Care for Women International, 23,* 820–834.

Medea, Andra, & Thompson, Kathleen. (1974). *Against rape; a survival manual for women: How to avoid entrapment and how to cope with rape physically and emotionally.* New York: Farrar, Straus, & Giroux.

Ramazanoglu, Caroline (with Holland, Janet). (2002). *Feminist methodology: Challenges and choices.* London: Sage.

Russell, Diana, E. H. (1975). *The politics of rape: The victims' perspective.* New York: Stein & Day. (Reprinted by iUniverse, On-Demand Book Service, New York, 2003. Available at Backinprint.com)

Russell, Diana. E. H. (1984). *Sexual exploitation: Rape, child sexual abuse, and workplace harassment* (8th printing). Newbury Park, CA: Sage.

Russell, Diana. E. H., & Bolen, Rebecca M. (2000). *The epidemic of rape and child sexual abuse in the United States.* Thousand Oaks, CA: Sage.

Schiebinger, Londa. (2003). Introduction: Feminism inside the sciences. *Signs, 28*(3), 859–886.

Spalter-Roth, Roberta, & Hartmann, Heidi. (1999). Small happiness: The feminist struggle to integrate social research with social activism. In Sharlene Hesse-Biber et al. (Eds.), *Feminist approaches to theory and methodology: An interdisciplinary reader* (pp. 333–347). New York: Oxford University Press.

Stockard, Jean, & Johnson, Miriam M. (1992). *Sex and gender in society.* Englewood Cliffs, NJ: Prentice Hall.

Unger, Rhoda Kesler. (1979). Toward a redefinition of sex and gender. *American Psychologist, 34*(11), 1085–1094.

Weasel, Lisa. (2001). Dismantling the self/other dichotomy in science: Towards a feminist model of the immune system. *Hypatia, 16*(1), 27–44.

THREE

FEMINIST STANDPOINT EPISTEMOLOGY

Building Knowledge and Empowerment Through Women's Lived Experience

Abigail Brooks

———•◦•———

I have . . . striven faithfully to give a true and just account of my own life in Slavery . . . to come to you just as I am a poor Slave Mother—not to tell you what I have heard but what I have seen— and what I have suffered.[1]

—Jacobs (1861/1987, p. 242)

These are the words of Harriet Jacobs, who, after escaping and eventually winning her freedom, took it upon herself to document her years spent as a slave in the American South during the first half of the 19th century. Speaking from a position of direct experience, Jacobs's words filled the widespread silence and ignorance about the condition of female slaves and challenged many of the misconceptions about slave women that were predominant at the time. Jacobs's goal, to educate Northerners about the cruelty and injustice of slavery and the particular suffering of female slaves within it, provided her with the courage, strength, and motivation to tell her story. She dared hope that by sharing her own life story as a female slave, by drawing on what she herself had witnessed and experienced, she would stand a chance of convincing Northerners about the brutal truths of slavery. As Jacobs (1861/1987) puts it,

> I have not written my experiences in order to attract attention to myself; on the contrary, it would have been more pleasant to me to have been silent about my own history. Neither do I care to excite sympathy for my own sufferings. But I do earnestly desire to arouse women of the North to a realizing sense of the condition of two millions of women at the South, still in bondage, suffering what I suffered, and most of them far worse. I want to add my testimony to that of abler pens to convince the people of the Free States what Slavery really is. Only by experience can any one realize how deep, and dark, and foul is that pit of abominations. May the blessing of God rest on this imperfect effort on behalf of my persecuted people! (pp. 1–2)

By revealing the acute exploitation, physical pain, and mental anguish she was forced to endure as a slave, including years of sexual harassment perpetrated by her owner, Dr. Flint, Jacobs succeeded in raising awareness among Northern women. Ultimately, the heightened awareness engendered by Jacobs's words about the horrors of slavery, and about the psychic and physical violence endured by female slaves in particular, inspired Northern white women to speak out against slavery and contributed to the growth of the Northern antislavery resistance movement.

Harriet Jacobs lived and wrote nearly 150 years ago, yet we look to her for guidance as we begin our discussion of contemporary feminist approaches to research and knowledge building. Why? Because Harriet Jacobs's life story—the strategies she applied and the goals she hoped to achieve in telling it—resonates strongly with the ongoing project of feminist research. Through sharing her own experiences as a slave girl, Harriet Jacobs opened people's eyes to what had been heretofore silenced and unknown—what life was like for slave women. As a firsthand account of slavery from the female perspective, Jacobs's story offered new insight into the brutality of the institution of slavery and helped to galvanize public critique and resistance against it. Similarly, much of contemporary feminist scholarship and research strive to give voice to women's lives that have been silenced and ignored, uncover hidden knowledge contained within women's experiences, and bring about women-centered solidarity and social change. This chapter focuses on a branch of feminist scholarship and research that was explicitly founded on these goals and that maintains an ongoing commitment to achieving them—namely, feminist standpoint epistemology.

Feminist standpoint epistemology is a unique philosophy of knowledge building that challenges us to (1) see and understand the world through the eyes and experiences of oppressed women and (2) apply the vision and knowledge of oppressed women to social activism and social change. Feminist standpoint epistemology requires the fusion of knowledge and practice. It is both a theory of knowledge building and a method of doing research—an approach to knowledge construction and a call to political action.

- But how do we actually go about integrating a feminist standpoint framework into our research practices?
- What are some of the new insights and perspectives that women's life experiences reveal about the larger social world?
- How do we translate what we learn from women's everyday lives, and from the different oppressed positions women inhabit in society, into political and social action?

These questions will prove useful guides as we trace the evolution of feminist standpoint epistemology, from its origins to its ongoing development, below.

BUILDING NEW KNOWLEDGE FROM WOMEN'S EXPERIENCES

While many thousands of men's lives have been recognized and recorded for centuries and across cultures, women's life stories have been documented far less often, even forgotten. As Joyce McCarl Nielsen (1990) puts it, women's culture, history, and lives have remained "underground and invisible," relegated to the "underside" of men's culture, history, and lives (p. 10). Beginning in the late 1960s and 1970s, however, and as a result of feminist consciousness-raising efforts both inside and outside of academia, women began to draw attention to the omission and exclusion of their voices and experiences in multiple arenas—politics; public policy; the professions of law, medicine, and business; and the disciplines of science, social science, and the humanities, to name a few. In sociology classrooms, for example, female students began to express frustration with the fact that the predominantly male-centered theories and concepts they were learning about failed to take their own experiences as women into account. In the words of feminist sociologist Dorothy Smith (1987), the sociological theories and methods being taught did not apply to "what was happening" as the female students "experienced it" (p. 86). Women's growing awareness of the contradiction between their own life experiences and the research studies and theoretical frameworks they were learning about—the failure of these studies and frameworks to accurately reflect their lives—inspired them to construct new models of knowledge building. These new models, or "alternative ways of thinking," would be developed by women for women, with the goal of granting authentic expression and representation to women's lives. One such alternative model of knowledge building came to be known as feminist standpoint epistemology.

Feminist standpoint epistemology requires us to place women at the center of the research process: Women's *concrete experiences* provide the starting point from which to build knowledge. Just as the reality about what life was like for slave women could come to light only through Harriet Jacobs's actual lived experience of it, feminist standpoint scholars emphasize the need to begin with women's lives, *as they themselves experience them,* in order to achieve an accurate and authentic understanding of what life is like for women today. Building knowledge from women's actual, or concrete, life experiences is acutely important, feminist standpoint scholars argue, if we hope to repair the historical trend of women's misrepresentation and exclusion from the dominant knowledge canons. And only by making women's concrete, life experiences the primary source of our investigations can we succeed in constructing knowledge that accurately reflects and represents women. As feminist standpoint scholar Patricia Hill Collins (1990) puts it, when making knowledge claims about women, we must always remember that it is women's "concrete experience" that provides the ultimate "criterion for credibility" of these knowledge claims (p. 209). But what exactly do we mean by women's concrete experience? How do feminist researchers go about uncovering women's concrete experiences? And what can we learn from these experiences? Let's turn now to some examples.

Women's concrete experiences consist of *what women do*. They are the wide and diverse range of activities that women engage in as part of their everyday lives. Just one aspect of women's lives, previously understudied and undervalued, that feminist researchers continue to shed light on is the myriad nurturing tasks that many women perform on a daily basis. These nurturing tasks, from cooking, cleaning, and taking care of their families (DeVault, 1991), to caring for the children of others (Collins, 1990), to caring for their own children from afar (Hondagneu-Sotelo & Avila, 1997), are examples of women's concrete experiences. Further, from each of these concrete experiences, women have cultivated particular knowledge and unique sets of skills.

To shed light on the lives and experiences of oppressed women, and to uncover women's knowledge and skills that are hidden and/or undervalued, feminist scholars often make innovative use of research methods, develop alternative research strategies, and even construct new methodological techniques altogether.[2] For example, in her research on women's experiences of shopping, planning, preparing, and cooking food for their families, Marjorie DeVault (1990, 1991) found that simply asking questions and listening to her respondents' answers was not working. Many women had not often had the opportunity to talk about their daily activities with an interested party and struggled with how to put their thoughts and feelings about their daily activities into words. DeVault (1990, 1991) moved beyond the traditional interview format to adopt what Kathryn Anderson and Dana Jack (1991) call the "interactive approach." She worked in collaboration with her respondents to "co-construct" new words that accurately reflected their experiences, thoughts, and feelings.

Marjorie DeVault's (1991) research documents the organizational and coordinating skills that women have developed from their work in planning, preparing, and cooking food for family members. The feminist standpoint scholar Alison Jaggar (1997) argues that through their ongoing practice as caretakers and nurturers, women have become especially skilled at expressing and reading emotion. Women's skill at expressing and reading emotion is important, because emotion serves several instrumental functions: "Emotion is necessary for human survival. Emotions prompt us to act appropriately, to approach some people and situations and to avoid others, to caress or cuddle, flight or flee. Without emotion, human life would be unthinkable" (Jaggar, 1997, pp. 190, 192).

Patricia Hill Collins's (1990) research reveals African American women's skill in community building, a skill derived from their unique role of caring for the children of extended family, friends, and neighbors. By performing a caretaking role that Collins calls "other mothering"—helping to fill in the gaps left by unaffordable child care, economic hardship, and overworked parents by caring for children other than their own—these "other mothers," known and trusted by many, may come to play an instrumental part in bringing different members of the community together and leading the community forward. In addition to other mothering, another innovative form of mothering called "transnational mothering" reflects women's cultivation of particular skills. Through Hondagneu-Sotelo and Avila's (1997) research, we learn about Latin American mothers who, separated from their children back home and often at great risk to themselves, live and work in the United States to provide financial support for their children. They send the bulk of their earnings home to ensure their children's well-being. Their earnings pay for their children's food, clothing, medical bills, and schooling. In this respect, these mothers have developed nurturing skills that lie outside of the traditional mother role of emotional support; although they do provide emotional support for their children through phone calls and letters, their primary method of nurturance becomes a financial one, a method traditionally reserved for fathers.

By making women's concrete experiences the "point of entry" for research and scholarship and exposing the rich array of new knowledge contained within women's experiences, feminist standpoint scholars begin to fill in the gaps on the subject of women in many disciplines. However, granting authentic expression to women's experiences, and to the knowledge that women have cultivated from these experiences, is not the only goal of feminist standpoint epistemology. Feminist standpoint epistemology also challenges us to critically examine society through women's eyes.

- What do women's experiences teach us about how society functions as a whole?
- Do women's experiences, and the knowledge gleaned from these experiences, offer us unique perspectives and insights into the world around us? If so, how?

UNDERSTANDING SOCIETY THROUGH THE LENS OF WOMEN'S EXPERIENCES

Like Harriet Jacobs, who pushed her readers to evaluate the institution of slavery through her eyes as a slave girl, feminist standpoint scholars encourage us to use women's experiences as a lens through which to examine society as a whole. Let's return to Patricia Hill Collins's (1990) research on African American mothering to illustrate this point. Collins exposes us to an important, and previously understudied, aspect of the everyday lives of African American women called other mothering, a practice in which women care for children of friends, neighbors, and family members whose biological mothers are working outside of the home. Collins illuminates the practice of other mothering as an indicator of the resourcefulness of African American women; it is a unique and useful skill developed for and by women. At the same time, however, and as Collins points out, African American women's daily experience of other mothering, and their reliance on it, throws light on larger social and economic issues—namely, the lack of quality, affordable child care in the United States and the difficulties faced by many poor mothers as a result.

Alison Jaggar's (1997) scholarship provides us with another example of how women's everyday experience, and the knowledge that accompanies that experience, can serve as a helpful tool for understanding the larger social world. When women engage in daily household activities, and comply with socially dictated roles such as that of caretaker, they cultivate a unique set of expertise that coincides with these activities and roles. Jaggar (1997) identifies "emotional acumen"—a unique, intuitive ability to read and interpret pain and hidden emotions and understand the genesis of those emotions—as one such unique set of expertise (p. 192). But the utility of women's emotional acumen is not limited to the realm of home and family. Instead, Jaggar argues, if extended outward and applied to the social world, emotional acumen can have many vital functions. Women's emotional acumen can help to "stimulate new insights" in the disciplines of sociology and philosophy and generate a new set of "psychotherapeutic tools" in the field of psychiatry (Jaggar, 1997, p. 192). Probably the most profound potential application of emotional acumen, however, is one of political analysis and accountability. Because emotional acumen enables women to tune in more quickly to situations of "cruelty, injustice, or danger," it can become a powerful vehicle for exposing political and social injustices. By providing the "first indication that something is wrong with the way alleged facts have been constructed, with the accepted understanding of how things are," emotional acumen can empower women to make "subversive observations that challenge dominant conceptions of the status quo" (Jaggar, 1997, p. 191).

Alison Jaggar (1997) and Patricia Hill Collins's (1990) research demonstrates that women's experiences, and the knowledge garnered from these experiences, can be used as a means to draw attention to the inequalities and injustices in society as a whole. In fact, as we come to understand society through the lens of women's experiences—let's say, for example, through the eyes of African American other mothers—we take the first step toward constructing a feminist standpoint. A feminist standpoint is a way of understanding the world, a point of view of social reality, that begins with, and is developed directly from, women's experiences. The next step is to draw on what have learned from women's experiences, to *apply* that feminist standpoint, toward bettering the condition of women and creating social change. Women's experiences not only point to us flaws in larger economic and political systems but also offer potential solutions to these flaws. As Alison Jaggar (1997) explains, because women's experiences, and the feminist standpoints that evolve from them, offer us a deep understanding of the "mechanisms of domination," they also help us "envision freer ways to live" (p. 193).

WOMEN'S EXPERIENCES AS
A MAP FOR SOCIAL CHANGE

Harriet Jacobs's (1861/1987) personal account of the sexual abuse and exploitation she was forced to endure as a female slave energized antislavery activism in the North. On learning about Jacobs's experience, people came to understand the institution of slavery as a whole through the eyes of slave women—from slave women's *standpoint.* The standpoint of slave women— with the knowledge and understanding of slavery it revealed—served as a powerful starting point, or position, from which to fight against the brutal institution. Similarly, by granting honest expression to women's contemporary experiences of oppression, feminist standpoint scholars and researchers seek to agitate resistance against these experiences of oppression and implement solutions to overcome them. African American women's experiences of other mothering teach us that the capitalist system as a whole fails to provide adequate support for poor working mothers. Further, as we come to view the capitalist system from the standpoint of African American other mothers, we are exposed not only to shortcomings in the system but also to the need for change and new solutions—solutions such as universally affordable, quality child care. In fact, often the very process of enabling women to articulate their own experiences of oppression raises awareness, among women and others, about the particular difficulties diverse women face and inspires movement toward change. Let's turn now to some more examples.

In her book *The Feminine Mystique*, Betty Friedan (1963) wrote about what it was like to live as a middle-class (white) housewife in mid-century America. Drawing directly from her own experience, and the experiences of many other middle-class women, Friedan challenged the dominant conceptions about American housewives at the time. Behind the cheerful media and magazine images of housewives pushing vacuum cleaners, doing laundry, and exclaiming over their new refrigerators with delight, Friedan uncovered widespread feelings of discontent. Many women, Friedan found, suffered from boredom and loneliness and encountered frustration with their everyday lives. And when women sought help to try to overcome these unhappy feelings, they would often blame themselves: "When a woman went to a psychiatrist for help, as many women did, she would say 'I'm so ashamed' or 'I must be hopelessly neurotic'" (p. 389). Women had been taught to aspire to the role of housewife: Compliance with the role of housewife was to bring them ultimate contentment and fulfillment. Therefore, women who didn't feel this way were left to worry: "Is there something wrong with me?"

But eventually, even the male psychiatric industry began to doubt that women's unhappiness could be attributed to individual or psychological factors alone. The problem was too widespread. "'I don't know what's wrong with women today,' a suburban psychiatrist said uneasily. 'I only know something is wrong because most of my patients happen to be women'" (Friedan, 1963, p. 390). Betty Friedan granted a name to this "strange stirring, dissatisfaction and yearning" felt by so many women. She called it, aptly, "the problem that has no name" (p. 387). By articulating the unhappiness experienced by many American housewives, Friedan helped women realize that they didn't have to struggle with these feelings alone. Moreover, by publicly naming the problem, Friedan *inspired women to take action to overcome it.*

As women came together and shared their stories of unhappiness and dissatisfaction, they stopped blaming themselves for failing to comply with the happy housewife image. Instead, they began to critically examine society through the lens of their own experiences and to challenge the social norms and expectations of the woman-as-housewife model. From their shared knowledge of what life was really like for American housewives, women developed a feminist standpoint—a critical perspective on reality and a position of political consciousness—that seriously questioned the legitimacy of the dominant worldview that women's natural and biological destiny was limited to the role of wife and mother. As Joyce McCarl Nielsen (1990) explains, "Without the conscious effort to reinterpret reality from one's own lived experience—that is, without political consciousness—the disadvantaged [women] are likely to accept their society's dominant world view" (p. 11). By drawing on their feminist standpoint, women were able to evaluate their experiences as housewives and mothers from a fresh perspective. They came to understand their experiences in the home not as an inescapable biological and natural destiny but instead as a role constructed and imposed on them by patriarchal society. This heightened awareness enabled women to resist dominant social perceptions that linked them exclusively to the roles of wife and mother and empowered them to pursue life and career paths outside of these roles.

Anita Hill's 1991 testimony about the sexual harassment she suffered from then judicial nominee Clarence Thomas, and the heightened awareness and legal protections against sexual harassment in the workforce that followed, provides another striking example of the vital relationship between granting voice to women's experiences of oppression and activating movement toward social change. In 1991, Hill articulated her experience of sexual harassment in a public hearing before the Senate judiciary committee. Humble and soft-spoken, Hill was a reluctant public witness. Yet her descriptions of the harassment she endured resonated with countless American women. On hearing Hill's story, thousands of American women came forward and told similar stories of abuse they had endured in the workplace. Women who had previously suffered in silence on the job filed a record number of sexual harassment complaints. Sexual harassment laws were rewritten or tightened in business and in government. The year following Hill's testimony, 1992, was hailed "the year of the woman," as a record number of women were elected to Congress, attributed largely to the "Anita Hill effect" (George-Graves, 2003, p. 16).

Anita Hill's testimony provided women with the courage and strength to build a critique of sexual harassment and to fight against it. As women came together and shared their stories, they stopped suffering alone and blaming themselves for the harassment they encountered. They stopped perceiving sexual harassment as a personal problem that they had to endure in private and questioning whether such harassment was a result of their own shortcomings.

Instead, drawing from their own experiences of sexual harassment, women developed a new point of view and position—a feminist standpoint—on the culture of the workplace as a whole. As women examined the workplace through the lens of their own experiences, they started to unpack connections between the harassment they suffered and several aspects of workplace structure—namely, widespread power imbalances based on gender and a blatant lack of laws prohibiting the sexual harassment of women and providing any serious recourse for women to fight against it. Thus, out of the process of sharing and articulating their experiences of harassment, women acquired a heightened level of consciousness about the issue and began to interpret their own experiences from a new perspective. This new perspective—or feminist standpoint—enabled women to locate the true root cause of sexual harassment and empowered them to do something to change it.

WOMEN'S EXPERIENCES AND DOUBLE CONSCIOUSNESS

Feminist standpoint scholarship and research teach us that women's experiences of oppression provide a powerful lens through which to evaluate society and a base from which to change it. In this section, we explore one aspect of the lens created from women's experiences of oppression in greater detail, an aspect feminist standpoint scholars call "double vision" or "double consciousness."

We now turn to the following questions:

- What is double consciousness?
- How does it develop out of women's experiences of oppression?
- Does it offer women unique insights into society as a whole?
- What about its utility for social change?

Feminist standpoint scholars argue that women, as members of an oppressed group, have cultivated a double consciousness—a heightened awareness not only of their own lives but of the lives of the dominant group (men) as well. Often, women's daily lives and labor remain invisible to the dominant group (men). Women, on the other hand, are tuned in to the "dominant worldview of the society *and* their own minority perspective" (Nielsen, 1990, p. 10). Put differently, women have a "working, active consciousness" of both perspectives (Smith, 1990, p. 19). In some cases, women's capacity for double consciousness grows out of their compliance with socially dictated roles, such as those of wife and mother. In other cases, women develop a double consciousness to ensure their own, and their family's, physical and economic survival.

Men do not necessarily recognize, nor are they always conscious of, the daily labor many women perform in the home and their dependence on it. But many women must attend to the everyday tasks of cooking, laundry, and child care, *and* learn to navigate, or at least become functionally familiar with, the (male-dominated) public sphere of the capitalist marketplace. In this respect, women mediate between two worlds, the world of "localized activities oriented toward particular others, keeping things clean, managing somehow the house and household and the children" and the male world of the marketplace, a world of abstraction and rationality (Smith, 1990, p. 20). Susan Ostrander's (1984) research shows, for example, that in addition to managing the household, women are often expected to be conversant in, and acquire a working knowledge of, their husbands' work activities. Familiarity with the names of coworkers and the daily goings on in their husbands' workplaces enables women to provide emotional support to their husbands, support that ultimately maintains their husbands' ongoing participation and success in the public sphere (Ostrander, 1984; Smith, 1999).

While some women develop a double consciousness as they attempt to conform to particular social roles and expectations, other women rely on their capacity for double consciousness to protect themselves and to ensure survival. As Joyce McCarl Nielsen (1990) explains, if a woman is in an oppressed position, it is often to her advantage to be "attuned and attentive" to the male perspective as well as to her own. To survive "socially and sometimes even physically," women must familiarize themselves with how "men view the world" and to be able to "read, predict, and understand the interests, motivations, expectations, and attitudes of men" (p. 10). Harriet Jacobs's (1861/1987) survival story serves as a striking case in point. To protect herself against the sexual abuse of her master as best she could, Jacobs had to become an expert knower of his mind and moods. As she explains, "He was a crafty man, and resorted to many means to accomplish his purposes"—sometimes he had "stormy, terrific ways, that made his victims tremble; sometimes he assumed a gentleness that he thought must surely subdue" (p. 27). Upon familiarizing herself with her master's psychology, Jacobs determined that his "quiet moods" were the most dangerous—"of the two, I preferred his stormy moods, although they left me trembling" (p. 27)—and found creative and skillful ways to avoid such moods.

bell hooks's (2004) account of growing up poor and black in Southern Kentucky provides another example of how double consciousness can develop as individuals fight to maintain survival, in particular material survival. Every day, hooks and her neighbors would cross the tracks to the white section of town where, working as maids, janitors, and prostitutes, they earned just enough money to obtain food, clothing, and shelter for themselves and their families. They were permitted to work in the white section of town, with its "paved streets, stores we were not allowed to enter, restaurants we could not eat in, and people we could not look directly in the face," as long as it was in the "service capacity" (p. 156). However, they were not allowed to live there. At the end of each day of work, hooks and her neighbors would cross the tracks to "shacks and abandoned houses on the edge of town." "There were laws to ensure our return. Not to return was to risk being punished" (p. 156). By crossing the tracks to work everyday, hooks and her neighbors developed a "working consciousness" of the white world as well as their own. Whites however, seldom crossed the tracks in the other direction.

hooks's (2004) account focuses more on African Americans as an oppressed group versus whites as a dominant group rather than women versus men. However, hooks's explanation of how double consciousness develops as individuals fight for material survival can be applied specifically to women as well. It is probable that some of the African American individuals that hooks describes were women who worked for white men and who depended on white men for their material survival. In fact, some feminist standpoint scholars draw parallels between women's capacity for double consciousness and the capacity for double consciousness among other oppressed groups, such as African Americans. Joyce McCarl Nielsen (1990) states:

> Given that blacks in our culture are exposed to dominant white culture in school and through mass media as well as in interaction with whites, we can see how it is possible that blacks could know both white and black culture while whites know only their own. The same might be said for women vis-à-vis men. (p. 10)[3]

It should be clear now that women's capacity for double consciousness grants them a unique perspective, or lens, through which to evaluate society as a whole. Out of their experiences of oppression and exploitation, and their enactment of gender specific (subordinate) roles, women have developed, in hooks's (2004) language, a "mode of seeing unknown to most of our oppressors" (p. 156). Women are tuned in to men's activities, attitudes, and behaviors *and* to their own. But men, as members of the dominant group, are not necessarily tuned in to women's activities and behaviors; instead men's mode of seeing reality is more likely to be rooted exclusively in their own experiences. Women's capacity for double consciousness enables them to see and understand "certain features of reality . . . from which others [men] are obscured" (Jaggar, 2004, p. 60). This unique "mode of seeing," this ability to know and understand the dominant group's attitudes and behaviors as well as their own, places women in an advantageous position from which to change society for the better. To improve a given society, it is necessary to comprehend how that society functions as a whole, become familiar with the everyday lives of the dominant groups and the oppressed groups, and understand the interrelations between them. Thus, the knowledge gleaned from women's double consciousness can be applied to diagnose social inequalities and injustices and to construct and implement solutions. bell hooks (2004) sums it up best when she says that double consciousness serves both as a powerful "space of resistance" and a "site of radical possibility" (p. 156).

WOMEN'S EXPERIENCES AND STRONG OBJECTIVITY

Some feminist standpoint scholars argue that women's subordinate status in society, and their capacity for double consciousness that evolves from it, places them in a privileged position from which to generate knowledge about the world. This feminist standpoint concept, sometimes called "strong objectivity,"[4] teaches us that women are more capable of producing an *accurate, comprehensive, and objective* interpretation of social reality than men are. As Alison Jaggar (2004) explains, women's "distinctive social position" makes possible a "view of the world that is more reliable and less distorted" than that available to the "ruling class" (or men; pp. 56, 57). Furthermore, some feminist standpoint scholars argue that research that begins from women's everyday lives as members of an oppressed group will lead to knowledge claims that are "less partial and distorted" than research that begins "from the lives of men in the dominant groups" (Harding, 1991, p. 185). Why? We turn now to a more detailed explanation, with examples.

In many societies, feminist standpoint scholars argue, knowledge is produced and controlled by the ruling class. Therefore, in a given society, the prevailing interpretation of reality will reflect the interests and values of the ruling class. Because of its commitment to maintaining power, the ruling class seeks to conceal the ways in which it dominates and exploits the rest of the population. The interpretation of reality the ruling class presents will be distorted such that the "suffering of the subordinate classes will be ignored, redescribed as enjoyment or justified as freely chosen, deserved, or inevitable" (Jaggar, 2004, p. 56). The positions of power and privilege that members of the ruling class inhabit allow them to separate and insulate themselves from the suffering of the oppressed, and to be more easily convinced by their own (distorted) ideology. Members of the ruling class experience the "current organization of society as basically satisfactory and so they accept the interpretation of reality that justifies that system of organization. They encounter little in their daily lives that conflicts with that interpretation" (p. 56).

Members of the ruling class are satisfied with the status quo and have no cause to question the prevailing interpretation of reality. The daily suffering faced by members of the oppressed groups, on the other hand, presents a series of "particularly significant *problems to be explained*" (Harding, 1993, p. 54) and demands further investigation. Sometimes the dominant (ruling-class-authored) ideology succeeds in temporarily convincing oppressed groups to accept their pain, to self-blame, or to deny it altogether. But ultimately, the pervasiveness, intensity, and relentlessness of their suffering push oppressed groups toward a

> realization that something is wrong with the social order. Their pain provides them with a motivation for finding out what is wrong, for criticizing accepted interpretations of reality, and for developing new and less distorted ways of understanding the world. (Jaggar, 2004, p. 56)[5]

Women, as members of an oppressed group, have no cause or motivation to misconstrue reality. Unlike men, who, as ruling class members, have constructed a distorted interpretation of reality to protect their interests and maintain their power, women's subordinate status means that they are likely to develop a "clearer and more trustworthy understanding of the world" (Jaggar, 2004, p. 62). Let's start with the example of Harriet Jacobs. If we examine the institution of slavery from her standpoint, through her eyes and her own lived experience of it, we obtain an interpretation of the institution that differs greatly from the dominant interpretations at the time. Slave owners constructed a paternalistic discourse about slavery: Slaves were helpless, weak minded, even subhuman, and masters were kindly father figures who took care of them and provided for them. Slave women were often portrayed as animal-like, hypersexualized, and in need of being "tamed" by the Victorian virtues and morals of their white mistresses. From Harriet Jacobs, we learn the truth about the widespread cruel and brutal treatment of slaves by their masters, and we learn about the humanity, suffering, and courage of slave women in particular. By exposing the reality of the sexual violence and exploitation that many slave women were forced to endure, Jacobs succeeded in challenging the (distorted) ideologies about slave women that held sway at the time.

Betty Friedan's (1963) research on American housewives in the 1950s and 1960s provides another example of how women's subordinate status in society places them in an advantageous position from which to build knowledge—to construct a more accurate picture of social reality. As we learned about in an earlier section, dominant ideologies and media images of the 1950s portrayed women as happy housewives—women's true and only calling in life was that of wife and mother. But in reality, many women were feeling unhappy, dissatisfied, and limited by that role. And these feelings of emotional pain and frustration motivated women to come forward and challenge the widespread happy housewife ideology. Women were able to successfully question the validity of an accepted interpretation of reality—that of the happy housewife—based on *their own knowledge and lived experience as housewives*. Finally, by overturning that (distorted) happy housewife ideology, women were free to step outside the boundaries and restrictions of the housewife role, to pursue other goals, interests, and skills—in short, to construct a new reality that more accurately reflected the full range of their potential as human beings.

In sum, the feminist standpoint concept of strong objectivity teaches us that the representation of reality from the standpoint of women is "more objective and unbiased than the prevailing representations that reflect the standpoint of men" (Jaggar, 2004, p. 62). Strong objectivity stems from women's oppressed position in society and from their capacity for double consciousness that evolves from that position. Because women can know and understand the dominant groups' behaviors and ideologies as well as their own, starting research from women's lives means that "certain areas or aspects of the world are not excluded" (Jaggar, 2004, p. 62). As Sandra Harding (2004b) puts it, "Starting off research from women's lives will generate less partial and distorted accounts not only of women's lives but also of men's lives and of the whole social order" (p. 128).

NEW COMPLEXITIES AND MULTIPLE STANDPOINTS

As we have learned above, some feminist standpoint scholars argue that women's subordinate status in society, combined with their capacity for double consciousness, grants them a kind of "epistemological privilege" (Jaggar, 1997; Narayan, 2004) from which new and critical research questions arise. These new and critical questions, if explored, may produce a less "distorted" and more "reliable" understanding of social reality (Harding, 1993; Jaggar, 1997, p. 192). Further, and perhaps most important, because research that starts from women's lives yields a more accurate picture of how a given society functions, it also uncovers the *necessary ingredients for social change*. Only by exposing the intraworkings of society as a whole do we learn about which elements require modification and reconstruction such that a more just, humane, and equitable society can be constructed. As Alison Jaggar (1997) explains, because research that begins with women's lives grants a more accurate and "reliable appraisal" of society, it *also* grants us a "better chance" of "ascertaining the possible beginnings" of a new society, a society in which all members can equally thrive (p. 192).

More recently, however, some feminist standpoint scholars have begun to challenge and rework the claim of women's capacity for a more complete understanding of social reality and the potentiality of producing more "objective" results by beginning research from the lives of women. As Joyce McCarl Nielsen (1990) puts it, feminist standpoint claims to accuracy and objectivity are both "promising and problematic" (p. 25). One the one hand, feminist standpoint scholars remain committed to the "liberating effect" of these claims and the goals of social justice and social change that accompany them. After all, the main purpose of attaining a more accurate, more complete understanding of society is to be able to change it for the "betterment of all" (p. 25). On the other hand, many object to the very notion, implicit within these feminist standpoint claims to accuracy and objectivity, that the experiences and perspectives of one group (in this case women's) are more "real (better or more accurate) than another's" (p. 25).

Beyond the difficulties of establishing that women as a group, unlike men as a group, have a unique and exclusive capacity for accurately reading the complexities of social reality, it is equally problematic to reduce all women to a group sharing one experience and a single point of view, or standpoint, based on that experience. This form of essentialism is a double-edged sword. Notions of objectivity, and the "more accurate" or "more reliable" standpoint of women, become increasingly difficult to negotiate as a diverse array of women's experiences are taken into account.

- How is the nature of feminist standpoint epistemology changing as racial, cultural, and class-based differences between women are exposed?
- As feminist standpoint scholars recognize women's multiple social realities, do they lose the capacity to produce truthful and meaningful research findings?
- Do the experiences and standpoints of some women offer a more objective and accurate assessment of social reality than those of others?
- If so, what are the criteria for determining the experiences and standpoints that are the most or the least reliable?

Let's turn to these critical questions in greater detail.

Most feminist standpoint scholars now acknowledge that women "occupy many different standpoints and inhabit many different realities" (Hekman, 2004, p. 227). In short, they take differences between women seriously. However, while the claim that women can be categorized into one group with uniform characteristics and a single standpoint has been discarded, feminist standpoint scholars continue to debate how best to incorporate women's differences into the research process. A range of strategies has been suggested. Sandra Harding (1991, 1993, 2004a) has proposed several, two of which are highlighted here. The first requires the consideration of women's different standpoints but at the same time maintains that some standpoints may generate more truthful, objective knowledge claims than others. Specifically, this tactic suggests that the higher the level of oppression, the more objective the account: The standpoint of the most oppressed group of women will generate the most truthful research findings. As Harding (1991) explains,

> It should be clear that if it is beneficial to start research, scholarship and theory in white women's situations, then we should be able to learn even more about the social and natural orders if we start from the situations of women in de-valued and oppressed races, classes and cultures. (pp. 179–180)

In this approach, Harding urges researchers and scholars to engage in a process of "critical evaluation" to determine which social situations "tend to generate the most objective knowledge claims" (Harding, 1991, p. 142).

In a second approach, Harding (1993, 2004a) calls for heightened attention to be paid to the differences and even the conflicts between women's standpoints:

> Feminist knowledge has started off from women's lives, but it has started off from many different women's lives; there is no typical or essential woman's life from which feminisms start their thought. Moreover, these different women's lives are in important respects opposed to each other. (Harding, 1993, p. 65)

In this approach, Harding (2004a) emphasizes that it is precisely in the differences, diversity, and even conflict between women's experiences that we can learn the most about society at large. As she explains,

> Each oppressed group will have its own critical insights about nature and the larger social order in order to contribute to the collection of human knowledge. Because different groups are oppressed in different ways, each has the possibility (not the certainty) of developing distinctive insights about systems of social relations in general in which their oppression is a feature. (p. 9)

And yet, despite Harding's call to recognize difference—the "subjects/agents of feminist standpoint theory" are "multiple, heterogeneous, and contradictory"—she continues to emphasize the fact that the experiences of the oppressed, no matter how diverse, produce more accurate accounts of the social order than the accounts of the dominant groups. She states, "Nevertheless, thought that starts off from each of these different kinds of lives can generate less partial and distorted accounts of nature and social life" (Harding, 1993, p. 65).

In contrast to Harding's concept of a "maximally objective" standpoint, but in resonance with Harding's recent emphasis on difference, other feminist scholars also focus on the *diverse array* of knowledge found within a multiplicity of standpoints. Instead of attempting to find tactics that reduce all standpoints to the "least distorted one," or to generate universal knowledge claims from an additive model of multiple standpoints, these feminist scholars question whether it is possible, or even desirable, to "produce a single, unified and complete description of the world" (Longino, 1999, p. 339). Each woman's standpoint presents a unique lived experience and perspective and *should be valued as such.* According to these feminist standpoint scholars, paying attention to the distinctive characteristics of each woman's standpoint, and the diversity among and between women's experiences, does not interfere with our capacity to build knowledge. In fact, it is precisely within the distinctive characteristics of a particular standpoint, or the uniqueness of a particular woman's experience, that we can hope to find new knowledge.

Donna Haraway (1991) and Helen Longino (1999) argue that knowledge grows out of women's unique lived experiences, and the specific interpretations of social reality (or standpoints) that accompany those experiences. Instead of attempting to glide over differences between women, Haraway (1991) points to the invaluable insights gleaned from the differences between women's standpoints and the "elaborate specificity" of each (p. 190). Similarly, Longino (1999) asserts that women's knowledge is located in "particular places, in particular times" (p. 333). Women have different standpoints, and embody different knowledges, depending on how they are oriented toward, and interact with, their environments. In this way, each woman's unique experience and standpoint directs our attention to details and features that we might otherwise overlook (p. 335).

By applying the knowledge-building strategies proposed by Sandra Harding, Donna Haraway, and Helen Longino to some of the women's lives that we have become familiar with throughout this chapter, we gain a clearer understanding of how each of their strategies actually work in practice. According to Sandra Harding's first tactic, for example, the lives and experiences of poor African American women (highlighted by Patricia Hill Collins's, 1990, research) potentially offer a more accurate and complete picture of social reality than the lives and experiences of white middle- and upper-middle-class housewives (highlighted by Betty Friedan's, 1963, research). The implication is not to deny any oppression or suffering experienced by white women. However, because the oppression and suffering experienced by African American women as a group tends to be greater than that of white women, it is by starting from the lives and experiences of

African American women that we achieve a more objective standpoint on society as a whole.

According to Donna Haraway (1991) and Helen Longino (1999), we can learn more by paying close attention to the unique perspective, or standpoint, on social reality that the experiences of African American women and white women offer us. Each of these women's experiences teaches us something different and valuable about society. By starting with the everyday lives of poor African American women, we learn about society from the perspective of women who have to work outside the home to make ends meet. We learn about low wages; the lack of quality, affordable child care; and the creative alternative child care strategies that African American women have developed. By starting with the everyday lives of white middle- and upper-middle-class housewives on the other hand, we learn about society from the perspective of women who do not have to work outside the home to make ends meet. We learn about the dissatisfaction and isolation these women experience as they perform their daily housekeeping and nurturing tasks in the home—and about the falseness of the happy housewife imagery and ideology. We also learn about women's desires to expand their lives beyond the roles of wife and mother—to enter the outside world of work.

OVERCOMING RELATIVISM

If, as Donna Haraway (1991), Helen Longino (1999), Sandra Harding (1991, 1993, 2004a, 2004b), and others encourage, we value the unique perspective on reality—or standpoint—produced by each woman's lived experience and respect the diversity of knowledge generated by women's many different experiences, do we also give up the opportunity for political activism?

- Is it possible to value a diverse range of women's perspectives and lived experiences *and* come together and create an organized force for social change?

Joyce McCarl Nielsen (1990) characterizes this dilemma as follows: "Once one rejects objectivism, the alternative seems to be a kind of relativism that is not very satisfying" (p. 28). It is difficult to combine women's many experiences into one universal standpoint without risking the repression of differences between women or the reduction of all women to a single group with uniform characteristics. On the other hand, by valuing the diversity of women's experiences and perspectives equally, feminist standpoint scholars must be careful to avoid a kind of paralysis that hinders women from moving forward together and taking a stand on social issues. If all groups produce "specialized thought and each group's thought is equally valid" and no group can claim to have a "better interpretation of 'the truth' than another" (Collins, 1993, p. 625), do we risk a state of apolitical relativism, a state of "being nowhere while claiming to be everywhere equally" (Haraway, 1991, p. 191)? It seems clear that if women are going to work to influence, change, and create new social policies, it is imperative that they develop some common ground or shared perspectives to meet with success. As Joyce McCarl Nielsen (1990) explains,

> One could argue that there is no need to determine one view as more correct, that plurality of views could prevail. But at some point—such as when important decisions have to be made—some view of social reality must be endorsed. To develop a policy about abortion, for example, one would have to take a stance in an area where there are conflicting, seemingly irreconcilable views. (p. 27)

But how can we facilitate the coming together of women with different lived experiences and unique perspectives and encourage the bridging of standpoints needed to wage a successful battle for social change without also suppressing the diversity and uniqueness of each?

Many feminist standpoint scholars emphasize the need for open dialogue between women and across different perspectives as a first step toward building the kinds of allied networks or solid bases needed to fight from. Helen Longino (1999) encourages the development of sites of "critical discourse" both within and between communities. In these sites, community members freely express their own perspectives *and* engage in dialogue with other communities whose "shared background is different" (p. 343). Similarly, bell hooks (1990) declares the need for "meaningful contestation and constructive confrontation" between different perspectives and urges the creation of safe spaces "where critical dialogues can take place between individuals who have not traditionally been compelled . . . to speak with one another" (p. 133).

The kind of dialogue that feminist standpoint scholars encourage is one in which every woman's unique lived experience and the perspective, or standpoint, based on her experience gains a hearing. Indeed, some feminist standpoint scholars argue that through the very process of constructing a space that is open to dialogue across women's different experiences and standpoints, a space where a multiplicity of women's voices are granted equal air time, we actually build *community*. Patricia Hill Collins (1990) urges us to hearken back to the African call and response tradition, whereby everyone must learn to speak and to listen to ensure membership in the community: "Everyone has a voice, but everyone must listen and respond to other voices in order to be allowed to remain in the community" (p. 625–626). In the context of such a community, a community that serves as a gathering site on which multiple standpoints converge, and where respectful listening and dialogic interchange is encouraged, we can begin to imagine the potential for increased under-standing among and between women from different backgrounds and cultures and from different life experiences.

Patricia Hill Collins (1993) describes the potential for community-driven growth of empathetic understanding between groups who hold different stand-points as follows:

> Each group speaks from its own standpoint and shares its own partial, situ-ated knowledge. But because each group perceives its own truth as partial, its knowledge is unfinished. Each group becomes better able to consider other groups' standpoints without relinquishing the uniqueness of its own stand-point or suppressing other groups' partial perspectives. (p. 626)

In this way, through communal dialogue, a multiplicity of views are shared and listened to. It is precisely because each community member is able to trust that her own unique perspective will be heard and respected that she is able to fully hear and respect the views of others. Such communal dialogue may enable us to reach a point at which, as Elsa Barkley Brown puts it, "all people can learn to center in another's experience, validate it, and judge it by its own standards without need of comparison or need to adopt that framework as their own" (cited in Collins, 1993, p. 625). But beyond facilitating empa-thetic understanding across women's standpoints *and* respecting the diversity and uniqueness of each, can such communal dialogue enable active alliances between standpoints?

In fact, as feminist standpoint scholars point out, communal dialogue that fosters interaction between women while also maintaining respect for the diversity of women's perspectives sets the stage for intragroup connections and enables the growth of alliances that are needed to wield power and forge social change. As women's diverse standpoints are shared, respectfully listened to, and validated, connections may be made "where none existed before" (Walker, cited in Collins, 1993, p. 625). As a woman shares her story of being sexually harassed in the workforce or being denied access to a safe and legal abortion, for example, other women who have not experienced these same events but have encountered gender-based exploitation and feelings of powerlessness in other contexts will probably connect to her experience.

These connections do not have to be made at the expense of diversity, nor do they risk the denial of women's different and unique lived experiences. Instead, women can connect with one another through identifying a "common thread," or a "unifying theme through immense diversity" (Walker, cited in Collins, 1993, p. 625). Let's say, for example, that working women from a range of socioeconomic, racial, and cultural backgrounds came together to share and listen to each other's experiences and perspectives on work and family issues. Without denying or disrespecting each other's differences, they could probably unite around some common problems and join together to fight for some common goals, such as equal pay to men, better maternity leave programs, more affordable and quality child care, and better protections against sexual harassment in the workforce. Joyce McCarl Nielsen (1990) describes this process as a "fusion of horizons": "With communication across and among a diversity of women's standpoints, each standpoint may be enlarged, enriched, or broadened such that a fusion, or synthesis, between standpoints may occur" (p. 29).[6]

By coming together and sharing their unique experiences and perspectives, women can build alliances, develop a common position, and take a stand on a particular issue without compromising their differences. Achieving a shared position, or standpoint, on a particular issue promotes the most promising course of action for social change—a solid base from which to fight. At the same time, we must also remember that women's experiences, perspectives, and the issues they face are constantly evolving and changing across space and time. Therefore, it is important that dialogue between and among women does not *end* with the achievement of a particular alliance, or shared standpoint. Instead, as many feminist standpoint scholars point out, dialogue must be *ongoing*. We must work to find ways to incorporate continuous listening and interchange into our communities of women—or, more simply, to construct *community* in Patricia Hill Collins's sense of the word. Such ongoing dialogue and debate, if successfully integrated into our communities, also drives, and even guarantees, a built-in process of healthy evaluation, a process Helen Longino (1999) calls "socializing justification." Maintaining a safe space for ongoing dialogue and debate—and for the creation and re-creation of new alliances and standpoints among and between women—remains acutely important as new issues arise and as women's struggles for justice take on new shape and form.

In many respects, committing to ongoing dialogic interchange and evaluative processes between and among women's standpoints is one and the same with committing to the ongoing struggle for women's empowerment. After all, women's struggles are not uniform or stagnant but ongoing and subject to change. For example, take the issue of women and work. In the 1960s and 1970s, women fought just to gain entry into the workforce.[7] Then, there were the struggles for equal pay. Now women are fighting for better maternity leave policies and more affordable quality child care.[8] The fact that women's experience, and their standpoint on reality that evolves from that experience, may change and evolve across space and time does not make it any less real or legitimate. As Linda Alcoff (1989) argues, women can achieve a positionality, or standpoint, that is simultaneously "determinate" *and* "mutable" (p. 325). In other words, we can treat women's standpoints on a particular issue or set of issues as legitimate, as serious, as grounded in social reality while also acknowledging these standpoints' location within a "moving historical context" (p. 325). Indeed, by highlighting "historical movement and the subject's ability to alter her context" (p. 325), we take women's standpoints seriously without reducing all women to a universal group with the same experiences, needs, and characteristics.

CONCLUSION

Feminist standpoint epistemology is an innovative approach to knowledge building that breaks down boundaries between academia and activism, between theory and practice. Feminist standpoint scholars seek to give voice to members of oppressed groups—namely, women—and to uncover the hidden knowledge that women have cultivated from living life "on the margins." Feminist standpoint epistemology asks not just that we take women seriously as knowers but that we translate women's knowledge into practice, that we apply what we learn from women's experiences toward social change and toward the elimination of the oppression not only of women but of all marginalized groups.

Feminist standpoint epistemology has become more complex and multi-faceted and continues to evolve over time. Feminist standpoint scholars no longer talk about *the* experience of women or conflate all women into one oppressed group. They recognize instead that women hail from a diverse range of class, cultural, and racial backgrounds, inhabit many different social realities, and endure oppression and exploitation in many different shapes and forms. As a result, the theoretical development of feminist standpoint episte-mology is multidimensional and ongoing, and scholars working within the feminist standpoint framework continue to apply new and innovative research methods to capture the diversity of women's lives and experiences. Some of these methods will be explored in other chapters in this volume. Finally, while feminist standpoint scholars understand and recognize differences between and among women—different experiences of oppression and different stand-points, or perspectives, based on those experiences—they also continue to emphasize the importance of dialogue between and among women, the need for empathetic understanding, and the potential for achieving alliances. After all, alliances between and among women are possible—*without risking the repression of difference*—and *necessary*, if we hope to fight for more just societies and to improve women's condition within them.

NOTES

1. This is excerpted from a letter written by Harriet Jacobs to her publisher in 1857. In it, Jacobs describes her motivation for writing her autobiography, titled *Incidents in the Life of a Slave Girl, Written by Herself.*

2. It is important to note that although feminist research methods are not the explicit focus of this chapter, feminist research methods were employed in many of the studies on women's lives and experiences that are cited throughout. The discussions of women's lives and experiences in this chapter are concerned more with content than with method. However, because many of the women's lives and experiences high-lighted here would not be known about except for the application of new and innova-tive feminist methods, the importance of such methods is implicit. After all, the framework of feminist standpoint epistemology demands that women's lives and expe-riences, "hitherto denied, repressed, and subordinated" (Smith, 1990, p. 12), break out and gain a hearing. To gain access to and uncover women's lives and experiences, new and innovative feminist methods are often required. Feminist interviewing,

autobiography, oral history techniques, and institutional ethnography are examples of the feminist methods used to acquire the information about women's lives and experiences cited in this chapter. These feminist methods, among others, will be discussed in greater detail and serve as the primary focus of later chapters in this volume.

3. The philosopher G.W. F. Hegel's (1967) concept of the "master-slave dialectic" easily applies here but transferred to the case of women and men. Hegel explains that the master is only able to have an illusion of independence, the illusion of an independent consciousness, precisely because of his dependence upon his slave. Without his slave's emotional and material labor, he would not be free to engage in "independent pursuits." While the slave, to ensure his own survival, must remain aware not only of his own world but the world of his master as well, the master, due to his privileged position, is able to remain unaware of the world of his slave. Indeed, just as many men remain unaware of their dependence upon women's labor (labor which sustains their dominance) so too is the master unaware of his dependence upon the slave.

4. The concept "strong objectivity" was developed and named by feminist standpoint scholar and philosopher Sandra Harding. For more from Harding on strong objectivity, see the first Behind-the-Scenes piece in Chapter 1 of this volume. See also Harding's book *Whose Science? Whose Knowledge?* (Harding, 1991) and her chapter "Rethinking Standpoint Epistemology: What is 'Strong Objectivity?'" in *Feminist Epistemologies* (Harding, 1993) and, in updated form, in *The Feminist Standpoint Theory Reader: Intellectual and Political Controversies* (Harding, 2004a), edited by Sandra Harding. Please also note that "strong reflexivity," an important aspect of Harding's "strong objectivity" that bears relevance to the method and practice of research, is not the focus of our discussion here. Strong reflexivity demands that researchers actively acknowledge, and reflect on, how their social locations, biographical histories, and worldviews interact with, influence, and are influenced by the research process. For more from Harding on strong reflexivity, see the second Behind-the-Scenes piece in Chapter 1 of this volume. Finally, some manifestations of strong reflexivity—namely, practicing reflexivity about one's own social location, biographical history, and worldview throughout the research process—are discussed in Chapter 5 of this volume.

5. In some instances however, while women's suffering plays a large role, it is not their pain alone that motivates them to begin to critique and challenge the status quo. As we have learned about in the case of American housewives of the 1950s or from the women who suffered from sexual harassment in the early 1990s, sometimes a process of consciousness-raising also needs to occur. As women come together and share their stories and begin to understand that they are not suffering alone, they stop blaming themselves for their own suffering and are empowered to look outward, toward society, and challenge the societal norms and dominant ideologies that are oppressing them. In this way, women's critical point of view—their position of political consciousness— their feminist standpoint—has to be *achieved* (Hartsock, 2004) through a process of consciousness-raising, as opposed to stemming directly and unproblematically from their pain and suffering.

6. Another hypothetical example of Walker's (cited in Collins, 1993) concept of a "unifying theme through immense diversity" and Nielsen's (1990) "fusion of horizons" is as follows: If a group of women get together to discuss abortion rights, each woman's standpoint may be deepened or broadened as she learns about other women's experiences, concerns, and perspectives. A woman who is socioeconomically privileged may focus solely on the legal right to choose to have an abortion. A woman who is from a rural area may also be worried about a literal lack of access to doctors' offices or clinics in her area that perform abortions. Finally, a poor woman may express concern about whether she can afford to pay for a safe and legal abortion. Through sharing and listening to each other's different concerns, these women might formulate a more complex, more developed standpoint on abortion rights—moving from a straightforward pro-choice position to a pro-choice position that demands a certain number of available clinics per region *and* governmental assistance to help ensure that poor women can obtain safe and legal abortions.

7. That is not to deny the many thousands of women who had been tilling the land and working in service, industry, education, and medicine prior to the 1960s and 1970s. After all, for hundreds of years many women across the globe have had to work to maintain their own, and their families', survival.

8. It is also important to note that each of these struggles are ongoing: Women still do not equal men's numbers in the higher-ranking professions, for example, and continue to make less money than men make in equivalent positions.

REFERENCES

Anderson, Kathryn, & Jack, Dana C. (1991). Learning to listen: Interview techniques and analysis. In Sherna B. Gluck & Daphne Patai (Eds.), *Women's words: The feminist practice of oral history* (pp. 11–26). New York: Routledge.

Alcoff, Linda. (1989). Cultural feminism versus post-structuralism: The identity crisis in feminist theory. In Micheline R. Malson, Jean F. O'Barr, Sarah Westphal-Wihl, & Mary Wyer (Eds.), *Feminist theory in practice and process* (pp. 295–326). Chicago: University of Chicago Press.

Collins, Patricia Hill. (1990). *Black feminist thought: Knowledge, consciousness, and the politics of empowerment.* Boston: Unwin Hyman.

Collins, Patricia Hill. (1993). Black feminist thought in the matrix of domination. In Charles Lemert, (Ed.), *Social theory: The multicultural and classic readings* (pp. 615–626). Boulder, CO: Westview Press.

DeVault, Marjorie. (1990). Talking and listening from women's standpoint: Feminist strategies for interviewing and analysis. *Social Problems, 37,* 96–116.

DeVault, Marjorie. (1991). *Feeding the family: The social organization of caring as gendered work.* Chicago: University of Chicago Press.

Friedan, Betty. (1963). *The feminine mystique.* New York: Norton.

George-Graves, Florence. (2003, January 16). The complete Anita Hill. *Boston Globe Magazine,* pp. 15–24.

Haraway, Donna J. (1991). *Simians, cyborgs, and women.* New York: Routledge.

Harding, Sandra. (1991). *Whose science? Whose knowledge?* Ithaca, NY: Cornell University Press.

Harding, Sandra. (1993). Rethinking standpoint epistemology: What is "strong objectivity"? In L. Alcoff & E. Potter (Eds.), *Feminist epistemologies* (pp. 49–82). New York: Routledge.

Harding, Sandra. (2004a). Introduction: Standpoint theory as a site of political, philosophic, and scientific debate. In Sandra Harding (Ed.), *The feminist standpoint theory reader: Intellectual and political controversies* (pp. 1–15). New York: Routledge.

Harding, Sandra. (2004b). Rethinking feminist standpoint epistemology: What is "strong objectivity"? In Sandra Harding, (Ed.), *The feminist standpoint theory reader: Intellectual and political controversies,* (pp. 127–140). New York: Routledge.

Hartsock, Nancy C. M. (2004). The feminist standpoint: developing the ground for a specifically feminist historical materialism. In Sandra Harding (Ed.), *The feminist standpoint theory reader: Intellectual and political controversies* (pp. 35–53). New York: Routledge.

Hegel, G. F. W. (1967). *The phenomenology of mind* (J. B. Baillie, Trans.). New York: Harper & Row.

Hekman, Susan. (2004). Truth and method: Feminist standpoint theory revisited. In Sandra Harding (Ed.), *The feminist standpoint theory reader: Intellectual and political controversies* (pp. 225–241). New York: Routledge.

Hondagneu-Sotelo, Pierrette, & Avila, Ernestine. (1997). "I'm here but I'm there:" The meanings of Latina transnational motherhood. *Gender and Society, 11*(5), 548–571.

hooks, bell. (1990). Culture to culture: Ethnography and cultural studies as critical intervention. In *Yearning: Race, gender, and cultural politics* (pp. 123–133). Boston: South End Press.

hooks, bell. (2004). Choosing the margin as a space of radical openness. In Sandra Harding (Ed.), *The feminist standpoint theory reader: Political and intellectual controversies* (pp. 153–159). New York: Routledge.

Jacobs, Harriet. (1987). *Incidents in the life of a slave girl, written by herself.* Cambridge, MA: Harvard University Press. (Original work published 1861)

Jaggar, Alison M. (1997). Love and knowledge: Emotion in feminist epistemology. In Sandra Kemp & Judith Squires (Eds.), *Feminisms* (pp. 188–193). Oxford, UK: Oxford University Press.

Jaggar, Alison M. (2004). Feminist politics and epistemology: The standpoint of women. In Sandra Harding (Ed.), *The feminist standpoint theory reader: Intellectual and political controversies* (pp. 55–66). New York: Routledge.

Longino, Helen E. (1999). Feminist epistemology. In John Grecco & Ernest Sosa (Eds.), *The Blackwell guide to epistemology* (pp. 327–353). Malden, MA: Blackwell.

Narayan, Uma. (2004). The project of feminist epistemology: Perspectives from a non-Western feminist. In Sandra Harding (Ed.), *The feminist standpoint theory reader: Political and intellectual controversies* (pp. 213–224). New York: Routledge.

Nielsen, Joyce McCarl. (Ed.). (1990). Introduction. In Joyce McCarl Nielsen (Ed.), *Feminist research methods* (pp. 1–37). Boulder, CO: Westview Press.

Ostrander, Susan A. (1984). *Women of the upper class*. Philadelphia: Temple University Press.

Smith, Dorothy E. (1987). Women's perspective as a radical critique of sociology. In Sandra Harding (Ed.), *Feminism and methodology* (pp. 84–96). Bloomington: Indiana University Press.

Smith, Dorothy E. (1990). *The conceptual practices of power: A feminist sociology of knowledge.* Boston: Northeastern University Press.

Smith, Dorothy E. (1999). *Writing the social: Critique, theory, and investigations.* Toronto, Ontario, Canada: University of Toronto Press.

FOUR

FEMINIST POSTMODERNISM AND POSTSTRUCTURALISM

Patricia Lina Leavy

———◈———

When "The Repressed" of their culture and their society come back, it is an explosive return, which is absolutely *shattering, staggering, overturning, with a force never let loose before.*

—Cixous & Clément (1996, p. ix)

Efforts of subversion . . . are conceived within culture, within the languages which speak us, which we must turn to our own purposes.

—Du Bois (1988, p. 188)

I don't know about the term "postmodern," but if there is a point, and a fine point, to what I perhaps understand better as post-structuralism, it is that power pervades the very conceptual apparatus that seeks to negotiate its terms, including the subject position of the critic; and further, that this implication of the terms of criticism in the field of power is not *the advent of a nihilistic relativism incapable of furnishing norms, but, rather, the very precondition of a politically engaged critique.*

—Butler (1992, pp. 6–7)

eminist empiricism is often viewed as one end of the continuum on which feminist research is grounded, postmodernism is the other end. Although postmodernism is often talked about as a theoretical perspective, I believe that it reflects an epistemological position. Perhaps one of the reasons that postmodernism has been the subject of so much conflict is that it takes feminist concerns out of the realm of methodology and into the realm of epistemology. That is, postmodernism asks vital questions about the nature of knowledge and knowledge building. This epistemological grounding is the focus of this chapter.

While it is later in this chapter that I review feminist postmodernism in detail, thus differentiating it from feminist empiricism and standpoint episte-mology, it is important to explain how feminist postmodernism sits on the epistemology continuum in relation to these other positions. Postmodern fem-inist researchers explain that, in their own ways, both feminist empiricism and feminist standpoint epistemology ultimately revert to essentialist claims in the way they use "women" as an identity category. In this vein, postmodern fem-inism posits a "false divide" between feminist empiricism and standpoint, both of which have failed to end women's oppression and both of which rely on the same essentialism, which has caused the oppression feminists seek to do away with (Cosgrove, 2003). In short, both feminist empiricists and feminist stand-point epistemologists revert to essentialism by viewing gender as an indepen-dent variable (add women and stir into preexisting models) in the former, and as an inherent trait in the latter (Cosgrove, 2003; Hekman, 1999). The post-modern critique of feminist empiricism focuses on the extent to which femi-nist empiricism relies on positivist science which has ultimately failed to bring about gender equality. In this regard Lisa Cosgrove (2003) writes,

> The continued focus on gender difference research, together with the failure to address how gender is symbolized and produced, have contributed to the belief that differences between men and women are essential, universal, and ahistorical. (p. 91)

According to postmodern feminism, while standpoint theory has alerted researchers to their location within the research project, which could potentially "radicalize" the research process, standpoint does not go far enough and resorts to essentialist claims like "women's voice." For example, drawing on the work of Layton (1998, p. 217), Cosgrove (2003) explains that there is a fundamental difference in saying that women are relational and that "femininity is symbolized as relational" (p. 89). Standpoint does the former without looking at how gender is produced within the symbolic realm. Standpoint theorists' focus on "voice" often deters a closer examination of difference and "disidentification" (Cosgrove, 2003; Pujal, 1998). Cosgrove (2003) sums up the limitations of standpoint as follows:

> The issue is not with standpoint theory or with the metaphor of voice per se. Rather, the problem is that the implicit assumptions made about gender, experience, and identity—do not allow for an analysis of the complexity of power relations of which gender, identity, and experience are embedded. (pp. 89–90)

Feminist postmodern theory has developed as an alternative to these two approaches, which are often presented as polarized views but in actuality resort to the essentialist logic from which women's oppression has flowed. Postmodern feminism is thus at the other end of the feminist epistemology continuum while also problematizing the polarization of feminist empiricism and feminist standpoint epistemology.

Postmodern theory has perhaps garnered more criticism within academia than any other movement in recent history. Furthermore, within feminist scholarship the relationship between feminism and postmodernism has been a source of major division and consternation for fear that just when women are beginning to be included in the research process and have been given "voice," this new view on knowledge building threatens to undermine the success feminism has achieved. In some ways, the strongest critique of postmodern feminism has come from within feminism. However, while this critique is important, it all too often overshadows feminist postmodern epistemology. In this vein, I will begin by discussing some background in the development of postmodern thought followed by a review of feminist interpretations of postmodernism. After establishing what postmodernism is and how feminists have contributed to this grounding, I will review the major critique of feminist postmodernism, which centers on issues of political pragmatism, identity, subject position, and agency.

It is also important to mention upfront that postmodernism is an umbrella category that has been used to categorize disparate theoretical and epistemological viewpoints. Alcoff (1997) refers to postmodernism as "an inherently fractured term" (p. 6). Oftentimes, scholars have the label postmodern placed on them but would not define their work as such. Other times, the views that are considered postmodern are so different that a binding thread is difficult to discern. Some in fact wonder if postmodernism refers to a historical moment, a theoretical framework, an epistemology, or a certain set of concerns. Given the unprecedented and impassioned criticism that postmodernism has drawn within feminism and the larger research community, the grouping together of theories under the rubric of postmodernism becomes more important than one might assume. Butler has been particularly outspoken on the lumping together of a variety of theoretical and epistemological positions under the rubric of the "postmodern" and questions the political intent of doing so. For example, when disparate views are falsely joined together to create a "whole" theoretical framework, any of the pieces of the whole (any individual theories) can be used to represent "postmodernism." This is highly problematic in Judith Butler's (1992) view and itself represents a violent reduction. Butler begins her famous essay "Contingent Foundations: Feminism and the Question of 'Postmodernism'" by asking about postmodernism. She then writes,

> Who are these postmodernists? Is this a name that one takes on for oneself, or is it more often a name that one is called if and when one offers a critique of the subject, a discursive analysis, or questions the integrity or coherence of totalizing social descriptions? (p. 3)

Butler, herself applying a postmodern perspective, then goes further by looking at how power shapes the umbrella category of postmodernism and whose interests are served by this classification.

> But if I understand part of the project of postmodernism, is to call into question the ways in which such "examples" and "paradigms" serve to subordinate and erase that which they seek to explain. For the "whole," the field of postmodernism in its supposed breadth, is effectively "produced" by the example which is made to stand as a symptom and exemplar of the whole . . . we have then forced a substitution of the example for the entire field, effecting a violent reduction of the field to one piece of the text the critic is willing to read, a piece which, conveniently, uses the term "postmodern." In a sense, this gesture of conceptual mastery that groups together a set of positions under the postmodern, that makes the postmodern into an epoch or a synthetic whole, and that claims that the part can stand for this artificially constructed whole, enacts a certain self-regulatory ruse of power. (1992, p. 5)

While Butler's point is important in the debate of postmodernism that persists within the academy, I do not find this debate particularly fruitful for the purposes of this book and as such will limit my engagement with it. However, I must acknowledge that I am guilty of using the term *postmodernism* as an umbrella category and even using it to describe work that some scholars themselves might not define as such. Some of the work I mention is perhaps better described under the smaller category of poststructuralism and perhaps yet some does not fit either of these categories. In this sense, I fully acknowledge that I am not doing justice to the range of work and disidentification within the field of "postmodernism." Furthermore, because the term is used so broadly, there is a great deal of work that I will not be able to highlight in this chapter. In this sense, there is a selection process that results in the privileging of some feminist postmodern thinkers over others, but this choice has to be made to present an overview of the main contributions of postmodern thinking to feminist praxis.

THE DEVELOPMENT OF
POSTMODERN THOUGHT: AN OVERVIEW

Postmodern theory emerged largely in response to the limitations of modernism and the grand theories, or metanarratives, produced by modernists. Lyotard (1984) uses *modernism* as the term to denote any science that self-legitimates with reference to a grand theory (and thus the theory is reified by virtue of a tautology). The theory thus retains its own discursive grounding and cycles within itself. In other words, grand theories are definitive statements about how something is—they are self-legitimating explanations and their claims go unchallenged. These grand narratives become taken-for-granted explanations about social reality. Postmodernism points to the social construction of reality and how some interests may be served by particular constructions (Layton, 1998). This is useful to feminist researchers who are concerned with the social construction of gender, gender difference, and so on. For example, many feminists are concerned with culturally and historically specific notions of femininity and masculinity, particularly how they have come to be and who is served by these dominant and taken-for-granted understandings of gender. I will elaborate on this when I discuss the blending of feminism and postmodernism.

Metanarratives are organizing stories or narratives which create a unifica-
tion of ideas and methodologies which may be used to understand all
aspects of the social world. (Hepburn, 1999, Postmodern Politics section,
para. 5)

The focus on metanarratives that characterizes modernism under this
perspective has also served as an "exclusionary force" that fails to consider
difference and disidentification (Hepburn, 1999). Linked to the weariness surrounding metanarratives, postmodernism rejects the positivist conception of
knowledge building based on objectivity, neutrality, causality, patterning, and
the scientific method opting for highly reflexive and power-sensitive practice
(Haraway, 1991; Pfohl, 1992). Instead of grand narratives and truth claims,
postmodernism proposes an expansive study of difference and the inextricable
relationship between power and knowledge. Postmodernists even go further
than the "situated knowledges" of standpoint theorists by looking at the social
world in flux. Postmodernism also rejects the binary thinking that has dominated during modernism. For example, as reviewed later in this chapter, postmodernists resist artificial splits between mind and body, male and female,
subject and object. Beyond resisting dichotomous thinking, postmodernism
provides entirely new ways of conceptualizing long taken-for-granted assumptions about the nature of the subject, the knower, and knowledge.

In addition to concerns with modernism's grand theories, postmodernism
also developed to merge theory and practice in the era of global capital.
Feminist scholar Poovey (1992) outlines the major changes to postmodernity
as follows:

Not just observable alterations in the U.S. economy and welfare system but
transformations in the global economy . . . technological innovations in the
electronic storage, retrieval, and transmission of information; medical
advances in genetic research and synthetic proteins; and the steady march of
new diseases across the planet. (p. 39)

So it can be said that postmodernism denotes a shift from the modern era
into the postmodern era that Frederic Jameson (1984) defines as the "cultural
logic of late capitalism," which constitutes a new pervasive form of
social power complete with major changes in the economy and technology/
communication. In this new era, there has been an implosion of media forms,
creating what Jean Baudrillard (1999) famously refers to as a "hyperreality" in

which "the real" and "the imaginary" have become blurred almost beyond (re)cognition.

> It is the generation by models of a real without origin or reality: a hyper-real ... the era of simulation is inaugurated by a liquidation of all referen-tials—worse: with their artificial resurrection in the systems of signs, a material more malleable than meaning, in that it lends itself to all systems of equivalences, to all binary oppositions, to all combinatory algebra. It is no longer a question of limitation, nor duplication, nor even parody. It is a ques-tion of substituting the signs of the real for the real. (pp. 1–2)

In this context, how is the symbolic constructed? How do symbolic con-structions serve particular interests? These questions are of course critical to feminists who might ask more specific questions like:

- How are symbolic constructions of femininity and masculinity created? Who is served by these particular constructions? Is patriarchy served, and if so, how?
- How are symbolic constructions of difference (gender, race, class, sexual orientation, etc.) created? Are these particular constructions of difference used in the service of inequality or oppression? Who is served by these particular constructions?
- What are the dimensions to symbolic constructions of gender and the above (i.e., extreme imagery, caricatures, fragmented bodies, particular language constructions, and so on)?

Foucault and Derrida's Influence on Feminist Thought: Power-Knowledge, Deconstruction, and Discourse Analysis

Michel Foucault (1978), whose body of work has largely influenced feminist thought, has radically altered the way many scholars conceptualize power. Foucault was principally interested in the micropolitics of power and he theorized that power and knowledge are inextricably linked in a complex web of power-knowledge relations. Put differently, Foucault's work professes that all knowledge is contextually bound and produced within a field of shift-ing power relations. Researchers in this tradition may interrogate cultural texts to unravel marks of the power relations that produced them, including traces of the dominant worldview embedded within the text as well as the "silences." Specifically, researchers in this tradition examine the discursive practices embedded in the text, referring to the specific ways that language is used within texts. Foucault proposed an archeological method of investigation to unravel how a text came to be as it is (Prior, 1997). This method, grounded in an epistemological view of power and knowledge, relies on tracing the texts process of production and distribution. A force in the interdisciplinary field of cultural studies, Stuart Hall (1981, cited in Storey, 1996) explains that it is within cultural texts that hegemony is enacted. Hall goes on to explain that popular texts also have an "oppositional" possibility and within texts hegemony is also contested, resisted, and challenged. Texts are thus an active, dynamic part of shaping social reality or "hyperreality."

Jacques Derrida (1966) has been at the forefront of developing poststructural theory. A key facet of poststructural theory is the research tool of deconstruction (again illustrating the link between developing theory and methods). Derrida coined the term *deconstruction* as a method of performing an *internal critique* of texts. Deconstruction is based on the notion that the meaning of words happens in relation to sameness and difference. In every text, some things are affirmed, such as truth, meaning, authorship, and authority; however, there is always an "other," something else, that contrasts that which is affirmed. That which has been left out or concealed, the "other," appears missing from the text but is actually contained within the text as a different or deferred meaning (Hesse-Biber & Leavy, 2006). Derrida theorized that through the process of deconstruction, these different and deferred meanings can be exposed. The aim of deconstruction is to displace assumptions within the text. Feminist scholar Luce Irigaray (1985), whose work I address in the section on "French Feminist Postmodernism," posits deconstruction as a way of "jamming the theoretical machinery" (p. 78). These theorists show that the meaning of a text is never single or static.

In addition to deconstruction, postmodernists also often employ discourse analysis.

> Influenced by poststructuralism, ethnomethodology, and linguistics, discourse analysis is a strategy employed when one is concerned with the social meanings within language and discursive practices. In other words, discourse analysis is concerned with the process of communication. For Foucault, discourses are practices that are comprised of ideas, ideologies, and referents, that systematically construct both the subjects and objects of which they speak, and thus discourses are integral to the construction of social reality. Many researchers perform discourse analysis when studying texts in order to

reveal the hidden ideas embedded within written language. Researchers can investigate how the dominant discourse is produced, how it is disseminated, what it excludes, how some knowledge becomes subjugated and so forth. This kind of research is rooted in the postmodern and poststructural conceptualization that language reflects power. Moreover, the structure of society is embedded within language (and representational forms). (Hesse-Biber & Leavy, 2006, p. 293)

Feminist researchers influenced by postmodern theory might be interested in studying the gendered discursive fields in which people operate and how patriarchal and male-centered ways of looking at the world are communicated via discourse, including language, symbols, ideology, and so forth.

POSTMODERN FEMINIST EPISTEMOLOGY: THE FLIGHT FROM METANARRATIVES

As seen in the last chapter on standpoint epistemology, feminist approaches to knowledge building have at times developed as a counter to positivism and interwoven conceptions of objectivity and truth. Postmodern feminism has also, in some ways, developed in contrast to the main tenets of positivism and like perspectives on knowledge construction. First and foremost, postmodernism looks at the knowledge-building process as one of creation versus the traditional science model of "discovery." As discussed earlier, Lyotard (1984) posits that modernism created self-referential grand narratives that were inattentive to difference and ultimately excluded those ideas and experiences that did not mesh with the particular theory. Herein lies a major intersection between feminism and postmodernism: a weariness as to how marginalization occurs as grand theories are produced and in turn become self-legitimating. Grand theories have historically been oppressive for women and all minorities because they do not account for difference in a nuanced way nor do they challenge the assumptions on which they rest (which are themselves the products of complex relations of power).

Lisa Cosgrove (2002) offers an example of how feminist psychologists have, at times, upheld the positivist assumptions about the social world that have oppressed women. As Cosgrove explains, to address androcentric bias and include women in research questions, some feminist psychologists have relied on and even championed concepts such as "women's experiences" and "sex roles" without working through the assumptions built within these concepts. In this way the notion of gender as something "one has" goes unchallenged, in fact, unnoticed. As a result, gender and experience both become "foundational" concepts upon which theory and data are built. For example, Cosgrove might want us to consider the following questions:

- On what assumptions is the term *women's experiences* based?
- When researchers refer to a concept like *sex roles* or *gender roles,* in what ways are they assuming gender or sex to be fixed?
- When we as researchers account for women and try to rectify sexist bias by adding "women's perspective" to the mix, do we reify the concept of gender in ways that are consistent with positivism?

The concepts that comprise grand theories have to be explored and challenged in social science research if women and others are to become more than an add-on to existing models of knowledge construction. Postmodernism offers feminist researchers an epistemological grounding from which to view knowledge building differently. Feminist author Hepburn (1999) writes the following regarding metatheories:

> These certainties re/create a "violence to the other," the marginalization of certain sectors of the population—e.g. women, children, ethnic minorities— leading to their consequent powerlessness. . . . It follows that a postmodern analysis of participants' discourse, in being sensitive to the ways that power can operate through metanarratives, can give us as feminists the tools we need to challenge the big stories that organize our lives. (Postmodern Politics section, para. 6)

In this way feminist postmodernism is very attentive to how totalizing theories have been complicit in the marginalization of women and other minorities, as well as the essentializing of difference. Postmodernism offers a method of deconstructing totalizing categories, including those of particular interest to feminists, like gender. Feminist postmodernism thus can challenge, for example, cultural narratives about femininity and masculinity that may otherwise go unchallenged, although examination reveals how varied ideas or parts of the narrative operate to reinforce each other.

Butler has been at the forefront of feminist theorizing in this area. Her work challenges the theoretical underpinnings of grand narratives while offering a powerful alternative for feminists, which at its core considers the contingency on which subjects are constituted.

POSTMODERN FEMINIST EPISTEMOLOGY: THE SUBJECT

Feminist scholars influenced by postmodern approaches to knowledge building, particularly the French school of thought, have drawn on the idea of the "death of man," which calls into question the subject-centered epistemology of modernism. The modernist subject derived from Cartesian philosophy is based on binary categorizations, such as mind/body and male/female, and this view of the subject has constructed women as inferior to men. Many postmodern feminists have held that until our conception of the "subject" changes, we cannot change the inequality inherent in modern social scientific knowledge building. As such, postmodern feminists view changing our conception of the subject as a vital undertaking if the goals of feminism are to be achieved. While the postmodern thinkers reviewed in the last section all have posed similar challenges to the Cartesian subject, the majority of this theorizing has done little by way of considering gender and, thus, feminist postmodern thinkers have added enormously to the literature by adding gender to the postmodern critique of the subject (Hekman, 1991, p. 46). Interest in conceptualizing the subject is not a new feminist concern. For decades, feminists have asked questions such as "How are women formed and informed by social, economic, political, and other conditions?" As Hekman (1991) notes, Simone de Beauvoir devoted much of her famed book *The Second Sex* (1972) to exploring such questions. Certainly standpoint epistemologists have also long been concerned with the subject and how in particular the female subject gains particular life experiences, vision, and voice based on occupying a disadvantaged social status. Despite feminists' long history of recognizing the centrality of conceptions of the subject, feminist research, postmodern thinkers argue, has not theorized a reformulation of the subject that ultimately dismantles Cartesian logic, which is based on binary constructions that have long oppressed women (and other minorities). Drawing on developments in postmodern theory (and psychoanalytic theory), feminists have posited a significant challenge to former views of the subject and offered multiple reformulations consistent with the tenets of both feminism and postmodernism. Hekman (1991) notes the influence of postmodernism on recent feminist scholarship in this area:

Several feminist theorists have turned to the theories of postmodernism to articulate a new approach to the subject. Postmodernism rejects the dichotomous epistemology of modernism by arguing that oppositions are only apparent, that the alleged polarities inhabit each other. The conception of language and meaning espoused by postmodernism entails the dethroning of the modernist subject and the dichotomies it has spawned. Postmoderns reject the notion that meaning derives from a connection between words and the world, positing instead that meaning is a product internal to the mechanisms of language. They argue that meaning derives from the interplay of sign and signified within the discursive formations of language. One of the consequences of the postmodern conception of language and meaning is that the subject is decentered as the origin of meaning and truth. Postmoderns emphasize the way in which subjects are constituted within discursive formations. But they do not replace the constituting subject with the constituted subject. Rather, they advance a conception of the subject that explodes the polarity between constituted and constituting by displacing the opposition. (p. 47)

In other words, in various ways, feminists influenced by postmodernism have developed new conceptions of the subject that typically view the subject as largely constituted (instead of constituting), although, as we will see, this does not negate agency. Butler (1992) encourages feminists not to fear the postmodern claim that the subject is "dead" as necessarily dangerous to the project of feminism, but rather to consider how subjects are produced and how a traditional conception of the "subject" may actually serve to oppress.

There is the refrain that, just now, when women are beginning to assume the place of subjects, postmodern positions come along to announce that the subject is dead. . . . Surely there is a caution offered here, that in the very struggle toward enfranchisement and democratization, we might adopt the very models of domination by which we were oppressed, not realizing that one way that domination works is through the regulation and production of subjects. Through what exclusions has the feminist subject been constructed, and how do those excluded domains return to haunt the "integrity" and "unity" of the feminist "we"? And how is it that the very category, the subject, the "we," that is supposed to be presumed for the purpose of solidarity, produces the very factionalization it is supposed to quell? Do women want to become subjects on the model which requires and produces an anterior region of abjection, or must feminism become a process which is self-critical about the processes that produce and destabilize identity categories? (pp. 14–15)

French Feminism and the Postmodern Subject

French feminists inspired by the backdrop of French postmodern and poststructural theory have been at the forefront of radically exploding and reconstructing the subject. Luce Irigaray, Hélène Cixous, and Julia Kristeva have all developed important theories of the subject, but due to space limitations I will focus on the work of Kristeva. Influenced by semiotics, poststructuralism, linguistics, and psychoanalysis Kristeva has been a leader (and a controversial one at that) in radicalizing the subject. Following a Lacanian tradition, Kristeva (1980) proposes that there are subjects (plural) that are constituted by different kinds of discourse. She writes,

> The subject never is. The *subject* is only the *signifying* process and he appears only as a *signifying practice,* that is, only when he is absent *within the position* out of which social, historical and signifying activity unfolds. There is no science of the subject. Any thought of mastering the subject is mystical: all that exists is the field of practice where, through his expenditure, the subject can be anticipated in an always anterior future. (p. 215)

In other words, subjects are not constituting but are, rather, constituted by a host of discursive practices. This is a radical departure from the Cartesian subject who creates knowledge, is a knower, a producer, and master of his knowledge. For Kristeva, the subject is a product of culture, and in particular, multiple discourses construct subjects. This is particularly important for feminists who grapple with the idea of whether there is an innate "femininity" (and if so, who gets to define it and for what purposes). Kristeva argues against this form of essentialism and consistent with the rest of her theory explains that the "feminine" is constructed through a multiplicity of discourses. She refers, then, not to the "subject" as a fixed entity but, rather, to "subjects in process." This is a critical component of her theory, as it allows the determined subject to retain revolutionary potential, that is, political capability, resistive possibility, indeed, agency. I will return to the politics of postmodern feminism later in this chapter and for now continue with feminist postmodern epistemology.

Feminist Postmodern Epistemology and Experience

Given the dismantling of the Cartesian subject that has shaped knowledge building for centuries, it is not surprising that postmodernism has inspired feminist researchers to rethink "experience" as a category of knowledge building.

- What is experience?

For the discursively constituted subject, who is no longer the center of knowledge building and the bearer of "truth," what is experience?

Feminists long concerned with the absence of "women's experience" in knowledge building (and society building more broadly) have gone to great lengths to account for women's experience(s) as evidence of women's unique standpoint in a hierarchically structured society and/or to provide evidence of women's situations, thoughts, feelings, and so forth. In short, experience is for many feminists the bedrock on which their work rests. Postmodernism and the conception of the "subject in process" problematizes this view of "experience" and has lead to the emergence of alternative ways that feminists can consider experience.

Joan Scott (1992) posits that by constructing experience as the central point of knowledge building, feminists have unwittingly rendered invisible the historical and discursive processes that serve as the base *for* that experience. Much like the discursively constituted subject, experience is shaped by discursive practices, and the "meanings" that we create from the telling of our experiences cannot emerge without a process of signification—experience is inextricably linked with discourse. Scott summarizes her position as follows:

> It is not individuals who have experience, but subjects who are constituted through experience. Experience in this definition then becomes not the origin of our explanation, not the authoritative (because seen or felt) evidence that grounds what is known, but rather that which we seek to explain, that about which knowledge is produced. (pp. 25–26)

When the Cartesian subject is called into question and dismantled and the subject is no longer the center of knowledge building and truth claims, then our view of experience also shifts. Experience in the feminist postmodern sense is part of the discursive field in which subjects are formed and transformed. Furthermore, Butler's theory of performativity posits that gender is something that is performed within discursive fields.

The connection between postmodernism and feminist goals is clear to some, but to others there seems to be a disjuncture between the two as postmodernism rejects the essentialist categories, such as "women's experience," that have been so useful to many feminist activists. In this vein, there has been great debate among feminists about the place of postmodern theory within their work. These concerns are countered in the next section, which discusses the political possibilities of postmodern feminism. However, before we get to that, it might be helpful to hear from a postmodern feminist who finds the marriage of postmodernism and feminism seamless in her psychological research. We now go behind-the-scenes with renowned feminist psychologist Lisa Cosgrove as she jumps right into this debate, talking about her early academic training, the larger epistemological debate among feminists, and an empirical research example, and ultimately beautifully illustrating that "postmodern feminism" is not an oxymoron and "the only way out is through."

Behind-the-Scenes With Lisa Cosgrove

"The Only Way Out Is Through" (Alanis Morissette)

When confronted with the difficulty of doing human science research, many feminists rely on tried and true methods. Simply put, when in doubt, count. The assumption is that "valid results" can only be obtained by designing studies in which multivariate statistical methods are used. If you can name drop—causal modeling, orthogonal rotation, linear regression, and so on—you must be a "real" researcher. Over the last two decades, a growing number of feminists have taken issue with this assumption, maintaining that qualitative, rather than quantitative, methods are more appropriate for studying gendered experiences. Numerous journal articles, countless essays, and probably hundreds of conference presentations have been devoted to the heated debate over how best to study women's experiences.

Trained as a clinical psychologist, I have conducted both quantitative and qualitative research, and I believe that epistemological issues are what's really at stake (see, e.g., Ussher, 1999) when we find ourselves arguing over the merits of either approach or even when we think we've solved the problem by saying, "Ok, both quantitative and qualitative methods should be used." There is no simple solution, the only way out of these epistemological deadlocks is to muddle through them; we must grapple with the inherent messiness and complexity of what it means to try to "do feminist research . . . and create empowering research designs"

(Continued)

(Continued)

(Lather, 1991, p. 71) in an unjust world. I have found postmodernism to be useful in terms of responding to the complicated issue of generating knowledge in an unjust world. By no means however, do I believe that postmodernism is "the" answer.

I was introduced to postmodern scholarship early on in my training, for unlike most clinical psychology programs, mine had a strong philosophical focus. The exposure to postmodern scholarship both helped and confused me as a feminist researcher. Specifically, I found the emphasis on the impossibility of value-neutral science to be congruent with feminist principles. Interests are always being served and the distinction between facts and values, politics and science, are artificial distinctions. Postmodernism has been described as a project that reveals the socially constructed nature of reality and the varied interests that are served by particular constructions (Layton, 1998, see also, Fairfield, Layton, & Stack, 2002). Postmodern scholars take seriously Nietzsche's contention that when someone asserts a truth, he or she should ask, "What's in it for me?" Thus, postmodernists maintain that it is impossible to discover universal truths about human behavior, and they question the very categories, such as mental disorder or gender, which social scientists hold dear. In this way, postmodernism brings epistemological, methodological, and political issues to the foreground.

From this brief description you may be thinking that there is a great congruence between feminism and postmodernism. And there is; both feminists and postmodernists recognize the richness and often contradictory character of experience, the importance of resisting easy answers, and the complexity of power and power relations. But there are also some major points of contention and these areas of conflict are not readily resolved. For example, it's one thing to contest the idea that "mental disorder" is a universal category that can be empirically defined and measured, but it's quite another thing to contest gender. Gender is, after all, the classic example of a dichotomous (vs. continuous) variable in an undergraduate methods class. To suggest that gender is not innate, that it's not an independent variable, but instead is best understood as a performance, as something we do rather than have (see, e.g., Butler, 1993), well isn't that going a bit too far? And if there are no universal truths, how can you argue for feminist principles? In other words, won't adopting a postmodern perspective depoliticize a feminist research agenda? Without denying the fact that there is an ambivalent relationship between feminism and postmodernism, in the next section I'll discuss why I've come to the conclusion that "feminist post-modernism" is not an oxymoron.

A few years ago I, along with some of my graduate students, began conducting menstrual cycle research. Specifically, we were interested in the relationship between constructions of feminine gender identity and experiences of menstrual distress. Well aware of the debate over the validity of "PMS"—some women argue strongly that PMS is a distinct clinical entity, a "real" disorder, while others argue that "PMS" does not exist—we wanted to design a study that avoided making that either/or choice. That is, we did not want to pathologize women's bodies and reproductive functioning, nor did we want to invalidate the experience of women who claim that they suffer from PMS. Taking a postmodern perspective helped us avoid this false binary because it is a perspective that emphasizes the constructed or mediated nature of experience; PMS is constituted or produced through the language of the medical model.[1] Women position themselves and are positioned by various practices (e.g., magazine with articles such as "Do you have PMS?"; drugs such as Prozac/Sarafem to "treat" PMS), metaphors (e.g., menstruation as shameful, dirty, etc.), and discourses (e.g., the medical model discourse of PMS). A postmodern framework helped us see that the question "Is PMS real?" is not the most useful research question to ask. This framework focused our attention on the ways in which women interpret their physical and emotional distress within the dominant discourses of femininity and PMS. In other words, rather than try to get at some underlying or universal truth about women's experience, we tried to design a study that addressed the sociopolitical context of that experience.

Therefore, we took as our starting point the idea that the meaning of "having PMS" is negotiated within dominant metaphors of both femininity and menstruation. One of the most striking aspects of our study was that PMS discourse has gained such cultural currency that women expect to have PMS; it is normative rather than atypical. Moreover, participants described their experience not only in terms of having PMS but also in terms of being a different self. That is, the PMS self was positioned as "bad" or problematic in some fundamental way in contrast to a woman's true or nonpremenstrual self. Feeling "irritable" or "angry," the two main emotional responses women identified as being symptomatic of their premenstrual selves, was not experienced as a valid emotional response that deserved attention. It is interesting to note that normative femininity requires a serene comportment

(Continued)

(Continued)

uncontaminated by the presence of negative emotions; it is virtually impossible to be both feminine and irritable. Positioning oneself in PMS discourse allows one to continue to live up to idealized representations of femininity. The "real me" or non-PMS self is the one who lives up to the ideal, while the PMS self is the disordered aberration. In this way, PMS discourse encourages women to disavow the negative affective experiences that disrupt culturally sanctioned representations of femininity (i.e., "I'm not truly angry; it's just my PMS"). Thus, the use of a postmodern approach helped us study women's experience without reifying or essentializing gender.

As I hope this brief example demonstrates, incorporating postmodern ideas into feminist research politicizes and enhances our work. It politicizes our research because we shift from intra-individual explanations of experience to structural and sociopolitical ones. Postmodernism enhances our work because it encourages us to resist dichotomous thinking, to reexamine our implicit assumptions, and to realize that the only way out is through.

Note

1. We were not trying to invalidate the experience of women who say that they experience distress prior to or during menses, nor were we suggesting that hormonal changes cannot ever have a negative impact. Indeed, it is not antifeminist to ask if women's hormones vary throughout the menstrual cycle. However, it *is* antifeminist to assume that the body is a natural object, "a relatively independent variable rather than a dependent ideological variable" (Zita, 1989, p. 200).

Cosgrove provided a powerful example of how postmodernism and feminism can be a part of the politicization of research, counter to many misinformed critiques. In this vein I move into a discussion of postmodern feminist activism and its various components.

POSTMODERNISM AND FEMINIST ACTIVISM: AGENCY, SUBVERSION, AND POLITICAL RESISTANCE/REVOLUTION

Somewhere every culture has an imaginary zone for what it excludes, and it is that zone we must try to remember today. (Cixous & Clément, 1996, p. 6)

Perhaps Sarah Herbold (1995) put it best—to some, postmodernism and feminism appear to have antithetical objectives. Feminism seeks to end women's oppression via identity politics, and postmodernism seeks to deconstruct terms like *women* as a falsely totalizing category (p. 85). I believe that the loud critique of postmodernism within the feminist community is a result of these seemingly divergent aims and a belief that they cannot be bridged. The central critique of feminist postmodernism centers on this question: Given postmodernism's view of the subject in process, and its position against essentialist categories, is postmodernism congruent with feminist political commitments?

The fear guiding this question is

- Will postmodernism set feminist activism backward?

For postmodern feminist researchers, the answer is a resounding no. In fact, postmodernism is deeply consistent with the political goals of feminism and complicates identity politics but doesn't abandon the work of feminist pioneers.

There is no doubt that feminists have made a great deal of progress via what is commonly referred to as *identity politics*. The critique and much larger fear of postmodern theory, beyond the intricacies that make it challenging to learn, is that somehow postmodernism denies women voice and for practical and pragmatic reasons essentialist categories such as "women's experience" have been useful in feminist struggles and thus feminists are concerned about letting go of what has been effective. Postmodern feminists are quick to warn that a reliance on categories such as "women's experience" seeks to reinforce hegemony and normalize dominant conceptions of gender without paying attention to the discursive fields in which gender becomes articulated. Postmodern feminism allows researchers to deconstruct gender norms rather than reifying or regulating them (Cosgrove, 2003). In this way, research conducted from a postmodern feminist perspective challenges the essentialism of feminist empiricism and standpoint epistemology. Postmodernism offers feminist scholars new ways of creating solidarity.

As discussed earlier, Foucault's work articulates that it is power and the discursive fields in which we operate that produce the subject. Butler (1993) extends this work and explains that gender identity is produced in a discursive matrix where femininity is an "idealized presence" (p. 232). It is possible to create a unifying feminist politics that views gender identity as a result of power effects, and identity as contingent (which does not make it less "real" in people's experiences of it). In this way, feminists can really begin to unravel the very ideas about gender that become dominant and shape individual subjects.

If there is a fear that, by no longer being able to take for granted the subject, its gender, its sex, or its materiality, feminism will founder, it might be wise to consider the political consequences of keeping in their place the very premises that have tried to secure our subordination from the start. (Butler, 1992, p. 19)

I have decided to conclude this chapter in perhaps an unconventional way, which I feel is congruent with the presentation of some postmodern scholarship. What follows is a Behind-the-Scenes piece from noted feminist scholar Patti Lather.

Behind-the-Scenes With Patti Lather

Front-Stage/Back-Stage: What Performance Where?

What follows are extracts from my 1996 to 1997 correspondence via e-mails and letters with Elliot Mishler, Professor of Social Psychology, Harvard Medical School, to whom I had sent a copy of a publication on the validity of angels (Lather, 1995) and the desktop published version of *Troubling the Angels* (Lather & Smithies, 1997). His response to the book was "cranky and testy," and I was not at all sure if "productive dialogue" was possible given his "discomfort with the book." A single-spaced four-plus-page letter delineated his "negative response." I do not believe I ever sent the following letter, although Elliot and I met for coffee in Columbus a few years later and he continued to send me "angel clippings," as he "hadn't exactly sworn an oath not to."

My title comes from Judith Butler (1990) who, in *Gender Trouble*, asks "What performance where?" in terms of subverting gender binaries (p. 139). It also comes from Erving Goffman's (1959) dramaturgical account of ethnography but inverts its assumptions that behind the scenes lies the more truthful and authentic. Extending the analogy to talk about a book, if "backstage" is where the unrehearsed, private performance not intended for public consumption takes place, then "front stage" is what gets published. Yet still very much playing to an audience in what I have staged in the following, my claim is not more truth or authenticity than the front-stage performance of *Troubling the Angels*, which is already quite replete with self-reflexivity. Instead, what I offer here is but another layer with the purpose of gesturing toward the limits of performances of self-reflexivity and what Foucault notes as the price we pay to tell the truth about ourselves. My goal is to "perform" the postmodern in this gesture of simultaneously using and troubling a concept or framework that we think we cannot think without: under erasure. (For the classic unpacking of deconstruction, see Gayatri Spivak, 1976; for an update, see Caputo, 1997; for an extended example, see Lather, 2007.)

Dear Elliot,

In reading your reading, I want to remain engaged with uncertainty, allowing no one reading to own the book. In a way that is very different than the self-criticism of modernism, I am trying to attend to how the book falls back into what it must refuse. So I thank you for your frank engagement.

It was the mawkish, banal and self-indulgent I was trying to avoid. To not be afraid of stirring up big emotions, but to do so responsibly, I frequently felt this task beyond me and perhaps I am not writer enough to carry it off. My ambitions for the book were many layered and I was very much up against my limits with a keen sense of the risks I ran with, for example, the angels. Perhaps I over-reached, embarrassed myself, the field, whatever, with some leaky feminist thing, a going too far. Having just sent final revisions off (October, 1996), I am mostly into the failures of the text to accomplish its ambitious goals and at a sort of peace with this. "Ruined from the start," as I have come to think through reading Walter Benjamin, it is what it is, "too much, too little, too soon, too late" to quote myself from the book.

You write that the book "presses readers to assent to its argument," full of "Ozhio" dimensions of "Chris and Patti skipping down the yellow brick road to see the Wizard, with added angel wings." This is similar to dance critic Arlene Croce (1994/1995), regarding Bill T. Jones's *Still Here*, where she writes of how a nonbeliever perspective is denied legitimacy regarding "oppression" art which positions a dissatisfied reader with no viable subject position.[1]

You particularly found the theological rhetoric coercive. It is my most Catholic book for sure, but I interrupted that with "god as an available discourse" and "post-wiccan spiritual sensibility." And I was very much invested in using the angels to interrupt our "disguised theologisms": progress, secular salvation through "knowledge as cure," the science that takes the place of god, etc.

You see angels as a mark of "facile transcendentalism" (Bloom, 1996). I use Benjamin and Rilke to try to do something else, some defamiliarizing move based on Benjamin's love for the Paul Klee painting *Angelus Novus* that Benjamin described as facing backwards the catastrophe of the past, wanting

(Continued)

(Continued)

to make whole what has been so broken, but caught up in the violence of the storm of progress that propels the angel into the future (Benjamin, 1968).

The key to Benjamin's angelology is what Paul de Man (1986) notes as Benjamin's tendency to both use familiar tropes and displace them to signal the all too human appeal that they make to us. He particularly used messianic appeals toward displacing our sense of what is human, destabilizing the original, translating beyond the original, keeping the text in circulation, decanonizing it by making us aware of certain disjunctions, disruptions, accommodations, weaknesses, cheatings, conventions (p. 97). Perverting familiar images to undo the claim that is associated with them, Benjamin works to desacralize. This is the paradoxical work of the angel: enacting how language cannot not mean and how it leads to identification, subjectification, and narrative, I use the angel not to recuperate for a familiar model but to deconstructively stage the angel as palimpsest, a failure at containing meaning. I wanted to empty out narrative in advance and make it generate itself over its impossibility.

In what you see as a "millennial decade lousy with angels," Bloom's point is not angels but what we do with them. I have also wrestled with this use of religious and spiritual themes in exploring Benjamin's juxtaposition of theology and Marxism in his theory of language and materiality. To situate the angel as a fraud, a staging that allows transcendence its final word only as "an emblem of illusion" (Rosen, 1977, p. 38), is to foreground the unavoidable discrepancy between a visual sign and its image or meaning. In this, I am following Benjamin in his attempt to appropriate what was left of a moribund religious culture, especially the largely untouched mystical strains, giving them a secular form, making them once again available via translation of their ruins.

I found it so interesting that it was research note in story series 3 that drew you in and on, what I saw as perhaps the most conventional scholarly move of the book, the "theorizing" of the lives of others, the "situating" them within a literature review, etc. This was a sort of "analysis under erasure" move. By presenting fragments from the interview transcripts woven together into a fiction of shared space and "emergent themes," the snippets from interview transcripts produce a parody of unmediated text, a representation by imitation. Filling with silence the interstices where researcher commentary is expected, as a strategy for resisting the authority of "expert testimony," and, then, juxtaposing this with some parts of the running subtext where Chris and I do, indeed, "say what things mean," we mime the forms of expert testimony, putting them under erasure, putting the gaze on display, making it accountable.

You raise concerns about not being able to follow the same person, a fragmentation where the women become anonymous, where we overwhelm their voices as "real" persons, the "press release" nature of their accounts. My effort here was to substitute a theory of deferral for one of essence. As a work of deferral rather than depiction, the book is irreducible to the terms of the real. A thinking of deferral, a complication of the language of presence: this is a terrible intellectual ambition that calls for a necessary indirectness, a detour and delay to interrupt the quest for presence. It is an imposition of radical complications for any story that promises to deliver a message to its proper receiver—surrendering the claim to the simplicity of presence. Without a center, what would such a thing look like?

My goal was a practice that exceeds both authorial intent and reader interpretive competence to produce non-mastery. Complex and ambitious, it is a place of ghosts and ruins versus consciousness. In this ambition, I worried about standards so exalted that work never actually gets made.

In assessing its effectivity, I presume we are delivered from certain loosely positivist questions. Making representations only to foreground their insufficiencies, my central message is how nothing can deliver us from our misrecognitions. This cannot be set aside, only recognized and wrestled with and in, figures we cannot read in the settled ways we'd like, perhaps, at best, shifting registers. Whatever detachment I had/have is in the work's separation from itself.

I hope for readers something other than a reading that can only find what it is looking for, perhaps a reading that surprises, a place where disjunction occurs, obliged by the text to see how we see, out of the over determined habits of reading, a reading that is other or more than we should like it to be, always more and other, protean.

In hearing readerly reactions, my goal is to be neither apologetic nor ironic in trying to map something of both the global and the body. Many risks were taken and embarrassments risked in the effort to enact interpretation's desire for mastery in the face of the recalcitrance of the object to be fully grasped by our interpretive machinery and a world that, partially, won't let us

(Continued)

(Continued)

in. Maurice Blanchot's "This work is beyond me" (1982, p. 126) was my mantra. Always feeling unable to do the subject justice, trying to block impulses to romanticize, I saw my central task as being purposefully not intelligible within standard frames in order to produce a book about multiple, shifting realities, a stubborn book that rubs against the desire for interpretive mastery and implicates an audience rather than persuades or seduces.

I see myself as a willful presence in the book rather than an authoritative knower of what can be said and done. Risking something "like a glory or a crime" (Melville, 1996, quoting Stanley Cavell), the stakes are a science constructed in a kind of materiality that recognizes the absence of things and the noninnocence of our efforts to know.

Note

1. Bill T. Jones's dance production *Still/Here* is about living with death-threatening illness. Arlene Croce (1994/1995), dance critic for the *New Yorker*, ignited a firestorm by refusing to review what she called "victim art." Unfortunately, what could have opened up interesting issues of how to position oneself in response to bone-shattering testimony was deflected by her decision to take her stand without seeing the production.

REFERENCES

Alcoff, Linda Martin. (1997). The politics of postmodern feminism, revisited. *Cultural Critique, 36*, 5–27.

Baudrillard, Jean. (1999). *Simulacra and simulation* (Sheila Faria Glaser, Trans.). Ann Arbor: University of Michigan Press. (Original work published 1981)

Benjamin, Walter. (1968). Theses on the philosophy of history. In Hanah Arendt (Ed.), *Illuminations* (pp. 253–264). New York: Schocken Books. (Original work published 1940)

Blanchot, Maurice. (1982). *The space of literature* (Ann Smock, Trans.). Lincoln: University of Nebraska Press. (Original work published 1955)

Bloom, Harold. (1996). *Omens of millennium: The gnosis of angels, dreams and resurrection*. New York: Riverhead Books.

Butler, Judith. (1990). *Gender trouble: Feminism and the subversion of identity*. New York: Routledge.

Butler, Judith. (1992). Contingent foundations. Feminism and the question of postmodernism. In Judith Butler & Joan W. Scott (Eds.), *Feminists theorize the political* (pp. 3–21). New York: Routledge.

Butler, Judith. (1993). *Bodies that matter: On the discursive limits of "sex."* New York: Routledge.

Caputo, John. (1997). *Deconstruction in a nutshell: A conversation with Jacques Derrida.* New York: Fordham University Press.

Cixous, Hélène, & Clément, Catherine. (1996). *The newly born woman* (Betsy Wing, Trans.; Introduction by Sandra M. Gilbert). Minneapolis: University of Minnesota Press. (Original work published 1975)

Cosgrove, Lisa. (2002). Resisting essentialism in feminist therapy theory: Some epistemological considerations. *Women and therapy, 25*(1), 89–112.

Cosgrove, Lisa. (2003). Feminism, postmodernism, and psychological research. *Hypatia, 18*, 85–247.

Croce, Arlene. (1994/1995, December–January). Discussing the undiscussable. *New Yorker,* pp. 54–60.

de Man, Paul. (1986). *The resistance to theory.* Minneapolis: University of Minnesota Press.

Derrida, Jacques. (1966). The decentering event and social thought. In A. Bass (Trans.), *Writing and difference* (pp. 278–282). Chicago: University of Chicago Press. (Original work published 1968)

Du Bois, Page. (1988). *Sowing the body: Psychoanalysis and ancient representations of women.* Chicago: University of Chicago Press.

Fairfield, Susan, Layton, Lynne, & Stack, Carolyn. (Eds.). (2002). *Bringing the plague: Toward a postmodern psychoanalysis.* New York: Other Press.

Foucault, Michel. (1978). *This history of sexuality: An introduction* (Vol. 1). New York: Vintage Books.

Goffman, Erving. (1959). *The presentation of self in everyday life.* Garden City, New York: Doubleday.

Haraway, Donna. (1991). *Simians, cyborgs, and women: The reinvention of nature.* New York: Routledge.

Hekman, Susan. (1991). Reconstituting the subject: Feminism, modernism, and postmodernism. *Hypatia, 6*, 44–63.

Hekman, Susan. (1999). *The future of differences: Truth and method in feminist theory.* Malden, MA: Blackwell.

Hepburn, Alexa. (1999). Postmodernity and the politics of feminist psychology. *Radical Psychology, 1*(2). Retrieved June 30, 2005, from www.radpsynet.org/journal/v011–2/hepburn.html

Herbold, Sarah. (1995). Well-placed reflections: (Post) modern woman as a symptom of (post) modern man. *Signs, 21*, 83–115.

Hesse-Biber, Sharlene Nagy, & Leavy, Patricia. (2006). *The practice of qualitative research.* Thousand Oaks, CA: Sage.

Irigaray, Luce. (1985). The power of discourse and the subordination of the feminine. In *This sex which is not one* (pp. 68–85, Catherine Porter & Carolyn Burke, Trans.). Ithaca, NY: Cornell University Press.

Jameson, Frederic. (1984). Postmodernism, or, the cultural logic of late capitalism. *New Left Review, 146*, 59–92.

Kristeva, Julia. (1980). *Desire in language: A semiotic approach to literature and art* (Thomas Goray, Alica Jardine, & Leon S. Roudiez, Trans.). New York: Columbia University Press.

Lather, Patti. (1991). *Getting smart: Feminist research and pedagogy within/in the postmodern.* New York: Routledge.

Lather, Patti. (1995). Troubling angels: Interpretive and textual strategies in researching the lives of women with HIV/AIDS. *Qualitative Inquiry, 1*(1), 41–68.

Lather, Patti. (2007). *Getting lost: Feminist efforts toward a double(d) science.* Albany: State University of New York Press.

Lather, Patti, & Smithies, Chris. (1997). *Troubling the angels: Women living with HIV/AIDS.* Boulder, CO: Westview Press.

Layton, Lynne. (1998). *Who's that girl? Who's that boy? Clinical practice meets postmodern gender theory.* Northvale, NJ: Jason Aronson.

Lyotard, Jean-François. (1984). *The postmodern condition: A report on knowledge* (Geoff Bennington & Brian Massumi, Trans.). Minneapolis: University of Minnesota Press. (Original work published 1979)

Melville, Stephen. (1996). Color has not yet been named: Objectivity in deconstruction. In Jeremy Gilbert-Rolfe & Stephen Melville (Eds.), *Seams: Art as a philosophical context (Critical voices in art, theory and culture)* (pp. 129–146). Amsterdam: G&B Arts. (Introduced by Jeremy Gilbert-Rolfe)

Pfohl, Stephen. (1992). *Death at the Parasite Café.* New York: St. Martin's Press.

Poovey, Mary. (1992). Feminism and postmodernism: Another view. *Boundary 2, 19,* 34–52.

Prior, Lindsay. (1997). Following in Foucault's footsteps: Text and context in qualitative research. In David Silverman (Ed.), *Qualitative research: Theory, method and practice* (pp. 63–79). Thousand Oaks, CA: Sage.

Pujal, i Llombart Margot. (1998). Feminist psychology or the history of a nonfeminist practice. In Erica Burman (Ed.), *Deconstructing feminist psychology.* Thousand Oaks, CA: Sage.

Rosen, Charles. (1977, November 10). The ruins of Walter Benjamin [Review of the book *The Origin of German Tragic Drama*]. *New York Review of Books, 24*(17), 30–40.

Scott, Joan W. (1992). Experience. In Judith Bulter & Joan W. Scott (Eds.), *Feminists theorize the political* (pp. 22–40). London: Routledge.

Spivak, Gayatri. (1976). Translator's preface. In Jacques Derrida, *Of grammatology* (pp. ix–xc). Baltimore: Johns Hopkins University Press.

Storey, John. (1996). *Cultural studies & the study of popular culture: Theories and methods.* Athens: University of Georgia Press.

Ussher, Jane M. (1999). Eclecticism and methodological pluralism: The way forward for feminist research. *Psychology of Women Quarterly, 23,* 41–46.

Zita, Jacquelyn N. (1989). The premenstrual syndrome: "Dis-easing" the female cycle. In Nancy Tuana (Ed.), *Feminism & science* (pp. 182–210). Bloomington: Indiana University Press.

PART II

FEMINIST APPROACHES
TO RESEARCH METHODS
AND METHODOLOGY

FIVE

THE PRACTICE OF FEMINIST IN-DEPTH INTERVIEWING

Sharlene Nagy Hesse-Biber

A FITNESS TALE

Setting the Scene

It is around 3 p.m. at my gym and I am waiting to interview Annette, a fitness trainer. She has been in the fitness industry for over 20 years and works as a personal trainer to mostly a well-to-do white female clientele. She herself is a picture of perfection, with not one ounce of fat on her body. Her 5-foot, 3-inch frame and well-defined arms, flat abdomen, and muscular all-over tone make her clients want to replicate her physique. I often hear her clients jokingly say "I want your body!" Annette has agreed to speak to me about her experiences as a trainer. I have known Annette for several years, and we have taken many gym classes together, mainly yoga. I have what I would call a casual gym friendship with her and consider her more of an acquaintance than a friend. I have explained to her that I am interested in understanding women's

---

Note: Portions of this chapter are reprinted with permission from Hesse-Biber and Leavy (2006), *The Practice of Qualitative Interviewing,* Sage Publications, Inc.

body image concerns and issues. We move to a quiet room upstairs, away from the hustle and bustle of the gym floor. Annette allows me to tape record the interview. The following is an excerpt from a longer interview I had with Annette that lasted almost 2 hours.

So what do women want from you when they come to you?

Annette: Well, different people want different things. A lot of women want to be altered totally. I try to find a place on their body that they like, one place on their body that they can relate to in a positive way. And some of them don't even have that one place they can relate to in a positive way. They want it changed.

In what way?

Annette: They want it smaller; they want it tighter. You know, they want it off, they want it on. For most of them, it's off.

Any specific areas?

Annette: The butt and the thighs.

OK. Do you think they are ever going to reach those ideals?

Annette: No. That's the insidious deception. They are impossible ideals to reach. They're unreachable goals. There's maybe what 1 in 500. How many perfect bodies, according to the standard. And how many beautiful bodies and beautiful people do you see walking around? One in 500?

So what do they come to you for?

Annette: Most anything. And hurt another person to achieve it as well. There are fights over treadmills, fights over spots on aerobic floors, and fights over benches. And I mean it's an intense environment.

Can you give me an example of the typical person who might come to train with you?

Annette: This morning is a good example. I had a woman come in. You know what I want to say. I try to teach people to enjoy the process. The end is immaterial really, because you'll just have this end in your mind that you want to be like and rather than saying to them you are never going to achieve it because that is very deflating. I rather focus in on the process and enjoying the process. But I had a woman come in this morning who was overweight. She used to be thinner. But you know the more overweight you are the thinner you were. And that's sort of the way the thing is, the better you were. . . . I think it's a lot that she just came in the gym. She wants to be thinner. She wants to get rid of the butt and thighs. Gains the weight in the butt and thighs. Weighs almost 200 pounds, which is reason to be concerned just even from a health standpoint. . . . She really wanted to alter her body. But I told her she would not be able to alter the genetic structure of her body but that we could make it tighter and that she should take her time. Because this is the thing that I gathered from her. She didn't even tell me that she wanted it right away. But you kinda get an instinct about it. That she was very anxious about the summer approaching and what was she going to do.

So she wanted to come to you for some kind of body alteration?

Annette: Right. If you are trying to achieve a goal that's unattainable, you're gonna be pretty unrealistic about yourself too. I mean you're not going to be able to see yourself either. You see yourself through the eyes of whatever you've come to that place with. If you come with a lot of dysfunction, you're going to look at yourself with a lot of dysfunction.

FEMINISM AND INTERVIEWING

As a feminist interviewer, I am interested in getting at the subjugated knowledge of the diversity of women's realities that often lie hidden and unarticulated. I am asking questions and exploring issues that are of particular concern to women's lives. I am interested in issues of social change and social justice for women and other oppressed groups. As a feminist interviewer, I am aware of the nature of my relationship to those whom I interview, careful to understand my particular personal and research standpoints and what role I play in the interview process in terms of my power and authority over the interview situation. I am cognizant, for example, in my interview with Annette, the fitness trainer, that I am both an "insider" and an "outsider." I am part of the fitness world, in that I am a member of Annette's gym, where she is a trainer and also one of my class members, but I am also a researcher, who inhabits a social world different from Annette's. I am asking Annette specific questions about her clients; I have a research agenda. I want to know "a something." Yet I am open in the types of questions I ask Annette, for they are not "yes" or "no" questions; I do not ask her to answer a question with a fixed number of choices. I am conducting what in interviewing terminology is called an *unstructured interview.* Sometimes my questions are in response to what she tells me or I am asking for clarification of one of her answers. However, I do have some specific ideas I want to find out, but I do not have a specific set of questionnaire items with which I begin. I tend to "go with the flow" of the interview, seeing where it takes me. In this interview, however, I do not probe for how Annette is feeling about her training of these women specifically, but through the conversation we are having, her own feelings about women and their bodies surfaces.

Interviewing is a particularly valuable research method feminist researchers can use to gain insight into the world of their respondents. It is a method used by feminists who are in a range of social and natural science disciplines, from an anthropology where the researcher conducts field work within a given culture, to a sociology where the feminist researcher wants to gain a new perspective on the lives of respondents living in a particular community or society, to the field of nursing and medicine where nurses and doctors want to understand, for example, the impact of certain illnesses and treatments on the ability of patients to cope in their daily lives. Interviews are also conducted by feminist survey and market researchers hoping to generalize their research findings concerning women's issues to a wider population. So, for example, feminist survey researchers are particularly interested in understanding the public's attitudes toward violence against women, whether or not the public supports increased spending for research into women's health issues. These are only a few disciplines where interviewing plays an important role in better understanding the human condition. We can see that the range of interviews feminists conduct span from the unstructured, in-depth variety to a much more specific set of questions that fit into a survey format.

TYPES OF INTERVIEWING

Interviews come in a series of formats. We can think of the interview method running along a "continuum" from "informal" to "formal." The *informal* interview has little structure. Very often this type of interview is used to build a relationship with your respondent, to explore what might be the relevant topics of interest to them, and to uncover topics that might otherwise be overlooked by the researcher. So, for example, if I didn't have any prior contact with Annette and I knew very little about the role of fitness training in relation to women's body image issues, I might start out my interview by asking a set of questions to establish some trust between myself and Annette. The questions would also seek to open up a space for her to speak about what she feels is important, to convey her own feelings about training in general and her training of specific clients. I might begin the interview with the following types of open-ended questions:

- "Can you tell me how you came to be a trainer?"
- "What is it like to train?"
- "How did you happen to train at this sports club?"

Unstructured interviews are like the one I conducted with Annette, in which I have a basic interview plan in mind, but I have a *minimum of control* over how the respondent should answer the question. I am often taking the lead from my respondents—going where they want to go, but keeping an overall topic in mind. Therefore, I might ask the following questions:

- "Do you think women have unrealistic expectations regarding what you can do for their bodies?"
- "Why do you think this is the case?"

In this interview example, I am interested in the general topic of how trainers think about their female clients and how they view their body change expectations during their training session.

A *semistructured* interview is conducted with a *specific interview guide*—a list of written questions that I need to cover within a particular interview. I am not too concerned about the order of these questions, but it is important that I cover them in the interview. I have *some control* then in how the interview is constructed and how I would like my respondent to respond, but I am still open to asking new questions throughout the interview. I have an agenda, but it is not tightly controlled and there is room left for spontaneity on the part of the researcher and interviewee.

- "Do you think women who come to see you have unrealistic body change expectations? Why?"
- "To what extent are women unrealistic about their bodies? Realistic?"
- "Why do you think that is the case?"
- "Would you train someone whom you thought has an eating disorder? Why or why not?"

These are some of the questions I might try to interject during the interview with Annette (my agenda), but I would not be very concerned about when I asked them. Ideally, I would try not to disrupt the flow of the interview but would do my best to interject them at a time when I felt some new space opened up in our conversation.

Structured interviewing is where the researcher has total control over the agenda of the interview. All respondents are asked the same set of questions in a specific order. Sometimes the questions are *open-ended*, such as the ones I asked Annette, but many of them are *closed-ended* questions with a set of fixed choices, such as

- "On the average, how many of your clients would you say have problems with their body image? 'Many,' 'some,' 'few,' 'none'?"
- "On the average, how many of your clients would you say suffer from an eating disorder? 'Many,' 'some,' 'few,' 'none'?"
- "Which of the following describes how you are currently feeling about your body image? 'Very happy,' 'happy,' 'somewhat happy,' 'unhappy'?"

I would ask a respondent to pick just one of these choices when answering the questions. We can use the first two questions to gauge the frequency with which certain behaviors occur among Annette's clients. Consequently, we are creating a more standardized profile of her clients in terms of the frequency of body image and eating issues among her clientele as a whole. We can think of the third item as more of an attitudinal question that captures Annette's feelings about her own body image. In this question, I am not asking Annette to go into detail about her feelings but, instead, I want her to respond to a specific *fixed-choice response.* I am asking for a single response that best captures her feelings. I would ask these questions in the order that they are presented here and would not waver from this sequence as I begin to interview other fitness trainers.

We can see that there are a variety of formats for interviewing. Which is best? The answer to this question depends on the *overall goals of your research project.* A move from the informal end of interviewing to the more formal, structured end is to move from an *exploratory data gathering and in-depth understanding* goal of a project to a more *theory testing set of goals.* Feminist researchers use both of these interview formats. As we shall observe in Chapter 10 (on survey research), feminists ask questions that require structured interviews to test out the relationships within their data. These structured interviews require large-scale data sets with fixed-choice items. Feminist who carry out mixed-methods research, as we will see in Chapter 9, may also have to integrate both types of interviewing styles, with one type of interview illuminating another. For example, feminists can gain insights from unstructured interviews. These interviews can reveal to them what specific questions they need to ask in a survey and what fixed-choice items they should include.

These interview styles, then, often complement one another or are even integrated in a given research project. What is feminist about each of these interview styles, however, are the *types of questions* feminists ask. Research that gets at *an understanding of women's lives and those of other oppressed groups*, research that promotes *social justice and social change*, and research that is mindful of the *researcher-researched relationship* and the *power and authority* imbued in the researcher's role are some of the issues that engage the feminist researcher. Feminist researchers practice *reflexivity* throughout the research process. This practice keeps the researcher mindful of his or her personal positionality and that of the respondent. Feminist researchers are also concerned with issues of representation of the researched. The interviewees and research subjects are presented in how the researcher interprets and presents the research findings. It is to these issues that we now turn.

IN-DEPTH INTERVIEWING: A FEMINIST PERSPECTIVE

In this chapter, we will focus on the in-depth interview, which is one of the three types of interviews covered in this book (in the next chapter we will review oral history and focus group interviews). The *in-depth interview* seeks to understand the "lived experiences" of the individual. We are interested in getting at the "subjective" understanding an individual brings to a given situation or set of circumstances. In-depth interviews are *issue-oriented*. In other words, a researcher might use this method to explore a particular topic and gain focused information on the issue from the respondents. The *oral history* method of interviewing usually covers a respondent's entire life story. A *focus group* interview provides the researcher with an opportunity to gain information from a group of people in a short period of time. The researcher can also observe the types of interactions among group members concerning a given topic or issue.

The In-Depth Interview

Feminists are particularly concerned with getting at experiences that are often hidden. In-depth interviewing allows the feminist researcher to access the voices of those who are marginalized in a society; women, people of color, homosexuals, and the poor are examples of marginalized groups. Shulamit Reinharz (1992) explains how interviewing is a way feminist researchers have attempted to access women's hidden knowledge:

> Interviewing offers researchers access to people's ideas, thoughts, and memories in their own words rather than in the words of the researcher. This asset is particularly important for the study of women because in this way learning from women is an antidote to centuries of ignoring women's ideas altogether or having men speak for women. (p. 19)

Designing an In-Depth Interview Study

- What is your research question?

It is important to point out that your research question will most often determine your research method. Suppose you want to study eating disorders among college students from a feminist standpoint. Given this perspective, your research goal becomes understanding from the point of view of those you are studying. So, for example, you might ask the following research question:

- What is the "lived experience" of college women's relationship to food and to their body image?

Conducting a survey with closed-ended questions gleaned from the research literature on this topic would *not* capture the lived experiences of these college students. We are interested in their story. We might decide to begin with an unstructured interview that would maximize our understanding of the process by which eating and body issues become gendered and perhaps even begin to build some *theoretical ideas* concerning this topic as we go along.

Sampling

The logic of qualitative research is concerned with in-depth understanding and usually involves working with *small samples*. The goal is to the look at a "process" or the "meanings" individuals attribute to their given social situation, not necessarily to make generalizations. For example, we investigate women's attitudes toward their bodies not to make overall generalizations about *how many* women have problems with their body image, but to understand how women *experience* being overweight, for example, in a thin culture. Here we would be interested in the process by which women do or do not cope with their body image and the ways in which they interact with cultural messages of thinness from the media and significant others in their lives.

Qualitative researchers are often interested in selecting *purposive* or *judgment samples*. The type of purposive sample chosen is based on the particular research question as well as consideration of the resources available to the researcher. Patton (2002, pp. 243–244), in fact, has identified 16 different types of purposive samples, and more than one purposive sampling procedure can be used within any given qualitative study.

While many qualitative interviews are conducted face to face, some may be conducted via telephone and even over the Internet. Interviews that are not conducted in person often make it more difficult for the interviewer to establish rapport with the respondent, and the researcher also loses the impact of visual and verbal cues, such as gestures and eye contact. In this chapter, we are going to focus on in-person interviewing, although we want to bring these other options to your attention as well. Patton (2002) notes that "there are no rules for sample size in qualitative inquiry" (p. 244). Patton goes on to note that part of determining the size of your sample depends on your research question, your specific economic resources, and the particular context within which you are practicing your research project (ask: Have you covered the phenomenon under investigation? If you are doing a grounded theory analysis: Did you add new samples based on emergent information?). If you are funded by a private or governmental agency, for example, they may have strict criteria established for what they believe to be a credible sample size for a qualitative project. Patton leaves us with the following advice with regard to sample size:

> Sample size adequacy, like all aspects of research, is subject to peer review, consensual validation, and judgment. What is crucial is that the sampling procedures and decisions be fully described, explained, and justified so that information users and peer reviewers have the appropriate context for judging the sample. The researcher or evaluator is obligated to discuss how the sample affected the findings, the strengths and weaknesses of the sampling procedures, and any other design decisions that are relevant for interpreting and understanding the reported results. Exercising care not to overgeneralize from purposeful samples, while maximizing to the full the advantages of in-depth, purposeful sampling, will do much to alleviate concerns about small sample size. (p. 246)

Obtaining Informed Consent

It is important to obtain the *informed consent* of each respondent after explaining the nature of your research project in advance. If your project is conducted under the auspices of a university or other organizations, each of these institutions will most likely have some type of review board that must approve your study to ensure that you are following the ethical guidelines set forth by that specific institution to protect human subjects. Even though the study and the participant's informed and voluntary participation have been discussed in advance, it is important to reiterate this prior to beginning the interview. Interviewees should be given every opportunity to ask questions and should also feel free not to answer any question they may not feel comfortable with.

When Would I Use an Interview Guide?

If you have a specific set of issues and concerns to discuss with your respondent, you might find a more structured interview to be the best research method for your purposes. In other words, if you have a specific agenda that you want to explore in the interview, you might find it helpful to prepare an *interview guide*. An interview guide is a set of topical areas and questions that the interviewer brings to the interview. Weiss (1994) suggests beginning with a "substantive frame" and then using that to create a guide for the interview process. It is often helpful to think topically before creating and choosing the specific questions you'd like to address in your interview. This can make the creative process of making an interview guide much simpler and better organized. In other words, guides can be constructed by first focusing on broader, more abstract areas of inquiry and then creating a series of interview questions. To begin, write down a "topics-to-learn-about" list. The topics you select become a "line of inquiry" or "domain of inquiry" that you might pursue during the interviews with respondents. You can then construct and organize your interview questions to "get at" the information that might relate to each of these "lines." The interview guide is ultimately a list of topics with or without specific questions under each topic that speak to the "lines of inquiry" that were suggested during the initial drafting of the guide (p. 48). The process of creating an interview guide, even if it remains unused, is an important tool that you might use in preparation for the interview, for it often helps the researcher isolate key issues and consider the kinds of things he or she might like to ask respondents. Pilot interviews are an opportunity for researchers to test out the effectiveness of their research guide:

- Is the guide clear and readable?
- Does the guide cover all of the topical areas you are interested in?
- Are there any topical areas or general questions missing from the guide?

Based on early experiences with an interview guide, you can then modify the guide to better suit your needs.

David Karp (Hesse-Biber & Leavy, 2006) talks about creating interview guides as an *analytical process* in the following Behind-the-Scenes piece:

Behind-the-Scenes With David Karp

[I'm] looking for major themes, what I think of as "domains of inquiry." Of course, they do not just come out of nowhere, because I have done so much preliminary work before this. And this is really critical, because too often when people do in-depth interviews, they see putting together the interview guide as, "Well, I've got to get this out of the way." And I see this task of discovering the areas of inquiry as an incredibly important analytical step in the process of doing this work. And if we talk about the full process, when you get to the point of writing, in my case books or articles, it comes full circle because the amount of time and energy that I put into getting this interview guide together really previews what will be the central pieces that I ultimately will write about. Now, in the end, it's just a guide, and in any interview, maybe 60% of the questions I ask are not on that guide. You are sitting, having a conversation with a person, and the artfulness of doing that in-depth interview is to know when to follow up on what a person is saying in the moment. By the end of the interview, I want to make sure that all the areas that I want to have covered are covered. But you would be missing the whole deal if the only questions you asked were the questions on your guide.

It is important that interview guides are not too lengthy or detailed. They are meant to serve as aids to the researcher but ideally will not be heavily relied on because too strong a focus on the interview guide itself can distract a researcher from paying full attention to the respondent. An interview guide is meant to be glanced at when needed and ideally remains unused or as a prompter for the researcher (Weiss, 1994, p. 48). The guide can also serve as a "checklist" for the researcher at the end of the interview, as a way of making sure all of the topics under investigation have been addressed even if not in the sequence suggested by the guide (p. 48).

CONDUCTING AN IN-DEPTH INTERVIEW

The in-depth interview can be particularly helpful when the feminist researcher wants to focus on a particular area of an individual's life. The interview tends to occur in one session, although multiple follow-up sessions may occur to expand or develop the ideas from the initial session. The goal of intensive interviews is to gain rich data from the perspectives of selected individuals on a particular subject. For example, in my own research on body image among different populations, I became interested in how young college-aged women experienced living with eating disorders while going to college. Let us take a look at a transcript excerpt from an interview with Alison, a white, middle-class, 20-year-old college student. I am interested in knowing more about Alison's experiences with eating disorders in college and specifically how her transition from high school to college affected how she negotiated her eating issues. She is Asian American and the second oldest of five sisters, one of whom is a half-sister from her father's second marriage. Alison has been binging and purging since she was in high school. Her father remarried when she was in the fifth grade, but in Alison's words, "That's about the time of the onset of my eating problem." In this excerpt, Alison talks about her eating problems and their current manifestation in her life as a college coed. Alison's mother is a compulsive binge eater whose eating issues apparently began after her divorce from Alison's father. We enter the conversation as Alison begins to talk about her binge-eating disorder and her mother's problems with food:

Alison: My mother was binge eating at night. She's a compulsive eater. And I'd watch her, and I thought it was normal. And just in spurts. At night, she'd get up by herself and get a big bowl of something, and just like, eat it all. I can remember the sounds very well. That, in addition to me thinking I was fat because I was eating so much, and my stomach was hurting and I would feel bad. You know . . . I was obsessed with food all throughout high school. I had not vomited except, you know, a good amount, but I wouldn't say it was bulimic. Once every month, 2 weeks, something like that.

So what happened when you made the transition from high school to college?

Alison: First year of college was OK. I was a little obsessed with food as I always am, but I never vomited. My sophomore year, after, you know, I told you about my boyfriend, and he wasn't there, but I was, you know, that was my crutch, you know, I used it exactly the way an alcoholic would alcohol. So that's what I was doing.

Can you tell me how you were feeling during this time?

Alison: A lonely Friday night, I was in a single room by myself at a school I didn't like, you know. I didn't have a big social life. I had a close friend but that wasn't enough. I had lots of good acquaintances, one close, best, trustworthy friend, but I don't know, it just didn't seem like enough somehow.

So when you said, "It didn't seem like enough somehow," what did you mean?

Alison: Mealtime was always hard because I'd always overeat, and the problem was I would always go to classes from like 9:00 until 12:00, or whatever, and then I would have like the whole rest of the day. And, like, I liked high school because you are supposed to do this from this time to that time, and then you're supposed to do homework, but then you have to organize your own time, set your own schedule, and I just don't know what to do, and I'm always thinking, am I studying too much? I feel like I've been studying forever, but if I don't then I'll feel guilty. And I just didn't know what to do with myself. Today it's easier, because I have a tight schedule now.

So you'd go home and eat?

Alison: So I guess around dinnertime I would eat and then, you know, being premed, you have to study all the time. And the only break you can take without feeling guilty is mealtime or exercise time. But I guess if you are binging, that's not really mealtime. I don't know. After dinner I would just, I think it was physical after a while. I honestly was compelled to go back down, you know, I have a food card. I can put anything on my food card. Of course, later I did spend lots of cash I didn't have, and then I would just go to the bathroom, which was the community bathroom for the floor.

Right after you ate?

Alison: Yes. And after, my friend and I would do study sessions. I would come back at like 10 p.m., and I had a refrigerator in my room, and

I grocery shopped, and I would make like bread with peanut butter and jelly, or jelly and butter, just whatever I had. I knew there was a vending machine in our building, and I would go down there and I'd come back up, and I'd go down there, and I'd come back up. And also, my best friend who lived next door to me in her single, she went home a couple of weekends, once a month or so, and I would be there. I felt alone. There were people I could hang out with. But nobody who really knew me, and so I would go down to the vending machines, and I can remember thinking, "This just isn't going to do it for me. It's not going to make my Friday night that exciting, but then again, why not?" So. . . . I would binge 4 times a week. Sometimes I stopped.

Uh-huh. So for how long?

Alison: Most of my sophomore year, and a good part of that summer.

So you also binged when you went home as well?

Alison: I remember when I went home for Christmas my sister. . . . Oh, Christmas was the worst at my house. That's where all the memories came back. My family left for Florida. I was there by myself with my brother. It was the house, the emptiness, the food. You know, it was just the worst. It was an awful Christmas. My boyfriend was seeing these other girls and I was in town, and I had no friends left that I kept in touch with. It was just really awful. My sister, I remember, mentioned it to me. She said, "Are you bulimic?" She knew I was defending my food. I told her, I said, "Yes." And she started crying and she got real upset, and she said, "Would you please make an effort, or something like that?" And so, when I went back to college, I stopped being bulimic for a couple of months.

In looking at Alison's transcript, several points can be made. First, the in-depth interview is a way of gaining information and understanding from individuals on a *specific topic*. In this example, we were interested in understanding Alison's transition from high school to college and her experience with bulimia. Second, the in-depth interview is a very particular kind of interaction, a particular kind of conversation. The in-depth interview dialogue is one where the researcher asks a question or seeks some clarification or amplification on what the respondent is saying. The role of the researcher is to listen to the respondent's story. If we look at the sheer number of words coming from the interviewer and the respondent, we cannot help but note that most of the conversation is coming from the respondent. The researcher often seeks to gain more insight into the respondent's life by asking questions that probe, in a neutral way, for more information or understanding. The researcher is engaged with the respondent and shows this by listening and providing signs of engagement. These include gestures such as nodding or asking the respondent to clarify a point or term. We can think of "probing" as an essential tool for an effective interview. *Probes* are also critical to a good interview, and you should be able to distinguish between when a marker has been dropped that you want to pick up on and when you should probe further into a respondent's response. Probes are particularly helpful and important during an in-depth interview; if it is a low-structure interview requiring you to ask fewer questions, you will find it very important to delve deeper into what the respondent is choosing to discuss. A probe is the researcher's way of getting a respondent to continue with what they are talking about, to go further or to elaborate, perhaps by virtue of an illustrative example. Sometimes a probe is simply a sign of understanding and interest that the researcher puts forward to the interviewee. Let's look back to a snippet of our talk with Alison to examine the various types of probing you might employ in this type of interview.

THE ART OF PROBING

Probes allow researchers to provide the respondent with support and encouragement without pushing their own agenda into the conversation. The following are some common ways you might use to employ probing in your own in-depth interviews:

A Silent Probe: You remain silent, but gesture with a nod. You might also convey your interest and support by maintaining eye contact with the respondent while she is speaking.

Echo Probe: This is where you may repeat what the respondent has just said and ask the respondent to continue. Such an example might be where I ask Alison, *So when you said "it didn't seem like enough somehow," what did you mean?* You can see that I repeated what she had said before asking her to clarify what she meant by this statement. I asked a new question but followed the direction of her general concern by asking her to elaborate on this. A neutral probe does not create a new agenda, but it is a way of keeping the conversation going and encouraging respondents to continue with their agendas.

Uh-Huh Probe: This is where you can encourage your respondents to continue to tell their stories by providing an affirmation sound like "uh-huh," "yes," or "uhmm, I understand." We can find an example of this probe in my interview with Alison. After she spoke, I said: *Uh-huh, so, for how long?* This is a "neutral probe," in that you are not trying to steer the conversation in a specific direction, but rather you are encouraging the respondents to continue with their stories. It is a sign that you are listening and supporting their telling of their story.

Probing by Leading the Respondent: Here you are being a bit more explicit about your probing. You want to lead the respondent toward a specific question or touch on a specific issue. In the interview with Alison, I might go on to ask a specific question about her relationship with her mother.

- "Was your mother ever critical about your body?"
- "If so, in what sense?"

I might probe further with this line of questioning by asking Alison a few more questions that would depend on her answer. If, for example, she tells me that her mother was critical and the ways in which she was critical about her body, I might be interested in knowing how often she was and when this tended to occur—as a young child, all throughout her childhood, and so on. I am taking a particular thread of the interview and following up with several other questions I consider pertinent to the specific issue. In this sense, I am following where Alison is taking me, but I am also mindful of my interests and research agenda regarding her mother's attitude toward her body.

RESEARCHER-RESEARCHED RELATIONSHIP
IN THE IN-DEPTH INTERVIEW

Feminist researchers are particularly concerned with reducing the hierarchy between the researcher and the researched. In fact, there is concern among feminists that the researcher and the researched are not on the same plane and there is much attention paid to the interview as a "co-construction" of meaning. Early on feminist researcher Ann Oakley (1981; see also Reinharz, 1983) advocated a "participatory model" that stresses the importance of the researcher sharing his or her own biography with the researched. The idea of sharing identities and stories with one another is thought to increase reciprocity and rapport in the interview process, thus breaking down the notions of power and authority invested in the role of the researcher. In particular, there is concern regarding the *power and authority* issues that can ensue between the researcher and the researched. These issues might interfere with the ability of those researched to provide a subjective account of their understanding on a specific issue, their life story, or a specific topic. To further balance out the inequities of power between the researcher and the researched, some feminist researchers and others advocate the process of giving back their research findings and interpretations to the respondent to get his or her input and to resolve possible disagreements between their interpretation and that of their respondents. However, there are some feminist researchers who caution against getting too close to your respondent. They argue that closeness alone can determine whether or not you will obtain the respondents' subjective understandings and perspectives. Feminist sociologist Judith Stacey (1991) suggests that while self-reflection is important to decreasing the power differentials between the researcher and the researched, being too personal with a respondent can provide a false illusion that there is no power and authority. This case might make the respondents more vulnerable, encouraging them to reveal the more intimate details of their lives. The researcher, however, still has the power to analyze and interpret the respondents' stories in a way that renders them with little or no voice in this process. Daphne Patai (1991) argues that giving back one's research findings to respondents as a way to address any power imbalances in the researcher-researched relationship may serve only as a "feel good measure." In doing so, the researcher may forgo his or her intellectual responsibility of interpretation to gain rapport and approval from the respondent (p. 147). Feminist researchers have suggested a number of important factors to consider throughout the interview process to make sure the respondent's stories are heard.

KNOWING YOUR OWN POSITION AS A RESEARCHER: REFLEXIVITY IN THE RESEARCH PROCESS

The feminist, reflexive researcher's perspective begins with an understanding of the importance of one's own values and attitudes in relation to the research process. This recognition begins prior to entering the field. Reflexivity means taking a critical look inward and reflecting on one's own lived reality and experiences; this self-reflection or journey can be extremely helpful in the research process. Consider the following questions: How does your own biography affect the research process; what shapes the questions you chose to study and your approach to studying them? How does the specific social, economic, and political context in which you reside affect the research process at all levels? Reflexivity is the process through which a researcher recognizes, examines, and understands how his or her own social background and assumptions can intervene in the research process. Like the researched or respondent, the researcher is a product of his or her society's social structures and institutions. Our beliefs, backgrounds, and feelings are part of the process of knowledge construction. To practice reflexivity means to acknowledge that "all knowledge is affected by the social conditions under which it is produced and that it is grounded in both the social location and the social biography of the observer and the observed" (Mann & Kelley, 1997, p. 392). The following is an excerpt from a reflection memo I wrote concerning being a white middle-class researcher who is interviewing young adolescent girls in the heart of an inner-city black community center.

Sharlene Nagy Hesse-Biber: Can a White Middle-Class Researcher Interview African American Teens of Color?

I walked into the community center in the heart of an African American community in a medium-sized inner city located in the Northeast. I was scheduled to meet with a group of African American teens between the ages of 13

(Continued)

(Continued)

> and 17 to talk with them about their experiences in "coming of age" in their
> community and their attitudes about school as well as their hopes and con-
> cerns for the future. I was definitely the "outsider." I was the researcher and
> the only white person in the community center that day. My concerns cen-
> tered around trying very hard not to have a strict agenda—a set of prepack-
> aged questions I would ask all of them, reminiscent of a survey where there
> is little room for the voices of those I interview to be heard outside of my own
> agenda of questions. I also wanted to find a way to position myself in the
> setting so that I would be able to break down somewhat the power and
> authority that is often inherent in the researcher-researched relationship.
> I remember the first day I came to the center. The director piled us all into a
> room she had reserved for us; after initial introductions, I provided more
> detailed information about myself, telling them I was a researcher and a
> teacher, that I was not the expert, but rather they were the experts on their
> own lives. I wanted to begin to shift the emphasis and flow of conversation
> around their concerns and hopes; I was to become the learner, bearing wit-
> ness to their lives. What was important to them? How did they see their lives
> unfolding at home? At school? During the course of the interview, they asked
> me questions: What do you teach? Are you married? Do you have children?
> Sometimes they would ask me to join them in playing basketball or to look
> at something they had drawn, and we would engage each other in conver-
> sation. I volunteered one day a week at one of the community centers, where
> I tutored several of the younger children, helping them with their homework
> assignments. Yet I was concerned about whether or not I was listening in a
> way that the girls felt they were being heard. How do I listen to them across
> the many differences I bumped up against with them—my race, my class, my
> age, my position as a researcher?

Reflexivity goes to the heart of the in-depth interview; it is a process whereby the researcher is sensitive to the important "situational" dynamics that exist between the researcher and the researched that can affect the creation of knowledge. To understand what biases you bring to a research project, and what specific power and privilege you might impose onto your own research, you might try the following exercise before you begin your research. This simulation could be particularly helpful as you prepare to begin the interviewing phase of your research:

Research Exercise: Finding Your Research Standpoint

Take 10 minutes and write down the various ways your social position affects the way you observe and perceive others in your daily life.

- What particular biases do you bring to and/or impose onto your research?
- How does this affect the types of questions you ask in your own research?
- How does this influence the research style you take on?

As reviewed in Chapter 3 on feminist standpoint epistemology, Sandra Harding (1993) introduces the concept of "strong objectivity" and argues that considering one's own standpoint during all phases of a research project "*maximizes* objectivity" for the researcher. This also ensures that the respondent's voice is represented, listened to, and understood throughout the research process. Harding urges researchers to examine the questions they ask during interviews and notes that these questions are not "value free," for they often reflect the values, attitudes, and agendas of the researcher. Researchers who practice "strong objectivity" might ask the following questions:

- How do my values and attitudes and beliefs enter into the research process? Do I only ask questions from my perspective?
- How does my own agenda shape what I ask and what I find?
- How does my positionality affect how I gather, analyze, and interpret my data, and from whose perspective?

THE IMPORTANCE OF LISTENING

Sociologist Marjorie DeVault (2004) urges researchers to pay attention to the language with which a respondent expresses his or her reality. She is particularly interested in not just what is said but what is not said or might come across as "muted" language. For example, in my interview with Alison, she uses the phrase "You know?" many times. Let's take a snippet from her interview to illustrate what DeVault means:

Alison: A lonely Friday night, I was in a single room by myself at a school I didn't like, you know. I didn't have a big social life. I had a close friend but that wasn't enough. I had lots of good acquaintances, one close, best, trustworthy friend, but I don't know, it just didn't seem like enough somehow.

What DeVault would note is the hesitation that becomes evident in Alison's interview through her use of language; this is especially clear when she begins to talk about her loneliness. She uses the term *you know* when she begins to describe the lonely Friday night in her dorm room. In transcribing Alison's interview, the researcher may in fact decide to omit the term *you know* since it appears to be irrelevant. Yet DeVault (2004) notes,

> I believe, this halting, hesitant, tentative talk signals the realm of not-quite-articulated experience, where standard vocabulary is inadequate, and where a respondent tries to speak from experience and finds language wanting. (p. 235)

DeVault (2004) suggests we should honor hesitant language and terms like *you know* during the interview process. This can be done by acknowledging this language not only when it occurs in the interview but also when the time comes to represent our respondent's voices in writing up our research findings. She discusses what she has done in a similar interview situation:

> I nodded, "um hmm," making the interview comfortable, doing with my respondent what we women have done for generations—understanding each other. But I fear that the request is too often forgotten when, as researchers, we move from woman talk to sociology, leaving the unspoken behind. In some sense, this is a betrayal of the respondent—I say I understand, but if I later "forget," her reality is not fully there in what I write. (p. 236)

A feminist perspective regarding in-depth interviewing would see the interview process as a *co-creation of meaning*. The researcher must stay on his or her toes and listen intently to what the interviewee has to say, for the researcher must be prepared to drop his or her agenda and follow the pace of the interview. The interview and conversations with the researched will assume an agenda independent of that of the researcher, and researchers should be ready to work with these changes. This can be difficult to do, and Kathryn Anderson ran into this kind of problem in her research. Anderson, a speech communications expert, wanted to document the lives of rural farm-women living in northwest Washington State for the Washington Women's Heritage Project (1991). During the course of her research, however, her focus on the rural farmwomen's attitudes and feelings was often displaced by her personal agenda. Anderson hoped to find specific descriptions of women's farm life activities that could be used as material for an exhibit. She notes,

> In retrospect, I can see how I listened with at least part of my attention focused on producing potential material for the exhibit—the concrete description of experiences that would accompany pictures of women's activities. As I rummage through the interviews long after the exhibit has been placed in storage, I am painfully aware of lost opportunities for women to reflect on the activities and events they described and to explain their terms more fully in their own words. (Anderson & Jack, 1991, p. 13)

Let us listen in on one of Anderson's interviews. She interviews a farm-woman named Verna, who candidly discusses how difficult life has been for her as a mother. Verna opens up to Anderson in the following excerpt, but notice Anderson's response to Verna's emotional remarks:

> [Verna:] There was times that I just wished I could get away from it all. And there were times when I would have liked to have taken the kids and left them someplace for a week—the whole bunch at one time—so that I wouldn't have to worry about them. I don't know whether anybody else had that feeling or not but there were times when I just felt like I needed to get away from everybody, even my husband, for a little while. Those were times when I just felt like I needed to get away. I would maybe take a walk back in the woods and look at the flowers, and maybe go down there and find an old cow that was real and gentle and walk up to her and pat her a while—kind of get away from it. I just had to, it seems like sometimes. . . .

> [Anderson:] Were you active in clubs? (Anderson & Jack, 1991, p. 16)

We can use this excerpt as an example of how a researcher's agenda can interfere with the interviewing process. This interview demonstrates Anderson's pursuit of her own agenda, and we can see that she did not really "listen" to Verna's heartfelt remarks. Instead, she follows her own agenda and fails to acknowledge the powerful emotions Verna has discussed. Anderson's follow-up question on clubs is an excellent example of how personal research agendas can conflict with the intimacy and spontaneity of the interviewing process.

A feminist perspective on the in-depth interview process reveals that it is more of a conversation between coparticipants than a simple question and answer session. Information flows back and forth throughout the interview, but it is important to underscore the role of the researcher in this process. The researcher's primary job is to listen carefully, discerningly, and intently to the comments of the researched. Researchers may want to ask specific questions that relate to their field or area of study, but it is important that their questions evolve as cues from the researched. This keeps the researcher from asserting his or her own agenda while emphasizing the researcher's role as a listener. Anderson and Jack (1991, p. 24) offer us a guide to sharpening our "listening" skills during the interview process. This guide is especially helpful in listening across our differences.

- Have an open-ended interview style to enable your interviewees to express their attitudes and feelings.
- Probe for feelings, not just facts. For example: How does the respondent understand what is happening? What meaning does she give to the course of events in her life?
- What is not said?

Anderson and Jack (1991) also suggest consulting the following checklist *before* you conduct your interviews:

- Be mindful of your own agenda.
- Go with your own "hunches, feelings, responses that arise through listening to others" (p. 24).
- If you are confused about something, don't be afraid to follow up on an issue or concern.
- What about your own discomfort and how this might affect the interview situation? Can your personal discomfort also provide you with a clue as to where you need to look at "what is being said" and what the respondent is feeling?

I have also provided you with a "listening exercise" you might want to practice with a researcher partner (see the following boxed text).

Developing Good Listening Skills

Introduction

Good interviewing starts with good listening. This exercise is intended to help you practice your listening skills. You will need one person who will be the interviewer, another who will be the respondent, and another who will serve as a timekeeper. The interviewer will start out by asking only one question of the respondent; after that it is important that the interviewer not think about what he or she wants to ask next (your agenda). The interviewer should concentrate on what is being said and try to remain silent during the interview process itself.

The Listening Exercise

1. Pair off with a research partner.

2. Position yourself in the interview situation so that you are facing one another at a distance that feels comfortable.

3. Flip a coin to decide who will first take on the role of interviewer, with the other taking on the role of respondent.

4. The respondent should talk for 30 seconds on a specific topic that the interviewer will determine. It should be a fairly neutral topic such as "my favorite restaurant" or "my favorite vacation spot."

5. A moderator will call time out after 30 seconds have elapsed.

6. At this point the interviewer should repeat what it is that he or she heard the respondent say.

7. Now reverse roles.

8. After this is complete, the time will increase to 60 seconds; you should inquire concerning a more personal issue, such as "something you are concerned with about yourself" or "the most difficult challenge faced in the past year."

9. Some questions you might want to ponder: What differences, if any, did you notice happening in the interview situation between the 30-second interviews and the 60-second interviews? Did your body language change? Did you make more or less eye contact? Did your verbal expressions change? How? How much were you able to recall in the 30-second encounters versus the 60-second interview? Was it hard to listen? In what sense?

There are other tools you can use to conduct a successful interview. Picking up on *markers* is one way to show a respondent that you are listening and interested in what is being said. Markers are also a valuable source of information and often lead to the thick descriptions that characterize and enrich qualitative interview data.

PICKING UP ON "MARKERS":
A STRATEGY FOR LISTENING

Markers are important pieces of information that respondents may offer while they are discussing something else. Weiss (1994) explains the marker and its appearance as

> a passing reference made by a respondent to an important or feeling state. . . . Because markers occur in the course of talking about something else, you may have to remember them and then return to them when you can, saying, "A few minutes ago you mentioned. . . ." But it is a good idea to pick up a marker as soon as you conveniently can if the material it hints at could in any way be relevant for your study. Letting the marker go will demonstrate to the respondent that the area is not of importance to you. It can also demonstrate that you are only interested in answers to your questions, not in the respondent's full experience. . . . Respondents sometimes offer markers by indicating that much has happened that they aren't talking about. They might say, for example, "Well there was a lot going on at that time." It is then reasonable to respond, "Could you tell me about that?" (p. 77)

Let's revisit the interview with Alison and examine the markers that appear in this discussion. There is a moment in the interview where Alison describes her loneliness. This issue comes up several times during the course of my interview with her. Here is one snippet from the excerpt you have already read:

Alison: Yes. And after, my friend and I would do study sessions. I would come back at like 10 p.m., and I had a refrigerator in my room, and I grocery shopped, and I would make like bread with peanut butter and jelly, or jelly and butter, just whatever I had. I knew there was a vending machine in our building, and I would go down there and I'd come back up, and I'd go down there, and I'd come back up. And also, my best friend who lived next door to me in her single, she went home a couple of weekends, once a month or so, and I would be there. I felt alone. There were people I could hang out with. But nobody who really knew me, and so I would go down to the vending machines, and I can remember thinking, "This just isn't going to do it for me. It is not going to make my Friday night that exciting, but then again, why not?" So. . . . I would binge four times a week. Sometimes I stopped.

Uh-huh. So for how long?

In this particular exchange, I heard Alison's concern about how empty and lonely she felt. She notes above, "I felt alone. There were people I could hang out with. But nobody who really knew me. . . ." It would be important for the interviewer to pick up on this "marker" shortly after she finished her response. I might follow her marker and ask, "Can you tell me more about your feeling lonely?" Alison mentions her loneliness at several points throughout the interview, but she never fully describes what she is feeling. It appears, however, that these feelings are strongly associated with her bulimic behaviors. By listening for these markers, you are showing the respondent that you are in fact listening very carefully to the hints and issues that matter to them.

At this point, let us join David Karp behind-the-scenes (Hesse-Biber & Leavy, 2006) to get a glimpse at how he conducts an interview and addresses some of the following issues:

- How do you get someone to start talking?
- Is it hard to be an active listener while in the role of interviewer?
- Do respondents want to share their stories?
- What do respondent's get out of this process?

Behind-the-Scenes With David Karp

Well, I think you should be making it easy on people. You should begin by asking the easy questions. You know, "What religion did you grow up with, etc.?" And not to ask threatening questions, and to give people a sense

(Continued)

(Continued)

about what you are doing because what they are trying to figure out, just like in any interaction, is, who is this guy? What is he after? Is he genuine? Are his intentions good? Does he listen? Does he seem to care about what I'm saying? And when you do an interview, you must make that person feel that he or she is the only person in the world at the time that you are talking to. I could never do more than one interview a day, never! Because the amount of energy that is required to really listen, to really pay attention, is enormous. And to know just when to ask a lot of questions.

Part of this conducting thing is to reach a balance between. . . . You should be respectful of the story that the person you're interviewing wants to tell. See, people come into your office and they have a story that they want to tell. And when they walk in, at the beginning, maybe they want to talk about how medicine screwed them over, or something like that. That's what they really want to talk about. I have to go with that at the beginning. I'm not going to turn them off. I'm not going to say, "Well, I didn't want to talk about that until 2 hours into the interview." And I think it's reaching balance between allowing people to be heard, to tell the parameters of the story that they really want to tell—and every story is to some degree idiosyncratic in meaning—and at the same time, as I said, to know what you want to get covered before you're done with this person.

I find in doing interviews that if you ask the right question at the beginning of the interview, once you really get into the substance of it, you often don't have to ask much more. In the depression stuff, the first question I typically asked people was, "You may not have called it depression, but tell me about the first moment it entered your head that something was wrong. What was the first time there was any kind of a consciousness that something was wrong?" Sometimes I didn't have to say much of anything else for the next 3 hours. People had a way of telling their story, and they spontaneously covered all of those domains of inquiry that I wanted to have covered. And the other thing I would say about this is that people really do want to tell their stories. Almost invariably, people thanked me at the end of their interview for giving them a chance to tell their story. And to have a sociologist ask them questions. . . . They often got a different perspective on their life than they could have gotten through years of therapy, because I was asking questions that only a sociologist would ask.

FEMINIST PERSPECTIVES ON
"DIFFERENCE" IN THE INTERVIEW PROCESS

Feminist researchers view social reality as complex and multidimensional, and this perspective shapes their opinion of the interview process. The researcher and the researched come together for an interview with different backgrounds in terms of gender, ethnicity, and sexual preference. Class status and other differences might also affect the flow and connection of the interview.

Researchers often pay little attention to how these differences might affect or define the interview situation. Positivist researchers are especially apt to overlook these differences, for traditional positivistic research deals with the issue of difference by *minimizing* its effects. Positivistic researchers standardize their participation in the interview situation by being "objective" or "bracketing off" these differences in their positionality vis-à-vis their respondent, so as not to influence the interview process itself. This minimizes the effects of difference, but it also means that the following questions are rarely considered:

- Can a single, white, middle-class, male researcher interview a black, working-class mother?
- Can a middle-class, white female interview a woman from the Third World who is living in poverty?
- Can a straight, white, middle-class male interview a gay working-class male?

Feminist researchers argue that "bracketing" off attitudes is not as easy as it may seem, for it is difficult to overlook the attitudes and values that emanate from any given individual's mix of positional ties. In fact, acknowledging the similarities and differences between the interviewer and the respondent allows the researcher to assess the impact of difference on the interview situation. Issues of difference affect all phases of the research process, from the selection of a particular research question, the formation of a hypothesis, to the overall process of data collection. The ultimate analysis, interpretation, and the writing up of our research findings are all affected by our perception of difference.

Insider or Outsider?

Some researchers have found ways to overcome the impact of difference in the interview process. One way this can be done is to "match" the interviewer's more important status characteristics (race, age, gender, or sexual preference) so that they use their *insider status* to gain access to an interview. This might also help the researcher obtain cooperation and rapport within the situation that would help him or her to better understand his or her respondents. After all, the researcher is an insider and should be familiar with the respondent's group situation. It is also important to achieve a balance in some of these status markers to decrease the possibility of power and authority imbalances negatively affecting the interview situation (Oakley, 1981). If the interviewer is perceived as an *outsider,* it is generally thought that his or her differences might make it more difficult to gain access to and understand the situation of "the other." But does an "insider" status guarantee a more valid and reliable interview? How might differences affect the research process?

Embedded in this example of difference is the realization that, from the beginning of our research project, who and what we choose to study is grounded in an appreciation of difference. *What* and *who* we study has affected our cognizance of difference and our general approaches to these issues. An appreciation of difference allows us to ask the questions: Which women? Are all women around the world the same? How are they different and what differences are important to my research question?

Difference is also critical in terms of the *interview situation.* Can a researcher from a First World country truly understand and relate to the plights of women working in the global marketplaces of the Third World? Suppose the researcher is a white middle-class male conducting a research project. How might his gender, race, ethnic background, and social class affect the interview process? Can the researchers "overcome" differences between themselves and those they research? Does the researcher want to "overcome" all of these differences?

If the interviewer and the interviewee are of the same gender, class, and ethnicity, it is easy to assume that an open dialogue would quickly be established. This situation might also provide a maximum opportunity for the voice of the respondent to be heard and represented. These are not unreasonable suppositions. In her field research among Gullah women, Beoku-Betts (1994) found that her research was enhanced when she informed her participants that she too was raised in a rural community with similar cultural practices. This revelation of her social positionality and background helped her to make contacts and gain data that would not otherwise have been available. Kath Weston (2004) is very reflexive about her identity as a lesbian and how it has influenced her research. She notes that while she still would have chosen to study gay families, her project would have been very different if she were not a lesbian. Weston also recognizes that her position within the homosexual community was the reason she had little trouble finding lesbian participants. These women seemed virtually invisible to her male colleagues who were also conducting sexuality research. She notes,

> In my case, being a woman also influenced how I spent my time in the field: I passed more hours in lesbian clubs and women's groups than gay men's bars or male gyms. (p. 202)

Sometimes sharing some insider characteristics with a respondent is not enough to ensure that the researcher can fully capture the lived experiences of those he or she researches. Catherine Kohler Riessman (1987) researched divorce narratives, and she provides an example of this instance. Riessman found that just being a woman was not enough for her to understand the experiences of divorced women whose class and ethnic backgrounds differed from hers. Her positionality as an Anglo, middle-class, highly educated individual prevented her from fully understanding the particular ways these women structured their divorce narratives (episodically instead of chronologically). The researcher realized the challenge of separating her own cultural expectations from the narratives that were shared with her from women of different ethnic and class backgrounds. Beoku-Betts (1994) confronted a similar scenario in her field research among Gullah women. Beoku-Betts is a black female researcher, and her race helped her secure insider status in the black community she was studying. Beoku-Betts relates how one of her respondents told her that "she preferred a black scholar like myself conducting research in her community because 'black scholars have a sense of soul for our people because they have lived through it'" (p. 416). However, Beoku-Betts found that her racial insider status was intertwined with other differences in class and cultural backgrounds. These differences created considerable resistance within the community toward her fieldwork activities:

> My shared racial background proved instrumental in providing access to research participants and in reducing the social distance at a critical stage of the researcher process. However, my identity as an outsider was also defined by other subgroups within that identity. For example, my gender, marital status (unmarried), and profession status as a university researcher often

operated separately and in combination with my race to facilitate and
complicate the research process. (p. 420)

Beoku-Betts (1994) also provides vivid illustrations of how difference
created conflict in her research. Her status as an unmarried female created
some tensions in one of the communities she studied, and she relays how difference created the following incidents in the field:

> In one community a local man visited the family with whom I was staying.
> When we were introduced, he recalled that he had heard about me and shared
> with me the rumor in the community that I was there to look for a
> husband. . . . Another incident occurred in church one Sunday with an
> African American minister who invoked the topic of the Anita Hill/Clarence
> Thomas hearing after I was asked to introduce myself to the congregation. At
> first, the minister was very supportive and welcomed me warmly into the
> community as an African coming to study aspects of a common historical
> heritage. However, he soon switched to the Hill/Thomas hearings and began
> to remark on the fact that Anita Hill was also an educated woman who had
> used that privilege to accuse and embarrass Clarence Thomas (whose home-
> town was not far from this community). (p. 428)

Beoku-Betts found that she must negotiate her differing statuses if she is
to obtain interviews with her respondents that reflect how they actually feel
about her. It was only after she completed this negotiation process that she was
given full access to her research subjects and could begin to co-create meaning and understanding.

While it is important to familiarize yourself with the challenges of difference, it should also be noted that being an outsider can actually be an advantage. This hinges on the research problem and population you have chosen to
study, but not belonging to a specific group can make you appear more unbiased to your respondent. Similarly, being an outsider might encourage you to
ask questions you might otherwise have taken for granted as "shared knowledge," and you might discover the unique perspectives your participants have
on a particular issue. Sociologist Robert Weiss (1994) comments on issues of
difference between the interviewer and the respondent as follows:

> One way to phrase this issue is to ask to what extent it is necessary for the
> interviewer to be an insider in the respondent's world in order to be effective
> as an interviewer. . . . It is difficult to anticipate what interviewer attributes
> will prove important to a respondent and how the respondent will react to

them. . . . There are so many different interviewer attributes to which a respondent can react that the interviewer will surely be an insider in some ways and an outsider in others. . . . I have generally found it better to be an insider to the milieu in which the respondent lives, because it is easier then for me to establish a research partnership with the respondent. But some of my most instructive interviews have been good just because I was an outsider who needed instruction in the respondent's milieu. (p. 137)

It is interesting and important to note that one's insider/outsider status is fluid and can change even in the course of a single interview. Your role/status might be shared with your respondent on some issues, but you might also discover glaring differences exist on other particularities of your research question or a topic of conversation. A good example of such a situation comes from research conducted by Rosalind Edwards (1990). Edwards is an educated, middle-class, white woman who is interested in conducting unstructured interviews with mature, Afro-Caribbean mothers who are also students. She wanted to understand the lived experiences of these women around issues of education, work, and family life, but she had trouble accessing the population and gaining their trust in interview scenarios. She and her respondents finally acknowledged these differences in an open discussion, and it was then that they were able to candidly discuss their experiences. Edwards experienced an ebb and flow feeling from insider to outsider status that shifted as she discussed different issues with her respondents. She notes that she felt more like an insider when the discussion was focused on motherhood: "The black women did indicate some common understandings and position between us" (p. 488). A noticeable shift occurred when the discussion reverted to a more "public" realm like their educational experiences. Even though Edwards also shared the positionality of having been a mature mother and student, the conversation became one where "black women were least likely to talk to me about what we had the most in common" (p. 488).

Reflexivity and Difference

The concept of reflexivity becomes important once again when we discuss studying across difference. Reflexivity can be an important tool that allows researchers to be aware of their positionalities, gender, race, ethnicity, class, and any other factors that might be important to the research process. We can use the previously discussed research projects to see how similarities and differences affect the interview process. Each of the above researchers had to face how they were like and different from those they researched and then channel these factors into their research. *Doing reflexivity* in fact empowered both the researcher and the researched within the interview situation. Reflecting on difference allowed Beoku-Betts (1994), Edwards (1990), Riessman (1987), Weston (2004), and Weiss (1994) to *negotiate their differences and similarities* with their respondents to *gain access* and *obtain data* that would not have been available to them otherwise. They were also able to *gain new insight* into their data from the perspective of difference. Kath Weston's (2004) reflexivity concerning her lesbian identity and its impact on her research allowed her to easily obtain access to the lesbian community. Edwards's (1990) recognition of the similarities and differences she shared with her Afro-Caribbean population offered her a more in-depth understanding of how her population talks about public and private issues. Weiss (1994) and Edwards (1990) also realized the fluidity of being an insider or outsider, which can shift depending on the given research topic and the individual current of the actual interview.

Reflexivity also reminds us of the important role difference plays in our research project as a whole. Difference enters every facet of our research process. It guides the projects we select, informs the questions we ask, and directs how we collect, analyze, write, and interpret our data. Differences should be explored and embraced, for ignoring and disavowing them could have negative effects on your data and overall project.

ANALYSIS AND INTERPRETATION OF INTERVIEW DATA

In this section, I will provide you with some general concepts to consider as you analyze your interview data. The sociologist David Karp (Hesse-Biber & Leavy, 2006, pp. 142–144) provides a step-by-step approach (see text box on the following page) to use as you begin the analysis of your interview data. He stresses the importance of starting your analysis early, for qualitative data analysis is an *iterative process* of data collection along with data analysis. These two processes should proceed almost simultaneously. Karp suggests *memoing* throughout your research process to trace how your data do or do not fit together. Memoing will help you track your project's progress, and it is also a fine time to jot down any hunches and ideas you might have about connections within your data. You can reflect on breakthroughs in your memos, but the memoing process will also help you become more reflexive about your own positionality and how it might affect your research. Karp also underscores the importance of purposely seeking "negative cases" that do not fit cohesively or create problems in your research. You can find these cases by asking yourself: What doesn't support my interpretation?

David Karp's Tips for Successful Analysis of Your In-Depth Interview Materials

Remember that the analytical work you do along the way is every bit as important as the task of data collection. Never subordinate the task of data collection to thinking about and analyzing your data. The great strength of methods such as in-depth interviewing is that you can engage simultaneously in the processes of data collection and analysis. The two processes should inform each other.

Start writing memos with the very first interview. Let your early data tell you which of your ideas seem sensible and which ones ought to be reevaluated. Especially at the beginning, you will hear people say things that you just had not thought about. Look carefully for major directions that it had just not occurred to you to take. The pace of short memo writing ought to be especially great toward the beginning of your work. I advocate "idea" or "concept" memos that introduce an emerging idea. Such memos typically run two to three pages.

Reevaluate your interview guide after about 10 interviews. Ten interviews ought to give you enough information to do a major assessment of what you are learning or failing to learn. This is probably a good point at which to take a close look at your research questions and emerging themes.

If you think that you have been able to grab onto a theme, it is time to write a "data" memo. By this, we mean a memo that integrates the theme with data and any available literature that fits. By a data memo, I mean something that begins to look like a paper. In a data memo, always use more data on a point than you would actually use in a research paper. If you make a broad point and feel that you have 10 good pieces of data that fit that point, lay them all out for inspection and later use. Also, make sure to lay out the words of people who do NOT fit the pattern.

(Continued)

(Continued)

Once themes begin to emerge, go out of your way to find cases that do not fit. You must try as hard as you can to disprove your ideas. Do not be afraid of complexity and ambiguity about themes. The world is complicated and your writing must reflect that complexity. There is a tendency of social scientists to describe patterns as if they were uniform and monolithic. To do that slights the complexity of things. Don't fall in love with early, plausible theories.

After 15 to 20 interviews, it is probably a good idea to create coding categories. Here the task is to begin by creating as many categories as you can that seem sensible. Coding is another way of "getting close to the data" and telling you what you know. You can eventually use these codes as you go through the data for paper and memo writing.

Write a fairly complete memo every time your work takes on a new direction (say, a major change in sampling procedure). Provide a full explanation for changes in analytical directions. Your memos can constitute an "audit trail" for people who want to retrace your steps. People who do qualitative research should be as fully accountable for their procedures as those who employ more standardized procedures.

If you think you have a theme significant enough to write a paper on for publication, do it. Getting papers published is very affirming and brings your ideas to a point of high refinement. You do not have to wait until all your data are in to write papers. You will find that some of your papers will be on "subsamples" within the larger sample.

Periodically, write outlines for what a book, thesis, or report from your data might look like. Draw up preliminary prospectuses. Pretend that you were about to sit down and write a book. This is a good exercise that requires you to paint the total picture.

Do not get crazy about getting exactly the same data from every respondent. You will find that each respondent's story is to some degree unique. In your writing, you will want to point out here and there the unique story. It is probably a good idea to write up a summary sheet of about one page that describes the main themes in each interview.

Test out your hypotheses on your respondents. Incorporate your hypotheses into questions ("You know, several of the people with whom I have talked tell me that. . . . Does this make sense to you?"). There is no reason to hide or conceal hypotheses, ideas, and concepts from subjects.

Pay attention to extreme cases, because they are often the most informative. Be on the lookout to do "negative case analysis."

In-depth interviews capture an individual's lived experiences. Feminist researchers bring a unique perspective to the practice of in-depth interviewing, for they are often cognizant of issues of power and authority that might affect the research process. These researchers are mindful that they must consider their own standpoints. Feminist researchers are able to discern how their own values and biases affect their research at all points along the research continuum. This includes the types of research questions that are asked and how data are to be gathered, analyzed, and interpreted. Feminist research is committed to getting at the subjugated knowledge that often lies hidden from mainstream knowledge building. Feminist researchers are particularly interested in issues of social justice and social change for women and other oppressed groups.

In the next chapter we turn to other forms of feminist research that involve interviewing as a means of data collection. We will first consider feminist oral history research and then turn to feminist focus group interviewing. We will focus on how these methods can be employed in the service of feminist concerns.

REFERENCES

Anderson, Kathryn, & Jack, Dana C. (1991). Learning to listen: Interview techniques and analyses. In Sherna B. Gluck & Daphne Patai (Eds.), *Women's words: The feminist practice of oral history* (pp. 11–26). New York: Routledge.

Beoku-Betts, Josephine. (1994). When black is not enough: Doing field research among Gullah women. *NWSA Journal, 6,* 413–433.

DeVault, Marjorie. (2004). Talking and listening from women's standpoint: Feminist strategies for interviewing and analysis. In Sharlene Hesse-Biber & Michelle Yaiser (Eds.), *Feminist perspectives on social research* (pp. 227–250). New York: Oxford University Press.

Edwards, Rosalind. (1990). Connecting methods and epistemology: A white woman interviewing black women. *Women's Studies International Forum, 13,* 477–490.

Harding, Sandra. (1993). Rethinking standpoint epistemology: What is "strong objectivity"? In Linda Alcoff & Elizabeth Potter (Eds.), *Feminist epistemologies* (pp. 49–82). New York: Routledge.

Hesse-Biber, Sharlene Nagy, & Leavy, Patricia. (2006). *The practice of qualitative research.* Thousand Oaks, CA: Sage.

Mann, Susan A., & Kelley, Lori R. (1997). Standing at the crossroads of modernist thought: Collins, Smith, and the new feminist epistemologies. *Gender & Society, 11*(4), 391–408.

Oakley, Ann. (1981). Interviewing women: A contradiction in terms. In Helen Roberts (Ed.), *Doing feminist research* (pp. 30–61). London: Routledge and Kegan Paul.

Patai, Daphne. (1991). U.S. academics and Third World women: Is ethical research possible? In Sherna Berger Gluck & Daphne Patai (Eds.), *Women's words: The feminist practice of oral history* (pp. 137–153). New York: Routledge.

Patton, Michael Q. (2002). *Qualitative research and evaluation methods* (3rd ed.). Thousand Oaks, CA: Sage.

Reinharz, Shulamit. (1983). Experiential analysis: A contribution to feminist research. In Gloria Bowles & Renate Duelli-Klein (Eds.), *Theories of women's studies* (pp. 162–191). New York: Routledge.

Reinharz, Shulamit. (1992). *Feminist methods in social research.* New York: Oxford University Press.

Riessman, Catherine K. (1987). When gender is not enough: Women interviewing women. *Gender and Society, 1,* 172–207.

Stacey, Judith. (1991). Can there be a feminist ethnography? In Sherna Gluck & Daphne Patai (Eds.), *Women's words: The feminist practice of oral history* (pp. 111–119). New York: Routledge.

Weiss, Robert S. (1994). *Learning from strangers: The art and method of qualitative interview studies.* New York: Free Press.

Weston, Kath. (2004). Fieldwork in lesbian and gay communities. In Sharlene Hesse-Biber & Michelle Yaiser (Eds.), *Feminist perspectives on social research* (pp. 198–205). New York: Oxford University Press.

SIX

THE PRACTICE OF FEMINIST ORAL HISTORY AND FOCUS GROUP INTERVIEWS

Patricia Lina Leavy

━━━━━•◆•━━━━━

In the following Behind-the-Scenes piece, feminist scholar Maxine Birch lets us behind the curtain of her research process, examining issues pertaining to her feminism in the practice of qualitative research. She describes how she personally negotiates some of the complex issues feminist researchers encounter as they build relationships in the field and during interviews, which is essential in oral history practice and which requires high degrees of rapport, trust, and collaborative spirit. In essence, Birch asks: "Can you spot the 'feminist' in the field?"

Behind-the-Scenes With Maxine Birch

The research role I adopt when interviewing or participating in the research context aims to appear as "ordinary" as possible. A role that is indebted to the ethnographic tradition and the many interactionist and feminist methodological contributions. Qualitative research offers the opportunity

(Continued)

Note: Portions of this chapter are reprinted with permission from Hesse-Biber and Leavy (2006), *The Practice of Qualitative Interviewing,* Sage Publications, Inc.

(Continued)

for conversations to move beyond generalized and public meanings to encourage more intimate and private expressions. I believe that a researcher who blends with the people and the social context of the research can access the depth of meanings required for adequate and trustworthy qualitative research. This naturalistic research role feels comfortable to me. I enjoy spending time with and finding out about people. I am also drawn to research the social contexts around me, where my experiences resonate with the experiences of others. For me being in the field feels like an extension of my everyday life.

Where my deep-seated curiosity for understanding people around me comes from, I am uncertain. I remember my childhood as distinctly lacking any political or cultural awareness. My family and friends, like everyone else just lived, never questioning their lives. To understand how my interest in research emerged I must address how feminism shapes who I am. As a young woman in the 1970s I absorbed many influential feminist novels and then went on to study feminism in the social sciences in the 1980s. Feminist stories made sense of my experiences and confirmed how the personal is political. A strong feminist identity emerged so that I now call myself a feminist. But am I a feminist researcher? I have called myself that in academic accounts, but a close examination of how I relate to participants in the field reveals that I do not declare myself as such when developing research relationships.

Here, I explore whether this is because I feel uncomfortable with declaring myself as a feminist in the field or because research relationships require a particular sensitivity to how the other person may respond to this information.

In "the therapy study" many of the male participants used therapy groups to understand their experiences of personal relationships with women. To encourage the male participants to express their feelings to me, I developed a particular sensitivity to how they viewed women, which often challenged the personal and academic values I hold on women and feminisms. I never disputed any assumptions made about me; I hoped I was seen as an "ordinary" woman because I deemed this role as facilitating their disclosure. I felt sure that a declaration of any explicit feminist views during this research relationship would alter their assumptions of me and potentially change their accounts. Therefore, I kept quiet about my feminist identity or how feminisms had shaped my research design. Conversely, the women in this study frequently expressed feminist values similar to mine, and so my feminist identity surfaced. For these women, being an "ordinary" woman did involve the expression of many feminist views regarding men in general and how personal relationships are formed and structured. Here, my feminist sense of self added to my role of encouraging them to tell me about their feelings and experiences. I still did not, however, add to any discussion encountered here as to how feminisms had influenced my research position. In another study, "Young People and Narratives of Smoking," I needed to sensitize myself to the different contexts and social relationships involved in the young people's lives. The young people saw me as being "ordinary" by being "a local," "a mum," and "an ex-smoker," and from this position, they felt I was able to appreciate aspects of their lives. This resulted in developing a research relationship where I was privileged to receive many personal and intimate accounts of their lives.

So when I look at the different research relationships I engage, build, and disengage, I do feel that I relate as myself, but with the appropriate boundaries of a professional researcher. The declaration of being a feminist researcher when developing a research relationship appears superfluous to this role. I willingly share aspects of myself to establish common ground; this sense of sharing encourages someone to talk to me. I keep parts of myself that could be viewed as too different, extreme, or challenging quiet; the research participant is not there to engage with who I might be in other aspects of my life. Yes, I shape the research, I coerce and co-construct the narratives told here, but I am not there as a catalyst. Yes, I respond to the questions about me when or if they arise. However, any contributions from me seek to explore more about what the other person is saying, or what is happening. I can liken this role to the therapist who adopts a person-centered approach. As a researcher, I am respondent-centered. I am in the field not to show how the person can make sense of his or her experiences but to facilitate the time and space for the person to show me and accommodate whatever insights or understandings may arise from this.

In the areas where I have undertaken research the private accounts told to me and the meanings I have observed are produced within the participants' personal worlds. The research world I have defined is part of their everyday lives. The participants make sense of their own life stories and at times indicate how some aspects can be considered at a political level. They do not need me to indicate this for them. I conclude that the research role I adopt is not deceptive due to any personal discomfort in calling

(Continued)

(Continued)

myself a feminist researcher. Rather, it lets me work toward achieving a more authentic and congruent role that fits with how the participants' want to locate me. Sometimes this research relationship grows into a sense of familiarity and ease as more experiences and life stories are shared. At other times, this results in a respectful but curious awareness of difference and strangeness. This "getting to know," engaging, building, and disengaging a research relationship with someone can occasionally end with feelings of distance and dislike. Rarely does any research encounter end without revealing something important to the research endeavor.

Feminist research texts alert us to the discrepancies that emerge between the academic production of knowledge and what went on in the field and provide methodological strategies, like autobiography, to counteract this tension. I suggest that there is a need for this tension, to remain as close and "real" to the research encounter as possible. This tension is automatically changed when the research relationship is disengaged. Feminism is part of my sense of who I am, and when appropriate I declare this. This declaration can impose a very strong sense of "who I am" to the other person before the relationship has had time to evolve. Research relationships require this time to be protected from any such imposition. The personal is political and feminist qualitative researchers know only too well the privileged position they hold to make the processes of politicization visible. I have not yet entered a research context with an explicit political intention to promote social change through the research relationship. I must let the participants make sense of their own accounts during the research process. This requires me to bear the ethical responsibility of choosing where, how, and when to express any knowledge, values, or beliefs I possess in the research encounter. It also requires me to take on the responsibility for the next stage, when I can politicize personal accounts to produce academic knowledge. So I will continue to call myself a feminist researcher, as this is the academic knowledge I choose to produce. In the field, I will continue to adopt a chameleon role in the hope to reflect how the research participants make sense for themselves.

Many of my life experiences indicate how a conversation is changed when I declare myself as holding some feminist principles and values. Therefore, when involved with "doing research" I choose to manage how my personal sense of feminism and knowledge of academic feminisms is presented. This management adapts how I locate myself as a feminist researcher in the varying research encounters and the production of the research account.

Note

With thanks and acknowledgment to Rebecca Jones and Nina Nissen, two feminist colleagues whose comments helped me develop my thoughts here.

In general terms, oral history is an intensive method of interview with anthropological roots that is also frequently used by sociologists and historians and is often associated with feminists. Eileen Clark (1999) explains that oral history is "located in the spaces between ethnography, sociology, and history" (p. 3). There is a performative aspect to oral history, because storytelling always involves a performance:

> Referring to performance in storytelling, Finnegan makes the point that this dynamic is what enables storytellers to choose settings for maximum impact, to create metaphor, to add emphasis, and to use rhythm to build dramatic and powerful meaning each time a story is told. She has fought against the tendency of scholars to reduce African stories purely to text and has continued to point out the literary value in the art of storytelling. (Schneider, 2002, p. 50)

While oral history can be conducted from any number of theoretical and epistemological commitments, it is true that for some feminists oral history might be a fitting tool for gaining knowledge about life experiences from women and others. Oral history, like feminism, has a political agenda (Turnbull, 2000, p. 16) and integrates women into scholarship (Sangster, 1994, p. 5). Oral history is based on a long tradition of the oral transmission of knowledge and relies on deep communication and storytelling. Oral histories differ from in-depth interviews in that they typically last longer and go into a much deeper conversation where the researcher serves as active listener and facilitator to the interview subject. Oral history interviews can become so in-depth that a researcher often spends multiple sessions with one respondent, sometimes working with one or a handful of respondents over a period of months or years. Projects that employ the oral history method often gain data from fewer respondents than in an in-depth interview project, but the researcher gains a deeper understanding of the respondent's experiences, often over a long period of time in their life.

- Why do feminists use the oral history method?
- What are the links between the oral history method and feminist concerns?
- How do feminists employ or conceptualize oral history differently from other researchers who use the method?

Feminists often use oral history as a way of gaining rich qualitative data from those whose experiences have not always been included in research agendas. In this regard it is a tool for accessing silenced or excluded knowledge, for unearthing and preserving this "missing" knowledge. For example, Rochelle Saidel's (2004) tour de force *The Jewish Women of Ravensbrück Concentration Camp* uses oral history among other methods for recording the previously silenced history of the Jewish people who suffered at Ravensbrück Concentration Camp, and in particular the experiences of Jewish women who suffered in very particular ways. This piece of history had been overlooked. Oral history is also often employed by feminists to study the experience of oppression or being a member of an oppressed group. Oral history provides feminists a tool for accessing the personal experience of oppression. For example, Sparkes (1994) conducted an oral history interview project with a female lesbian physical education teacher to examine the ways that discrimination and heterosexism fashioned her workplace experiences. Some feminists feel that personalizing the experience of oppression is enabled in very unique ways through oral history. This method also allows feminists, who are centrally committed with the voices of women, an opportunity to challenge their own preconceived ways of thinking and categorizing experiences, and allowing the diverse voices of women and others to come through. This aspect of feminist oral history research is elaborated when discussing the role of the researcher as listener and the research participant as storyteller.

The organic affinity between oral history and feminism extends beyond the inclusion of women's knowledge and the study of oppression and also speaks to the way feminism conceptualizes experience. More specifically, it speaks to the way many feminists conceptualize the relationship between agency and structure, or the individual and the larger society. As feminism is a necessarily engaged political perspective, and women's oppression is bound to the social construction of reality, women's lives and experiences are linked to larger symbolic and institutional structures. Oral history is generally employed by feminists as a way of bridging the personal biography of women with the social context in which that biography is written. Oral history explicitly allows for the politicizing of individual experience and thus has a deep connection with the project of feminism. Looked at slightly differently, oral history can merge the public and private, individual and social, illustrating the falseness of these dichotomous constructs, and the relationship between them in lived reality. Christine Heward's (1994) research provides an empirical example of how many feminists use oral history as a way of locating the individual within a structural context. Heward conducted an oral history with a female academic to study the underrepresentation of women to study the "glass ceiling" phenomenon in academia (referring to the halting of women's careers, underrepresentation of women in higher positions, etc.). Through the oral history method Heward was able to give voice to the experience of an individual, who remains at the center of her narrative, while simultaneously studying the glass ceiling concept as a way of understanding the structural circumstances in which women in academia operate. Another example of using oral history to understand individual life experiences within a larger social context comes from Rachel Slater's (2000) research in which she conducted life histories with four women in Cape Town, South Africa. Slater's research indicates that oral histories are useful for understanding how individuals are differently constrained by their social and economic contexts. Furthermore, Slater contends that oral history research can be useful for development researchers interested in understanding the impact of social change on individual biographies. Some feminists use oral history to document how women's constructions and interpretations of history differ from men's documented accounts. The results can be surprising, and feminist oral historians must be willing to let go of previously held assumptions. Z. Kabasakal Arat (2003) discovered this firsthand in her oral history, where she discovered Turkish women recounted particular past events regarding education in the same way that men had. This may overturn some assumptions regarding gender inequality in this particular context, or it may be an indicator of the pervasiveness of male ideology.

Assumptions can come in many forms, and as we have seen throughout this book, feminism itself has been shaped by different assumptions at different times. The feminist scholar Shirley A. Hill speaks about the exclusion of

African American women from early feminism and speaks to the ways this history and issues of difference more broadly inform her interview research. Let's join Dr. Hill behind-the-scenes.

Behind-the-Scenes With Shirley A. Hill

Finding Our Voice

Decades of social science research that denigrated and/or marginalized African Americans was challenged during the 1960s by a spate of new scholars determined not only to allow black people to speak for themselves but also to honor their perspectives and lived experiences. Black women were prominent among those demanding change, yet their voices were frequently subordinated to those of black men and white women. The politically contentious claim that black women were strong, emasculating "matriarchs" was publicly rejected by African American leaders but privately invoked to silence black women and encouraged them to assume a lower profile in the civil rights movement. This fostered an increasingly "masculinized" view of racial oppression, with black men seen as its major victims. The egregious gender politics among African Americans were matched by the racial politics evident in liberal feminism. Second-wave feminism initially spoke to the concerns of middle-class white women and sometimes deliberately tried to avoid sullying its agenda by addressing issues of racial oppression.

African American women resisted their marginalization in the black liberation and feminist movements, and due largely to the painstaking work of scholars like Paula Giddings and Jacqueline Jones, their stories gradually began to emerge. *Black Feminist Thought: Knowledge, Consciousness, and the Politics of Empowerment*, written by Patricia Hill Collins (1990), was a seminal work in making theoretical sense of the experiences of black women. Collins contended that African American women had a unique standpoint that was shaped by their social location, cultural heritage, and material circumstances and that enabled them to reject the negative evaluations of their lives found in the dominant society. Expressing that standpoint, however, often proved difficult. African American scholars who tried to do so were frustrated by the demand that they use the tools, theories, and language of the dominant group, at least if they wanted their work accepted in academic circles. For many other black people, the struggles of everyday life left little opportunity for developing and/or articulating a self-defined standpoint.

Feminist theorizing has now evolved remarkably and supports understanding the interlocking systems of race, class, and gender oppression. Moreover, feminism offers epistemologies and methodologies that have often helped give voice to this distinct black feminist standpoint. There is ongoing discourse on what constitutes "feminist" research, but one of its central objectives has been to dethrone the positivistic pursuit of objective "truth" by advocating a broader array of research methods, especially those capable of elucidating social processes. Feminists have also criticized the hierarchal relationship that often exists between researcher and subject and sought ways to make the process more democratic. For some scholars, like myself, this has meant an emphasis on qualitative research, especially interviews and participant observation.

The basic theoretical approach in my work is grounded on the tradition of symbolic interactionism, which urges researchers to get inside of the defining processes of people whose lives they seek to understand. Closely related are approaches referred to as social constructionist and/or interpretive, which view realities and meanings as socially created through human interaction. I also draw on intersectionality theory to explicate how race, class, and gender shape the construction of meaning. For example, my research on how black families cope with having children diagnosed with sickle cell disease sought to understand issues like family caregiving, access to medical care, and the racial politics and myths that surrounded the disease. I conducted in-depth interviews with mothers whose children had been diagnosed with sickle cell disease and spent time sitting in on their support group meetings. I also interviewed health care professionals and social service workers and observed their interactions with these children and their families. These data enabled me to understand differences in medical and lay conceptions of the disease, how values like motherhood affected reproductive choices, and how gender—in this case, the sex of the child—influenced their caregiving work.

I have probably conducted more than 100 interviews for various research projects, and have an appreciation for the pitfalls and advantages of interviewing and ethnography. One problem has always been asking people who often lived hurried and stressful lives to take the time to sit down and share their experiences, and to allow me to intrude on the private spaces of their lives. A related issue is what they are to receive in return for their time. In one project, I offered respondents a $10 token of thanks; some gratefully received it, others were reluctant or said they

(Continued)

(Continued)

would donate it to a sickle cell fundraiser. In the kind of research I have done, what respondents more often (if more tacitly) ask for is advice and/or support, which I try to offer in thoughtful yet careful ways. My goals are always to be an interested and attentive listener, to accept the legitimacy of their values, and to share my own views when asked to do so. Developing a self-defined standpoint is powerful, and I believe the best way to encourage it is to give people the opportunity to reflect on life situations, voice their opinions, and have their opinions validated. This is what I hope to give my respondents in return for their help.

FEMINISM AND ACTIVE LISTENING IN ORAL HISTORY INTERVIEWS

During the oral history interview process the researcher assumes the role of active listener. The kind of listening required by this method necessitates a willingness on the part of the researcher to let go of her possible desire to control the flow of conversation and to listen with a completion and devotion more rigorous and attentive to nuance than would be used in normal speaking situations. The feminist oral historian Dana Jack (Anderson & Jack, 1991) explains that we need to "immerse ourselves in the interview" (p. 18) to gain meaning from the perspective of the interviewee. As oral historians, we listen to many things, including how our narrator is creating meaning. The oral historian is not simply there to collect preexisting data but is rather a part of the construction of meaning that occurs as the narrator tells her story.

> In the oral tradition, the decision to tell a story and the way a story is told and understood is a dynamic process that involves continuous attention to "what is going on in their minds." Dialogue, response, and restating over a period of time in different settings and with different implied reasons for telling can give us the background to understand. Our interpretations get tested as we become familiar with the teller and how he or she uses story to "negotiate meaning" in each telling. The notion that in oral tradition meaning is negotiated in the telling is commonly understood by folklorists. (Schneider, 2002, p. 51)

Feminist researchers who employ oral history in service of gaining data from their respondents and in their respondents' frameworks are particularly likely to try and *hear* the story of others, not just the words, but also the spaces between the words, the meanings, the process of meaning-making, the emotion, and even the silence.

Silences are particularly important for feminist researchers for several reasons. Mainly, feminists are concerned with accessing subjugated voices, and this is a primary reason a researcher might employ oral history from a feminist grounding. By accessing subjugated voices and experiences feminist researchers are often trying to make connections between individual biographies and the larger cultural and institutional contexts that serve as the backdrop for those experiences, as Collins (1990) explains. In this vein, paying attention to what is left out of the narrator's story can give the researcher insight into her struggles and conflicts. For example, silences may indicate differences between her explicit and implicit attitudes that are derived from the relationship between the larger culture and her biography as well as the retelling of that biography. Blatant omissions, for example, may indicate that there is a disjuncture between what the respondent thinks and what she feels is appropriate to say. This may be the result of her perception of social norms and values or her feeling that they are in violation of normative ways of thinking, feeling, and behaving, which may be linked to gendering. For feminist researchers the research endeavor is imbued with an intent to access marginalized voices and the perspectives of people who are forced to the peripheries of a gendered social order. Listening for silences may also indicate that the categories and concepts we have available to interpret and explain our life experiences do not in fact reflect the full range of experiences out there, such as the experiences of women, people of color, and the sexually disenfranchised. A feminist researcher working from a postmodern approach, for example, who is interested in the discursive matrix in which we all operate, may feel that the silence indicates something about the larger culture and a disassociation between ways of framing experience and the experience of the particular gendered and sexed individual. As feminist research has shown, a society does not necessarily provide all of its members with appropriate tools with which they fully and freely express what meaning something has for them. This is one reason why feminist researchers might be inclined toward the oral history method when it is appropriate to their research objectives. Deep listening to the voices of individuals, particularly those long excluded from the production of culture, is vital to the production of a larger more diverse knowledge base about human experience.

The process of becoming true listeners who are nonjudgmental and open to hearing a great many things requires reflexivity on the part of the researcher and may involve the questioning and disavowing of previously held concepts and categories that frame our understanding of social reality (Hesse-Biber & Leavy, 2006).

Feminist scholar Antoinette Errante uses her personal research experience to bring these issues to light in the following Behind-the-Scenes piece. In this powerful and reflexive piece Errante talks critically and candidly about her own process of questioning and disavowing previously held assumptions, as a feminist scholar, as she engaged in an oral history and ethnography project. Using her reflexive journey she asks us to consider not what add-on makes oral history feminist, but how could one conceive of the practice of oral history as other than feminist.

Behind-the-Scenes With Antoinette Errante

Experience and Oral History

On June 1, 2001, I excitedly arrived in Beira, Mozambique, along with 200 pounds of excess baggage, ready for a month-long trek into central Mozambique's interior to conduct oral histories of Mozambicans' colonial and postcolonial educational experiences. The cost of lugging my state-of-the-art Sony video and Marantz recording equipment, tripods, batteries, and tapes had been three times the price of my airline ticket, but it seemed well worth it because I had spent nearly 6 months planning this trip and 10 years dreaming about it. I had been in Mozambique since October 2000 doing fieldwork for a book on Mozambican colonial and postcolonial education. It was an auspicious time: I had a grant, and Mozambique was at peace. This meant it was the first time since my first trip to Mozambique in 1989 that I had the time and opportunity to travel safely through the countryside by car. My hope was to collect additional oral histories, particularly those of women. The literacy rate among black Mozambicans at the time of independence from Portugal in 1975 was only 2%—so the pool of people with any kind of institutionalized schooling was relatively small. Women had even fewer opportunities. Nevertheless, I was anxious to speak with women about their *formação*, which in Portuguese literally means "formation" but also means education or rearing in its broadest sense. I wanted to know how they had experienced colonialism, the revolution, and the years since Independence.

And so, I was especially anxious to arrive in Beira. From there, I was to meet up with my driver and translator/guide. My guide was an older gentleman who knew extensively the geography and languages of the central part of the country as well as all the local chiefs and leaders. He was vitally important because I would need someone whom local leaders and people trusted to introduce me and vouch for my integrity. My plan was to spend about 4 weeks in his company traveling central and north central Mozambique.

Dragging myself and 200 pounds of baggage out of the Beira airport, I met up with my Beira contact, who very regretfully informed me that my guide had just been hospitalized the night before with appendicitis. Well. . . . No guide and translator, no road trip. I tried my best to regroup and find either another guide or some other contacts, but to no avail. To offset the price of excess baggage, I had booked a discount ticket, which meant I could not leave Beira for another 3 weeks. The upfront costs and time spent planning the trip had been such that I knew it would be difficult to arrange another one.

What to do? I took my sorry self down to a bar on the beach just in front of the friend's apartment where I was staying. It was a popular local hangout, and I had visited my friend enough to recognize several friendly faces. We sat, watched the sun set, and exchanged several hours of laughter and storytelling.

And storytelling. It suddenly occurred to me that if I wanted to talk to people, there were plenty all around me. And so I turned to the young women sitting next to me and said, "Hi, I'm Antoinette." Thus began my "Beira beachfront interviews" with anyone who would speak with me. Some were my bar mates; some were friends of bar mates who told them I could be trusted. I ditched my big fancy recorder for my trusty little Sony cassette; no room on the tables for the Marantz and the plates of grilled chicken.

Most of the women I spoke to lived in the shantytowns around Beira. Most had not been able to go past the fourth grade. My 2-hour protocol turned into 4- and 5-hour conversations. We talked late into the afternoons. I met Dina; of the revolution she remembered only that her mother had died shortly before it and that the beloved Portuguese teacher who had become a surrogate mom was forced to return to Portugal with her military husband. "For me, the revolution just means I lost two mothers," she

(Continued)

(Continued)

shrugged. Her mother became a second-class wife to her brother-in-law when Dina's father died; she remembered how she escaped a life of servitude in her uncle's house by escaping with men—those who beat her and those who stole from her. She spoke to me with clarity of her choice to date only white men, about what she got from them and what they got from her. There was Joana, the woman whose mother was African and whose father was Greek and married to her aunt as well as her mother. She remembered her mother hiding from her father the fact that she had her daughter do all the traditional rituals of initiation. She described her girlhood as a shadow world that was visible only to the women living in her family's compound. I learned there was a difference between city polygamy (infidelity arising from male vanity) and country polygamy (a practical and economic arrangement). These women not only told me their life stories; they took pains to explain them to me—to theorize their lives.

Every day I sent little blessings to my guide's appendix. I was forced to confront my own arrogance, despite my feminist leanings, because why else would I be surprised these women could articulate highly sophisticated theories of their experiences of race, class, and gender? Obviously somewhere deep, I harbored the beliefs that theory was something created on university campuses by people with advanced degrees, that "key informants" make history (and that I knew who those might be), and that social scientists have a monopoly on defining or understanding the world. In Beira, I learned that grand historical events like a revolution are not necessarily the things that change people's lives. For most of those I interviewed, the revolution and independence came and went without fanfare. Until then, most of my informants had been selected because of their experiences with colonial and postcolonial schools, but in a country where only 2% were literate at the time of independence (1975), this made them all "key informants" in that they had all actively participated in the revolution. My random beach sample had revealed how my perspective had been skewed by my recursive logic: Key informants were key to an event (the revolution) I had defined as key. So much for grand theories of revolution.

How does this tale from the field reflect a feminist perspective of oral history? The difficult question for me is *not* how we might conceive the practice of oral history from a feminist perspective but how we might conceive of the practice of oral history that was not feminist. Oral history is organic and intimate, revealing simultaneously the power of one and of the collective, the uniqueness of our individual experiences, as well as the ways in which our experiences connect us all together. Good oral history may get you published. It may even get you on *Good Morning America*. But a *certain* outcome of good oral history practice is that it will lead you to individuals from whom you will learn immensely not just as a scholar but as a human being. Each one will contribute to your own biography and the stories you may someday tell if you are ever asked to be interviewed as part of someone else's oral history project.

I knew all this when I arrived in Beira. But I left Beira with a lesson that deepened my appreciation of multiple voices and ways of knowing the world: Don't let your theories and years of schooling interfere with your ability to appreciate the power of experience—yours as well as others. Fieldwork never goes as you think it should. Do it anyway.

As seen in this piece, feminist oral history requires a particular and comprehensive listening on the part of the researcher. Dana Jack (Anderson & Jack, 1991) suggests specific things feminist oral historians must listen for. First, feminist researchers in particular should consider a respondent's "moral language" (p. 19), which refers to self-evaluative comments:

> Although very different in tone, these moral self-evaluative statements allow us to examine the relationship between self-concept and cultural norms, between what we value and what others value, between how we are told to act and how we feel about ourselves when we do or do not act that way. (p. 20)

What Jack refers to as moral language may signal a host of issues to the active listener, but of feminist concern are the interviewee's statements that may point to the cultural context in which she lives. For example, being embarrassed discussing some component of sexuality may reveal something about the larger culture. More specifically, a woman talking about sexual dissatisfaction with her partner, which perhaps she has not shared with her male lover, may speak to the patriarchal context in which sexuality is lived and sexual scripts that reinforce heterosexual male versions of sexuality are emphasized.

Jack (Anderson & Jack, 1991) also encourages feminist researchers to listen for "meta-statements" (p. 21) or moments in the interview where the interviewee will double-back to critically reflect on something she just said:

Meta-statements alert us to the individual's awareness of discrepancy within the self—or between what is expected and what is being said. They inform the interviewer about what categories the individual is using to monitor her thoughts, and allow observation of how the person socializes feelings or thoughts according to certain norms. (p. 22)

These kinds of statements can be particularly important to feminist researchers who may be studying sexism, racism, or some part of living in a gendered and raced world. For example, someone might make a statement that they then perceive as sexist, homophobic, or racist. At that point they may stop to clarify, revise, or contextualize their claim. For an attentive feminist listener these kinds of moments may reveal not only how a respondent feels about a particular issue but how she thinks she *should* feel per social norms.

Feminists also understand that language helps shape social experience, and in fact, language has shaped each of us. Therefore, the language women use to tell their stories is doubly revealing, involving not only their own biography but how their personal biography has been shaped by the social world.

In addition to the content of an interview, researchers need to listen to the form in which the content is told. Different people talk in different ways, so listening to the way a respondent frames her story can also reveal important information. For example, in a patriarchal society, male forms of communication are normalized and thus influence how people tell their stories. Researchers should be attentive to male ways of thinking, categories, and talk styles as well as sexist language. Furthermore, feminist researchers should be open to styles of communication rooted in women-centered ways of thinking and knowing.

Although some women narrators have adapted well to this male interviewing system that female oral historians must acquire, we will not hear what women deem essential to their lives unless we legitimate a female socio-communication context for the oral history situation. . . . We will not be able to hear and interpret what women value if we do not know how to watch and how to listen and how to speak with women as women. We first need to know consciously how women do communicate privately and with each other. (Minister, 1991, pp. 31–32)

It is also imperative that feminist researchers who work with the oral history method of interview do not replicate past biases within feminist research by essentializing women's experience. It is important not to assume a common kind of speech to women, just as we must not assume a common experience or perspective. In this vein, feminist oral historians need to be attentive to the ways different narrators frame their experiences. In other words, feminist oral historians must look across difference and be open to many different communication styles if we are to unearth previously subjugated knowledges. Feminists who often work from postmodern, multicultural, and Third-World perspectives are interested in understanding the experiences of those marginalized within the society. How has their position within the culture influenced their life experiences as they interpret them, and how have these experiences in turn affected their method of storytelling?

Speech patterns inherent in oral narrative can reveal status, interpersonal relationships, and perceptions of language, self, and the world. In the case of black women, we must ask what their narrative patterns reveal about their lives. How do their unique experiences influence the manner in which they tell their own life stories (Etter-Lewis, 1991, pp. 44–45)?

When conducting an oral history interview, some of the things feminist researchers might think about include the following:

- What do my respondent's silences indicate? What is she not saying and why?
- What kinds of moral judgments are a part of how my respondent talks about her life and experiences? Is she reflecting on comments as she shares her story?
- What categories is she employing that serve as the basis for her thinking and storytelling? For example, what ideas about normality, sexuality, gender, and such shape her thinking?
- How are social norms about gender shaping her thoughts?
- What is my respondent's speech style? Does she use slang language or language I need clarification of? Is she speaking chronologically or in vignettes or in some other narrative structure? What does her speech style reveal about her perspective?
- How do I feel about what my respondent is saying? What does my internal monitor tell me about silences, omissions, her emphasis, and the like?

While feminist researchers have traditionally used oral history as a method of hearing women's stories, in the following Behind-the-Scenes piece

Kristin L. Anderson takes us into her vantage point as she employed oral history to study a particular group of men from whom she was different in more ways than one. In this provocative piece, Anderson addresses issues such as gender dynamics and power within the research process, building knowledge across difference, and the challenge of questioning previously held assumptions.

Behind-the-Scenes With Kristin L. Anderson

Feminists have long viewed the practice of oral history as a means to allow people who have been silenced to speak. What does it then mean to use this method with people who, in feminist terms, would be more appropriately thought of as silencers? This is the difficult question that struck me as I was conducting oral histories with men who were court-mandated to attend a treatment program for abusing their female partners or wives. Could I listen to the stories of men who did things that disgusted and frightened me? What could I learn from their histories?

Before I started the interviews, I expected that the dynamics of gender (as a woman interviewing men) would predominate; I recall today with embarrassment that I wore a "mock" wedding band to the first few interviews, out of a misplaced fear that an interviewee might ask me out. Instead, I found that issues of race/ethnicity, class, and institutional power felt more central to the dynamics of the conversations that I had with these men. I was the one wielding the tape recorder and the informed consent statement on impressive stationery. I was the one asking the questions. I was the one holding the $30.00 cash that we offered as "compensation" (read "motivation") for their participation in the study. The men that I talked to were, in many cases, struggling with unemployment, poverty, and substance abuse. We were talking across powerful differences of race/class and, in a few cases, across differences of native language. These differences mattered.

What I learned from these conversations is that power is complex. Feminists, for the past 30 years, have been struggling to understand the relationships between structures of power—the ways in which systems of patriarchal, racist, classist, and heterosexist power interact (and sometimes contradict each other). A crucial lesson for me was that people can have institutional or structural power without realizing it. In my relations with many of these men, I was structurally privileged by my middle-class, white, university-affiliated structural location. These privileges helped me feel at ease and in control of the interview process. The men that I spoke with often appeared hesitant, uncertain, and eager to help with our project. As I reflected on the ways in which the actual experience of interviewing differed from my expectations, I began to think about subjective and objective power, and how we miss the complexity of power if we are attentive to only one type of power. Why did I initially think that I would feel powerless in relation to these men? When I privileged a gender analysis, I was thinking of myself as a woman in relation to violent men. When I privileged a class or race analysis, I realized that I felt powerful during these interviews because I was literally protected by the power of classed institutions. The interviews with male batterers were conducted in the offices of a domestic violence treatment program, in the daytime, with members of the program staff nearby. Although it wasn't "my turf" per se, it was turf on which I felt safe and comfortable. This was not the case for the majority of the men that I interviewed, who were mandated by the court to attend the program.

The same lesson was taught to me through the stories these men told of the violence in their relationships. These batterers did not recognize the power granted to them by their maleness—they perceived themselves as powerless, as controlled by the women in their lives, as victims of a biased criminal justice system. This subjective sense of powerlessness blinded them, in many cases, to the power they abused when they lashed out against the women in their lives. It was only through a feminist lens—a lens that made the relationship between gender and violence problematic—that their privileged position became visible. But at the same time, feminist insights into the ways that gender cannot be understood in isolation from other types of power helped me understand that these men's experiences of power differed depending on their class and racial/ethnic locations. In the end, then, I learned that feminist insights into the complexity of power as it shapes women's lives must also be used to help us understand men's lives.

COLLABORATION, AUTHORITY, AND EMPOWERMENT IN FEMINIST ORAL HISTORY

Oral history depends on the co-building of knowledge between the researcher and narrator; however, the extent to which different phases of the research project, and thus the resulting knowledge, are collaborative is grounded in the epistemological underpinnings of a given project. Feminist researchers are particularly attentive to these issues because they are concerned with power in the research process and how relations of power shape knowledge building. Oral history offers feminist researchers a way of decentering authority, depending on how a study is designed. The decentering of authority resonates with many feminists, and particularly feminists who are interested in the emancipatory possibilities and conditions of empowerment of research practice and collaborative knowledge building.

How do feminists who practice oral history think about the following issues?

- Does the collaborative process that shapes data collection continue on during analysis and representation?
- Who gets to put their mark on the story that emerges out of this process?
- Who has authority over the narrative?
- What does "shared authority" mean in practice? Is it always possible or even desirable? What are the ethical considerations involved when determining the scope to which a project will be collaborative? What impact does collaboration have on the researcher, the narrator, and the research?
- Who has authority over the data? How do we think about meaning making and collaborative knowledge building?

The collaborative potential of oral history is not simply a choice about methodology but also carries with it a set of politics and a host of ethical considerations linked to the empowerment of research subjects and the social activist component of feminist research. Collaboration and authority ultimately speak to how a narrative is constructed and who has ownership over the narrative and how it is represented. During the storytelling process the co-construction of meaning occurs as the researcher actively listens and probes the narrator. Collaboration can continue during analysis and interpretation, which is something that oral historians need to consider. Feminists bring a certain set of concerns to issues about collaboration and authority. Some feminists prioritize coauthorship during all phases of the project because of their commitment to attending to and reclaiming the "voice" of their participants and challenging their categories and concepts that they use to make meaning. Jennifer Scanlon (1993) advocates research *with* women and not *on* women as a means of empowering narrators. Scanlon further suggests that feminist researchers are obliged to create a real "take-and-give" methodology where research participants are provided with time, money, or resources for their participation (p. 640). Other feminists who are centrally concerned with politicizing the experiences of marginalized persons might see great value in retaining an authoritative voice in their work so that they can use the narrative to speak effectively to feminist concerns. It is important to understand two things. First, collaboration exists on a continuum. All oral history projects require collaboration, but there are various degrees and ways in which that collaboration can occur. Second, for feminists in particular, who are committed both to reclaiming women's history and to social and political change, there is a real tension between giving voice and authority to our narrators and using our feminist lens and categories of understanding to try to effect positive social change. Turnbull (2000) also reminds us that collaboration and censorship are inextricably linked:

> In preparing for and undertaking oral history interviews the research is enmeshed from the outset, in complex decisions involving censorship and collaboration. The amount and quality of information about the research that will be shared with the interviewees prior to the interviews may vary enormously from project to project. How far knowledge of the project's intellectual origins, or precise details of the methodology is believed to be relevant information to share with participants may have important repercussions. The preparation, content and timing of the interviews themselves raise two further issues, first how the subject matter of the interviews is negotiated both prior to and during the interview and secondly, the extent to which the interviewer or interviewee orchestrated the interview; for example, in its location and timing and in the selection or emphasis of the content. (p. 19)

As you can see, when thinking about issues of collaboration there are ethical considerations, practical considerations, political considerations, not to mention the countless decisions made during the research process that researchers may not even realize they are making or may not recognize as important.

Katherine Borland's (1991) research provides an excellent and, I think, classic example of the tension between an acquired feminist vision and a desire to build knowledge that is true to the narrator's understanding of her own story. Borland conducted an oral history interview project with her grandmother. Borland experienced a conflict in the interpretive phase of the project as she shared her early interpretations with her grandmother. Borland had read her grandmother's story through the lens of contemporary feminism and thus paid critical attention to the patriarchal backdrop of her grandmother's story. Borland's respondent, Beatrice, however, was not pleased to see her story interpreted as a female struggle for autonomy in a male environment and wrote to Borland that her story had been lost and Borland had taken ownership of it and read into it to such an extent that the story was now Borland's, not Beatrice's. In the end Borland's "interpretive conflict" brings to light many of the issues feminists confront as they try to reconcile their desire to be true to their narrators with their own achieved feminist vision with its political possibilities and, no doubt, limitations.

It is not difficult to understand how sharing authority has the effect of narrator empowerment. Certainly, people are more likely to feel empowered when they are fully included and values are operating on an even playing field. Likewise, as feminism is an earned political perspective, the value of retaining ownership over the resulting knowledge so that it can best serve the greater goals of feminism also makes sense for many researchers and their participants. The various sets of choices all have ethical considerations, and none are simply right or wrong, better or worse, more or less "feminist."

PRESERVING SUBJUGATED KNOWLEDGE: ARCHIVING ORAL HISTORIES

The archiving of oral history transcripts is an important part of feminist praxis that at its center wants to recover and include women's experiences in the historical record. As a part of ethical practice, and for feminists this may also be linked to issues of social justice, the words of the respondents who share their stories must be archived and made accessible for future generations. This is critical in feminist practice because voices that have historically been silenced are being heard, and their knowledge must then be transmitted, made available, made a part of the historical record, and, thus, *preserved.*

Researchers need to think about how a transcript will be handled and to what extent the researcher will put her fingerprint on the finished transcript. These considerations have to do with if and how a transcript will be edited, which may be a part of the analysis and preservation processes. Researchers need to consider the following:

- Will you edit the transcript, and if so, how? What assumptions and goals are guiding your choices? Is your narrator a part of this process?
- Will you "clean it up" in terms of pauses, "ums," "likes," and the other informal ways people speak? Will you fix grammar?
- Will you change the particulars of their way of speaking, and if so, how does this affect meaning? How do these changes reflect feminist tenets?
- Will you alter emphasis to convey meaning? If so, meaning from which perspective—yours, the narrator's, or your interpretation of the narrator's meaning? How are these choices influenced by the feminist grounding of your work?
- How are these choices influenced by social class, race, gender, sexuality, nationality, and other characteristics?
- What are the implications of changing, or adding your own explanations for, slang words that may be the product of ethnic background and other social characteristics?

The handling of transcripts is critical for ethical feminist research because editing is tied up with meaning-making and, furthermore, because feminists know these choices are interlinked with social power and knowledge production (Wilmsen, 2001):

> A significant feature of the social relations of oral history interviews is the power relations between the interviewer and the narrator. Gender, class, race, and other social considerations enter into every interview situation to a greater or lesser extent. They affect editing through narrator and interviewer/ editor perceptions of the social status similarities or differences between them, which in turn shape their understandings of their respective roles. The importance this has for editing is the way in which power relations are interwoven with differing experience with the written word. The fact that narrators have varying experience with the written word, the world of publishing, research archives, libraries, et cetera, affects what editing decisions are made, who makes them, and why. (pp. 75–76)

Feminist researchers consider issues of difference and research power relations as a part of ethical praxis and make choices that are consistent with their ideological commitments, theoretical frameworks, and practical research goals. The extent to which a researcher prioritizes shared authority and collaboration or the political possibilities of retaining authority over the text is inextricably bound to decisions about editing, meaning-making, and the preservation of oral history transcripts.

THE PRACTICE OF FEMINIST
FOCUS GROUP INTERVIEW RESEARCH

Focus groups differ from in-depth interviews and oral histories in that multiple respondents are interviewed together in a group setting. While focus groups largely developed in market research as a way to gain consumer data, this unique method of interview is now widely used in the social sciences, health care, and education. Focus groups are generally used in academic research in three kinds of research projects: (1) evaluation research, (2) exploratory research, and (3) multimethod research projects. Before I briefly explain how focus groups are used in the aforementioned ways, I would like to note that as with the other methods of interview discussed in this chapter, focus groups can yield descriptive data and be used to generate theory.

Focus groups are employed in evaluation research when a program or organizational structure needs to be examined. New educational programs, early intervention programs (Brotherson, 1994), and community programs (Matoesian & Coldren, 2002) are often evaluated with focus groups. Focus groups are also often appropriate in exploratory research where little is known about a topic. This method allows the researcher to gain data, such as attitudes, thoughts, feelings, and personal experiences, from a range of respondents at once. This may help direct future research on a subject about which little is known. Furthermore, the data gained in this kind of exploratory research may provide important information about key issues or informal styles of language within a particular group. The latter point is one of the reasons why focus groups are well suited to multimethod designs. While research design should always be consistent with research objectives, focus groups are most frequently combined with in-depth interviews and quantitative surveys (where focus group data are used to help develop appropriate survey questions or qualitatively explain survey results). Now that I have reviewed some of the broad applications of focus groups, I will turn to a discussion of feminist focus groups highlighting some of the main features of this data collection technique.

- Why might feminist researchers use focus groups?
- How do focus groups serve feminist principles?
- How might feminist researchers think about design issues such as sampling, standardization, and moderator control?

FEMINISM AND FOCUS GROUPS

Feminists are often researching topics and populations that have been ignored by the larger research community and thus may employ focus groups in exploratory research. However, I think the major appeals of this method for feminists are the ability to conduct research with disenfranchised groups and the ability to access "subjugated voices."

Kitzinger (1994) shows that focus group interviews are particularly helpful in gaining data from "difficult" populations (p. 112). By *difficult*, Kitzinger is referring to people who may feel disenfranchised, unsafe, or otherwise weary of participating in a research study, such as people with sexually transmitted diseases or drug users (Hesse-Biber & Leavy, 2006, p. 197). Additionally, focus groups are useful in accessing the attitudes, feelings, and experiences of groups who have been marginalized or silenced within society. This includes women, sexual minorities, ethnic/racial minorities, and other groups of interest to feminist researchers.

- How are focus groups useful in gaining knowledge from disenfranchised or marginalized groups?

The kind of group interaction and multivocal narrative that occurs within focus group interviews appeals to feminist researchers interested in unearthing subjugated knowledge. Focus group interviews produce what is referred to as a "happening" (Hesse-Biber & Leavy, 2006, p. 199). A happening is a conversation that, while prearranged and "focused" by the researcher, remains a dynamic narrative process. Within the context, group members communicate their thoughts, feelings, and experiences on their own terms.

> Group work ensures that priority is given to the respondents' hierarchy of importance, *their* language and concepts, *their* frameworks for understanding the world. . . . Everyday forms of communication . . . may tell us *as much,* if not *more,* about what people "know." In this sense focus groups "reach that

part other methods cannot reach"—revealing dimensions of understanding that often remain untapped by the more conventional on-to-one interview or questionnaire. (Kitzinger, 1994, pp. 108–109)

For feminist researchers working with disenfranchised populations and/or attempting to access previously silenced knowledge about social reality, the group happening may be a productive knowledge-building path. For example, let's say we are interested in working mothers' daily experience balancing work and family. In a survey or intensive interview, some of the details of daily experiences, as well as how women process those experiences, may not surface. However, in a group conversation these important pieces of knowledge may be expressed through the sharing or comparing of experiences. For instance, one woman in the group may talk about how rushed she is dropping her child off at daycare and getting to work. At this point, another woman may say something like "and the guilt when he wants me to stay and I have to go"; this may then prompt the expression of similar feelings and experiences resulting in more in-depth data from the initial respondent as well as other women in the group. Furthermore, the women are explaining their daily life experiences by using their own concepts and frameworks for understanding, such as the loaded term *guilty* in this example.

Feminists are using focus groups in many different ways as a part of accessing knowledge from marginalized groups. In the following Behind-the-Scenes piece, Lisa Dodson, Leah Schmalzbauer, and Deborah Piatelli discuss their experiences conducting a particular kind of "feminist-infused" focus group research project in which participants take part in multiple levels of the knowledge-building process. They have written their insightful piece as a conversation, much like a focus group transcript would read.

Behind-the-Scenes With Lisa Dodson, Leah Schmalzbauer, and Deborah Piatelli

A Conversation About Interpretive Focus Groups

In these pages, we briefly share an ongoing conversation about practicing feminist, participatory methodology with a focus on the interpretive stage of social inquiry. Similar to other "feminist-infused" participatory research (Lykes & Coquillon, 2006) our work seeks to reflexively engage participants in research collaborations that treat lived experiences as central to building knowledge. In all our work, we address the historical absence of women, people of color, and other groups that have been disregarded, and sometimes distorted, in how we know our world. While we employ various participative methods, an area of focus for us has been the "ethics of interpreting" data from other people's lives. Behind the scenes, and recently on the front stage, we have used a method called interpretive focus groups (IFGs) that seeks to keep local knowledge and "subjects'" vantage of the world at the center of data analysis.

IFGs are gatherings of people who live or work in the same overall socioeconomic condition as do the people "under study," to assist in data analysis (for a full discussion, see Dodson & Schmalzbauer, 2005). In these gatherings participants are asked to analyze various kinds of data: words, vignettes, themes, numeric trends, tape-recorded discussions, and other expressions, and to collaboratively interpret "meaning in context." As such, they engage in unraveling the meanings behind the immediate forces that affect respondents' everyday lives.

Telling Lives

LD: Very early on in my work it seemed clear to me that most research that inquired into life in poor America was designed on social fault lines. At the time, working in public health, I assisted in complicated studies researching teen childbearing and maternal and child health conditions. While thoughtful theoretical work went into the formulation of research hypotheses, sampling schemes, and methods for gathering data, I found myself wondering why we imagined the "subjects," teen mothers and low-income women with new babies, would tell us what we wanted to know. Having worked in community-based organizations in low-income neighborhoods, I understood a common code that divulging accurate accounts of everyday life was generally considered foolhardy, probably a disservice to one's immediate material interests and, in some cases, dangerous. "I keep my business to myself" is a mantra heard where people experience economic, racial, and other kinds of marginalization. The most "neutral" of the research questions to adolescent mothers—"Where do you live?" and "What child care do you use when you go to school?"—brought with them a host of potentially punitive overseers. In Section 8 (federal housing subsidy program), there are rules about cohabitation; break them and you may

(Continued)

(Continued)

lose your home. The state investigates the whereabouts of fathers to seek repayment for welfare, and so identifying a young father, who may be providing critical child care but not money, could put him in trouble, if not jail. And these just scratch the outer shell of an oblique place people tend to occupy when they don't have enough income to sustain themselves, or when they are stretching the definition of eligibility for food stamps and health insurance, or they are in the United States "illegally," or in some other way have learned to obscure their social reality. At best, promises of confidentiality sound tenuous in much of this society.

Over the years, reflecting on the dilemma of seeking information that people have good reason not to tell, I modeled my work on a feminist participatory approach, incorporating the people under study in designing, critiquing, and even conducting research. Yet I was convinced that to gain a deeper understanding demanded the inclusion of people from "the community" when data are transformed into meaning or during the interpretive stage of social inquiry. More than 10 years ago I began to systematically engage people as experts in analyzing their worlds, but I made only glancing reference to the practice. While IFGs seemed to clearly elucidate hidden accounts of life and society, the approach was not well received in conventional research forums.

Several years ago, when Leah and I began to discuss her research with Honduran immigrants in Boston (much the same process unfolded with Deb 2 years later), she wanted to know more about IFGs and related methodology that grappled with "habits of hiding" data of daily life.

Elaborations: Listening for the Ground Truth With Honduran Immigrants

LS: For my dissertation, I embarked on a project looking at the survival strategies of poor Honduran transnational families, families divided between the United States and Honduras. The majority of the family members in my research were poor and undocumented immigrants working in the United States, and thus living in what the anthropologist Leo Chavez (1998) so appropriately characterized as "the shadows." Inspired in great part by Lisa, I was determined from the start to do research that was rooted in the community, reflexive, and collaborative—namely, participatory feminist research. I was supported and guided in this endeavor by Lisa and Deb, as we talked often about how to take feminist discourse out of our textbooks and into the field and the unique struggles this presented when the field was an extremely marginalized place.

From the initial conception of my research idea I was confronted with the practical and emotional challenges related to my status as a privileged outsider in relationship to the Honduran community. I am a white, middle-class academic. I speak Spanish and have worked for many years in the Central American solidarity movement. Yet despite my personal commitment to and involvement in this community, I could never and would never pretend to truly understand the "ground truth" (Dodson, 1998) that Central Americans live every day. I knew that a couple of years of field research would not be able to change that, no matter how rigorous my methods. And so I spent hours upon hours contemplating issues of representation and participation and trying to construct a methodology that would contribute to the social justice struggles of immigrants while not causing harm via misrepresentation. I was also certain that I wanted to do research in which the community collaborated with me and ultimately guided me in the analysis and interpretation of data; I didn't want to simply be a mouthpiece. I decided to pursue participant observation, in-depth interviews, and IFGs.

After a year of participant observation in a grassroots immigrant rights organization, I began conducting in-depth interviews with community members. This was shortly after the events of September 11, and immigrant communities throughout the country were immersed in a culture of fear: fear of deportation, fear of discrimination, and fear of violence. Even though I felt trusted by the community, I at times sensed this fear lurking in the minds and hearts of my respondents.

The fear I intuited seemed to reveal itself when I asked respondents to talk about how they perceived their opportunities in the United States. In interview after interview, they shared stories about discrimination in the workplace, homesickness, racism, and unfair and abusive treatment by employers. Yet when I asked my respondents if they felt there were barriers to social and economic mobility in the United States, only a couple of them answered in the affirmative. Baffled, I presented the discussion in an IFG that included Honduran immigrants, service providers, and community workers.

This IFG resulted in a modification of my data analysis. From Honduran community members I learned how to decipher the codes of politeness and security that characterize the topic of "opportunity" for many immigrants,

(Continued)

(Continued)

especially the undocumented. I also gained a deeper understanding of the implicit influence my race, class, and citizenship status had in my communication with respondents. Finally, and perhaps most important, through this process I felt power shift as Honduran community members took on the role of analytical experts and I stepped back into the role of student. This power shift enabled a clearer, sharper analysis of the data, and altered my relationship with the community.

I know from my conversations with Lisa and Deb that they have gained similar insights from their own IFGs, and I continue to reap inspiration from their experiences.

Adaptation: Revealing "Habits of Hiding" With Privileged Populations Around Racial Discourse

DP: In my dissertation work, I set out to document the challenges that a predominately white, middle-class peace and justice network encountered as it worked to transform itself into a multicultural movement. Early on in the research, I sensed that there was more to the story of how people approached organizing than I was observing or being told. I needed to find more creative ways, other than the conventional forms of sharing transcripts and researcher interpretations with participants, to interpret the data. Reading and conversing with Lisa and Leah about their work, I was intrigued by the potential of IFGs to enhance and engage community experts in the interpretive process. I used IFGs both in the early and latter stages of the research process and found that this method was useful in revealing the hidden discourses of the privileged population of this network. IFGs also revealed new lines of inquiry as well as provided an avenue for engaging community members in the research.

Conversations around race and class were challenging and difficult. When conversing with people about their experiences working across differences, we explored the difficulties working within a highly charged racial social structure. What was surprising to me was the candid nature of the conversations with people of color around issues of race. Our conversations were straightforward and comfortable. They spoke about the importance of understanding the "real issues," valuing "community work as political work," and knowing what it's like to "walk in my shoes." One person in particular, Ken, said he felt silenced many times in groups of white people. He said, "White people don't want to get into political conversations because they don't want to have to address racism and classism; racism particularly. . . . white people just don't want to go there . . . I don't think they even see it." When conversing with whites, the experience was very different and very difficult. With many, the conversations were strained, uncomfortable, vague, and contradictory. I encountered awkward silences, attempts to divert the conversation—a general feeling of tension. I remembered both Lisa and Leah relaying similar experiences when venturing into topics with participants that raised fear of exposure. When approaching topics of racism, white people often fell into color-blind discourse. They emphasized the critical nature of building multicultural movements, yet when I asked why there weren't any people of color in their group, they said, "They are unorganized, and not very political" and "It's too hard and too time-consuming to build those relationships." However, with other whites it was different. They acknowledged their privileges and stressed the importance of working with people of color and lower-income populations on the "day-to-day issues that oppress them," rather than "asking people of color to join them." One woman, Pauline, said, "If we fight injustice here in this country [as well as in Iraq], we are forced to look at how we, as white people, contribute to that injustice. Many whites do not want to do that."

I wondered why some whites were so polarized in their views from others, and if people were committed to working across difference why it wasn't happening, especially in diverse communities. I took these conundrums to the IFG setting, where we discussed themes that emerged from these conversations. These modified IFGs of three to four white people revealed that people's definitions of peace and organizing practices were products of not only different political experiences but different structural, lived experiences in a racialized, classed, and gendered society. The atmosphere in these sessions was much more comfortable than in the personal interviews. In some instances, this led to the interrogation of their own privileges and beliefs. People were more open in speaking about racism and privilege when interpreting other white people's voices rather than their own, because there was a distancing from the privilege that provided a safe environment.

Demands and Dilemmas of the IFG: Is It Worth the Effort?

LD: Over the years, I have encountered criticism of this interpretive strategy generally falling into two areas. The IFG approach is constructivist

(Continued)

(Continued)

(Charmaz, 2000) and intrinsically participatory and thus cannot be replicated exactly. The method invites collaboration between researchers and respondents and also among members of the respondent community. As Leah and Deb reveal, this interpretive approach welcomes elaboration and adaptation, albeit at considerable effort, particularly at the end of all other data gathering. Some researchers are not comfortable with "methodological spontaneity" because it is hard to replicate in neat or precise steps.

The other criticism that I have encountered is that IFGs shift the discovery process—interpreting meaning to make a claim of knowledge—from the researcher to a collective of people who are not research experts; as Leah pointed, out there was a moment when "power shifted" in the room. I have recognized that while feminist participatory methods are theoretically accepted (at least among many social researchers), the notion of opening up and sharing the "intellectual moments" of the research process may come as heretical practice. Academia places great value on "original thinkers," those who quickly stake out their intellectual territory are the most successful. Graduate students are trained to find, claim, and author originality, explicitly not with others, rather, asserting intellectual individuality, if not superiority. And social researchers, whether in university or not, know that ongoing support for their work is highly correlated with identity as the expert. These are elite communities that have long taught jealous guarding of intellectual property and identity as expert and the IFG approach runs counter to these tenets. Yet we have found it is precisely the act of asking for the wisdom of others, acknowledging and demonstrating our limitations, that opens the possibility of community members claiming knowledge and making meaning with us. Our experience suggests that, reflecting the principles of feminist participatory theory, IFGs challenge conventional lines of authority in interpreting social phenomena and can contribute to transforming how a society is "known."

LS: As my research within the transnational Honduran community has continued, the importance of employing participatory methods in general and IFGs in particular has become clearer. The very methodological point that Lisa mentions as having sparked criticism about IFGs, "opening up the intellectual moments of the research process," is exactly what I believe makes my research viable and important—that is, it has been my collaboration with and guidance from "others" who do not have traditional research credentials that has shaped my analysis and theorizing in the most critical ways.

Some academics have suggested that IFGs are no different from traditional focus groups. But I would argue that they are indeed different! They are different in the very important senses that they shift power by making collaboration a core element of the research process from the beginning and that they bring community members into the process as "experts" at the interpretive stage. As such, I feel them to be a beneficial, if not necessary, tool to strengthen analytical validity when research is rooted in marginalized communities.

I will forever struggle with the dilemmas of doing qualitative research within a community to which I cannot claim membership. But I do not see this struggle as negative. Rooting my work in a participatory feminist framework keeps me in touch with the vulnerability and risk that are implicit in my research. It mandates constant reflexivity and power checking. My engagement with participatory methods, and specifically with IFGs, has also facilitated my commitment to an ongoing collaboration with my community of respondents. Whereas my dissertation is completed, the process that set it into motion continues, and my partnership with the community grows stronger. I believe that it is only from this base of strength and trust that I will be able to participate in the creation of new knowledge in the future, knowledge that has sprouted from the margins and not the center.

DP: In my research, I found that desiring a participatory research relationship is not enough to make it happen. Overcoming an environment of mistrust and discomfort with outsiders, as well as the belief that academic research is irrelevant to the needs of activists, was the dilemma I faced on entering the field. I struggled for many months before gaining the respect and trust needed to prove that I was dedicated to producing useful research with and for them, not just about them. IFGs were able to engage many people in the research and highlight important ways these findings could be integrated into their work. IFGs opened the door for building participatory relationships, and fostered greater trust and acceptance of my presence within the network. Attempting to talk an unwilling community into a participatory project or asking people to act as interpreters of my data would have been inappropriate. By investing many hours into the work that mattered most to them and treating community members as valuable knowers, this research project organically unfolded into a participatory venture. IFGs provided a way for people to examine their processes and beliefs and, on their own terms, determine how and in what forms this research would benefit them.

(Continued)

(Continued)

Like Lisa and Leah, I believe that IFGs validate lived experience and acknowledge that participants in our research are knowing bodies. Although time-consuming and often leading us into uncharted territory, IFGs provide greater depth and understanding to our work and foster less hierarchical and participatory ways of building knowledge.

Let's take one more example to illustrate how feminists might employ focus groups as a means of accessing subjugated knowledge.

The focus group happening can be an extremely useful tool for understanding the experience of oppression—the daily experience of which may appear as a "second skin" to individuals and thus go partly unnoticed or uninterrogated. For example, the daily experience of racism, homophobia, or sexual harassment may remain largely invisible to those culturally privileged to society, and daily experiences, thoughts, and feelings may be repressed or quickly forgotten by members of minority groups for whom such experiences are a routine part of daily life. This "double invisibility" may make this critical knowledge difficult to reach; however, the group happening may allow the researcher to unearth some of this hidden knowledge. As one group member notes her difficulty finding a book for her child representative of their "alternative family" (e.g., a single-parent home or homosexual parents), this may jar other members of the group who have dealt with many similar issues but hadn't connected them or simply wouldn't have remembered to bring them up. In this way, the group dynamic can produce very rich data. The group dynamic can be a complex thing, however, and design choices made by the researcher play a significant role in how well an interview runs per the researcher's goals:

- How does the dynamic of a group develop?
- What design choices are feminist researchers confronted with?

The group dynamic that develops in focus groups is commonly termed the "group effect" (Carey, 1994; Morgan, 1996; Morgan & Krueger, 1993). The group effect can have both positive and negative outcomes, and in ways that are particularly central to feminist practice. On the positive side, the group dynamic may have the effect of opening up conversation around a difficult topic and producing important discussion, understanding, and even debate among diverse or similar participants. For example, Frances Montell (1999) found the group dynamic to be integral to the success of her study of gender, sexuality, and the mass media. The group environment created a comfort level around very personal subject matters because no one felt all of the attention was on her alone. Likewise, the group interaction allowed for some beliefs and assumptions to be challenged and thus denaturalized, which is an important aspect of feminist research.

> Participants can help each other figure out what the questions mean to them, and the researcher can examine how different participants hear possibly vague or ambiguous questions. This is important in studying sex and gender because these issues are "naturalized" to such an extent that it is very difficult to recognize one's own preconceived notions, much less challenge others' taken-for-granted assumptions. The expansion of the roles available to women in a group interview, beyond the strict separation between "interviewer" and "interviewee" allows for interactions that are likely to reveal and even challenge these taken-for-granted assumptions. (p. 49)

While the "group effect" can help facilitate feminist knowledge building, it can also impede it while making visible the very concerns feminists raise. Sometimes group members can actually silence others in the group by dominating the conversation or making it difficult for others to comfortably express their own viewpoints. In a focus group where some members have a majority standpoint and some have a minority standpoint, social relations of dominance may be replicated (Hesse-Biber & Leavy, 2006, p. 214). This occurs because minority voices are often "muted" in majority populations (Kitzinger, 1994, p. 110). For example, in a focus group comprising both women and men, there may be a tendency for men to dominate, which would then produce knowledge from a privileged position that is incongruent with feminism. Feminist researchers much consider these issues when designing their studies. In particular, feminists carefully consider sampling, standardization, and their role as a moderator.

Feminist Approaches to Research Design

Sampling refers to who the members of your focus group will be. It is important to recruit people with an interest in the topic. Feminists are likely to recruit members of marginalized or disenfranchised groups that may be accustomed to experiencing social inequality. Beyond sampling, one must consider standardization across groups. This is a critical decision for feminist scholars. *Standardization* refers to whether group members will be similar or dissimilar from one another. Groups with members who are alike in terms of relevant status characteristics (such as gender, sexuality, race, or social class) are referred to as *homogeneous*. Groups with dissimilar members are called *heterogeneous*. Heterogeneous groups yield data about how a diverse range of people respond to a particular topic. While there is certainly a place for this kind of design, feminist scholars are more likely to opt for homogeneous groups where group members' similarities make them comfortable, members are likely to share minority status characteristics, and minority voices are privileged rather than silenced. In short, homogeneity serves the group dynamic in ways that are integral in feminist research.

Segmentation is a popular strategy feminists use to maximize the benefits of homogeneity while building a comparative dimension into a project. *Segmentation* means that a study has multiple focus groups, each group comprising similar members, but there is difference across the groups. For example, in a study where gender is central, as in most feminist research, two focus groups might consist of women and two of men, for a total of four homogeneous groups that are "segmented" based on gender. This is an important technique for feminist researchers because it allows us to compare how groups differentially positioned in the culture think about and experience a range of topics while it minimizes power imbalances.

Finally, researchers adopt a particular role during focus group interviewing, that of "moderator." The style of moderation adopted is linked to the research question but also the researcher's theoretical framework and epistemological position. Feminism thus plays a significant role in the level of moderation imposed. *Moderation* refers to the degree of control the interviewer exercises. Control comes in various forms, including guiding the conversation, letting people speak as they choose or ensuring each member speaks to each question, and standardization (the extent to which each group follows the same interview guide). Feminist scholars who are explicitly interested in accessing subjugated knowledge might be inclined toward a low level of moderation where participants have more control in focusing the conversation on topics of importance to them, in their language and with their flow. However, a feminist researcher performing evaluation research, perhaps on a new sex education program or domestic violence intervention program, might opt for a higher degree of control and standardization to more effectively lobby for programming or policy changes. Here, we can see how the specific research question and feminist epistemology (such as standpoint or empiricism) play a role in focus group design.

In conclusion, focus groups are one of the three major forms of interview employed by feminists. In this distinct form of interview multiple participants produce a multivocal narrative larger than the sum of its parts. Just as feminist epistemologies are diverse, so too are the ways diverse feminists employ focus groups in the study of a range of social issues.

REFERENCES

Anderson, K., & Jack, D. C. (1991). Learning to listen: Interview techniques and analysis. In S. Gluck & D. Patai (Eds.), *Women's words: The feminist practice of oral history* (pp. 11–26). New York: Routledge.

Arat, Z. Kabasakal. (2003). Where to look for the truth: Memory and interpretation in assessing the impact of Turkish women's education. *Women's Studies International Forum, 6*(1), 57–68.

Borland, K. (1991). That's not what I said: Interpretive conflict in oral narrative research. In S. Gluck & D. Patai (Eds.), *Women's words: The feminist practice of oral history* (pp. 63–75). New York: Routledge.

Brotherson, M. (1994). Interactive focus group interviewing: A qualitative research method in early intervention. *Topics in Early Childhood Special Education, 14*(1), 101–118.

Carey, M. (1994). Forms of interviewing. *Qualitative Health Research, 5*(4), 413–416.

Charmaz, K. (2000). Grounded theory: Objectivist and constructivist methods. In N. Denzin & Y. Lincoln (Eds.), *Handbook of qualitative methods* (pp. 509–535). Thousand Oaks, CA: Sage.

Chavez, Leo. (1998). *Shadowed lives: Undocumented immigrants in American society.* New York: Harcourt Brace.

Clark, Eileen. (1999). Getting at the truth in oral history. *Social Research and Social Change, 6,* 1–18.

Collins, Patricia Hill. (1990). *Black feminist thought: Knowledge, consciousness, and the politics of empowerment.* Boston: Unwin Hyman.

Dodson, Lisa. (1998). *Don't call us out of name: The untold lives of women and girls in poor America.* Boston: Beacon Press.

Dodson, Lisa, & Schmalzbauer, Leah. (2005). Poor mothers and habits of hiding: Participatory methods in poverty research. *Journal of Marriage and Family, 67,* 949–959.

Etter-Lewis, G. (1991). Black women's life stories: Reclaiming self in narrative texts. In S. Gluck & D. Patai (Eds.), *Women's words: The feminist practice of oral history* (pp. 43–58). New York: Routledge.

Hesse-Biber, S. N. & Leavy, P. (2006). *The practice of qualitative research.* Thousand Oaks, CA: Sage.

Heward, C. (1994). Academic snakes and merit ladders: Reconceptualising the glass ceiling. *Gender & Education, 6*(3), 249–262.

Kitzinger, J. (1994). The methodology of focus groups: The importance of interaction between research participants. *Sociology of Health & Illness, 16*(1), 103–121.

Lykes, M. Brinton, & Coquillon, Erzulie. (2006). Participatory and action research and feminisms: Towards transformative praxis. In Sharlene Nagy Hesse-Biber (Ed.), *Handbook of feminist research: Theory and praxis.* Thousand Oaks, CA: Sage.

Matoesian, G., & Coldren, J. (2002). Language and bodily conduct in focus group evaluations of legal policy. *Discourse & Society, 13*(4), 469–493.

Minister, K. (1991). A feminist frame for the oral history interview. In S. Gluck & D. Patai (Eds.), *Women's words: The feminist practice of oral history* (pp. 27–41). New York: Routledge.

Montell, F. (1999). Focus group interviews: A new feminist method. *NWSA Journal, 11*(1), 44–70.

Morgan, D. (1996). Focus groups. *Annual Review of Sociology, 22,* 129–152.

Morgan, D., & Krueger, R. (1993). When to use focus groups and why. In D. Morgan (Ed.), *Successful focus groups: Advancing the state of the art* (pp. 3–19). Newbury Park, CA: Sage.

Saidel, Rochelle G. (2004). *The Jewish women of Ravensbrück concentration camp.* Madison: University of Wisconsin Press.

Sangster, Joan. (1994). Telling our stories: Feminist debates and the use of oral history. *Women's History Review, 3,* 5–28.

Scanlon, Jennifer. (1993). Challenging the imbalances of power in feminist oral history: Developing a take-and-give methodology. *Women's Studies International Forum, 16*(6), 639–645.

Schneider, W. (2002). *. . . So they understand: Cultural issues in oral history.* Logan: Utah State University Press.

Slater, R. (2000). Using life histories to explore change: Women's urban struggles in Cape Town, South Africa. *Gender and Development, 8*(2), 38–46.

Sparkes, A. (1994). Self, silence, and invisibility as a beginning teacher: A life history of lesbian experience. *British Journal of Sociology of Education, 15*(1), 93–119.

Turnbull, Annmarie. (2000). Collaboration and censorship in the oral history interview. *International Journal of Research Methodology, 3*(1), 15–34.

Wilmsen, C. (2001). For the record: Editing and the production of meaning in oral history. *Oral History Review, 28*(1), 65–85.

SEVEN

THE FEMINIST PRACTICE
OF ETHNOGRAPHY

Elana D. Buch

Karen M. Staller

O ne of the difficult things about defining feminist ethnography is that in practice, the forms of feminist ethnography are nearly as diverse as feminist ethnographers themselves. This is not to say that feminist ethnographies do not share many things, but that the kinds of ethnographies feminists write reflect the wide variety of feminist theories and ethics presented elsewhere in this book. Ethnography is a flexible, responsive, and *iterative* form of research and is well suited to answering many of the kinds of questions feminists are interested in.

Ethnography, in general, is a form of research that asks questions about the social and cultural practices of groups of people. Sherry Ortner (1995) notes that "minimally (ethnography) has always meant the attempt to understand another life world using the self—as much of it as possible—as the instrument of knowing" (p. 173). There are two significant parts of this "minimal" definition of ethnography. First, it is the "attempt to understand another life world." Thus, ethnographers study the lived experiences, daily activities, and social context of everyday life from the perspectives of those being studied to gain an understanding of their life world. Ethnographies provide holistic understandings of people's everyday lives, which means that ethnographers strive to describe and analyze systematic connections between domains of social life such as religion, economy, and kinship.

Second, ethnographers gain this knowledge by "using the self as much as possible." They conduct their research by going to the environments or *natural settings* where social life occurs and becoming immersed in those environments for long periods to gain an understanding of people's cultural practices. One goal of ethnographers is to look at the world with unfamiliar eyes. This means that rather than making sense of everyday activities through common-sense intuitions, ethnographers view even mundane, common actions and beliefs as unusual and worthy of extended analysis. In short, "Ethnographic research aims to get an in-depth understanding of how individuals in different cultures and subcultures make sense of their lived reality" (Hesse-Biber & Leavy, 2006, p. 230).

Ethnography is well suited to the study of everyday life in local places, though recently ethnographers are developing methods of studying global and interconnected processes in multiple places. Like all forms of research, there are also limitations to ethnography. It is difficult to make broad generalizations based on ethnographic work because ethnography does not use random or representative sampling. Rather, ethnographic studies can be used comparatively to see what is shared and what is unique in communities. Although ethnographies often provide narrative explanations for certain events or processes, it is difficult to prove causation of specific events using ethnography because it does not test the degree to which various factors influence outcomes. Ethnographies are also virtually impossible to replicate and verify because so much of ethnographic work depends on personal interactions between the ethnographer and the community she studies.

Although ethnography is closely tied to anthropology, researchers in disciplines such as sociology, social work, public health, women's studies, political science, psychology, nursing, education, and even business have used it extensively. Researchers with both humanistic and social science backgrounds have found ethnography useful for gathering information about and analyzing social life around the world.

Common accounts usually trace the origins of the ethnographic method to the early 20th century when European and American sociologists and anthropologists sought to understand ways of living very different from their own.

Shulamit Reinharz (1992), however, documents the earlier contributions of women such as Harriet Martineau, Alice Fletcher, Helen Merrell Lynd, and Faith Williams to the advent of fieldwork and the foundations of ethnographic method. These women's innovative research methods emphasized the importance of the ethnographer actually going to the *field* and relied on interviewing and observing local people to find out about their beliefs and customs. In the midst of World War I, during a famous and extended stay in the Trobriand Islands, Bronislaw Malinowski further developed what is now considered the cornerstone of the ethnographic method, *participant observation.* Malinowski (cited in Stocking, 1983) argued,

> Direct questioning of the native about a custom or belief never discloses their attitude of mind as thoroughly as the discussion of facts connected with the direct observation of a custom or with a concrete occurrence, in which both parties are materially concerned. (p. 97)

Traditionally, ethnography involved Westerners traveling to conduct research in small villages in exotic and remote locations with people from very different backgrounds than the ethnographer. Since Malinowski, various forms of ethnography have been developed. *Native ethnographers* conduct their research in familiar settings. Thus, while traditional ethnography strove to describe foreign ways of life in a manner that Western readers would find familiar, *native ethnographers* work to denaturalize taken-for-granted aspects of their own social worlds, often revealing the unseen workings of power or shared social norms. *Urban ethnography* studies aspects of social life in cities. *Multisited* and *global ethnography* seek to describe how people in multiple places are tied together through global processes. In *critical ethnography* and *applied ethnography* the researcher engages the community to help solve a problem or evaluate a policy of some sort. According to Robert Trotter and Jean Schensul (2000), the goal of the applied ethnographer is to "conduct research so that the implications of their research can be used for direct interventions or to lead to recommendations for policy change" (p. 691). In *auto-ethnography*, the researcher uses personal lived experiences as the primary source of ethnographic data.

Feminist researchers of the 1970s and 1980s often extolled the virtues of ethnography and other qualitative forms of research for their potential to create interpretive and intersubjective understanding of social lives. "Discussions of feminist methodology generally assaulted the hierarchical, exploitive relations of conventional research, urging feminist researchers to seek instead an egalitarian research process characterized by authenticity, reciprocity, and intersubjectivity between the researcher and her subjects" (Stacey, 1991, p. 112). *Intersubjective knowledge* is knowledge co-created by the researcher and those she researches. These forms of knowledge were thought to be more consistent with feminist critiques of expert knowledge, which were seen as reflecting and reinforcing the power of academic elites over those they study (Stacey, 1991). As an interactive process, ethnography is often seen as offering a more egalitarian means of generating knowledge and understanding than other research methods. More recently, feminist ethnographers have challenged the assumption that ethnographic methods are necessarily more egalitarian or intersubjective and have heightened aware-ness of the ways in which feminist ethnographers must remain attuned to issues of power and dominance in their own research practices (Patai, 1991; Reinharz, 1992; Stacey, 1991).

What makes ethnography a *feminist ethnography* is a contested issue. Hesse-Biber and Leavy (2006) note,

> There are a range of feminist approaches to ethnography depending on the particular disciplinary perspective, theoretical stance, and political goals of any given feminist ethnographer. What unites these approaches is a deep commitment to understanding the issues and concerns of women from their perspective, and being especially attentive to activities and the "goings on" of women in the research setting. The work of early feminist ethnography did much to unearth the "invisible" aspects of women's roles in the ethnographic setting. (p. 237)

There are three principal ways in which *feminist ethnography* might be distinguished from other ethnography. Feminist ethnography includes

- Ethnography focused on women's lives, activities, and experiences
- Ethnographic methods or writing styles informed by feminist theories and ethics
- Ethnographic analysis that uses a feminist theoretical lens and/or pays particular attention to interplays between gender and other forms of power and difference

We briefly consider some examples of each of these approaches.

ETHNOGRAPHY FOCUSED ON WOMEN'S LIVES AND EXPERIENCES

One of the earliest academic ethnographies to include detailed description and analysis of women's activities was Audrey I. Richards's (1939/1995) *Land, Labour and Diet in Northern Rhodesia*. Richards was one of Malinowski's students, and her study of agriculture and nutrition among the Bemba tribe is one of the first to provide a detailed account of women's domestic labor and responsibilities. Richards (1956) also supplemented the many accounts of male initiation rituals when she published one of the first ethnographic accounts of female initiation ceremonies, describing the Bemba "Chisungu" ceremony.

In *Am I Thin Enough Yet?* Hesse-Biber (1996) uses ethnographic methods to study the impact of cultural ideals about the female body on young women. Hesse-Biber argues that a "cult of thinness" pervades U.S. culture. She found that this female body ideal is perpetuated by patriarchal constructions of women as decorative objects and supported by the interests of the diet and fitness industry. Hesse-Biber uses interviews and ethnographic research with college-age women to elaborate on the impact of this "cult of thinness" on their lives and to recommend possible strategies to improve women's lives.

ETHNOGRAPHIC METHODS AND WRITING STYLES INFORMED BY FEMINIST THEORIES AND ETHICS

In the classic and controversial feminist ethnography *Translated Woman*, Ruth Behar (1993) weaves together the life story of Esperanza, a Mexican peddler woman and her own experiences as a woman, immigrant, and academic. Behar's approach to her fieldwork with Esperanza, her chosen writing style, and genre are deeply personal and reveal the ways in which Esperanza and Behar share experiences of rage, power, and redemption. Behar's inclusion of her personal narrative promotes a feminist agenda of breaking down analytic boundaries between women's experiences through writing that is explicitly *intersubjective*.

Billie Isabell (1995) uses the form of a dramatic play to capture the dialogue of female family members describing transforming experiences shaped by migration from small Andean villages to Lima, Peru. Isabell argues that using this kind of dialogic text to capture women's voices partially transfers the interpretive authority of the ethnographer back to those whose lives she describes.

ETHNOGRAPHIC ANALYSIS THAT USES A FEMINIST THEORETICAL LENS AND/OR PAYS PARTICULAR ATTENTION TO INTERPLAYS BETWEEN GENDER AND OTHER FORMS OF POWER AND DIFFERENCE

Ellen Lewin (1993) studied lesbian mothers' experiences to understand how their experiences of motherhood were similar to or different from those of heterosexual mothers. Lewin's study reflects feminist theory that acknowledges forms of power and difference that operate between and among women as well as between women and men.

Pierrette Hondagneu-Sotelo (2001) conducted ethnographic interviews and participant observation with Latina maids in Los Angeles. She studied the uneasy relationship between the affluent women who employ domestic workers and the working-class women who work and sometimes live among them. Through this ethnography, Hondagneu-Sotelo provides detailed description and analysis of relations of race and class between women as well as between Latina maids and the wider society.

A pioneer in considering feminist methods in social research, Reinharz (1992) wrote this of feminist ethnography: "My view on this matter is that there is no agreed on definition of feminism, but that there are many people who call themselves feminists and whose ethnographic research follows their own definition of feminism" (p. 74). In the end this might be the best way to think about and judge feminist ethnography. Rather than try to isolate a single definition, it is best to embrace a diversity of approaches—we can evaluate the scholar and the scholarship by understanding how the ethnographer situates herself and integrates her feminist views with her methodological approach. Reinharz concludes that it isn't the ethnography per se that is feminist, but rather, it is "ethnography in the hands of feminists that renders it feminist" (p. 48).

HOW CAN WE DO FEMINIST ETHNOGRAPHY?

As can be seen from the examples above, feminist ethnography is an open and flexible method. Each ethnographer tailors her methodological choices to reflect both her theoretical interests and the particular constraints of the questions and field she chooses. Despite the diversity of ways in which one can do feminist ethnography, most ethnographers follow similar steps and face similar choices throughout the ethnographic process. In this part of the chapter, we outline the following steps in doing ethnography: choosing an ethnographic problem, choosing the field, gaining access to the field, making decisions about roles and relationships, collecting ethnographic data, analyzing ethnographic data, and writing ethnographic reports.

No textbook chapter can tell you how to make the myriad decisions that face the ethnographer because such decisions will ultimately be informed by your theoretical and ethical positions. Feminist theory can inform the research questions you choose to study, the way you conduct yourself in the field, the relationships you develop with the people you study, the analytical tools you use to make sense of ethnographic data, and your final analysis and description. Different ethnographers will use theory at different stages of the ethnographic process. Thus, this chapter is intended to help you prepare for ethnographic research by giving you a sense of the common choices and problems most ethnographers encounter, as well as the strategies and techniques commonly used to gather and analyze ethnographic evidence.

What Is an Ethnographic Problem?

Every research project starts with a question, puzzlement, something that the researcher is curious about. Of course, the type of question and the way it is framed depend on the subject material. Often ethnographers don't start with a specific inflexible question. Ethnographers are more likely to start with large and intersecting domains of interest. These domains can include an interest in certain types of people, places, customs, practices, or attitudes, among other things. For example, Beth Montemurro (2005) was interested in changing gender roles and social practices and thus examined what happens when men are included in bridal showers, a ritual that had historically been reserved for women. Elana Buch is interested in the ways in which transformations in the organization of work and family affect working-class women, and thus is currently designing a study of women who do paid caregiving of elders to see how this form of labor influences their own families and elders' families. Through the process of ethnographic research, these general domains of interest often begin to give way to more specific questions. In fact, researchers frequently use ethnographic methods because they don't yet know enough about a community to frame good research questions; thus, the ethnography can be used to explore broadly and to develop better, more nuanced questions.

Theory often guides the researcher's choice of an ethnographic problem. A researcher's theoretical orientation often leads her to want to study particular domains and ask certain kinds of questions. When defining an ethnographic problem, most researchers rely either implicitly or explicitly on theory to help them decide which domains of social life they are interested in studying. Personal or informal theories about how the world works are often drawn from the ethnographer's understanding of her own everyday experiences—her common sense. Such theories usually inform how the ethnographer decides which aspects of social life she finds interesting enough to study for an extended period of time. These informal theories can be useful in helping define a research problem; the ethnographer should expect that her experiences in the field will challenge the cultural assumptions that often lie underneath informal theories. Formal theories are explicit explanations or interpretations of the relations between domains of social life often drawn from the works of other scholars. Sometimes researchers design their research problems in ways that are intended to challenge or refine formal theories and contribute to theory development as well as provide information about an unstudied people or phenomenon. Other scholars draw from formal theory to find out if it is applicable to a specific situation. When doing applied ethnography, scholars use theory both to help them understand the social phenomenon they are studying and to guide their thinking about programs or interventions that might benefit the people they work with. Because ethnography often involves an *iterative* process in which ethnographic data cause the ethnographer to refine or reformulate her theoretical ideas, ethnographers find it useful to enter the field with an awareness of a variety of formal and informal theories that can help them understand what they encounter in the field.

Feminist theories often direct ethnographers to ask questions about the contexts of women's lives, the ways in which women experience and resist gender norms and the ways in which difference is organized across lines of gender, race, class, and sexuality. For example, Emily Martin's (1992) *The Woman in the Body* is informed by feminist theories about how popular medical discourse constructs gender and ideas about women's bodies. This ethnography shows how women both subscribe to and resist dominant medical discourses (created by male doctors) that alienate women's bodies by describing them as productive machines. In her ethnographic study of a women's self-defense course, Kristine De Welde (2003) both framed the study using "feminist theories that focus on women's power and agency" and used a feminist lens to aid her in making "conclusions" about her data (p. 248). Thus, De Welde's feminist perspective influenced the way she designed the study at the outset and the way she interpreted her data at the end.

Sometimes feminist ideas and areas of interest are met with resistance in university environments and minimized as less than serious scholarly research. Frida Furman (1997), who asked important questions about the "meaning and experience of the female body for older—mostly Jewish—women in the context of a youth-loving, male-dominated society" (p. 5) by studying a beauty salon where the customers were primarily older Jewish women, wrote of her own initial concern about the study:

> I remember asking a friend, an academic also involved in feminist work, "Do you think it is serious enough?" I had evidently internalized mainstream values and was nervous about how such work would be perceived in the academy. My friend was encouraging, and I quickly moved ahead, but my misgivings were not without foundation. I soon discovered that on the face of it, a study of a beauty salon populated by older Jewish women was not taken seriously by everyone, for some, it was a source of amusement. For example, when I answered my home phone one day, a male university colleague's first words were "is this Frida Furman's beauty parlor?" . . . When I told a colleague in sociology about the study, he assured me, with a laugh, that he knew all about that generation of Jewish women; he was alluding to his mother. Another sociologist seemed intrigued and encouraging, yet he laughed as he described older Jewish women's "blue hair," suggesting that their hairstyles—and by extension, they themselves were in a "time warp." (p. 4)

Though feminist ethnographers (like other feminist researchers) may experience resistance within the academy regarding the legitimacy of their research, feminists are likely to agree that such resistance indicates the importance and necessity of their research rather than be discouraged by it. Such resistance might even make for a fascinating ethnographic problem!

Choosing the Field

Once an ethnographer has decided on a general area of study, she must decide where to go to investigate it. The *field* refers to the community, institution, or setting in which the ethnographer will go to study the problem of interest. So *fieldwork* can be done in an urban neighborhood, a rural village, a beauty parlor, a clothing store, a displaced persons camp, and so on. In multisited ethnography, the field is constructed by tracing how widespread processes or the circulation of objects connect people in a variety of places. For example, Janet Finn (1998) used a multisited approach to study women's participation in labor organizing in copper mines owned by the same company in Butte, Montana and Chuquicamata, Chile. Rayna Rapp (2000) also used a multisited approach to study how the medical technology of amniocentesis places women on uncharted moral ground. In both multisited and single-sited ethnographies, the field is the natural setting of the people and processes the ethnographer is interested in learning about. Rather than bringing people into neutral settings such as laboratories, the ethnographer travels to the places where the people she is interested in studying already are. Thus, one of the first decisions that you must make as an ethnographer is where to situate the study.

Several criteria may influence an ethnographer's selection of the field. These include aspects directly related to the area of inquiry and answer the question, *Where can I go to see the phenomena in which I am interested?* Given Furman's (1997) interest in women's experiences of aging in a culture that tends to worship youth, it made great sense to select a beauty parlor frequented by older women as a place to start her research. Or when feminist ethnographer De Welde (2003) identified an interest in the "tradition of feminists who reconceptualize power and place women's agency and resistance at the forefront" (p. 249), it made sense that the field she selected for her research was a dojo that specialized in women's self-defense courses.

Reinharz (1992) argues that feminist ethnography is

> Research carried out by feminists who focus on gender issues in female-homogeneous traditions or nontraditional settings, and in heterogeneous traditional and nontraditional settings. In feminist ethnography, the researchers are women, the field sites are sometimes women's settings, and the key informants are typically women. (p. 55)

So selection of the field is often but not always part of a feminist approach to the ethnographic project. Consider the differences between Marisa Corrado (2002), who studied a bridal shop, and Montemurro (2005), who studied bridal showers. On the face of it, both meet Reinharz's characterization of "female-homogeneous traditions" and settings. However, Corrado was interested in the way salespeople control their customers' behavior. She selected a bridal dress shop as the field in which to study this "generic social process" because it offered an "unfamiliar sales setting" and therefore a unique site in which to witness the interactions between customer and salesperson. Corrado specifically denies an interest in studying the "gendered processes of buying and selling wedding dress[es]." She chooses instead to examine the generic social processes at play. In contrast, Montemurro (2005) studied bridal showers specifically to examine the gendered nature of the ritual. Specifically, she was interested in the increasing practice of men attending showers to see whether this practice "is indicative of gender convergence or if couples showers replicate traditional gender roles" (p. 7), so she studied a traditionally female-homogenous tradition (wedding showers) in a nontraditional setting (coed wedding showers).

There are also several practical considerations that go into selecting a field. "To do intensive ethnography frequently requires the ability to suspend personal and work obligations, to travel, and to expose oneself to risk" (Reinharz, 1992, p. 73). Ethnographies require a great deal of time, frequently years, to conduct and require firsthand observation. Thus, time and money are very practical issues that must be factored into the field selection decision. Language skills are another important practical issue because ethnography relies heavily on ongoing interactions between the ethnographer and those she is studying. It is very difficult to conduct fieldwork among people whose language you don't speak. Distance and access to transportation can be other important practical considerations in choosing the field. Positionality and status are important considerations. Feminist ethnographers also pay keen attention to issues of power and exploitation when choosing the field (Nader, 1988; Spivak, 1988). It is important to consider how who you are will influence what kinds of information you are able to gather in a particular field. How might your class, gender, or race influence how people in the field interact with you? How likely is it that your presence in the field could get those you are working with in trouble?

Safety concerns are another critical and practical concern every ethnographer must consider before choosing a field. Reinharz (1992) writes,

> Much feminist ethnographic writing includes a frank, reflexive discussion of these problems, particularly sexual harassment, physical danger, and sex stereotyping. In a society that is ageist, sexist, and heterosexist, the researcher who is female and young may be defined as a sex object to be seduced by heterosexual males. (p. 58)

Thus, the relative safety of the field site is a reasonable and important consideration. Even seemingly safe settings can be unsafe at times. Ethnographers may choose to study refugee camps rather than war because it is safer to do so. Other ethnographers have studied topics that put them in harm's way—such as drug cultures, gangs, prostitution, or disease epidemics. In evaluating how safety concerns affect your field choice, it is important to consider if there are safer ways to study your questions or if danger is an inherent aspect of your questions (e.g., studying disease or war). How much risk are you willing to assume for the knowledge you might gain? Regardless of how dangerous you anticipate the field may be, it is essential to think ahead about backup plans and ways to extricate yourself from the field if you find it unsafe. It is also important to think about what kinds of training or knowledge will help you remain safe in your field of choice.

In short, it is critical for an ethnographic researcher to select the field with care. Consider all the possible field sites where you could see intersections between the domains of life you are interested in and then ask the following:

- Who am I?
- Where can I conduct my study safely?
- What personal risks am I willing to take?
- What privileges am I assuming when I think I can gain access to the field?
- Where can I successfully answer my research questions?

Gaining Access to the Field

Just because an ethnographer has decided that a certain field location would be the perfect place to conduct a study does not mean she will automatically have access to it. Sometimes gaining access to the field can be a much more difficult and lengthy process than you might imagine. Brooke Harrington (2003) draws distinctions between the concepts of access, entry, and rapport. She argues that "access" relates to the "social scientific goals of ethnography" specifically gaining *access to information*. She notes that *entry* commonly refers to "the initial act of entering the field or gaining permission from participants to start a study" (p. 599). Finally, *rapport* refers to "the quality of the researcher-participant relationship itself and is often likened to friendship" (p. 599). For example, Jennifer Lois (2001), who studied a mountain search and rescue team made up of volunteers, describes each of these ideas in her methodology section, although she does not use Harrington's terminology. Lois began the process of gaining access by volunteering with the search and rescue group herself. She attended "bi-weekly business meetings, weekly training sessions, social hours at the local bar and some missions" (p. 136) for several months before she even approached the board of directors about the possibility of conducting a research project. She received permission from the Board to proceed, thus gaining entry into the field. Finally, she spent 5½ years going on search and rescue missions with volunteers, building *rapport* with them over time. This rapport building continued to help deepen her *access to information*. The process of gaining access to the field and to information has several features and is ongoing.

Similarly, De Welde (2003) describes her experiences gaining access to her field site, a women's self-defense course, which took place over time and included an evolution in her relationship with the people in her field site:

> My entrance to the setting began when I attended the course in July 1998. Subsequently, I joined the school as a martial arts student. I established a close friendship with the owner of the school, Elaine, as well as with the other members of the setting. After approximately one year of attending classes at the dojo, I became engaged in helping Elaine with the self-defense courses for both personal and research purposes. My affiliation with the school allowed me to participate easily in the self-defense classes, enabling me to conduct opportunistic research (Reimer 1977). Although there was an assistant instructor role previously established and held by another member of the school, Marie, I had to create a secondary assistant role, one that did not exist. My gender and my previous participation were assets in gaining access to the setting (Warren 1988), as the course is typically limited to women, and I had been quite involved at the school as a student. As I became a complete member of the setting (Adler and Adler 1987), my status as a student and as a teacher was enhanced. I built on these roles while simultaneously strengthening my friendship with the instructor, Elaine. (p. 252)

Ethnographers frequently refer to individuals who hold key positions either formally or informally within the environment and help facilitate the researcher's access to people and information as *gatekeepers*. So in De Welde's study, Elaine was certainly a gatekeeper. De Welde earned her way into the environment by befriending Elaine and others and by becoming a full participant in the dojo environment. However, sometimes gatekeepers also participate in a *gatekeeping* function that can potentially exclude or hinder researchers rather than facilitate their access to the setting. They can challenge a researcher to public performances or tests as part of earning their way into the community, which can ultimately either hinder or facilitate an ethnographer's access. For example, Alexandra Murphy (2003) was tested by the manager of the strip club she was studying. She reports,

> During those initial visits, I felt uncomfortable, conspicuous, I felt like I had entered a male fantasy cliché: football played on a gigantic television screen adjacent to a main stage where a topless woman danced around a pole filled with bubbling water. My fourth visit marked a turning point in my research. At one point in the evening, Bob, the manager of the club, came over and told me to take a seat in a chair he had retrieved from a nearby table. In front of me was a blonde woman wearing a black Lycra bra and G-string bottoms and holding a tray full of shots in test tubes. "What do you want, sex on the beach?" Bob asked as I tried to figure out what was going on. "Sex on the beach is fine," I replied, still not knowing the full implications of that response. The woman took one of the liquid-filled test tubes off her tray and with her head tilted back lowered the test tube down her throat and back up again; then, with the end of the tube still in her mouth, she leaned over me putting the other end in my mouth, forcing the alcohol down my throat. Cheers rang out as I finished the shot. I was no longer watching the spectacle; I had become part of the show. Later, I realized the importance of that shot. If I had turned it down, I would have rejected the lifestyle of the organizational members I was trying to understand. After that evening, I had open access to the club. (p. 332)

Not only can gaining access be very time-consuming and cumbersome, sometimes it may not yield entry. Some field sites will prove difficult to gain access into, sometimes for unexpected reasons. For example, Buch continues to struggle to figure out a way to gain access to the home care workers she is interested in studying in the future, primarily because of the decentralized nature of this employment context and the hesitancy of home care agencies to allow a researcher to study their employees. Often ethnographers will have to work very hard to establish trust among those they wish to study, for ethnographer's motives and intentions may be unclear and communities sometimes suspect ethnographers of acting as spies or informants for more powerful interests. For example, one reason agencies might be unwilling to allow Buch to study their workers is that they are concerned that she will evaluate the workers, the care they provide, or the agencies' administrative practices negatively. Workers might be equally unwilling to allow Buch to work with them because they fear she will report unsanctioned practices to their supervisors and jeopardize their jobs.

To ease access to the field, sometimes ethnographers will rely on gate-keepers who seem to make access easier, such as friends, family, or other personal acquaintances. There are risks associated with this method of gaining access that are worth considering at the outset as well. While using a familiar insider as a gatekeeper may seem to save time and hassle, it can create other kinds of problems. It may be harder to gain access to people with opposing points of view if the researcher is perceived by the community to be too closely allied with a particular person. For example, Karen Staller (2002) attempted to conduct an ethnographic study of a police unit by relying on "permission" from a friend who was a sergeant in the unit. Police organizations, like military units or some businesses, are very hierarchical. In Staller's study the beat officers were reluctant to cooperate with the research project because they feared consequences from the unit's lieutenant, who ranked higher in the departmental pecking order than the sergeant who had first permitted access. Thus, working through a known gatekeeper who had apparent authority to grant access did not guarantee the ability to conduct the study successfully.

In keeping with feminist interest in power dynamics, the feminist ethnographer must always be aware of the power dynamics, including formal and informal relationships between and among the people that she wants to study. Of course it may not be possible to have equal access to all community members under all circumstances. Gaining entrance through one set of institutional players may preclude or impede gaining access to another set that may have different kinds of information, as was demonstrated in Staller's failure to win over the beat police officers. Therefore, you should give careful thought to how you gain access because it can be directly related to the kind of information (or "data") that will be available for analysis and therefore to the "results" that can be reported. So if entry is gained to a hospital setting through an administrator, or a doctor, a nurse, an orderly, a social worker, a custodian, or a patient, it is likely that you will be exposed to very different kinds of experiences and interpretations. While you may want to obtain all the perspectives, choosing access through one entry point may end up precluding or limiting access to other viewpoints. Instead, it is useful to consider the pros and cons of the entry methods you've chosen and recognize the limitations on the data that will be collected. Furthermore, you should be on the lookout for both the formal social relationships of the community or institution that you are studying and the informal ones that are in operation. In short, you should be aware at the outset that the pathway you use to get into the community can have a direct relationship on what information you gather during the course of your fieldwork.

Questions that must be asked before entering the field include the following:

- What is my relationship with the community?
- What pathway will I use to gain access?
- What are the benefits and risks of my choice of access?
- How will the methods I use to gain access affect the data I am able to collect?
- What is my backup plan if things don't work they way I've planned or I find myself in an unsafe situation?

Role and Relationships: Researcher, Observer, and Participant

Another decision that you must make has to do with your role in the community and how actively engaged you will become in the community. Ethnographers must decide on what kind of role they will play before they begin their research, although that role may evolve during their time in the field.

As noted earlier, Malinowski first developed the notion of *participant-observation*, the most frequently used ethnographic approach, though there is a range of possible roles within this approach. One measure of the variety of roles that an ethnographer can play involves the degree to which the researcher becomes involved in the day-to-day activities of those people and institutions under investigation. Sometimes these different *researcher roles* are described as complete observer, observer-as-participant, participant-as-observer, and complete participant (Hesse-Biber & Leavy, 2006, pp. 245–251). Note that this ranges from a complete, detached observer to a complete and fully integrated participant. Choices about how to balance participation versus observation are likely to be based partly on your research questions, partly on your theoretical position, and partly on what is possible in the field. No one balance of these roles will work equally well in all sites or to answer all questions. For example, in Murphy's (2003) study of a strip club, she was forced to participate to a small degree in order to help gain trust; however, for the most part she remained an observer of the club (although some might argue she "participated" as patron of the club). At the other extreme, Lois (2001) became a complete participant in the search and rescue team. Arguably, De Welde's (2003) role in her study of self-defense classes fell somewhere in between these extremes because she created a new role for herself that did not exist prior to her participation.

Oftentimes the researcher's role will evolve as she becomes increasingly familiar with her field site and her informants become increasingly accepting of her. For example, Corrado's (2002) role changed with time, as she grew more familiar with the community. In her study of a bridal shop, she started out as a complete observer. However, as time passed and she came to know the social actors and the business, she began to help out as an "assistant" to the two women who ran the shop performing tasks such as "fetching and restocking dresses the workers needed" (p. 38). In doing so her role became more participatory in nature. However, Corrado never became a full-time employee of the shop being studied and thus never reached a "complete participant" status.

Another role dimension to consider that is related to participation level is whether the researcher is an *insider* or an *outsider* of the community under investigation. Murphy (2003) chose not to become a stripper herself in her study of the strip club, thus remaining an *outsider*. Alternatively, Lois (2001) and De Welde (2003) were community insiders and played active roles in their respective communities. Often these choices regarding how much of an insider to become can have complicated ethical, legal, or moral aspects. Considering the various choices of roles and relationships raises a number of thorny questions. If you want to study homeless women must you become homeless yourself? If you are studying low-income workers who travel to work on public transportation must you forsake the use of your car? If you are studying drug use must you experiment with the drugs yourself? Of course, making these decisions, like the choice of whom you use to gain access to the field discussed above, has a direct impact on the data that will be available to you. This requires careful and thoughtful balancing of alternatives.

Another dimension to consider has to do with the characteristics of the researcher herself and attributes that the community may ascribe to her. So while the ethnographer may enter the field with a general idea of the role she would like to play in the community she studies, often members of the community will have other ideas about appropriate roles for the researcher to play.

When the researcher is a woman, it is likely that community members will expect that she play roles similar to those of other women in the community, which might include the role of daughter or caretaker. As discussed above, it is fairly common that single women doing ethnographic fieldwork are approached as possible partners for marriage, dating, or sexual activity. As illustrated in the examples above, the choice to accept or reject the roles the ethnographer is placed in can have a significant effect on the kind of access the ethnographer will have in the community. Moreover, conscious attention should be paid to the processes involved when a community places the ethnographer in particular social roles, for these processes can illuminate a great deal about gender and other roles in community life.

As the ethnographer negotiates these complicated and difficult decisions regarding her role in the field, a number of very important and often difficult ethical questions are encountered while in (and after leaving) the field. One of these ethical dilemmas involves the level of intervention or assistance you are willing to provide. For example, if the people you are studying use public transportation daily to get to work, should you offer to give them a ride in your car on a cold, snowy day? What if they ask for a ride? This seemingly innocent intervention changes the environment and experiences of those you are studying. What if you witness an act of violence, such as domestic violence, elder abuse, or child abuse? Or what if you are studying a teenage gang that plans to engage in criminal activity? As a researcher, should you intervene by calling the police, reporting the case to child welfare authorities, taking the victim to a shelter, or warning potential victims? It is important to be aware of the legal, ethical, and research implications of your answers to these questions. For example, in choosing to give a person you are working with a ride, you change the experience you are studying, but do you change it in significant or important ways? If you witness some form of abuse, you may have to balance between confidentiality agreements you've made with those you are studying, legal reporting requirements (which may apply to health, education, and social work researchers, among others), and your own ethical stance.

Another significant ethical dilemma can arise from the personal relationships that develop during the period of your fieldwork. Oftentimes the people you are "studying" forget that you are "researching" them. The process of gaining access does not really end after initial contacts. Since the ethnographer is in the field for long periods of time and will continually meet new people in new situations, she will have an ongoing responsibility of considering how to introduce herself and her project to those she is studying. How often should she remind them?

The role of the researcher in the field is always bound to a constant awareness of ethics and ethical practice. For feminists these issues are particularly salient. Judith Preissle discusses this and other experiences in the following Behind-the-Scenes piece.

Behind-the-Scenes With Judith Preissle

Regrets of a Women's Libber

My niece once said she envied my young adulthood—civil rights, anti-war protests, women's liberation. She saw the exciting times and progressive solidarity. I see all the work yet to be done and feel the frustration of reaching toward goals constantly changing. Among those goals are feminists' visions of a society enriching for girls and women and feminist scholars' visions of research ethics, a moral framework for doing the right thing in research. This latter task has been my preoccupation in recent years, and here I reflect on my own ethical research dilemmas through the lens of a developing feminist research ethic. As I show, I have regretted some of the choices I've made over the years, but I excuse myself by thinking that the developing ideals may have been possible only through these bumbling errors in judgment.

What are feminist research ethics? I view them as self-conscious frameworks for moral decision making—helping decide whether decisions are right or wrong by feminist values and standards. The tricky part is that there are likely as many different feminist ethical frameworks as there are feminisms. For me, the framework involves justice for women, care for human relationships, and a commitment to finding the political in the personal. My feminist research ethic requires me to consider all elements in my formulation of research goals, in the roles I take during research and how I conduct it, and in how I represent others, especially women, in my research reports. The ethic requires that I change myself before I presume to change others. I have disappointed myself in all these moral imperatives.

My 4 years of doctoral preparation during the early 1970s concentrated on anthropology and education at Indiana University, aided by my

(Continued)

(Continued)

committee chairs, the social studies educator Dorothy J. Skeel, and the anthropologist Judith Friedman Hansen. My discretionary reading, however, was the core curriculum of women's liberation—Friedan, de Beauvior, Greer, Firestone, *The Women's Room, Ms. Magazine.* As a teacher, a citizen, and a family member, I knew where I stood and what values I sought. As a novice researcher, however, I had difficulty figuring out how to integrate my strong political values with scholarship I wanted to be balanced, open-minded, and skeptical. Only with the repeated urging of my roommate Carole Hahn, a social studies educator and comparative scholar now at Emory University, did Judith and I reconsider how we were representing scholars in the article we wrote together in the 1970s on theoretical perspectives in the anthropology of education (Goetz & Hansen, 1974). Instead of using inclusive alternatives, we depended on the generic masculine: The anthropologist, the observer, and the educational researcher were all *hes* and *hims* with a rare "he or she" thrown in to mollify our budding feminist selves. This is my first regret.

What is ethical about pronouns? *The Publication Manual of the American Psychological Association* (American Psychological Association [APA], 2001) now comments, "Fair treatment of individuals and groups . . . requires authors of APA publications to avoid perpetuating attitudes and biased assumptions about people in their writing" (p. 61). Changing writing patterns took time and practice, but I now reflect more self-consciously on how I portray groups and individuals and how I write about sex, gender, and the presentation of women. In the meantime my initial foray into anthropology and education stands for my students and colleagues to read, with its embarrassing masculine generic.

Finishing a dissertation on the social organization and shared meanings among a group of third graders and their teacher, a study that left gender unexplored, I considered how my scholarship might contribute to a better world for women and girls. However, my research self, like my writing self, was immersed in a taken-for-granted world of gendered assumptions and biases, so "seeing" these patterns also took time and practice. I read avidly the literature of the times on sex differences and their origins. As I supervised elementary preservice teachers in the urban-suburban district where my university was located, I began to notice—to "see"—children being socialized to be "girls" and "boys" by each other, their teachers, and the schools.

Meanwhile, I had arranged to follow up my first ethnography in the Midwest with a study of social behavior in two first-grade classrooms in the South—in a rural school district beyond where I was supervising. Two other ethical regrets occurred during this study. As a result of a review of research on sex-role cultures in schools that I had put together from all that avid reading (Goetz, 1978), I was asked to contribute a chapter on sex-role culture from my own research and observations. My dilemmas centered on research purpose and research conduct and role. First, I had plenty of observations— the midwestern ethnographic data, the supervision sites, and the new rural site—but limited clearance on the material. Because I had not collected data from the midwestern site with any intention to analyze for sex roles, or what we now call gender roles, and because I had no agreements for conducting research in my supervision sites, dismissing that material was an easy moral decision. Of course, I was influenced by those experiences and especially by what seemed to me to be exaggerated differentiation between girls and boys in the urban-suburban district. In retrospect I might have sought permission for a study to "expose" these practices, but the more subtle and complex patterns in the rural site seemed more interesting to document, and I was already committed to researching there.

Reformulating goals for this site seemed simple. I had permission to study what first-grade teachers were teaching, what first graders were learning, and how children were being socialized and were socializing each other into the public role of students in school. The principal and the teachers knew I was interested in the history and the demographics of the school. Race, socioeconomic class, and sex were part of this, but the focus was open-ended. Peer review through an institutional review board (IRB), which we depend on now as we make these decisions, was just then getting organized at my university and was preoccupied with experimental interventions. I don't think that I even knew about IRBs at that time.

My dilemmas were, first, how much to tell the principal and the teachers about my narrowing focus and, second, how much to involve them in this topic. Having sought and established a rapport that permitted me to talk candidly about race and class, how openly could I share a shift into sex? I believed at the time that I ought to tell these welcoming women that the children in their school seemed far less pressed into conventional sex roles than students in neighboring districts, that I viewed this as positive, and that I sought to account for this pattern. But I feared to be so open:

(Continued)

(Continued)

What if they didn't intend such an environment? What if they felt misled by my initially broader research goals? What if they found my interpretation of the site objectionable? I hedged. One of the first-grade teachers self-consciously engaged children in questioning conventional gender roles; the other was ambivalent. Only toward the end of the fieldwork did I start revealing interest in this topic, and when I shared my two publications (Goetz, 1981a, 1981b) about sex-role culture in their school with them, the teachers and the principal were only mildly interested.

A feminist research purpose, exploring what happens in schools to restrict girls and boys, seemed to be far more important to me than to these three women. Likewise, their notion of role reciprocity was different from mine. They had their own goals and pursuits. I believe I could have been straightforward earlier about my interests in children's socialization to conventional sex roles, but I suspect that only the one teacher would have been interested in examining this with me cooperatively. I regret that I was less than honest and that I didn't give her that opportunity. I believe she might have found my interest affirming. What I now view as the importance of being clear about purposes and seeking collaboration with participants were hard-won lessons to a libber turned feminist. Even more crucial is reaffirming through reflections such as these how my feminist ethics have always been developmental and dynamic, rather than static, and dependent at any given time on what I am learning from research practice and from other scholars. Our regrets can be ways we bring our practice into dialogue with our theory and learn to change both.

Collecting Ethnographic Data

When conducting participant observation, the ethnographer actively engages in the everyday lives of those she studies while simultaneously observing the details about the social dynamics and patterns she encounters. Ethnographers often use participant observation in conjunction with *interviews* and *social artifacts* to compare what people say and the documents they produce with the ways they act and talk in their natural environments. In short, ethnographers are likely to rely on three basic forms of empirical evidence. The first is *ethnographic talking* to *informants*, or people in the field. Gathering data through talking with people can be done through formal interviews but is more likely to consist of informal conversations that occur during the ethnographer's time in the field. Ethnographers often rely on some key informants who provide significant information but rarely exclusively rely on information from these individuals. Ethnographers are keen observers of social settings. They watch how people conduct their daily lives and how they interact with each other, gathering *observations*. They usually do this by watching mundane, everyday activities as well as special events and rituals that have particular significance. The third form of empirical evidence is the *social artifact*. Social artifacts are things that people produce, such as documents, photographs, shopping lists, and diaries.

Most ethnographers use a rich combination of empirical evidence. For example, Corrado (2002) spent many hours observing bridal store salespersons interact with brides, fiancés, bridesmaids, mothers, and other members of the bridal party in one particular bridal shop; she conducted formal semi-structured interviews with the sales help; she traveled to five other bridal shops in the region as a client and used secondary resources such as bridal magazines, videotapes, and Internet bulletin board postings, which helped contribute to her understanding of people's experiences in bridal shops. Lois (2001) spent 5½ years as a volunteer in the mountain rescue group she was studying, keeping detailed *field notes* of her experiences, as well as collecting thank-you notes from victims and conducting in-depth interviews with rescue team members. Martin (1992) interviewed women in the Baltimore area and conducted textual analysis of numerous documents, including medical textbooks, scholarly articles, and popular books on women's reproductive health. In addition to extensive participant observations in a beauty shop serving older Jewish women, Furman (1997) used photo elicitation as a research tool because she discovered "that asking women to reflect on their facial wrinkles and other marks of aging was too intrusive and intimidating." She asked them to select photographs of themselves from youth, middle age, and current periods and asked them about their lives and their thoughts about their appearance (p. 10). She noted, "By treating the photograph as a kind of artifact, participants were able to gain some distance from it and to feel less self-conscious" (p. 10).

The kinds of ethnographic evidence needed for your project will depend largely on your research problem and questions. Often ethnographers find themselves in unexpected places or gathering unexpected kinds of information as they recognize new connections and possibilities in their field site. It is important to think broadly and creatively about the ways you might obtain evidence and what types of documents, observations, or interviews might count as information that answers your questions.

While the primary empirical evidence used by ethnographers is obtained by talking to people and observing people, it is important that this evidence is systematically and thoroughly collected and preserved. Thus, ethnographers rely on field notes to preserve their day-to-day observations. Field notes must be recorded as soon after the experience as possible; events must be fresh in the ethnographer's mind. This is particularly true because ethnographic analysis and writing depend on vivid and detailed descriptions of everyday life that are likely to be forgotten if not immediately recorded.

Field notes are often written as a two-part process. While in the field, many ethnographers write *jottings* in a pocket-sized notebook or on scrap paper to help them remember unique turns of phrase or interactions that they will describe and elaborate on in field notes written up later. Jottings help the ethnographer capture the immediacy of field experiences in an accurate manner. Often the significance of a particular conversation or event may not be evident at the time it occurs. It is only during the process of reviewing the entire field experience that its relevance becomes apparent. Thus, field notes serve as a comprehensive, chronological log of the ethnographer's perceptions of everything that has happened in the field. They can be extremely tedious to write, and sometimes what to focus on in field notes is not apparent. Ethnographers frequently spend a long day in the field only to have to spend hours into the night writing down what happened.

Field notes may be descriptive as well as analytical. The field notes might record what the ethnographer observed (who was there, what they were wearing, what happened). They may also include interpretations, hypothesis, or speculations about what was happening. The ethnographer may begin to record tentative interpretations (perhaps beginning hypotheses) after a day in the field, but these may change over time. In this way, the process of ethnographic analysis begins immediately and is ongoing. Furthermore, good ethnographers will continue to challenge their own interpretations as they spend more time in the field.

For example, Murphy (2003) reports the following observations in her field notes of a strip club:

> A football game on a big-screen TV silhouettes a half-nude woman dancing
> for a row of cheering men. Waitresses wander through the club in white lace

G-string lingerie. One asks what I want to drink. Her name is Ilona, and she speaks with a soft Spanish accent. $4.50 for a Miller Lite! "PUT THE GREENERY ON THE SCENERY," I hear an amplified voice ring out over the sound of Madonna singing, "Like a Virgin." "COME ON GENTLEMEN, THESE WOMEN DON'T GET A SALARY FROM THIS ESTABLISH-MENT. THEY RELY ON GENEROUS TIPS FROM YOU!" Though stimu-lated by vision, the customers are controlled by sound. A dancer performs a table dance for the man next to me. He is alone. She is called the "Polynesian Queen." In this dark room full of smoke, he can pretend to be her king. Her breasts appear too round. Are they real? He doesn't seem to care. He watches her body move to the beat as Janet Jackson sings "Nasty Girl." She leans for-ward and presses perfectly round breasts together—in his face. She bends down—her head in his lap. Her hair hides what she is not doing—mock fel-latio. She turns around. With her back to the patron, she bends over again. This time I see her face. She looks disinterested. He looks impressed. I'm impressed with her ability to walk in four-inch heels. Music pounds so loudly it vibrates my chair. "Welcome to Paper Dolls," a sign out front declares. "The Hottest Show on Earth." (p. 306)

In writing these notes Murphy creates a rich description of what she observed. We get a sense of the sights and sounds of the place. Note that Murphy records factual observations, such as the price of a can of Miller Lite, but by using the exclamation point she also records her interpretation, opinion, and responses to this pricing. Note how she adds to her interpretation that patrons are "stimulated by vision" but "controlled by sound" and reproduces the sound control in capital letters in her field notes. Also, notice how she offers an interpretation of how three different individuals are responding in the moment, writing that the dancer "looks disinterested" and the patron "impressed," and about her own passing thought about the skill it takes to walk in "four-inch heels."

Ethnographers also use field notes to reflect on their own position in the field. This might include describing and creating preliminary analyses about how the method used to gain access or build rapport in the field is influencing the ethnographer's experiences. Field notes might also record the roles the ethnographer has been given or chosen in the field and the ways this seems to be influencing what kinds of interactions she is able to observe and participate in. This kind of reflection about the ethnographer's own power, position, and influence in the field is known as *reflexivity*. So, for example, in Furman's (1997) study of older women and beauty shop culture, she records the follow-ing in her field notes:

What is so safe there? Is it something about the shop culture that reminds me of my childhood in its more positive moments—time with grandmothers, aunts? What is so comforting and satisfying about talking about coat sales? Or exchanging, in a somewhat competitive mood, our latest physical maladies? There is something very affirming there. It is as if one feels nurtured without having to do anything in exchange, save nurture others, which comes naturally and is self-confirming, too. Why does the concern expressed feel so warming? (p. 1)

Note that Furman uses reflexivity to relate the way she feels in the field to her own childhood experiences. In this way, she is attempting to make sense of her field experiences. However, she is also posing important questions for herself—such as, "Why does the concern expressed feel so warming?"— which will drive her study forward. She will continue to seek answers to this question and therefore a better understanding of the culture in which she is immersed.

Feminist ethnographers are likely to be very attentive to the subjective experiences of their informants as well as paying heed to power relationships and to sharing interpretive authority. For example, De Welde (2003) noted, "Consistent with feminist interviewing methods (Reinharz, 1992), the interviews provided insights into the subjective experiences of the women in the program, as well as an opportunity for their involvement with the research process and emerging theory" (p. 253). In addition, De Welde (2003) used her own personal experiences as a student in the self-defense classes in a reflexive manner reporting:

My own experiences in the program and its lasting effects permeated the data as well. My emotions and perceptions served as part of the research experience (Coffey 1999). As a "complete member researcher," I was able to highlight retrospective accounts of my own strategies, emotion conflicts, identity, and body work. (p. 253)

Perhaps the most important thing to remember about collecting data as an ethnographer is to remember that it is an active, not passive, process. The ethnographer must always be watchful and mindful of what is going on. She must continually observe with a critical and analytical eye, even while participating in everyday social life. She needs to actively remember or make jottings of conversations while in the field. There is a continual back-and-forth process of participating and observing that has to be maintained. Ethnography requires a very special kind of "being there" that involves much more than just hanging out.

Ethnographic Analysis

Analysis of ethnographic data, as noted above, starts immediately as an iterative part of the process of data collection. Good ethnographers start to ask questions to themselves about what they are seeing and experiencing, thus beginning the *interpretive process*. However, at some point all ethnographers are faced with the nearly overwhelming prospect of returning to all their data (which can include years of chronological jottings and field notes, thousands of pages of interview transcripts, and collections of artifacts, including documents, photographs, and so on) and somehow make sense of it all. This part of the ethnographic process is both interpretive and analytical. Ethnographic analysis techniques are sometimes borrowed from, or at least shared with, other methodological discussions. For example, some use grounded theory, others narrative analysis, and many a more generic thematic approach.

In its most basic form, analysis frequently involves some steps shared with other qualitative researchers such as coding, looking for patterns or themes, comparing and contrasting, and placing incidents and experiences into broader social and political contexts. *Coding* is a process by which a researcher goes through her data and attaches a code (a word or brief description) that represents something that she sees happening in the data. *Pattern* or *thematic analysis* refers to the process of identifying how similar processes or worldviews recur repeatedly in the data. *Comparing and contrasting* can refer to processes of looking for similarities and differences between different actors encountered in the field, as well as similarities and differences between how some situations or interactions were handled in the field. Ethnographers will frequently compare and contrast ideas during their analyses to establish what kinds of behaviors or ideas are similar to or different from other kinds of behaviors or ideas. Feminist analysis in ethnography often involves sustained attention to the ways in which similarity and difference are organized through sex and/or gender. *Contextualizing* incidents and experiences refers to analysis that ties the ways in which domains of social life are organized and experienced in the field to broader social and political trends in the nation or world. Feminist ethnographers often pay particular attention to the ways in which social and political contexts contribute to or are influenced by the organization of gendered difference and other kinds of discrimination.

Lois (2001) was interested in how mountain rescue volunteers managed emotions, intimacy, and relationships with victims and their families during missions. In her analysis she developed the idea of "tightness," which she defined as "interpersonal management to refer to situations in which emotion managers require emoters to conform to specific emotional directives" (p. 139) to consider how victims' emotions were managed. In contrast she determined the families emotions were managed using "looseness." Furthermore, she determined that "tightness" in managing victims' emotions included neutralizing embarrassment, alleviating anxiety, and preventing a psychosomatic crash. On the other hand, managing families' emotions included validating grief and balancing hope and reality. Although Lois did not explain her analysis strategy, we can speculate about her process because of her clear reporting. For example, she may have coded the data by identifying specific incidents (such as the use of humor during a rescue). These codes might have led her to find patterns that led to themes such as neutralizing embarrassment. Ultimately, by comparing and contrasting, she noticed a difference between how rescuers managed the emotions of victims and families, leading her to conclude that the former was managed tightly and the latter loosely. She ultimately contextualized her study within a larger body of literature on socioemotional economy. Although Lois did not cast herself specifically in the role of "feminist" researcher, she did take special note of the differences ascribed to male and female rescuers. For example, she writes, "Women were given the same opportunities as men to perform physically demanding tasks, but when it came to controlling their emotions, women were stereotyped as weaker than men and thus less able to perform critical missions" (p. 175). While Lois didn't start her research with a problem directly informed by feminist theory, she did pay attention to matters of gender in her analysis and in reporting her findings.

There is some folklore among anthropologists about sorting ethnographic data by using index cards with holes punched to represent topical or theoretical codes and then grouping them by pulling a knitting needle through the holes. More recently, these kinds of low-tech, physical approaches have been supplemented (and in some cases supplanted) by electronic versions of coding and sorting offered by computer software programs. Some ethnographers join other qualitative researchers by using qualitative analysis computer software to help manage and to analyze the massive amounts of data. Computers can be a great help in maintaining, organizing, and sorting large amounts of data. However, it is critical to remember when using qualitative software that unlike quantitative software analysis (in which the researcher essentially feeds in numerical data, asks the software to perform a mathematical function, and then interprets the results), there are no mechanical steps in the process of qualitative analysis. Thus, ethnographic researchers who use qualitative software must be constantly interacting with their data and interpretations.

As ethnographers work, and rework, their way through the data, they often find themselves refining the questions that they are asking and answering. While they may have entered the field with broad intersecting domains of interest in mind, during analysis these ideas become more focused, more concrete, more complicated, and often more interesting. It is hoped that the ideas and questions that emerge from ethnographic fieldwork more closely reflect the experiences and understandings of the people studied rather than the a priori beliefs of the ethnographer. Some argue that one purpose of ethnographic studies is not only to answer some questions the researcher had in mind but also to learn enough to ask better, more sophisticated, and more nuanced questions at the end.

Reinharz (1992) argued that

> a feminist perspective on data analysis includes many components such as understanding women in their social contexts and using women's language and behavior to understand the relation between self and context. It includes the problem of finding a way not to omit any person's voice while still having a manuscript of manageable length. It includes the use of feminist theory to analyze data. (p. 71)

In short, one of the big projects during analysis is to move from having piles and piles of chronological data, individual people, events to reorganizing it all in a way that is topical, thematic, and interpretative. This also involves the often painful process of data reduction, which necessitates that the ethnographer take complicated, rich, and contextual information and reduce it down to smaller sets of ideas that can be reported to an audience. Buch refers to this decision-making process as choosing "which thread she will pull" to make sense of and report her study after she has first been confronted with an entire interwoven tapestry of ideas. There are always many threads from which to choose. So ethnographers, like all other researchers, face decisions about which stories get told. There are always also political forces at play when making these decisions, and feminist ethnographers often choose which stories to tell in ways that reflect their feminist theoretical and ethical positions.

Writing Up Ethnographic Reports: Representation and Presentation

As with any research project, the goal of an ethnographer is to write up an interesting and accurate (although what constitutes accuracy is contested) narrative report about what the researcher discovered. Ethnographers pride themselves on providing *thick descriptions* of social life that include rich contextual detail along with clear analysis (Geertz, 1972). This is easier said than done. Ethnographers may consider such questions as the following:

- How do I tell an interesting and accurate story?
- How should I represent the voices and the perspectives of the people I study?
- What are the ethical and political implications of telling the story the way that I do?
- How much control should the community have over the final interpretation?
- How much control should I have over the final interpretation?

These questions are fundamentally about how the ethnographer goes about *representing* her participants and community in her final *presentation*. Ortner (1995) writes,

> The anthropologist and the historian are charged with representing the lives of people who are living or once lived, and as we attempt to push these people into the molds of our texts, they push back. The final text is a product of our pushing and their pushing back, and no text, however dominant, lacks the traces of this counterforce. (p. 189)

Feminist ethnographers have particularly struggled over methods of representing the people they study in ways that seek to balance the visions of the author with the visions of those they study. In this vein, feminist ethnographers have pioneered several alternative methods of writing ethnographies, some of which more closely approach humanistic writing (e.g., poetry, novel, and biography) than traditional scientific reporting. These kinds of ethnographies emphasize the subjective and intersubjective aspects of human experience and attempt to capture such aspects by using emotive and personal language rather than detached or analytical prose. Nevertheless, such forms of ethnography share with others the goal of portraying the rich and varied experiences of people in their social contexts.

Ultimately, the ethnographic report makes use of the analysis described above to place findings in social, political, and historical contexts. Ethnographies are usually very engaging to read because they tell stories about people, places, and events that give the reader an insider view of communities that might not otherwise be familiar. Even when the communities studied are familiar, ethnographies often present and analyze aspects of community life that challenge common sense ideas about these people and places. Of course the best way of learning about "writing up" ethnographic research is to read some of the wonderful studies that women have produced both historically and currently. Only a very small number of such studies are described in this chapter.

Ethics and Responsibilities

Feminist ethnography requires that the researcher pay particular attention to her ethical practices and responsibilities both in collecting data and in reporting the results of her studies. There are a plethora of ethical questions that arise at every stage of the ethnographic research project. Frequently, these ethical dilemmas are not well addressed by the university IRBs, which usually frame ethical issues within other kinds of research paradigms. Thus, sensitive issues of gaining access, informing participants and gaining their consent, trading on friendships, protecting privacy, and the politics of reporting are frequently not resolved even after obtaining IRB approval to conduct research. Resolving ethical dilemmas in research can be particularly challenging, especially when feminist researchers consider the relative positions of power and authority between themselves and those they study. Daphne Patai (1991) writes that if the idea of feminism is to have any meaning,

> it must involve a critique of traditional concepts and structures that have marginalized women materially and psychologically, in the world and even in their own souls. . . . Because feminism has challenged the pose of neutrality and objectivity that for so long governed positivist social science, it has forced us to scrutinize our own practice as scholars . . . [whether it is]

possible—not in theory but in the actual conditions of the real world today—to write about the oppressed without becoming one of the oppressors. (p. 138)

Patai further argues that feminists often make the mistake of imagining that simple participation in the discourse of feminism protects them from the possibility of exploiting other women even when their research practices are predicated on privilege. Regardless of your feminist positions, it is essential that you consider how dynamics of power, including hierarchies of class, race, education, and access, will affect the lives of those you study. Many feminist ethnographers, such as Paley (2001), view the people they study as experts on their own lives and communities and thus consider the people they work with active collaborators in the research project rather than passive research subjects. Different kinds of feminists will respond to power differences according to their theoretical and ethical positions, and solutions to ethical dilemmas are often difficult and inconvenient. Thus, it is particularly important that we concern ourselves with careful navigation of ethical issues that arise during the research process.

Given the fact that ethnographers spend so much time with the people they work with in the field, most want and feel obligated to continue important relationships from the field for many years. It is critical to be aware of how the research you write and publish might affect both the people you worked with and the possibility of working with them in the future. Some ethnographers have been surprised by the response that they encountered when they returned to the communities in which they had spent a great deal of time (Ellis, 1995; Scheper-Hughes, 2000). Even the most well-intentioned ethnographers sometimes describe communities or people in ways that those they write about find unfair or hurtful, often for reasons the ethnographer did not anticipate. At other times, the ethnographer may find herself intentionally critiquing practices of dominance, discrimination, or coercion in the community. Each ethnographer must make her own decision about publishing potentially hurtful analyses of the community she studies. Many ethnographers emphasize the importance of obligation and responsibility in deciding what to publicize. Such ethnographers argue that their ability to do research depended (and in the future depends) on the voluntary contributions and participation of those she studies. Without them, she would have nothing to write about.

Most ethnographers agree that it is important not to publicize material that would put those they work with at risk of violence, economic hardship, or severe emotional trauma. Many ethnographers also share their findings with the community they study before they publish any writing in order to get feedback from the community, both about the accuracy of their portrayal and about the potential risks involved for community members if the work is published. Regardless of how you choose to negotiate the many ethical challenges of ethnographic fieldwork, it is important to be aware that what you do in the field and write about it afterward can have serious consequences for your research and those you work with in the field. For feminists, this is a central concern.

REFERENCES

American Psychological Association. (2001). *Publication manual of the American Psychological Association.* Washington, DC: Author.

Behar, R. (1993). *Translated woman: Crossing the border with Esperanza's story.* Boston: Beacon Press.

Coffey, A. (1999). *The ethnographic self.* London: Sage.

Corrado, M. (2002). Teaching wedding rituals: How bridal workers negotiate control over their customers. *Journal of Contemporary Ethnography, 31*(1), 33–67.

De Welde, K. (2003). Getting physical: Subverting gender through self-defense. *Journal of Contemporary Ethnography, 32*(3), 247–278.

Ellis, C. (1995). Emotional and ethical quagmires in returning to the field. *Journal of Contemporary Ethnography, 24*(1), 68–95.

Finn, J. (1998). *Tracing the veins: Of copper, culture, and community from Butte to Chuquicamata.* Berkeley: University of California Press.

Furman, F. K. (1997). *Facing the mirror: Older women and beauty shop culture.* New York: Routledge.

Geertz, C. (1972). *The interpretation of cultures.* New York: Basic Books.

Goetz, J. P. (1978). Theoretical approaches to the study of sex-role culture in schools. *Anthropology and Education Quarterly, 9*(1), 3–21.

Goetz, J. P. (1981a). Children's sex-role knowledge and behavior: An ethnographic study of first graders in the rural South. *Theory and Research in Social Education, 8*(4), 31–54.

Goetz, J. P. (1981b). Sex-role systems in Rose Elementary School: Change and tradition in the rural-transitional South. In R. T. Sieber & A. J. Gordon (Eds.), *Children and their organizations: Investigations in American culture* (pp. 58–73). Boston: Hall.

Goetz, J. P., & Hansen, J. F. (1974). The cultural analysis of schooling. *Anthropology and Education Quarterly, 5*(4), 1–8.

Harrington, B. (2003). The social psychology of access in ethnographic research. *Journal of Contemporary Ethnography, 32*(5), 592–625.

Hesse-Biber, S. (1996). *Am I thin enough yet? The cult of thinness and the commercialization of identity.* New York: Oxford University Press.

Hesse-Biber, S. N., & Leavy, P. (2006). *The practice of qualitative research.* Thousand Oaks, CA: Sage.

Hondagneu-Sotelo, P. (2001). *Domestica: Immigrant workers cleaning and caring in the shadows of affluence.* Berkeley: University of California Press.

Isabell, B. (1995). Women's voices: Lima 1975. In D. Tedlock & B. Mannheim (Eds.), *The dialogic emergence of culture.* Chicago: University of Illinois Press.

Lewin, E. (1993). *Lesbian mothers: Accounts of gender in American culture.* Ithaca, NY: Cornell University Press.

Lois, J. (2001). Managing emotions, intimacy, and relationships in a volunteer search and rescue group. *Journal of Contemporary Ethnography, 30*(2), 131–179.

Martin, E. (1992). *The woman in the body: A cultural analysis of reproduction.* Boston: Beacon Press.

Montemurro, B. (2005). Add men, don't stir: Reproducing traditional gender roles in modern wedding showers. *Journal of Contemporary Ethnography, 34*(1), 6–35.

Murphy, A. G. (2003). The dialectical gaze: Exploring the subject-object tension in the performances of women who strip. *Journal of Contemporary Ethnography, 32*(3), 305–335.

Nader, L. (1988). Up the anthropologist—Perspectives gained from studying up. In J. B. Cale (Ed.), *Anthropology for the nineties* (pp. 470–485). New York: Free Press.

Ortner, S. B. (1995). Resistance and the problem of ethnographic refusal. *Comparative Studies in Society and History, 37*(1), 173–193.

Paley, J. (2001). *Marketing democracy: Power and social movements in post-dictatorship Chile.* Berkeley: University of California Press.

Patai, D. (1991). U.S. academics and Third World women: Is ethical research possible? In S. B. Gluck & D. Patai (Eds.), *Women's words: The feminist practice of oral history.* New York: Routledge.

Rapp, R. (2000). *Testing women, testing the fetus: The social impact of amniocentesis in America.* New York: Routledge.

Reinharz, S. (1992). *Feminist methods in social research.* Oxford, UK: Oxford University Press.

Richards, A. I. (1956). *Chisungu: A girls' initiation ceremony among the Bemba of Northern Rhodesia.* London: Faber & Faber.

Richards, A. I. (1995). *Land, labour and diet in Northern Rhodesia* (2nd ed.). Munster-Hamburg: LIT with the IAI. (Original work published 1939)

Scheper-Hughes, N. (2000). Ire in Ireland. *Ethnography, 1*(1), 117–140.

Spivak, G. C. (1988). Can the subaltern speak? In C. Nelson & L. Grossberg (Ed.), *Marxism and the interpretation of culture* (pp. 271–316). Basingstoke, UK: Macmillan Education.

Stacey, J. (1991). Can there be a feminist ethnography? In S. B. Gluck & D. Patai (Eds.), *Women's words: The feminist practice of oral history* (pp. 111–119). New York: Routledge.

Staller, K. M. (2002). Working the scam: Policing urban street youth. *Qualitative Inquiry, 8*(5), 550–574.

Stocking, G. W., Jr. (1983). Fieldwork in British anthropology. In G. W. Stocking Jr. (Ed.), *Observers observed* (pp. 70–120). Madison: University of Wisconsin Press.

Trotter, R., & Schensul, J. J. (2000). Methods in applied anthropology. In H. Russell Bernard (Ed.), *Handbook of methods in cultural anthropology* (pp. 691–735). New York: AltaMira Press.

EIGHT

THE FEMINIST PRACTICE OF
CONTENT ANALYSIS

Patricia Lina Leavy

———◄●►———

By discovering patterns between existing and missing documents, and with power/gender relations in the society of the time, and by bringing this material to the attention of people today, new ties are made that help explain the current relation between gender and power and give some groups a greater sense of their own history. To make this connection vivid, some feminists reprint texts and photographs so others can formulate their own interpretations and ties.

—Shulamit Reinharz (1992, p. 163)

Feminist intervention in popular culture might offer feminist politics a pragmatic strategy to shift the balance of power and prepare the ground for change, and thus help transform society. Since popular culture is a significant site for struggle over meaning, which offers the culture's dominant definitions of women and men, it is therefore crucial to intervene in the mainstream to make feminist meanings a part of everyday common sense.

—Süheyla Kirca (1999, p. 105)

Culture is a site where struggles over meaning are played out and later embedded into a host of cultural artifacts such as texts and products. Particular cultural struggles over meaning might result in a collective or national memory of an event or time, or, the result might be broader, such as a set of ideas about a group. The repository of artifacts containing these visions and ideas may also contain implicit or explicit contradictions. By investigating culture in general, and popular culture more specifically, dominant narratives, images, ideas, and stereotyped representations can be exposed and challenged.

For example, some feminists have used content analysis to examine the idea of "postfeminism" which rose to popularity in the 1980s and 1990s. Hall and Rodriguez (2003) observed that the popular media in the United States have claimed a new era of postfeminism, and they conducted content analysis to develop a definition of a "postfeminist perspective" and to determine what kind of empirical evidence there is of such a perspective. Their research, only enabled by content analysis, refuted the claims that postfeminism exists and argues that this popular notion or ideology has actually served to undermine efforts at feminist unity, and thus feminism has lost support from 1980 to 1990. Feminism has been viewed as less relevant, antifeminism has increased in relevance for some young women, and new versions of feminism have not developed as the term *postfeminism* falsely implies. Hall and Rodriguez write, "The mere existence of a post feminist perspective in public discourse dramatically alters the social landscape in which discussions about and actions to improve the status of women occur" (p. 884).

This research illustrates how a feminist perspective on culture can challenge dominant ideologies, even those about feminism itself.

Feminists are at the forefront of critically interrogating the texts and products that comprise culture to resist patriarchal understandings of social reality that push women and other minorities to the peripheries of their culture and social interpretive processes. By bringing a feminist lens and feminist concerns such as women's status, equality, and social justice to the study of material culture (products) and symbolic culture (multimedium images and representations), feminist researchers employ content analysis in very unique ways and ask questions that would otherwise go unexplored. Furthermore, as culture is a site where ideas are created, disseminated, and consumed (often including extreme and stereotypical imagery), feminists have a particular stake in unraveling the texts and products that become an integral component in how women and men are viewed. Content analysis offers feminist researchers a flexible and wide-reaching method for engaging in this intellectual and political process. As culture is extremely far-reaching, it is not possible to cover all the ways that feminists can unobtrusively study it, so this chapter is meant to introduce you to some of the issues and practices out there.

As you are already getting a sense of, feminist content analysis is particularly broad, so to have a solid point of departure let's begin with research questions:

- How is gender represented in popular film?
- Furthermore, how does the representation of gender in popular film affect both an "objectified public" and subjective individuals?
- Is it true that popular culture recycles gendered stereotypes, and if so, what is the nature of these stereotypes?

These questions guided Mark Hedley's (2002) research in which he performed an inductive content analysis of a sampling of popular films from 1986 to 2000. Drawing from feminist and critical theories, Hedley posits the following:

> Through its application of technological advances, popular culture in modernity has been able to define what is real. A system-world of ideological control, therefore, has replaced the life-world of authentic experience as the primary source of meaning. Furthermore, those that control the relevant media are cognizant of the power that this control provides. (p. 202)

Using content analysis grounded in feminist scholarship, Hedley explains,

> I am exploring representations of gendered conflict as they are communicated from the psychic systems of those individuals who create films to the psychic systems of those who experience films via the societal system of the motion picture industry in the United States. (p. 202)

The results of Hedley's expansive content analysis are multifaceted. The broadest finding is that the "gendered point of view" across these diverse films shows an "overwhelming preference for men's perspectives" (Hedley, 2002, p. 211). This is a significant finding as we try to make sense of whose perspectives are highlighted and whose perspectives, voices, and visions of the world are silenced or marginalized in contemporary film. Furthermore, Hedley's research reveals numerous patterns within popular film that can help us to better understand how gender and heterosexual relationships are portrayed. For example, Hedley found that female characters were represented as consistently advantaged in terms of "moral status" in comparison with male characters, while male characters were consistently advantaged in terms of "social power" in comparison with female characters (p. 207). Hedley also found that in male-centered triangles the moral backdrop invoked a Madonna/whore dualism while in female-centered triangles the moral backdrop relied on a hero/villain or prince/scoundrel dualism. This research also found that there was overwhelming conflict between men and women in these films, thus making gendered conflict appear normal. The nature of this conflict was generally romantic and/or sexual, and often in the context of sexual competition, indicating that this is a large basis for relations between men and women. This kind of nuanced analysis, only possible through a systematic content analysis of cultural texts, is important to our understanding of the ways that men and women are differently represented in American culture. Beyond helping us to understand the themes through which gender is articulated, Hedley's research offers a range of issues to be explored in future research if we are to take this analysis and move it forward toward feminist goals of equality. Hedley proposes that researchers continue this research by asking the following questions:

> What kinds of women's participation are most significant in transcending the norms of the system? How much of these kinds of participation is needed if system transcendence is to be accomplished? What contexts prevent women's participation of any kind or amount from challenging normative patterns? And what contexts allow men's participation to pose such challenges to the system even when women's participation is minimal or absent? (p. 213)

Hedley's research on gender in popular film is an example of how content analysis can merge with feminist concerns and principles to address a range of issues regarding the social construction of gender and difference more broadly.

Content analysis can be employed by feminists to examine the presence of feminism in a range of cultural artifacts. Another example comes from Shindler Zimmerman, Holm, and Starrels (2001), who performed a content analysis of 11 self-help books to examine how much the content of these books is feminist or nonfeminist. Their results indicated that best-selling books have become less feminist over time. This kind of research may counter popular conceptions about the presence of feminism in popular culture.

Content analysis offers a method for how a feminist researcher might approach research questions such as:

- Whose point of view is represented in popular and commercial culture?
- How is difference represented in culture? For example, how is gender represented in culture? How is sexuality represented? Race and ethnicity?
- How are messages distributed to people via popular culture?
- How are ideas about masculinity and femininity constructed, reconstructed, and contested within culture via texts produced within the culture?
- Whose viewpoints are silenced or marginalized within particular cultural artifacts?
- What does an examination of the texts produced in a given culture tell us about how men and women are valued?

CONTENT ANALYSIS: AN OVERVIEW

Content analysis is the systematic study of texts and other cultural products or nonliving data forms. The data used in this kind of research thus exist independently of the research process. In other words, the researcher does not create or co-create the raw data through surveys, ethnography, or interviews but rather collects preexisting data, such as newspapers, books, magazines, pictures, television programs, and so forth. The nature of the data garners them two unique qualities: (1) the data are preexisting and thus naturalistic, and (2) the data are noninteractive (Reinharz, 1992, p. 147). These qualities give the data a built-in level of authenticity (Reinhraz, 1992; Hesse-Biber & Leavy, 2006). The level of authenticity afforded to preexisting artifacts is critical to feminist researchers, who are particularly harangued with questions of quality and validity from the larger scientific community in which feminism is devalued. "By using such documents, feminist researchers identify social norms without using interactive methods that may affect the norms they are trying to study" (Reinharz, 1992, p. 151).

Furthermore, content analysis can be employed both quantitatively and qualitatively and from any number of theoretical and epistemological positions, including many kinds of feminism. Feminist researchers might employ quantitative content analysis to "identify patterns in authorship, subject matter, methods, and interpretation" (Reinharz, 1992, p. 155). This kind of approach might build data that can be used toward advancing social change in the areas of public policy or education. For example, feminist quantitative content analysis might reveal statistically significant patterns of gender and race bias in national standardized tests. Researchers could use their findings to lobby for change. On the other hand, qualitative content analysis can help feminist scholars interpret a document as a whole or in parts (p. 159), often from a grounded theory approach where "analytic categories emerge" from the data (p. 161). Under this qualitative feminist approach researchers would, for example, use words directly from the text under investigation to form their code categories. This kind of approach produces a thematic analysis with rich descriptive data that can be used to generate theory.

In addition to general quantitative and qualitative applications of content analysis, many feminists also apply postmodern and poststructural theory and principles to their content analysis projects. While feminist scholars can draw on a range of theories as they design studies using content analysis, I think it is important to make a link between postmodernism and feminist content analysis because I consider this a growing practice within feminism. As we saw in Chapter 4, in recent decades there has been a surge in the development of postmodern feminist epistemology and theory. This surge has not occurred in a vacuum, but is rather linked to an overall increase in cultural studies within academia (Hesse-Biber & Leavy, 2004).

Over the past few decades, new conceptions about the nature of social reality and the nature of social inquiry have led to an increased use of and expansion of content analysis within the interdisciplinary field of cultural stud-ies. In particular, the postmodern and poststructural critiques of knowledge construction have influenced the practice of unobtrusive research by changing the theoretical perspective from which many researchers practice these methodologies. Feminist scholars have drawn on the major developments in this area to merge postmodern and feminist concerns and practices, which have resulted in an increase in feminist content analysis. In particular, many feminist researchers perform textual analysis from a deconstruction perspec-tive in which a text is analyzed to see not only what is there but also what is missing, silenced, or absent. The goal of this kind of research is not to create conjecture about what should be there, but rather to deconstruct the text to see what is revealed, what emerges, what juxtapositions develop.

- How did content analysis develop?

Content analysis, and more broadly, unobtrusive methods, developed out of the assumption that we can learn about our society by interrogating the material items produced within the culture. In other words, we can learn about social life, such as norms, values, socialization, or social stratification, by looking at the texts we produce, which reflect macrosocial processes and our worldview. Furthermore, cultural artifacts do not simply reflect social norms and values; texts are central to how norms and values come to be shaped (Reinharz, 1992, p. 151). The texts and objects that groups of humans produce are embedded with larger ideas those groups have, whether shared or contested, such as ideas about sex and gender. Unobtrusive methods differ from other research methods covered in this book in that they use texts and other nonliving artifacts as the starting point of the research process. This distinguishes content analysis from surveys, interviews, and ethnography, all of which rely on subjective individuals, who have been "imprinted" by societal norms and values, as the primary starting point for knowledge building. "Social science research has to confront a dimension of human activity that cannot be contained in the consciousness of the isolated subject. In short, it has to look at something that lies beyond the world of atomistic individuals" (Prior, 2004, p. 318).

Researchers do not intrude into social life by observing, surveying, or interviewing, but rather examine existing noninteractive texts, which classifies the research process as "unobtrusive." Many different kinds of texts and artifacts can be studied, including but not limited to historical documents, newspapers, magazines, photographs, books, diaries, literature, music, cinema, television, and Web sites.

Feminist researchers view cultural artifacts through a particular framework, which likely draws their attention to the artifact itself, as a whole and/or in parts, *as well as the origin of production.* "Contemporary feminist scholars of cultural texts are likely to see meaning as mediated, and therefore to examine both the text and the processes of its production" (Reinharz, 1992, p. 145).

Feminists realize that texts are not produced within a vacuum but are the products of a given time and space with all that entails from technologies of production and reproduction, to differential access to those technologies, to the cultural norms and values that guide all aspects of social life. For example, in a patriarchal society texts produced in dominant venues are likely to contain traces of gendered ideas about social reality. "Cultural artifacts are the products of individual activity, social organization, technology, and cultural patterns" (Reinharz, 1992, p. 147).

Just as texts can be an integral part in creating and maintaining the status quo, so too can they help challenge long-held beliefs and practices. Texts can be sources of resistance, including feminist resistance, which may also be a part of a feminist textual analysis project.

In this vein, some researchers employ deconstruction from a feminist point of view. Luce Irigaray (1985) posits deconstruction a method of "jamming the theoretical machinery" by exposing what is absent within a representation, what is taken-for-granted, and what is centrally located versus what is forced to the peripheries. These efforts don't always focus on dominant representations but may include resistive texts. As popular culture is a site of struggle over meaning, there are traces of resistance within many kinds of representations. Feminists are widely concerned with studying the varied ways that resistance and feminist perspectives emerge in different representational forms.

While unobtrusive methods encompass a wide range of methodological possibilities, historically, "content analysis" was the major method under this rubric. Content analysis traditionally referred to the examination of written texts. Originally, this practice was quantitative in nature and researchers would count the occurrence of a particular thing they were interested in, such as gendered or racialized terms in a newspaper. Many researchers now do not think qualitative or quantitative when they think about content analysis—content analysis merges these categories and can be considered a "hybrid." Content analysis can be conceptualized as an inherently mixed method of analysis, or, a method that always contains the possibility of both qualitative and quantitative applications. Bauer (2000) refers to content analysis as a "hybrid technique," which has always been, even when performed quantitatively, an implicitly hybridized approach to inquiry. He explains as follows:

> While most classical content analyses culminate in numerical descriptions of some features of the text corpus, considerable thought is given to the "kinds," "qualities," and "distinctions" in the text before any quantification takes place. In this way, content analysis bridges statistical formalism and the qualitative analysis of the materials. In the quantity/quality divide in social research, content analysis is a hybrid technique that can mediate in this unproductive dispute over virtues and methods. (p. 132)

Regardless of the extent to which we think about content analysis as implicitly hybridized or a method with deductive and inductive capabilities, there is no doubt that with this method of inquiry social scientists have contributed to our overall body of knowledge in significant ways with statistical and descriptive power.

The process one follows when using content analysis will depend on the research question, epistemological grounding, methodological approach, and the extent to which the project is inductive or deductive (or qualitative or quantitative). However, generally speaking, content analysis requires a sampling of data, which are then broken down into "units of analysis" (such as lines of text, scenes of films, and so forth). The data are then coded, which means they are categorized into preconceived or inductively generated code categories, which may be very literal/specific or larger metacodes that are more conceptual in nature. The results from the coding are then represented in any number of ways. The chart on pages 232 and 233, reprinted from *The Practice of Qualitative Research* (Hesse-Biber & Leavy, 2006) illustrates typical models of content analysis from quantitative and qualitative perspectives.

The appeal of content analysis for feminist researchers is multifaceted. Feminist researchers may use content analysis to examine the extent to which women's issues or feminist perspectives are explored in a particular medium, as well as the nature of the content (history textbooks, sitcoms, medical literature, etc.). Feminist scholars might also be interested in using content analysis to explore diversity and difference within a particular medium.

- To what extent are women, or any oppressed group, visible or invisible in a particular medium?
- How is language gendered in a particular medium? How do representations draw on gendered, sexualized, or racialized stereotypes?

These are just some of the questions feminist content analysts might have when thinking about using this approach to data collection.

Given the kinds of issues feminist scholars might be interested in, how have feminist researchers used this unique method? How can feminist researchers use nonliving materials to study the social world? How can texts, in their varied forms, be used as the starting point for understanding social processes and generating theories about social life from a feminist perspective? What are the benefits of using nonliving data in feminist praxis?

Content Analysis Flowchart

Quantitative model
(Deductive)

1. Research question and hypothesis
   ⇓

2. Conceptualization
   (What variables are used and how they will be defined)
   ⇓

3. Operational measures
   (Aimed at gaining internal validity and face validity)
   3a. Unit of analysis
   3b. Measurement

— categories can be: exhaustive
and mutually exclusive
or
"a priori"
   ⇓

4. Coding
   ⇓

5. Sampling
   (Randomly sampling a subset of content)
   ⇓

6. Reliability
   Can use: Two codes for intercoder reliability
   or
   computer program for validation
   ⇓

7. If reliability was determined by hand (Step 6)
   then apply a statistical check
   ⇓

8. Tabulation and representation

Qualitative model
(Inductive)

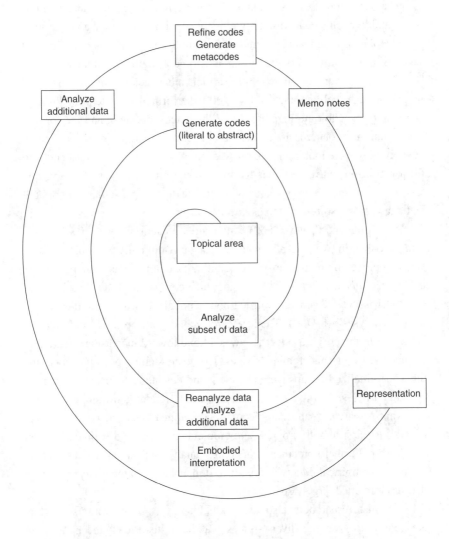

SOURCE: From *The Practice of Qualitative Interviewing*, adapted from Neuendorf, K. Reprinted with permission.

Feminist Textual Analysis

Feminist researchers have used content analysis across media forms to explore a range of issues that are central to our understanding of gender and difference, as well as research aimed at social action. In fact, feminist scholars have even employed content analysis to examine the extent to which feminist concerns are researched within academia.

There has long been speculation among feminist scholars that feminist issues and women's concerns are marginalized within academia and that feminist scholarship isn't always funded and published at the rate nonfeminist scholarship is, putting pressure on scholars to publish outside of the bounds of feminism. Unfortunately, much of this criticism has lacked empirical backing. In this vein, Angelique and Culley (2000) performed a content analysis on community psychology literature to see the extent to which, and the form in which, feminist concerns are addressed in peer-reviewed journals in this field. In short, they were looking for feminist content. This research was intended to fill a gap in our current knowledge by drawing on the power of preexisting texts. Because their data consisted of written texts, this particular kind of content analysis is also referred to as *textual analysis.*

Angelique and Culley (2000) conducted a content analysis of 2,178 articles published in two peer-reviewed journals in community psychology. Their study employed both qualitative and quantitative components. The researchers defined *feminist content* as the following three components: "1) consciousness of gender issues, 2) gender stratified power imbalances or 3) multilevel contextual analyses" (p. 797). Their research noted both progress and areas of concern. On the positive side, there was a trend toward increasing attention to "women-relevant" and feminist issues. However, stereotypes of women and other marginalized groups were prevalent and despite an increase in women-centered articles, overall women were frequently rendered invisible.

This research is an example of how feminist researchers use content analysis to explore both progress and problems in the area of women-relevant scholarship. Furthermore, the use of content analysis allowed these researchers to produce empirical data with a built-in dimension of authenticity in an area that has remained largely speculative.

Feminist researchers also use textual analysis to explore issues that are central to women's lives—issues that have historically been made to appear invisible within academic literature. Hall and Shepherd Stolley (1997) conducted a longitudinal content analysis of marriage and family textbooks from 1950 to 1987 to examine how abortion and adoption are represented within these kinds of texts, and, how representation changes over time. Using both quantitative and qualitative coding strategies, Hall and Shepherd Stolley examined the extent of coverage in these two areas and also conducted a thematic analysis to investigate the type of coverage. Explaining their research goals, Hall and Shepherd Stolley state, "This research seeks to determine whether the kinds of depictions we find over time reflect changes in the theoretical perspectives used in family studies, or reflect changes in the societal content of abortion and adoption as social issues" (p. 74).

Incorporating a feminist perspective into their research affected the kinds of themes that emerged from the data. Their research indicated that abortion received significantly more coverage than did adoption; however, the qualitative component of their research helped illuminate the nature of the coverage. In short, Hall and Shepherd Stolley found that the nature of portrayals about abortion changed after the legalization of abortion. The researchers also found that a functionalist theoretical perspective dominated these texts. This perspective largely omits women's voices and personal experiences, privileges nuclear family ideals while negatively depicting "alternative" families, and treats abortion as deviant. The shift after *Roe v. Wade* in conjunction with emphasizing a functionalist perspective indicates that both social and disciplinary forces are at work and thus shape the perspective from which these books are written. Of particular interest to feminist scholars is the extent to which feminist perspectives are marginalized within these texts, which is of course noteworthy given that these topics are considered women centered. In this regard, Hall and Shepherd Stolley (1997) write,

> We argue that a generic theory of functionalism has become part of the phenomena of family life itself rather than only one of several perspectives we bring to the study of family life. The taken-for-granted quality of the functionalist perspective tends to limit the potential for bringing diverse perspectives to family studies. In disciplines rooted in a functionalist perspective, feminist and multi-cultural perspectives have been incorporated but tend to be ghettoized . . . or relegated to the periphery. . . . Even though alternative feminist and multi-cultural perspectives of family life are now available, we believe their impact on us as scholars and as teachers probably will be limited until critical theories that challenge the preeminence of the functionalists' "traditional family" are more widely acknowledged and accepted. (p. 81)

In addition to explaining how feminist perspectives in this area have been marginalized, these researchers also highlight the interplay between theoretical perspectives and research practices.

There are numerous examples of feminists conducting textual analyses of popular texts to study the perspectives that are emphasized or marginalized in particular texts. For example, Schlenker, Caron, and Halteman (1998) conducted a longitudinal content analysis of *Seventeen Magazine* from 1945 to 1995 to determine the effect of the feminist movement on this publication, at different points in time. Commeyras and Alvermann (1996) conducted a content analysis of world history textbooks to examine many aspects of the content on women. Wachholz and Mullaly (2000) conducted a content analysis of American introductory social work textbooks to examine the extent of feminist, radical, and antiracist scholarship in these texts.

Feminist textual analysis is important because when looking through a feminist lens, researchers are likely to ask different research questions, approach the data differently, and use their resulting knowledge to effect intellectual, social, and political change. Furthermore, this kind of research often looks at text from the viewpoint of women who may not otherwise be considered.

Feminist scholar Süheyla Kirca Schroeder addresses some of these issues, including viewing women as producers of popular culture and not simply consumers, as well as other vital issues in the following Behind-the-Scenes piece.

Behind-the-Scenes With Süheyla Kirca Schroeder

A Methodological Approach to the Study of Feminism and Popular Culture: The Case of Women's Magazines

There is no standard agreement over what constitutes feminism as theory and practice or what constitutes feminist research. We find a variety of approaches to study and challenge gender inequality in the social world. As my work falls into the field of cultural studies, I employ the cultural studies approach of the Birmingham School to study gender, media, and contemporary culture. According to this perspective, media texts are seen as central sites in which negotiation over gender takes place, and in which contradictory cultural representations of gender are accommodated, modified, reconstructed, and reproduced. Media texts are viewed as a field of both conflict and contestation. If such position is taken, cultural texts appear significant for feminist analyses as they are involved intimately in producing and perpetuating the dominant meanings of the categories of man and woman and of sexual difference. However, contestations over these meanings cannot only be seen as textual representations of gender relations in particular popular cultural forms, but they are significant also "in the lives of actual women and men who consume, use, and make sense of them in the contexts of their daily practices and social relations" (Roman & Christian-Smith, 1988, p. 4). Cultural forms, then, appear to be important sources for providing the contexts of the conflicting power relations within which women and men learn their gender roles in the process of becoming feminine and masculine.

How can we study these cultural texts that contain conflicting and contradictory representations of men and women? I argue that we should approach the subject in a way that will enable us to investigate how gendered subjectivities are reproduced, by whom they are reproduced, in whose interests they work, and how they are constructed. I would like to suggest a methodology to study representations of traditional gender identities and feminist images and values articulated, constructed, and (re)defined in a particular popular culture form that is women's magazines. (Note: In fact, I have employed this methodology in a work of mine in which I study the dynamic interchange between feminist politics and mainstream or consumer women's interest and to examine the relationship between the concepts of feminism and femininity in contemporary women's magazines [see Kirca, 2001].)

The methodology is derived from feminist critical theory and cultural studies. It is mainly qualitative in nature and includes semiology, discourse analysis, psychoanalysis, and structured interviews. I also apply content analysis to the written texts. The reason for doing content analysis is first to find out which topics appear and how often they are repeated in women's magazines. Second and more important is to discover how these topics work as a signifying system and a bearer of a certain ideology, and how this ideology deals with the construction of contemporary femininity and of feminist concepts and images. This methodology allows us to examine the various ways in which feminist values and broader debates about nontraditional roles for women are incorporated into national, large circulation women's magazines.

(Continued)

(Continued)

While content analysis is an accepted method in the field of social sciences, there are no fixed rules which determine its framework. The forms, the units and level of analysis, vary from one text to another, depending on the aim of the research. I intend to use the content analysis of the women's magazines to produce a quantitative base for qualitative analysis. It is a collation of the frequency of occurrence of various content characteristics—words or texts—and thus operates at the surface level. This method helps identify which issues are covered or left out of specific magazines. The qualitative approach, on the other hand, permits an investigation of deeper levels of meaning and is concerned more with content as a mediator or reflector of hidden cultural phenomena. Furthermore, this qualitative approach permits a more complex analysis of themes on a sub-textual level. However, there is a certain crossover between the two approaches, and this it is hoped brings new insights.

Statistical information on the number of current women's periodicals and their circulations are also taken into consideration. These figures enable us to draw a picture of the market size and to show how the magazines in question fit into the range of other women's magazines available. Considering texts within given markets and production dynamics can help, as Douglas Kellner (1995) points out, "to elucidate features and effects of the texts that textual analysis alone might miss or downplay" (p. 9). It is the production, distribution, and structure of the market that often determines what sort of cultural texts are produced and what structural limits there are.

Analysis of any cultural product or of media representations cannot be isolated from the wider context of ownership and editorial control of media products. Thus the editors of the women's magazines are interviewed to provide their own accounts of women's magazines and feminist issues. The information gathered from the interviews is used in addition to the textual analysis of women's magazines to examine to what extent editors' accounts overlap with the actual content of the magazines, and furthermore, how influential they are in shaping the content of the magazines and what their characteristics and strategies might signify for the future of women's magazines from the viewpoint of feminist politics.

The methodology suggested here points to a critical issue in feminist theory. The tradition of textual analysis and reception analysis positions women merely as consumers of popular culture. Such an approach not only drives women increasingly toward questions of pleasure and consumption but also maintains the theoretical division between femininity and masculinity. As Modleski (1986) puts it, "Countless critics . . . persist in equating femininity, consumption and reading on the one hand and masculinity, production and writing on the other" (p. 41). To challenge these dichotomies or establish a productive relation between women and cultural commodities, it is crucial for feminist criticism to conceptualize the experiences of women as producers of cultural meanings. This feminist approach to popular culture and gender helps open up popular cultural texts to a wider debate by shifting the emphasis from consumption to production, which allows more effective ways of delivering a feminist politics and developing theories that would address the experience of women as both producers and consumers of cultural meanings.

FEMINIST VISUAL CONTENT ANALYSIS

- What is visual content analysis?
- What do images reveal about how women and men are regarded in a given time and place?

Visual content analysis involves the study of visual images. The kinds of images that can serve as data vary and include computer-generated images, art, and photography. Culture has a visual landscape of images, which through increased technologies of production and reproduction infuse many cultural spaces. Interrogating these images can help us to understand differential representation, for example, mass-mediated images such as those found in magazines can tell us a great deal about ideal body types for women and men across racial and ethnic groups. If as feminists we were to examine parenting magazines to examine how girls and boys are represented, or if we were interested in studying fashion magazines to examine how women are represented, we might look at some of the following features: posture, stance, prominent in the image or photo, roles, clothing, stature, centrality of each figure, race, and so forth. Looking at some examples of feminist visual content analyses, we can gain a richer understanding of both why and how feminists study visual images.

Pederson (2002) was interested in newspaper photographic coverage of female and male high school athletics. Pederson conceptualized the mass media and sports as two of the "most prominent and hegemonic social institutions" (p. 304). Pederson wanted to compare male and female sports coverage to examine to what degree hegemonic masculinity is portrayed in newspaper sports coverage. Pederson's study used 827 photographs taken from 602 randomly selected newspapers and examined the amount and type of photographs given to cover male and female athletics. This study employed a "descriptive analysis" of the photos to ascertain information such as whether the photos were still or action shots, which is very important in the study of gender and media representation. Ultimately, Pederson found that there is inequity in sports coverage across gender lines and argued that photographic coverage reaffirms hegemonic masculinity. Visual content analysis allowed Pederson to ask and answer a research question about social inequality that would otherwise be inaccessible.

This is an example of how mass media images can be used as the starting point for research. When you decide what topic you want to investigate and what data you will use, research design becomes critical to the practice of visual studies. The process of analysis is particularly salient in this kind of research project. There are many strategies qualitative researchers can employ for coding visual data. As we saw in the Pederson example, codes such as "still" and "action shot" can be employed. Likewise, feminist researchers interested in the representation of difference can code for gender, race, sexuality, and other social attributes. This process can occur from an inductive approach where code categories emerge from analysis or from a deductive approach where preconceived code categories are employed.

Visual content analysis has repeatedly been employed through a feminist lens to study gender representation in children's books and school textbooks, which feminists acknowledge as a critical component in the socialization process, gender socialization, and identity development. This research has provided statistical and descriptive evidence that, indeed, children's reading books often rely on sex stereotyping. Even publishing houses have been influenced by feminist analysis, as evidenced by Macmillan's statement: "Children are not simply being taught mathematics and reading; they are also learning, sometimes subliminally, how society regards certain groups of people" (Britton & Lumpkin, quoted in Evans & Davies, 2000, p. 256).

- If a picture speaks a thousand words then what kinds of gendered images are young children being exposed to as they develop their self identity?

Evans and Davies (2000) conducted research on the representation of masculinity in elementary school textbooks with three goals in mind:

> In this research, we set out to answer three questions. First, are males in text-books portrayed in a manner in which they cross traditional boundaries of masculinity? In other words, are males depicted with both stereotypically masculine and feminine traits? Or are the males in elementary school reading textbooks more likely to be depicted with masculine characteristics only. . . . Second, do two of the leading publishers differ in how they portray males in their textbooks? Could it be that one publisher portrays males in a more stereotypical light than another? Third, does the portrayal of masculine and feminine traits in males vary by grade? (p. 259)

The results of this research are multifaceted and also illustrate an area where social change is still needed—change which can be pushed through the results of studies such as this one:

> Even though our results indicate a greater number of numerical equality of males and females displayed in textbooks as compared with previous studies, the manner in which males and females are depicted through personality traits is still sexist. Males are overwhelmingly more often portrayed as aggressive, argumentative, and competitive, whereas females are more likely to be characterized as affectionate, emotionally expressive, and passive. These findings contrast with the expectations that publishing house guide-lines established in their efforts to create nonsexist literature in textbooks. (Evans & Davies, 2000, pp. 268–269)

These findings illustrate how important it is for feminist research to continue in any given area, as the "discovery" that children's textbooks contained sexist representations was not enough to change the situation in its entirety, nor was a "promise" by publishers to eradicate this difference. This is why continued feminist research that can be applied to social issues is so necessary. Other kinds of textbooks also contain photographs that can be content analyzed. For example, Low and Sherrard (1999) performed a content analysis of photographs to see how women are portrayed with respect to sexuality and marriage in family textbooks. They specifically focused on the visual images in the textbooks because images can be viewed with authority, as readers may view them as snippets of reality.

FEMINIST AUDIOVISUAL CONTENT ANALYSIS

We live in a cultural landscape in which audiovisual narratives constantly flow from television sets and movie screens. The *content* of these narratives emerges from the interplay or fusion of the visual, sound, and textual components. Given the normative nature of audiovisual material in people's daily lives, feminists have a real stake in investigating how different genres of television and film portray women, people of color, and sexual minorities.

- How are girls and women portrayed in the evening news, sitcoms, or dramatic television series?
- What do visual shots, the motion of the camera, the camera angle, and the dialogue imply about female versus male characters?
- Is there a disjuncture between dialogue and image, and if so, what is the nature of the mixed messages?

These questions barely scratch the surface of why feminist researchers might be interested in content analyzing audiovisual texts. Audiovisual data also has a set of particular characteristics that makes working with it special and challenging for any researcher, of course including feminists, who bring their own set of concerns to the research endeavor.

Audiovisual data are unique because they comprise multiple components, each in their own medium or language, including visual, sound, and dialogue. The data are further complicated in that they are *moving* (Hesse-Biber & Leavy, 2006, p. 304). Rose (2000) conceptualized audiovisual texts as "multiple fields" because they comprise distinct and interrelated textual forms (the audio, visual, and dialogue/textual narrative). Two major issues when working with data that are complicated in these ways are determining the unit of analysis and the coding strategy.

The *unit of analysis* refers to each segment of audiovisual data that will be examined and coded. There is no one-fits-all method for defining the unit of analysis, but some standards include scene change and camera change. As always, the procedure should fit the research goals. Feminists who are centrally concerned with the way female bodies are filmed (angles, lighting, fragmentation, etc.) may find camera change an appropriate demarcation of data segments as the analysis *follows the camera* on multiple levels. When considering this aspect of research design, you will also have to construct an operational definition of just what is meant by "scene change" or "camera change" in your particular study.

Coding audiovisual data presents many challenges and considerations because of the multifield nature of the material. Some considerations are as follows:

- Will all "fields" be coded (sound, visual image, dialogue) or will the study be more limited in scope? What about color, mood, film quality/texture, and other more "abstract" parts of the data?
- Will the data be viewed in their entirety prior to coding each unit of analysis, and if so, will this initial step inform code categories and will memo notes be taken?
- Will the multiple "fields" be coded together as they appear in the text or will they be coded as distinct? What procedures will be followed?
- How will gender, sexual, and racial differences be coded?

In addition to the complexity of the data, one must determine the extent to which the coding will be deductive or inductive. Feminists use approaches ranging from highly deductive to highly inductive depending on their research objectives and epistemological position. As feminist researchers conduct politically and socially engaged research, and typically work to actively locate themselves within their projects, coding style selection is informed by many things. When thinking about deductive and inductive coding procedures, it is important to realize that this is not an either/or decision because deductive and inductive approaches exist on a long continuum (Hesse-Biber & Leavy, 2006, p. 306), as discussed in the epistemology section earlier in this book. Furthermore, deductive and inductive approaches can be employed "to degrees" or in combination with one another.

Deductive approaches rely on preconceived code categories. So for example, let's say you're interested in revisiting a research topic that has previously been studied. You are doing so to see what a feminist lens reveals about a topic that might have been studied by a nonfeminist, and/or you want to see how something has changed over time. Let's take the portrayal of women in music videos as our working example. Research in the early 1990s showed several patterns in how women are represented in music videos, including but not limited to fragmenting women's bodies; shooting from below or above; panoramic camera shots; women wearing certain kinds of clothing, including underwear and garter belts; and women in certain roles, including back-up singers, girlfriends of musicians, prostitutes, dominatrix, and models (Jhally & Bartone, 1991). A feminist researcher, perhaps a feminist empiricist, interested in how women are portrayed in this same genre 10 years later might create a list of code categories based on earlier research (deductive codes) and perhaps some additional categories (also deductive) informed by feminist scholarship, and then code a sample of videos counting the number of times each code is present. A deductive researcher who is also interested in "unexpected" results may add additional inductive categories that emerge during the coding process, or may follow up the deductive coding with an inductive approach to see how code categories differ.

Inductive approaches to coding, often employed from a grounded theory perspective, allow the researcher to develop code categories directly out of the data during the coding and analysis process. In other words, the categories actually emerge as you sift through the data. This approach allows researchers to use the language of text itself and help the data emerge, which is appealing to feminists who are drawn to the naturalistic quality afforded by preexisting texts. Inductive approaches are also congruent with feminist scholars who challenge positivist approaches to knowledge building, such as those who work from feminist postmodern and standpoint perspectives.

As discussed in the opening of this section, feminist researchers have many reasons for conducting audiovisual content analysis. One of the overarching reasons for this kind of work is feminists' concern with what Tuchman, Daniels, and Benet (1978) called the "symbolic annihilation" of women in television (and film). This description refers to the overall exclusion of women as well as distorted and stereotypical representations where women's perspectives are invisible. Concerned with changes in the "symbolic annihilation" of women in prime-time television, Signorielli and Bacue (1999) conducted a longitudinal content analysis of lead prime-time television characters from 1967 to 1998. Their research pointed to some positive changes in representation but a lagging problem of under- and misrepresentation. The number of women on television has increased but remains disproportionate to the number of men, and women still appear younger than their male counterparts, but women are less frequently shown in traditionally "feminine" occupations and are more frequently shown in "masculine" or gender neutral occupations. This kind of longitudinal research is important because it often contradicts public perception that "great change" has occurred and instead allows us to see precisely what has improved and what has yet to improve.

CONCLUSION

Content analysis is a broad method that can be employed from qualitative or quantitative paradigms, from the spectrum of theoretical perspectives, with single or multimethod designs, and in service of a wide range of research questions and objectives. Within this expansive landscape of content analysis, feminist research plays a critical role in how we come to interrogate and understand the cultural world. Feminists employ content analysis from a range of perspectives, but regardless of the multiplicity of projects in which they use content analysis, the feminist lens remains at the core of the work. The content analysis work done by feminists has shed light on the gendered dimensions of culture and popular culture in particular. Feminists have asked questions about representation, stereotyping, extreme imagery, language, and more to under-stand the relationship between the lives of women and men and the textual environments they create and inhabit. Because feminists are centrally con-cerned with women and other minorities, they have asked questions of popu-lar culture in ways that would not be possible from a perspective other than feminism. As the small sampling of studies in this chapter indicates, the knowledge derived from these efforts has added to our understanding of gen-der inequality, social power, and taken-for-granted assumptions about femi-ninity and masculinity.

In addition to exploring the dominant representations of gender that flow from a patriarchal social structure and worldview, feminists may employ con-tent analysis to study or expose the resistive possibilities of popular culture. While extreme imagery that stereotypes, sexualizes, racializes, and objectifies women and other minorities occupies a prominent role within contemporary popular culture and receives considerable attention from feminist researchers, feminists and other critical scholars such as those working in the field of cultural studies, also show how popular culture can be an important site of resistance to patriarchal and other destructive forces. For example, the recent Dove brand "campaign for real beauty" has received considerable media atten-tion as an advertising campaign aiming to change impossible standards of female beauty through more diverse and realistic imagery. This is merely one small example of the resistive possibilities of popular culture: a sphere where dominant ideas about femininity, sexuality, and race can be exposed, challenged, and altered.

Technological developments, including the advent of the Internet and its ever-increasing components (virtual pornography, online dating services, chat rooms, message boards, clip art, etc.), as well as digital imaging and the like, change the cultural landscape and thus provide important opportunities for new images and narratives, which may challenge or reinforce patriarchy. Seidman Milburn, Carney, and Ramirez (2001) discuss how computer-driven imagery, for example, has become increasingly present in business and educational environments. For example, clip art is now frequently used in presentations as a way of dressing up informational presentations. Seidman Milburn et al. (2001) conducted a quantitative content analysis of the portrayal of human beings in popular computer clip art to study how this new form of popular imagery represents gender and race (whether, for example, stereotypical images are used or if this new medium contains more egalitarian images). This groundbreaking study revealed that clip art mirrors other media in that women and people of color are underrepresented and women are primarily shown engaged in passive activities and nurturing activities while men are frequently imaged in activity in nonnurturing settings, such as work or athletics. This research indicates, among other things, the important work of feminist content analyzers in the future in terms of questioning and examining new media.

Feminist content analysis will continue to offer a perspective and tool for investigating technological developments and the complex ways they may come to stifle and/or promote equality for women. In this vein, as culture changes, grows, and transforms, so too will the questions that feminists ask of it via the method of content analysis.

REFERENCES

Angelique, Holly L., & Culley, Marci R. (2000). Searching for feminism: An analysis of community psychology literature relevant to women's concerns. *American Journal of Community Psychology, 28,* 793–813.

Bauer, M. (2000). Classical content analysis: A review. In M. Bauer & G. Gaskell (Eds.), *Qualitative researching with text, image and sound* (pp. 131–151). London: Sage.

Commeyras, M., & Alvermann, D. (1996). Reading about women in world history textbooks from one feminist perspective. *Gender and Education, 8*(1), 31–48.

Evans, L., & Davies, K. (2000). No sissy boys here: A content analysis of the representation of masculinity in elementary school reading textbooks. *Sex Roles: A Journal of Research, 42,* 255–270.

Hall, E. J., & Rodriguez, M. (2003). The myth of postfeminism. *Gender & Society, 17*(6), 878–902.

Hall, E. J., & Shepherd Stolley, K. (1997). A historical analysis of the presentation of abortion and adoption in marriage and family textbooks: 1950–1987. *Family Relations, 46,* 73–82.

Hedley, Mark. (2002). The geometry of gendered conflict in popular film: 1986–2000. *Sex roles: A Journal of Research, 17,* 201–217.

Hesse-Biber, S. N., & Leavy, P. (Eds.). (2004). *Approaches to qualitative research: A reader on theory and practice.* New York: Oxford University Press.

Hesse-Biber, S. N., & Leavy, P. (2006). *The practice of qualitative research.* Thousand Oaks, CA: Sage.

Irigaray, L. (1985). The power of discourse and the subordination of the feminine. In *This sex which is not one* (pp. 68–85; C. Porter & C. Burke, Trans.). Ithaca, NY: Cornell University Press.

Jhally, Sut. (Producer), & Bartone, Joe. (Director). (1991). *Dream worlds II* [Motion picture]. United States: Media Education Foundation.

Kellner, D. (1995). Cultural studies, multiculturalism and media culture. In G. Dines & J. M. Humez (Eds.), *Gender, race and class in media* (pp. 5–17). Thousand Oaks, CA: Sage.

Kirca, Süheyla. (1999). Popular culture: From being an enemy of the "feminist movement" to a tool for women's "liberation"? *Journal of American Culture, 2*(3), 101–107.

Kirca, Süheyla. (2001). Turkish women's magazines: The popular meets the political. *Women's Studies International Forum, 24*(3/4), 457–468.

Low, J., & Sherrard P. (1999). Portrayal of women in sexuality and marriage family textbooks: A content analysis of photographs from the 1970s to the 1990s. *Sex Role: A Journal of Research, 40*(3–4), 309–318.

Modleski, T. (1986). Femininity as mas(s)querade: A feminist approach to mass culture. In C. MacCabe (Ed.), *High theory/low culture: Analysing popular television and film* (pp. 37–52). Manchester, UK: Manchester University Press.

Neuendorf, K. A. (2001). *The content analysis guidebook.* Thousand Oaks, CA: Sage.

Pederson, P. M. (2002). Examining equity in newspaper photographs. *International Review for the Sociology of Sport, 34,* 303–318.

Prior, L. (2004). Following in Foucault's footsteps: Text and context in qualitative research. In S. N. Hesse-Biber & P. Leavy (Eds.), *Approaches to qualitative research: A reader on theory and practice* (pp. 317–333). New York: Oxford University Press.

Reinharz, S. (1992). *Feminist methods in social research.* New York: Oxford University Press.

Roman, L., & Christian-Smith, L. K. (1988). Introduction. In L. Roman, L. K. Christian-Smith, & E. Ellsworth (Eds.), *Becoming feminine: The politics of popular culture* (pp. 1–34). London: Falmer Press.

Rose, D. (2000). Analysis of moving images. In M. W. Bauer & G. Gaskell (Eds.), *Qualitative researching with text, image, and sound* (pp. 246–262). London: Sage.

Schlenker, J., Caron, W., & Halteman, W. (1998). A feminist analysis of *Seventeen Magazine:* Content analysis from 1945–1995. *Sex Roles: A Journal of Research, 38*(1–2), 135–149.

Seidman Milburn, S., Carney, D. R., & Ramirez, A. M. (2001). Even in modern media, the picture is still the same: A content analysis of clip art images. *Sex Roles: A Journal of Research, 44,* 277–294.

Shindler Zimmerman, T., Holm, K., & Starrels, M. (2001). A feminist analysis of self-help bestsellers for improving relationships: A decade review. *Journal of Marital and Family Therapy, 27*(2), 165–175.

Signorielli, N., & Bacue, A. (1999). Recognition and respect: A content analysis of prime-time television characters across three decades. *Sex Roles: A Journal of Research, 40,* 527–540.

Tuchman, G., Daniels, A. K., & Benet, J. (Eds.). (1978). *Hearth and home: Images of women in the mass media.* New York: Oxford University Press.

Wachholz, S., & Mullaly, B. (2000). The politics of a textbook: A content analysis of the coverage and treatment of feminist, radical, and anti-racist social work scholarship in American introductory social work textbooks published between 1988 and 1997. *Journal of Progressive Human Services, 11*(2), 51–76.

NINE

FEMINIST APPROACHES TO MIXED-METHODS RESEARCH

Denise Leckenby

Sharlene Nagy Hesse-Biber

———◦●◦———

A MIXED-METHODS TALE

> ***Zoe, a white suburban teen, speaking on sexuality and desire:***
> *"I don't know if you can feel it (desire) if you did it with someone you didn't love."*

> ***Beverly, an African American teen, speaking on sexuality and desire:*** *"If you want to do it, do it. If you don't want to, don't do it. . . . My body was saying yes, but my mouth was saying no."*

> —Tolman and Szalacha (1999, pp. 114–115)

Zoe and Beverly, two adolescent girls from different social class and racial and ethnic backgrounds, relate very different aspects of their experiences of sexuality and desire. Suppose you are interested in studying adolescent girls' sexuality and sexual experiences. You want to know how girls are experiencing their own sexuality, how they view their bodies, and how they negotiate the many choices that they are required to make as sexual beings. Suppose within your discipline of research, let's say psychology, you find that many empirical studies typically conducted are quantitative in nature,[1] employing survey research.[2] The picture presented by these studies, although important in your field for understanding the broad picture of sexuality and sexual activity within a given population of girls, does not seem to capture subtleties that you suspect are at play within the lives of those you want to study. You feel that methodologically[3] there are pieces of information and meaning that cannot be fully captured by survey research where there is a rigid, and in your view, patriarchal picture presented within the framework of typically positivist research.

Let's further suppose that you are a feminist—both in terms of the critical epistemological[4] lens that helps you approach your work and in your political perspective. You want to produce research *for* women and girls, not *on* women and girls. Your feminist lens provides you with a set of tools that help you to question and critique quantitative methods, particularly the ways in which quantitative methods are often used for research that is *on* women, girls, and other subjugated populations. Such a distinction is important to you because of the feminist lens through which you view your work, and your intention is to produce research that may provide space for social change. The perspective you have on the world encourages you to thoroughly explore the work being done by other feminists inside and outside your discipline. You are aware of a number of studies conducted by feminists about girls and women's sexuality that are grounded in a qualitative tradition (Fine, 1988; Welsh, Rostosky, & Kawaguchi, 2000; White, Bondurant, & Travis, 2000). You feel that the qualitative research produced about girls and women's experiences of their sexuality does a good job of remedying one of the major problems with quantitative research, namely, it does not reduce girls' actions and behaviors as sexual beings into categories of "good" or "bad" (Tolman & Szalacha, 1999, p. 8).[5] Qualitative research studies focus on the subjective meaning, reflection on experiences, and a great deal of exploratory insight into sexualities of girls and women.

In reflecting on the methodological choices you have before you, you find that there are strengths to be found in *both* methods. Quantitative methods are particularly well suited to looking at "cause and effect" relationships between a set of factors that are referred to as variables. Quantitative methods help you to test hypotheses and deductively examine theories about girls' sexuality that are already available to you. There is an abundance of theoretical arguments within the field of psychology that you feel are partly at play within your research question and research population. On the other hand, you find that much of the quantitative research and theory in your field presents an over-simplified picture of girls' behavior and actions. Viewing the world through a feminist lens causes you to be concerned about the representation of women and girls in research. Your political perspective makes you aware that public policy advocates, funding agencies, the government, and even educational institutions use a great deal of the quantitative social science research about girls' sexuality. You know that the research conducted *on* girls affects their lives. The power imbued in quantitative research gives you pause; you look deeply into the research that is being conducted in your field. For example, you might notice that in a survey of adolescent girls' sexuality, a quantitative questionnaire might ask whether or not a girl has had sexual intercourse. The question would have two possible answers, yes or no. As a feminist, you are interested in what is left out when the question is framed as such. For instance, in such a survey, what answer would a girl mark down who is not sure of whether or not she has had intercourse? What answer would be marked down if a girl is not a heterosexual but is sexually active? Which answer should a respondent mark if she says she has had sexual intercourse but does not use contraception? What are the policy implications of such data?

Many feminist researchers feel that quantitative data produced about such topics have "framed and limited for girls what the pertinent questions and pos-sible answers are about what is important in the development of their sexual-ity" (Tolman & Szalacha, 1999, p. 8).[6] The types of questions asked that *fit* into a survey framework simply do not capture the issues that you want to under-stand. Due to some of these limitations found within quantitative methods, feminist researchers have been an integral force in exploring new qualitative methods that avoid the pitfalls of survey research. For instance, Joyce A. Ladner's (1971) *Tomorrow's Tomorrow* is a groundbreaking qualitative study about young black girls and their ideas, attitudes, and experiences of becom-ing a woman that illustrates the impact that breaking out of "good" and "bad" categories can have on a research endeavor. Ladner remarks that ideas about premarital sex among women were traditionally marked by "regulative norms that govern sexual behavior" stemming from American society's views about the standards for behavior (p. 196). Ladner quotes Ira Reiss, stating, "The double standard in premarital sexual behavior is obvious in our norms which state that premarital coitus is wrong for all women, and thus women who indulge are bad women" (p. 197). Ladner purposively avoids this intersection between mainstream white societal views on morality and her own research, remarking that such moral statements rely on a powerful "moral-immoral dichotomy" (p. 198). The influence of such categories and dichotomies had led to the classification of black girls as having *loose morals* and engaging in *promiscuous behavior,* which categorized them as "bad" without digging deeper into their ideas and attitudes. Research such as that of Ladner, as well as Tolman and Szalacha (1999), seeks to avoid a moralistic agenda that shapes the research findings into discrete deviant and normal categories.[7] Although Ladner (1971) engaged with qualitative interviewing and ethnographic tools exclusively, her work questioned the boundaries that had previously separated girls' sexuality into tightly knit boxes of moral judgment. Her work also pushed against theoretical paradigms that supported deviance models of girls' sexuality. Her research opened up spaces that direct quantitative analysis of sexual activity could not touch. She found various and complex reasons for girls' engagement in premarital sex that she saw as leading towards an increase in maturity and "aids in the process of achieving womanhood" (p. 211). Ladner's work, along with other qualitative methods explored in previous chapters, has helped bring new empirical questions to the social sciences that generate new types of knowledge about women and girls' experiences.

Imagine that during your exploration of your field's literature, you see that qualitative studies such as Ladner's help avoid stereotypical or ideological assumptions that you see infused in many of the quantitative studies produced in your discipline, such as those described above, that categorize girls in reductive ways that don't capture their subjectivity or the context of their lives. Yet in spite of the rich complexity that the qualitative research provides you, perhaps you are not entirely sure that a qualitative study would *fulfill all* your research goals. Your research goals *also* include an interest in using quantifiable data to explore statistically significant differences among groups of girls that can help policy makers and educators apply their expertise and funds to addressing issues and needs found among a certain population of girls.[8] You are also interested in using qualitative methods to identify pertinent issues in your subject of study that will be used to inform and adapt the survey research questions to better measure what you seek to understand. If this is the case, you might want to mix qualitative and quantitative methods.

This chapter will examine the ways feminist researchers are using mixed methods and how mixed methods might expand or limit the ability for feminist knowledge building. Having gained knowledge of the range of mixed-methods designs, we then return to the issue of studying girls. Later on in this chapter, we look at the new layers of epistemological and methodological questions that are brought to the fore by feminist researchers when deciding whether or not to employ mixed methods.

WHAT ARE MIXED METHODS?

In general, researchers who use mixed methods employ a type of research design that uses both quantitative and qualitative data collection and analysis to answer a particular question or set of questions in a single research design (Lackey & Moberg, 1998; Tolman & Szalacha, 1999; Westmarland, 2001). For some researchers, mixed methods can also refer to the use of two or more qualitative methods in a single research study or, similarly, the use of two or more quantitative methods in a single research study. The timing of data gathering of different types also varies within mixed methods. For instance, the researcher might "collect both the quantitative and qualitative data in phases (sequentially)," or he or she might "gather it at the same time (concurrently)" (Creswell, 2003, p. 211). Researchers, both feminist and nonfeminist, are using mixed methods in a variety of ways that are both innovative and creative.

Like all methods discussed in this book, none are particularly feminist or nonfeminist.[9] Methods are tools that are used in the hands of a researcher who may or may not *use* them as a feminist, with a feminist focus, or with a feminist lens. Mixed methods, in and of themselves, are not feminist in nature, but we can identify certain *ways* that feminist researchers are mixing methods. Although feminist researchers have increasingly been associated with qualitative research methods, developing new strategies and the innovative uses of traditional qualitative research methods, feminist researchers do not limit themselves to qualitative methods entirely. As evidenced in earlier chapters, feminist researchers are epistemologically and methodologically attuned to issues of power, difference, voice, silence, and the complexities of the knowable world. The innovations developed through the uses of qualitative methods are being carried forth into the realm of mixed methods in interesting ways that illuminate and interrogate the strengths of both methods while grappling with feminist-oriented foci (Deem, 2002; Manfredi, Lacey, Warnecke, & Balch, 1997; Reinharz, 1992). Let's look at the ways feminists use mixed methods.

PUTTING MIXED METHODS INTO PRACTICE: MIXED-METHODS DESIGNS

David Morgan's (1998) work offers a set of research designs for conducting a mixed-methods study and provides a four-method research design based on the sequencing (time ordering) and relative importance (priority) of each method. Morgan suggests that each researcher ask the following questions as they contemplate mixing methods:

- What is your primary research method and what is the secondary (complementary) method?
- What method comes first? Second?

Your answer to each of these questions leads to four possible mixed-methods research designs, as depicted in Table 9.1.

Let's examine some of the research where mixed methods have been fruitful for feminist researchers following David Morgan's design for a mixed-methods project.

qual Followed by QUANT

The first design (qual followed by QUANT) involves conducting the qualitative component of the research project first but keeping it secondary

Table 9.1   Combining Qualitative and Quantitative Methods

Design 1	qual followed by QUANT[a]
Design 2	quant followed by QUAL
Design 3	QUANT followed by qual
Design 4	QUAL followed by quant

SOURCE: Adapted from David Morgan (1998).

a. All lowercase means secondary method and all uppercase denotes primary method.

(designated by lowercase letters) to the project's goals. The quantitative method is primary (all uppercase letters), but it is administered as a follow-up to the qualitative study. Using a qualitative design before a quantitative one provides the researcher who is unfamiliar with a given topic the opportunity to generate specific ideas or hypotheses that he or she might address more specifically in the quantitative part of the project. An illustrative example of this comes from a mixed-methods study design used in a research project conducted by Lackey and Moberg (1998). They were interested in understanding the sexuality of urban American adolescents. They began their research by conducting prefocus groups in 10 community-based organizations focusing on youth and parents who were asked to "define topics they thought needed to be studied" as a basis for a wider survey (QUANT) of 593 youths and 95 of their parents. In addition, 13 more formal focus groups (qual) consisting of 6 to 10 youth, some in coed groups and others in single-sexed focus groups, were asked to "describe their experiences in contexts known to influence teen behavior . . . and to describe what, if any, messages these contexts project about sexual standards and practices" (p. 494). The findings from both the informal and formal focus groups (qual) enabled the researchers to create questionnaire items for the larger survey (QUANT) that reflected the community's experience, especially items that dealt with "youth exposure to the media and popular culture, time spent with peers and ecological factors" (p. 495). In fact, the research findings from the survey (QUANT) revealed that several of the variables that the focus and prefocus groups suggested ended up "comprising important scales" in the survey study (p. 499).

quant Followed by QUAL

In the second design—quant followed by QUAL—the quantitative study is used secondarily (quant), and the qualitative study is used primarily (QUAL). In this case, the quantitative study is used to *identify specific populations or issues* that need to be further explored in depth. The quantitative (quant) study complements the qualitative (QUAL). A good example of this comes from the work of feminist geographer Kim England (1993). She takes on the "spatial entrapment thesis" as an explanation for the segmentation of the labor force and, more specifically, why women become entrapped in pink-collar ghettos. The conventional wisdom of geographers of the time noted that firms employed pink-collar women located to suburban areas to take

advantage of women workers' spatial entrapment; women's dual roles as wives
and mothers prevented them from taking advantage of wider job opportunities.
Women workers remained stuck in pink-collar suburban jobs. Early geographical research on the commuting time of American workers concluded
that the commute of female clerical workers tended to be a shorter distance
compared with their male counterparts—because women's family obligations
restricted their ability to travel to better jobs. Using the case study of
Columbus, Ohio, whose industries are "heavily reliant upon pink collar workers" (p. 228), Kim England seeks to test out the "spatial entrapment" thesis.
She conducts a mixed-methods study, using her quantitative data (quant) to
determine the commuting times of men and women within the greater
Columbus suburbs by gathering commuting data obtained from a compilation
of workplace- and residence-based data drawn from personnel records, a
survey questionnaire, and a suburban directory. She finds that whereas these
data show women are somewhat more spatially entrapped compared with their
male counterparts, this is less true for women in two-adult households where
there were dependent children! She is led by her quantitative findings to conduct a qualitative study (QUAL). She conducts a series of in-depth interviews
with personnel managers within suburban companies as well as suburban
women pink-collar clerical workers. As a feminist geographer, she is interested in the *lived experiences* of women workers. She notes,

> The central purpose of my research is not to obtain empirical generalizations;
> rather it is to develop an in-depth understanding of a particular local inter-
> section of the changing geography of office locations, gender division of
> labor, and urban labor markets, grounded in an acceptance of people as
> knowledgeable agents. The interviews, in particular, allowed me to develop
> an understanding based on the interviewee's frame of reference and to
> explore specific issues within the context of the interviewees' set of
> meanings. (England, 1993, p. 227)

In interviews with personnel managers, she wants to assess why their firms
tended to relocate to the suburbs and to examine whether or not a manager's
motivation was to take advantage of entrapped workers. Managers were
selected from the city of Columbus's business directories, and interviews were
conducted with personnel managers of the 10 private firms that had an extensive clerical labor force. She conducted 30 interviews with women from the
quantitative sample of 200 women drawn from the suburban directory (these

residential data on 200 women originally composed part of her quantitative study to assess commuting times). These 30 women created a purposive sample of women who lived in suburban towns known to be "popular destinations for relocating firms," and Kim made efforts to select women "whose commutes were representative of the broader sample" (p. 234).

In conducting her qualitative study, Kim England's (1993) research questions stem directly from anomalies of her quantitative findings: Why didn't the spatial entrapment thesis hold up for dual worker women? How do women negotiate a given commute within the context of their family and career? In articulating these questions, England assumes a degree of agency on the part of women; something that the traditional entrapment hypothesis, with its assumptions of a traditional gendered division of labor, does not. What her qualitative findings actually reveal is the presence of *human agency at the center of understanding* larger macrostructures, like commuting patterns. It is only by focusing on the context of women's lives that England can better understand and begin to break down long held stereotypes of macro commuting data. The author concludes that women workers are not "passive victims of spatial structures," but instead they weigh a variety of workplace (e.g., career ladders, career aspirations) and family factors (e.g., child care arrangements, good neighborhood schools) in their commuting decisions. She notes, "Women's journeys-to-work should be reconceptualized as an effort to juggle a multiplicity of overlapping and often contradictory roles and spatial factors" (p. 237).

QUANT Followed by qual

The third design, QUANT followed by qual, is designed to have the quantitative study be the primary mode of inquiry, with the qualitative study second. This type of design is often used when there is a need to provide clarification or elaboration of research results from quantitative findings. The qualitative study assists in understanding such things as negative results and what are called "outliers" (findings that do not appear to fit the overall hypothesis or theoretical perspective). In essence, qualitative data can be used to supplement quantitative data to help the quantitative researcher "salvage" the data by understanding "erroneous results" in his or her survey data (Weinholtz, Kacer, & Rocklin, 1995). An example of this type of study comes from research conducted by feminist psychologist Paula Nicholson (2004), who examines clinical studies on postnatal depression. She notes that research in this area is traditionally quantitative and often uses clinical research trials by randomizing respondents into categories including a control group. Following this clinical model, known as a randomized control trial (RCT), women with postpartum depression (PPD) are randomly assigned to an experimental group, for example, those receiving an antidepressant or those receiving a placebo. A control group is also formed for the study. These methods are often funded by the federal government or drug companies to test for the viability of certain drugs in treating a specific condition. In this case, Nicholson is testing how well antidepressants treat PPD. What researchers are looking for is some "quantified" way of measuring how effective the drug treatment is for depression. What Nicholson's research shows, however, is the lack of "listening" to the concerns of mothers. Instead of launching into a randomized study, Nicholson decided to do a pilot project with mothers experiencing PPD. She conducted qualitative interviews with a small sample of women who experienced PPD in hopes of *understanding their experiences.* She interviewed 17 women four times during a 6-month period starting after their delivery. What her pilot study reveals is that doing a qualitative study after a quantitative study (QUANT followed by qual) gives more credence to the quantitative component. She also notes a number of important benefits that the qualitative component may bring to the overall research project. The researcher is empowered to decide when a particular "outcome should be evaluated." She notes that by longitudinally following the women more than 6 months, "although behavior and mood might be similar at 3 and 6 months after the birth, the construction and meaning of the experiences are different." She notes that this has important implications on "when and what is evaluated" (p. 224). A qualitative component also provides a context for the researcher's results. For example, if the quantitative results showed that the variable of a "poor marital relationship" was highly related to PPD, the qualitative component could provide a more grounded idea of what that meant in the context of a given mother's life. In addition, the researchers have an opportunity to understand the extent to which respondents evaluate a specific drug intervention as well as how they evaluate the entire research experience itself, providing the researchers with valuable information that will "lead to more effective intervention and preventative measures" (p. 226).

Nicholson's research takes a feminist psychological approach to the issue of PPD by focusing on the lived experiences of mothers with depression.

Arguing for a mixed-methods approach that combines quantitative with qualitative data, she challenges the sole use of a randomized controlled trials approach that she sees as reinforcing clinicians' tendency "to pathologise the female body and mind, paying no regard to women's experiences of child care and the context in which that care occurs" (p. 210).

QUAL Followed by quant

In the fourth research design—QUAL followed by quant—the qualitative research study is primary (QUAL) and is followed up with a quantitative study (quant). The quantitative study can add to or clarify the results of the qualitative study or be used to test results on different populations to ascertain whether or not the qualitative findings "transfer" to other populations (Morgan, 1998, p. 370). A study by Cuyvers, Wets, Zuallaert, and Van Gils, started in 2003, is part of an ongoing research action project sponsored by the Belgian Federal Social Policy Office (FEDRA). The authors envision an interdisciplinary study and note that it is "at the crossroads of two recent and rapidly developing scientific disciplines: the sociology of childhood, and (the sociological dimension of) traffic sciences." Between the ages of 10 and 13, children reach a more independent stage, with their mobility "growing significantly more autonomous." Yet there is a paucity of research on how children view the issue of transportation and the extent of their experiences with regard to transportation autonomy and transportation dependency. The authors' perspective places children's concerns at the center of their research inquiry. They take on an interpretive perspective in understanding aspects of children's development, in particular their experience of transition from dependency to independence. They capture these ideas through the lens of children's mobility perceptions. How do children view mobility? What are their needs? Preferences? What are the actual practices of mobility of children in their daily lives? To what extent is independent mobility of importance to children, and what factors do they think have impeded or contributed to their autonomy? One might also consider their project emancipatory and feminist in the sense that children, whose voices are often muted in this type of research, have the opportunity to be heard, and in addition, the research goals of the authors are oriented to seek action and social change. These researchers hope to translate children's needs and concerns into social policy initiatives in planning for future transportation and urban planning policy. The authors' primary data collection consisted of interviews and focus groups with boys and girls 10 to 13 years of age living in both urban and rural environments. The authors followed this with a quantitative study on a representative sample of 5,000 children throughout Flanders to "check the results obtained in the qualitative phase" and to "weigh the factors that were defined as relevant in the qualitative research." The authors hope to follow up their study with an action research component in two rural and two urban areas with the goal of encouraging children to participate in mobility projects in their communities (Cuyvers et al., 2003).

There is, however, a multitude of other designs that combine qualitative and quantitative methods using different criteria. Some mixed-methods designs combine methods concurrently but maintain the primary/secondary distinction (see Creswell, 2003). Morgan's (1998) design considers sequential (time ordering) studies—one after the other. Yet other mixed-methods researchers conduct their studies concurrently (at the same time), often placing both methods on an equal footing without distinguishing between a primary and a secondary method (Creswell, Fetters, & Ivankova, 2004). This appears to be the case in the mixed-methods design that Tolman and Szalacha (1999) employed, and we will examine their design in more depth in the following section. Other researchers place one method (qualitative or quantitative) nested or "embedded" in the other. In this case, the nested method is often given a lower priority. This method may even answer a different research question, yet both methods are used to analyze the data (Creswell, Plano Clark, Gutmann, & Hanson, 2003, p. 229). There is also the possibility of mixing two qualitative and two quantitative studies.

CASE STUDY ON THE USE OF MIXED METHODS: STUDYING GIRLS' SEXUALITY

Deborah L. Tolman and Laura A. Szalacha provide an innovative and illustrative example of the type of research that emerges when one uses mixed methods with a feminist perspective. We now return to the example we introduced at the beginning of this chapter, but the example is now infused with knowledge regarding the range of mixed-methods designs feminists have used and their motivations for engaging in mixed-methods research.

Tolman and Szalacha (1999) sought to provide a picture of female adolescent sexuality that uses the strengths of *both* types of research method.

They took a long and thorough look at the types of research that were being conducted in the social sciences, focusing specifically on psychology, and looked for the stories that these studies tell about female sexuality. What they found was a relatively singular, objectivist, and powerful perspective on girls' sexuality, for there was a "historical denial and denigration of female adolescent sexuality (p. 8)."[10] Like the research critiques by Ladner, the quantitative research tended to *fit* girls into two categories and labeled them either *bad* or *good*. These objective, patriarchal voices never told the stories about girls whose lives were complex and complicated, who were neither good nor bad. This body of research, in Tolman and Szalacha's view, was lacking in depth, complexity, and thoroughness. Centering themselves within their feminist perspective, Tolman and Szalacha decided that the only way to provide a more multifaceted story about girls' sexuality was to use qualitative methods as well as quantitative methods in the *same study*. They used *"a sequential integration" of methods* and worked to create an intricate and vivid understanding about the development of young girls' sexuality. This brought the researchers to a space where they realized that "the challenge of grappling with increasingly complex social problems . . . demands that we investigate further the hidden potential in combining quantitative and qualitative research methods (p. 8)." This commitment to seeking out and using methods that reflect the complex and multifaceted world around us makes a particularly powerful case for using mixed methods. For some feminist researchers, the case for mixed methods is underscored when they realize the meaningful ways they are able to gain access to women's and girls' voices and experiences with mixed methods.

Tolman and Szalacha (1999), like many feminist researchers, brought their interests and questions to the table before setting out to identify the research method necessary to attend to such issues. They brought their political and epistemological lenses as feminists, intent on listening to girls' voices and stories. The context for their research design is situated within a predominantly quantitative field, where bridging the divide between qualitative and quantitative can illuminate, layer, and enrich already established theories about girls' sexuality. Furthermore, the context that Tolman and Szalacha aim for is within the gaps of existing research. Through qualitative and quantitative data and careful analysis, the researchers are able to create a dynamic and synergistic account of adolescent girls' narratives about their bodies, desires, and sexuality. This idea of bridging two methods within one research endeavor, all the while holding true to the goals of feminist research of seeking access into women's and girls' experiences, gives us our first example of what feminist mixed-methods research might look like. Just as the intent of using a particular method, such as an oral history, requires a particular type of research question, so too the desire to employ mixed methods, for most feminists, does not come out of thin air.

Though many of the empirical studies in their field were lacking and they hoped to use qualitative research methods, Tolman and Szalacha (1999) did not want to remedy the problems produced by exclusively working in a qualitative methodology. They sought instead to dynamically illustrate the ways in which their field, and their own research, can benefit from a mixed-methods approach, and they succeeded beyond expectation. As feminists, Tolman and Szalacha placed at the center of their research a feminist concern to make women's voices central while blending in quantitative data that empirically "enabled us to answer each emerging question, the result has been an eclectic merging of both approaches to feminist methodology, producing a kind of feminist eclecticism that has at its heart the perspectives and experiences of these young women" (p. 11).

For example, Tolman and Szalacha (1999) engaged first with intensive interviews and, through their narrative analysis, found four voices involved in girls' experiences of sexual desire: "A voice of the self, an erotic voice, a voice of the body, and a voice of response to one's own desire" (p. 14). These qualitative narratives were then restructured and organized to compare urban with suburban contexts. The qualitative distinctions found between these two groups of girls, particularly in the narratives that speak about vulnerability, led to the researchers' next phase of research. In this part of the research process, the narratives were quantified. Specifically, the researchers sought to examine "how pleasure and vulnerability were associated differently for these two groups of girls . . . [and] . . . whether there was an interactive effect of sexual abuse or violence" (p. 17). Moving from intensive interviewing with 30 girls, they reestablished their unit of analysis into the number of narratives found within their data, equaling 128. These narratives were coded for themes of vulnerability and pleasure such that the quantitative associations could be explored. Such an integrative approach fits well with a dialectical epistemological vision of how methods can be mixed.[11] However, we must remember that not all feminist researchers are comfortable with the idea of mixing research methods. This is partly because they want to avoid the use of a quantitative research paradigm. Some feel that this paradigm neglects the concerns and interests of those who are most oppressed within the social system—women and other oppressed groups. Others argue that to mix methods means to cross basic epistemological assumptions regarding the very nature of the social reality—what can be known and by whom. It is to these and other issues that we now turn our attention. In our Behind-the-Scenes interview excerpt, Janice Morse, a leading qualitative researcher, talks with Mexican sociologist César Cisneros-Puebla (Cisneros-Puebla, 2004). Janice Morse is the founder of the International Institute for Qualitative Methodology at the University of Alberta, Canada. In this excerpt, Morse provides important insights into the problems and prospects of mixing methods.

Behind-the-Scenes With César Cisneros-Puebla and Janet Morse

Mixed Methods and "Theoretical Drive"

CISNEROS-PUEBLA: In what ways do you see multimethods evolving? How will qualitative researchers deal with such diversity?

MORSE: I think it is going to get into a terrible mess, but it will sort itself out in the end.

CISNEROS-PUEBLA: What kind of "terrible mess" are you talking about?

MORSE: I think people lack analytic skills to handle both qualitative and quantitative data. I don't think there has been enough work done on theory development, I think that not enough people even want to do theoretical development and are content with their descriptions. I think the pressure to do mixed methods, to get funding, overwhelms or overrides the goals of qualitative inquiry. I think the funding agencies say they fund qualitative inquiry, meaning that they really do fund mixed methods. This still places qualitative inquiry in an inferior position.

CISNEROS-PUEBLA: What are the empirical implications of using mixed methods? I mean, facing the complexity of the actual world, every one of us for sure will be more in need of mixed and multiple methods.

MORSE: I do not think we all have to give into these pressures. I feel I use multimethods if required in the design, not simply to please funding agencies.

CISNEROS-PUEBLA: Because we need this kind of multimethod research to produce knowledge?

(Continued)

(Continued)

MORSE: Nonsense. Fiddlesticks. Basic knowledge also comes from doing qualitative research alone.

CISNEROS-PUEBLA: But qualitative research needs multimethods?

MORSE: No, it does not need multimethods; the funding agencies need multimethods and some questions need multimethods.

CISNEROS-PUEBLA: Using multimethods is not a question for qualitative research—multimethods is in your view an answer for the agencies?

MORSE: No. You are asking me loaded questions. I did not say either of those two things! I think the biggest advances can come from qualitatively derived knowledge. Some problems lend themselves to some mixed-method designs. Why would funding agencies still fund qualitative research if it could not stand alone?

CISNEROS-PUEBLA: What is your view about the contemporary discussion on multimethods?

MORSE: I do not think that those who write about multiple methods understand the concept of *theoretical drive;* I think the literature lacks the specific instructions for how, when, where, and why one should transpose qualitative data to numeric data, and it lacks good guidelines for synthesizing the findings.

SOURCE: Reprinted with permission of *Forum: Qualitative Social Research.*

METHODS: TO MIX OR NOT TO MIX?
WHAT ARE THE ISSUES?

The next section of this chapter will explore the way epistemological paradigms engage and employ mixed methods. There are epistemological perspectives that are closed off to mixed-methods approaches, whereas others fully embrace it as an option. Paradigmatic choices made by researchers on the path to mixing their methods will be examined in this section. The third section of this chapter will explore the reasons why feminist researchers might mix methods. The final section of this chapter will look at how feminists deal with the sometimes-messy outcomes of mixed-methods research. Mixed methods is a burgeoning field of research methods, and past decades have witnessed the innovative and emergent ways mixed methods are being discussed, developed, and employed. In the hands of feminists, these methods take on different intentions and different questions. They are used in the service of questions that seek empowerment, or an expansion of possibility, for women. They seek answers to questions that matter to women, especially those exploring boundaries between race, class, and gender. Furthermore, looking at mixed methods from a feminist perspective can help us examine the links between theory and method where epistemology, methodology, and method are deeply intertwined in efforts to engage such issues. Exploration of these linkages draws our conversation into the realm of epistemological challenges to the use of mixed methods.

EPISTEMOLOGICAL CHALLENGES— PARADIGMATIC APPROACHES TO MIXED METHODS: PURIST, PRAGMATIC, AND DIALECTICAL

A wide range of feminist and nonfeminist research faces the challenge of mixed methods. Should mixed methods be used? When? These questions and others form the base of one argument against the use of mixed methods. Implications arise from epistemological perspectives about whether or not mixed methods *should* be used at all. Feminists hold no singular epistemological perspective. They do not stand on unified ground when asked, "How can we know the world around us?" Feminists cross all epistemological boundaries, and their multitude of voices speak from positivist, postpositivist, critical, constructivist, and poststructural epistemologies (Lincoln & Guba, 2000). Each of these epistemological perspectives, explored within earlier chapters in more detail, holds differing perspectives about the ability of a single researcher to employ mixed methods. The question is now focused on which paradigms are most open to acknowledging, recognizing, and employing mixed methods. Quantitative research methodologies tend to be predicated on a positivist or postpositivist paradigm where research is hypothesis driven and deductive. Empirical research in the positivist and postpositivist paradigm seeks objective knowledge about the world around us. Qualitative research is often predicated on a critical, interpretive, constructionist, or poststructuralist paradigm where research is inductive and grounded in the experiences and meanings individuals attribute to the world around them.[12] It must, however, be recognized that some qualitative researchers are positivist or postpositivist in their epistemological approach. The two poles of epistemology are often artificially positioned in opposition to one another; this positioning will be further explored in the next section of this chapter. Mixing methods requires reaching across what has been traditionally a paradigmatic chasm to engage two types of methods. Issues such as listening to women's voices, exploring and empowering their experiences, and examining the connections between power and knowledge have all led to a sound and powerful critique of the positivist paradigm of science. Feminist social scientists have been at the forefront of these critiques, and there are many efforts to develop new, critical epistemological perspectives, including those explored in the prior chapters. The varied and dynamic ways in which feminists engage their epistemological perspectives and the ways in which their politics have interacted with their methodological choices illuminate many of the paradigmatic challenges that are being grappled with by many mixed-methods researchers.

Paradigmatic Approach: The Purist

Intersecting each paradigmatic perspective about the nature of knowledge and the ways in which we can know the world leads to an important question: *Does our epistemological lens allow for mixing methods?* Greene and Caracelli (1997) summarize the three main epistemological approaches to applying and using mixed methods. The first approach outlined is the "purist" approach.

> Proponents of the *purist* stance argue that different inquiry frameworks or paradigms embody fundamentally different and incompatible assumptions about human nature, the world, the nature of knowledge claims, and what it is possible to know and, moreover, that these assumptions form an interconnected whole that cannot be meaningfully divided. Hence, it is neither possible nor sensible to mix different inquiry paradigms within a single study or project. (p. 8)

The purists are perhaps the most powerful figures to have built the epistemological and methodological chasm between qualitative and quantitative methods. The purists argue that we are either positivists employing quantitative methods *or* we are critical constructionists employing qualitative methodologies. In their opinion, there is no boundary that would allow for mixed methods use while simultaneously maintaining an honest and reflexive stance on the question of epistemology.

A purist approach to our example on girls' sexuality would require researchers to choose either qualitative or quantitative methodologies. This epistemological perspective would examine the research question from either a positivist stance that would employ quantifiable and objectivist standards of measure that are generalizable across a particular population or from a critical perspective that would see girls' sexuality as only captured by qualitative research methods. There is no "in between," no mixing, from this perspective. The purists are entirely skeptical of attempts to cross the divide between the two methodologies and see mixed methods as incompatible with a strongly formulated sense of epistemological perspective. For the purist, a researcher would be avoiding questioning the nature of knowledge claims and shunning any question of how humans can come to know the world around them. Purists must choose one side of the divide or the other and approach their work accordingly from their chosen side. They cannot use both sides or combinations of approaches to examine a research question.

Epistemological purism responds to the question of young girls' sexuality with a focused either/or approach. A qualitative purist would examine the question, grounded in a vision of a critical, constructionist, or interpretive lens, open to all data and meaning that a qualitative interview or focus group would allow. This purist would argue that survey research that deductively tests hypotheses about girls' sexuality could never fully capture the complex realities that are meaningful and experiential. A qualitative purist who is also a feminist might argue that survey research would inherently disempower young girls by silencing them and flattening their experiences into two-dimensional, quantifiable answers. On the other hand, a quantitative purist would likely argue that qualitative research methods require a view of girls' sexuality that neither is good science nor helps to build important and objective research standards. For this purist, valid, trustworthy, and objective research that describes generalizable research findings is the most important aspect of knowledge building. For the purist, research needs to be generalizable such that statements can be made about the population as a whole. Sometimes quantitative purism is also related to organizational, institutional, and disciplinary structures that help maintain the consistent, enforced, and encouraged use of quantitative research methods. For example, Tolman and Szalacha (1999) note that within the discipline of research psychology, the standard approach to answering questions is that of a purely quantitative approach. Furthermore, enforcing the quantitative purist's stance is the long tradition of positivism within the social sciences that was examined in earlier chapters. For the purist of either sort, the philosophical differences about the nature of social reality cannot be compromised. To mix methods for some purists is a violation of philosophical and epistemological standards.

In spite of the purist's powerful argument, this stance has been critiqued from both inside and outside feminist circles. Feminists Joey Sprague and Mary K. Zimmerman (2004) notably argue that in fact, "too often the methodological alternatives offered by feminists have been simply a mirror image of positivism" (p. 39). They argue that both positivist and feminist commitments to *either* quantitative *or* qualitative purity serve to rebuild and reenforce longstanding dualisms. Sprague and Zimmerman continue and suggest,

> Both positivistic and common feminist approaches are organized around four dualisms—object/subject, rational/emotional, abstract/concrete, and quantitative/qualitative—but that the two approaches differ in which half of each dualism is emphasized and normatively valued. Positivism claims an objective reality, perceivable independently of subjective experience, and values the rational, abstract, and quantitative. Feminists, in contrast, give priority to actors' own subjective experience and emphasize the emotional aspects of social life grounded in concrete, daily experiences. For them, data must be qualitative in order to reveal these aspects. (p. 39)

Their concern over the dualistic nature that is inherent to the purist's approach to these epistemological questions brings us to the first approach that finds space to mix their methods, namely that of the pragmatists. The pragmatists avoid the binary ranking of one method over another; instead, they seek methods that are most appropriate for the research question at hand.

Paradigmatic Approach: The Pragmatic

The second grouping of approaches, the *pragmatic* position,

> maintains that there are philosophical differences between various paradigms of inquiry. But, for the pragmatist, these philosophical assumptions are logically independent and therefore can be mixed and matched, in conjunction with choices about methods, to achieve the combination most appropriate for a given inquiry problem. (Greene & Caracelli, 1997, p. 8)

In other words, this epistemological perspective to mixing methods requires that there be a fluid approach grounded entirely on the needs of the research design. In some ways, this pragmatic approach depicts a researcher who assesses and accepts the important articulation of an epistemological stance, but when it comes to conducting the research, these philosophical assumptions are separate from what is required to do the work at hand to answer his or her question.

A pragmatist might approach our recurring example and ask, "*What is needed* to answer the questions I hold about girls' sexuality?" To answer this question, a pragmatist does not look to his or her epistemological perspective for guidance but looks instead to the questions of the study and seeks the best method or methods for solving the research question. A pragmatist seeks to engage the subject of inquiry from all possible angles of vision while using all her available tools to fully answer the question. A pragmatist approach to mixed methods would fit well with the varied, complex tools used by feminist empiricists when the goals of good research are flush with objectivist standards of procedure that require the research design be driven by the best way of addressing a hypothesis.

How would pragmatists approach the research questions in our example of girls' sexuality? Perhaps the researchers' focus is to compare two types of sex education programs in a particular school district. To carefully and thoroughly examine the content of the sex education curriculum, these researchers might use qualitative analyses, such as participant observation, interviewing, and detailed case studies. Within this side of the research design, their practical intention is to catalog, describe, and explore the qualitative differences between the two programs. The second aspect of their research design might include a quantitative survey that assesses the students' behavioral changes with regard to sexual experience and knowledge gained from within each of the two programs. These researchers might then choose to integrate their mixed methods in a final analytical text that makes correlations between the content and the outcome of the educational programs on girls' sexuality. If our hypothetical researchers are focused on how well certain types of sex education programming are working and what their content and outcomes are, they might employ the pragmatic approach to mixing their methods to obtain the most comprehensive answer. Lackey and Moberg's (1998) study (previously mentioned as an example of qual followed by QUANT) fits well with the pragmatic epistemological stance. Their research joins in a larger body of work in looking at ways of preventing risky sexual behavior among adolescents. They argued that most researchers "limit their inquiries and analyses to antecedent factors such as individual skills, family relationships, and peer pressure" (p. 491). Lackey and Moberg, however, found these factors ineffective in telling the *whole* story about sexual risk taking. Like those using other pragmatic approaches, they simply sought the "best" pathway with which to answer their question, rather than grappling with epistemological chasms that engage other methodological debates. They sought a valid and more complex understanding and measurement of urban American adolescent engagement with intercourse, but the researchers did not limit themselves to the more structural analyses that arise from survey research conducted in the past. They chose instead to incorporate a mixed-methods approach that acknowledges the importance of structural factors of individual, family, and peer constructs, while also drawing in a nuanced understanding of a cultural framework that is accessed through qualitative methods. The aspect distinguishing the pragmatic from other epistemological approaches to mixing methods is that the researchers do not feel the need to create an analysis of their epistemological position. They seek to answer the question at hand most fully and deliberately without, in their view, losing themselves in epistemological debates. In some ways, it is easier for the pragmatists to mix methods, as they are not bound by the epistemological debates that purists and dialectic researchers might engage in—rather, they are concerned with the outcome of their research. However, for some researchers, many benefits can be derived from acknowledging the differences between the methods being mixed. Some researchers argue that there are political and epistemological implications to choosing to mix methods and that mixing methods ought to be difficult and challenging. Some researchers find great strength in the dissonance and harmony they uncover in mixing methods, namely those that subscribe to the dialectical approach.

Paradigmatic Approach: The Dialectical

The third approach outlined by Greene and Caracelli (1997) is the *dialectical* position, which

> argues that differences between philosophical paradigms of logics of justification for social scientific inquiry not only exist but are important. These differences cannot be ignored or reconciled, but rather must be honored in ways that maintain the integrity of the disparate paradigms. Moreover, the differences should be deliberately used both within and across studies toward a dialectical discovery of enhanced understandings, of new and revisioned perspectives and meanings. (p. 8)

Here, the dialectical position creates a spiraling conversation between the epistemological paradigms and the methods themselves. Within these spaces of spirals, researchers tend to interrogate both sides of the research, seeking to articulate and explore the gains and losses of both methods and the outcome of their mixing. The research design builds in moments when the two methods speak to one another, traversing but not breaking down epistemological perspectives that hold qualitative and quantitative methodologies apart from one another. These are border crossings where the tension between the methods and the processes of mixing them becomes apparent, and useful ideas often emerge. The interpretive and constructionist frameworks that inform qualitative research also inform the types of quantitative measures used. The positivist and postpositivist perspectives that build quantitative methodologies aim to draw generalizable content to the qualitative sides of the research.

This dialectical approach best fits the intent and outcome of Tolman and Szalacha's (1999) research endeavor. These researchers built into their research design "three iterations that are organized by three separate and synergistically related research questions, which emerged sequentially in response to the findings generated by pursuing the previous research question" (p. 13). At each stage of their research, and at each shift of research focus, they continued to dialectically spiral their research findings into focus. They built a multilayered picture of girls' sexuality that began in a qualitative framework focusing on the question, "How do girls describe their experiences of sexual desire?"

Like many researchers who stand on the epistemological question of whether or not one can, and how, to mix methods, Tolman and Szalacha (1999) sought the strengths found in both methods. Rather than detaching their research endeavor from the philosophical questions associated with the project, as might be seen among some pragmatists,[13] Tolman and Szalacha directly address the philosophical issues present. They comment,

> Quantitative and qualitative approaches are often understood as separate paradigms of research, with radically differing assumptions, requirements, and procedures that are rooted in completely different epistemologies. One position of the philosophical debate contends that the integration of quantitative and qualitative paradigms is impossible, as they represent irreconcilable worldviews. The opposite position, maintained on both philosophic and pragmatic grounds, is that not only *can* the two paradigms be combined at the hands-on level of research practice, at the sociological level of methodological assumptions, they *should* be combined, because these concerns are

superseded in importance by political goals about how research findings should be used. (Firestone, 1993; Tashakkori & Teddlie, 1998, cited in Tolman & Szalacha, 1999, p. 9)

They are intently focused on building a bridge between qualitative and quantitative methods to access and engage the benefits of both methods, rather than position them in opposition to one another. The epistemological commonalities that Tolman and Szalacha (1999) outline are premised on the fact that "the challenge of grappling with increasingly complex social problems, particularly those that confront activist and applied psychologies like feminist psychology, demands that we investigate further the potential in combining quantitative and qualitative methods" (p. 10). Only with the potential for synergistically and dynamically uniting these two forms of research methods, Tolman and Szalacha argue, can the complexities of our social world come into focus. These researchers set out to *know* something about the world, something that they epistemologically felt could be realized only through the union of these two methodologies and the bridging of these two paradigms.

Questions of whether, how, and when methods should be combined are directly informed by the epistemological perspective. The debate about these questions is alive and well within methodological circles. The boundaries between purist, pragmatist, and dialectical epistemological stances with regards to mixed methods, like most other categories, are not without blurring. In some cases, as Tolman and Szalacha note, there are many researchers who are finding the need to disregard the political and epistemological discussion and simply go forward with mixed methods as deemed appropriate to their research question. However, this is a difficult proposition for many feminist researchers to face, for they believe that the chosen methods have a real, lasting, and powerful impact on the world that they are seeking to engage and understand.

METHODOLOGICAL CONVERSATIONS ACROSS BORDERS: WHY FEMINISTS ARE CHOOSING TO MIX METHODS

Based on its ability to address or avoid the theoretical, political, and epistemological traps built by positivist qualitative science, feminist research has steadily become more synonymous with qualitative research, and many feminist researchers have pushed forward to employ both quantitative and qualitative research methodologies (Brannen, 1992; Devine & Heath, 1999; Maynard & Purvis, 1994). The discussions and debates, equipped with enough force and eloquence to form strong divisions within the feminist community, have made many people reluctant to enforce such dualisms. Compromises, bridges between the two methodologies, and an urgency to attend to the research question at hand have softened the gulf between the methods. Working the borders and working the hyphens (Fine, 1994) illuminate the complexities of methodological choices. Working the hyphen, in the context of mixed methods, builds bridges that increase the expanse of answers that can be accessed when asking what we can look at and how we can understand the realities of our world. Working the hyphens can fit with a feminist agenda that "propose[s] an inclusive feminist methodology based on the premise that social research is both collective and processual" (Sprague & Zimmerman, 2004, p. 39). In the methodological spirit of integrating these dualisms, breaking down the either/or dichotomy might include mixing qualitative and quantitative methods. Such bridges involve widening the scope of meaning that can be accessed within a single research setting. The reasons for, or purposes behind, the choice of using mixed methods are as varied as the researchers and research subjects explored. However, within some of the mixed methods discussed in this chapter, we can look at a number of reasons why a feminist might choose to work the hyphen and mix research methods.[14]

Some feminists might choose mixed methods for the same reasons that nonfeminist researchers choose mixed methods, namely for purposes of: falsification, triangulation, interrogation of measures, casting the net as widely as possible, and disciplinary tradition. In addition to general reasons for mixing methods, feminists tend to add new layers of reason behind the choices made at the outset of their research design. These reasons include a sense of double consciousness, interest in subjugated knowledge and silenced voices, and empowerment of researcher and participant.[15]

Falsification

Exploring the reasons that a researcher might undertake a mixed-methods approach brings us to the goal of seeking to falsify or test a particular hypothesis. An example of this purpose is illuminated by the work of Ladner (1971) as well as Tolman and Szalacha (1999). Both these research designs set out to examine and falsify the prevailing notions that adolescent girls' sexual activity is deviant or abnormal. Tolman and Szalacha also show us that mixed methods can build bridges between macro and micro sets of theories about sexuality. Tolman and Szalacha develop new micromeasures grounded in qualitative data about young girls' voices of the body and desire. They then show how these micromeasures might be united with new ways of understanding and examining macrostructures that shape theories about deviance and sexuality.

Triangulation

Triangulation is another reason why researchers might seek to undertake mixed methods. Triangulation, in general, refers to the use of two methods to get at a singular data set that answers a particular question. Although the concept of triangulation takes on various meanings for different researchers, we can think through the reasons why triangulation might be important to a feminist researcher in this discussion.[16] For a pragmatist, triangulation is a powerful justification for using mixed methods. A pragmatist would be most concerned with showing the most thorough picture; Lackey and Moberg (1998) illustrated this concern as they tried to gather the most complete data set surrounding the question of girls' sexuality as is possible. For feminists,

> the use of multiple methods reflects the multifaceted identity of many feminist researchers. We are multifaceted because we are working during a feminist renaissance that transcends disciplinary boundaries and challenges many of our capacities at once. Our multifacetedness makes single-method research seem flat and inadequate to explore and express the complexities of women's lives. (Reinharz, 1992, p. 202)

Reinharz's perspective on reasons for mixing methods reflects the desire of many feminists to create the most multifaceted and complex layering of data analysis possible.

Interrogating Research Measures

Feminist and nonfeminist researchers often use mixed methods to interrogate and improve their data-gathering measures. Some researchers develop survey questions *after* they have undertaken intensive qualitative data gathering. They use the issues, language, and terms that arise from qualitative data to construct their survey questions. Lackey and Moberg (1998) provide us with an example where methods are mixed "to explore participant views with the intent of using these views to develop and test an instrument with a sample from a population" (Creswell, 2003, p. 100). Lackey and Moberg (1998) began their research with qualitative focus groups, which consequently led them to add survey questions that measured and attended to issues mentioned in those groups. Most of the additions they made to their survey deal with "exposure to the media and popular culture" (p. 495). These researchers discovered an overwhelming theme that arose out of their focus groups, namely that of the pervasiveness of messages *to have sex* found in media and popular culture; this theme led them to pragmatically add and alter their survey research measures.[17]

Casting a Wide Net

Another reason for mixing methods that is often related to triangulation is described by Shulamit Reinharz (1992), who describes feminist researchers who engage both quantitative and qualitative methods

> so as to cast their net as widely as possible in the search for understanding critical issues in women's lives. The multimethod approach increased the likelihood that these researchers will understand what they are studying, and what they will be able to persuade others of the veracity of their findings. Multiple methods work to enhance understanding, both by adding layers of information and by using one type of data to validate or refine another. (p. 201)

Casting our nets as widely as possible is one particularly powerful and pragmatic reason for using mixed methods. The intention of leaving all doors open frees the researcher to choose any method that might improve the situation for women or answer important questions is a powerful one. The ability of feminists to test and improve on chosen methods by engaging with methods from a different methodology is also an important argument for mixing methods.

Disciplinary Frameworks

Certain aspects of methodological perspective are also informed simply by the disciplinary framework that a particular feminist researcher is working within. Shulamit Reinharz (1992) states that "feminism supplies the perspective and the disciplines supply the method. The feminist researcher exists at their intersection" (p. 243). For Tolman and Szalacha (1999), psychology as a discipline favors and encourages quantitative research methodologies. For other researchers, whose disciplines are more accepting of inductive and qualitative research strategies, qualitative research methods might provide the initial base for a mixed-methods research design.

Double-Consciousness

When it comes to understanding why feminists would want to mix methods, we might also briefly posit that feminist research can be a particularly fruitful space in which mixed methods might be explored. Feminist researchers have long been discussing women's multiple ways of knowing and the multiple sites of vision on which women come to know the world at large. Reasons to break down and avoid the false dichotomy between qualitative and quantitative methods include feminist disciplinary goals that aim to avoid hierarchies and unearned privileging of quantitative methodologies.[18] Mixed methods might afford feminists a new space in which these multiple ways of knowing are articulated and employed. Barbara DuBois (1983) discusses the general intent of feminist scholarship as a passionate one, which aims "to see what is *there;* not what we've been taught is there, not even what we might wish to find, but what is. We literally *cannot see women* through traditional science and theory" (pp. 109–110). She notes that feminist scholarship is a

> communal, not individual task where women develop a "double-consciousness" where women are in and of our society but in important ways also not "of" it. . . . We are aware, however inchoately, of the reality of our own perceptions and experience; we are aware that this reality has often been not only unnamed but unnamable; we understand that our invisibility and silence hold the germs of both madness and power, of both dissolution and creation. (pp. 111–112)

Subjugated Knowledges and Silenced Voices

Flowing from Barbara DuBois's ideas of double-consciousness, we can think about how mixed methods can access subjugated knowledges and silenced voices. Like Ladner, and Tolman and Szalacha, DuBois is touching on the feminist goals of seeking to name the unnamable and to make visible that which has traditionally been invisible when rendered by traditional modes of knowledge production. It is possible that using women's "double consciousness" in an effort to expand

and employ mixed methods may provide innovative ways with which knowledge can be created. To further illuminate what dimensions, concerns, and contexts feminist researchers add to the discussion of mixed methods, we will return to our example of mixed-methods research regarding adolescent girls' sexuality and sexual activities. A nonfeminist researcher's mixed-methods approach might be less engaged with the epistemological and methodological assumptions that are required by using quantitative research as well as qualitative research. A feminist researcher is likely, due to his or her concerns about women's voices and experiences, to be initiating his or her research from a qualitative perspective. From this stance, the researcher might pragmatically build quantitative measures into the research design or dialectically integrate the two sides of his or her research methodologies.

Tolman and Szalacha's (1999) research first sought out the voices of the girls in their study through intensive interviews. Their narratives were then recontextualized quantitatively to compare urban with suburban settings. The narratives were quantified further to compare girls' sexuality on several dimensions of pleasure and vulnerability and the association of this with sexual abuse or violence. Such an integrative approach fits well with a dialectical epistemological vision of how methods can be mixed.[19]

Empowerment

In many ways, feminist research, engaging in qualitative, quantitative, or mixed methods, always grounds itself in seeking the betterment of humanity in general and women in particular. Feminist researchers bring to mixed methods a central focus of women's issues that draws on their political focuses to illuminate institutions and social ills that affect women's lives. Feminist researchers of all types are particularly *present* in their research endeavor. They position themselves, through political perspective within the research process, engaging and interacting with their epistemological perspective, the methodologies employed, and the methods at hand. A sense of reoccurring and intensive reflection on the methods that they choose is required of these researchers. Many feminists are specifically concerned about the role their methods might have in altering and engaging power in the research process. They ask, "Are mixed methods useful in accomplishing my research goals, and are they useful to me?" They seek methods that empower their respondents and participants as well as their research. Feminist researchers are bridging the divide because it is worth being traversed. A feminist perspective allows the researcher to be synergistically engaged with the three moments of research, such that they are never divorced from one another as might be seen more frequently in nonfeminist research.[20] Mixed methods promote insight into methodology by drawing from both ends of the continuum. They allow feminist researchers to fulfill many goals of research, including upending biases, working for social change, and exposing women's voices.

For example, feminist researchers are likely to interrogate their quantitative survey research measures and examine the ways in which their questions might serve to silence women and disempower them. Feminist researchers would likely regard the survey question "Have you ever had sexual intercourse?" as problematic. Attuned to issues of power and essentialism, they would likely be concerned that a girl who does not identify as heterosexual might be sexually active and not be accurately or appropriately measured by such a survey question. A feminist researcher might rephrase the survey questionnaire to ask specific questions about sexual activity that account for a broad array of sexual engagement between individuals. His or her research questionnaire would likely not begin or end in terms of heterosexual intercourse.

Sensitivity to girls' issues of empowerment, self-esteem, and confidentiality would be present at all stages of the crafting of the research measures. For example, Tolman and Szalacha (1999) discuss the reasons why they did *not* collect information on socioeconomic status. They worry that asking questions about class, money, and household status might lead to a silencing of information about other sensitive topics, such as sexual desire and sexual violence. They state that because Tolman was "asking girls to speak about something that is essentially unspeakable, she made careful choices about what she did and did not ask so as to enhance the development of trust" (p. 12). They found that, in many cases, socioeconomic status came out in the focus group discussions but that, in fact, urban and suburban locations became better indicators of difference regarding sexual desire. Instead of seeking out socioeconomic information and ending their analysis there, the voices of urban and suburban differences spoke powerfully from their data:

> The magnitude of difference we noted qualitatively between urban and suburban girls' experiences of desire. We are also able to highlight that an interplay between these girls' social locations and personal histories of sexual violation figures significantly in how they experience and give meaning to their own desire, specifically pinpointing how they are limited and supported in the possibility of associating their own sexual desire with pleasure. (p. 21)

On the other hand, a nonfeminist quantitative research methodology using survey research methods might include a question about economic status. A non-feminist researcher would likely not interrogate the data resulting from this question. There would be little concern for the ways in which a respondent might approach this question and its impact on trust. Openness in the context of the interview, trust, and emotional consideration for the feelings of the respondents was important to Tolman and Szalacha, as it is to many feminist researchers.

They *thought through* their methodology and the employment of their methods before engaging with their respondents. They wanted their respondents to be as comfortable as possible within the research setting, so as to gain as much insight into their experiences and feelings as possible. They thought through their epistemological and political concerns that might further silence the voices of the girls if they were to ask such probing questions on their survey. The subject matter of sexuality and sexual activity was approached with sensitivity and careful clarity that aimed to increase the avenues through which these girls could be empowered and reduce the avenues by which the research tools and researchers could silence them.

While feminists flow across all epistemological boundaries, there are particular nuances and concerns that go into shaping feminist methodologies. Attention to women's voices, difference between and within groups of women, women's contextual and concrete experiences, and researcher positionality often are part of feminists' discussions of methodology, whether they are engaging in qualitative, quantitative, or mixed methods. These concerns make feminist uses of mixed methods distinct from nonfeminist approaches. The mixed-methods approach fits many of the tenets of feminist research, particularly as a way of opening up many choices to women researchers. Furthermore, mixed-methods research designs lend themselves to many goals that, when wisely chosen, serve to empower feminist research.

MIXING THE METHOD: FEMINISTS LIVING IN THE MESSINESS OF MIXED-METHODS RESULTS

For feminist researchers, the method used is all about choices. When making these choices, feminists are seeking tools that empower them to do their work. They are examining the impact that their research can have in epistemologically dynamic ways. What happens when methods are mixed? Methods of data collection are without politics, power, or paradigmatic focus in their own right. Methods give researchers access to the world around them, allowing them to engage, listen, and collect information. It is in the hands of a particular researcher that methods hold the prospect of silencing or empowering the world at large. Feminist researchers are particularly attuned to the actions and power that their methods hold when put out into the world. How methods are actually mixed and how a researcher deals with the results are avenues through which both epistemological perspectives and methodological choices come into play. These methods are tools in the hands of feminists that are in the service of social justice and social change. Yet these multifaceted and complex layers are not without their perils. Often the complex layers found in mixed-methods research are inconsistent with one another.

MIXING INCONSISTENCIES: WHAT DILEMMAS AND DISAGREEABLE RESULTS TELL US

The reasons behind mixing methods do not always lead to consistent and uncontroversial results, as seen in Tolman and Szalacha's example. Feminists have been particularly willing and able to discuss the complexities of mixing methods. Feminist researchers' awareness and reflexivity have often led to examination of the inconsistencies and dilemmas found within mixed-methods research. Nonfeminist researchers who conducted mixed-methods research and found inconsistent results might be inclined to throw out the qualitative research findings. Feminist researchers push on the boundaries of right and wrong and analyze what these inconsistencies mean.

Integrating qualitative and quantitative methods through one overarching research question can sometimes lead to messy results. Feminist researchers are well suited to residing in the multiple realities found within one research design. Sprague and Zimmerman (2004) comment about feminist researchers, in efforts to integrate qualitative and quantitative research methods, "when we encounter apparently different findings from each method, we need not immediately assume that one should be refuted and the other accepted" (p. 53).[21] An example of researchers who illuminate both the consistencies and inconsistencies in their research findings is provided by Manfredi et al. (1997), whose survey research and focus group interviews were conducted with African American women to understand motivations to quit or continue smoking. The research examined the different contextual meanings women applied to their experiences as smokers. They found contradictory results between the quantitative and qualitative research findings. They state, "Much of the inconsistency is understandable only in the situational contexts in which smoking occurs and which did not emerge from the survey data. Without this contextual reference, the survey responses did not accurately reflect the respondents' dependence on smoking for managing endemic stress in their lives" (p. 796). The qualitative descriptions of the context in which women are choosing to smoke illuminated aspects that typically were hidden and sometimes subjugated from the view of survey data collection. The contexts described are resonant to everyday experiences, arenas that have typically been silenced by nonfeminist research methods. The everyday experiences of routine, household chores and child care duties all created a context of stress that encircled the space in which women were choosing to smoke. These everyday experiences were not part of the survey research questions and were completely obscured from the data collection procedures. "Smoking in this context is a concrete response to reality, grounded in events and behavior, and not necessarily mediated by the cognitive processes postulated by the theoretical models" (p. 796). The cognitive processes and theoretical models are well addressed, however, by the quantitative research methods. The union of these two research methods, in spite of sometimes-contradictory findings, illuminates some of the important and dynamic reasons for engaging with mixed methods. Manfredi et al. are clear on their distinctions between the types of data collection and analysis that they chose to use.

Survey collection is not designed to assess topic salience; it presumes it. Contextual meaning does not emerge in the survey but must be built into the design of the questionnaire. Survey questions are structured and designed to assess generality and covariation. In turn, the focus group is qualitative and is more useful for identifying perspectives than for assessing their generalizability. Focus groups measure the subjective viewpoint of the participants in a context that the actor creates; this, in turn, may exaggerate or overstate the importance of certain themes because of their relevance to the ongoing group context (Manfredi et al., 1997, p. 798).

Manfredi et al. do not approach their research with an intention to critique a paradigm or methodology. They approach the work from what seems to be a pragmatic approach and, in part, a dialectical position that aims to provide the best research and build the most thorough knowledge possible. They see the integration of qualitative and quantitative research to be beneficial, not just in their disciplinary framework but also in the health and public policy fields that can benefit from these multilayered findings.

Another example of inconsistent findings among qualitative and quantitative methodologies is located within women's ways of *naming* their experiences that are often silenced or obscured in survey research. Westmarland (2001) performed a survey and interviewed female taxi drivers about sexual harassment and violence on the job. She found that women taxi drivers "rarely *named* their experiences as 'violent' in the survey, but follow-up unstructured interviews revealed that women frequently invalidated and normalized their experiences of violence." Westmarland's survey research did not measure what she set out to examine because women were not willing or able to categorize their experiences as violent unless they included physical attack. Other forms of violence that Westmarland was seeking to examine were not identified *as* violence by the women in their survey responses. Westmarland was challenged by the complex inconsistencies existing in her research findings. She questions, "Whose definition would I be using? If I used my definition of violence am I implying that my definition of violence is more accurate (more 'true'?) that the taxi drivers' own definitions? Would I then be labeling their experiences for them?" Westmarland further questions herself as a researcher and her survey method through the findings of her intensive interviews.[22] Again, her feminist approach leads her to be a *thoughtfully present* participant in her analysis. Her approach is one based on quantitative research design that integrates and puts into conversation a small intensive interviewing procedure to increase the validity of her findings and the ability of her survey to measure what she seeks to measure.

Similarly, Tolman and Szalacha (1999) try to bring voice and experience into a quantifiable and statistical research question.

> Acknowledging the possibility of female adolescent sexual agency, desire, pleasure, and fantasies through the act of asking about these realms of experience renders this approach a feminist research method. This method departs from a survey design by creating an opportunity for girls to put into words and to name their experience in and questions about a realm of their lives that remains unspoken in the larger culture. (p. 13)

When differences are found amongst and between methodological findings, the presence of a feminist perspective often helps to remedy, reinterpret, and coalesce the inconsistencies and voices of the data. Researchers in every field make choices about which research findings are most important, most powerful, and most interesting. But for a feminist, the answers to these questions when discrepancies occur require that their feminist lens be a part of the untangling process.

CONCLUSION[23]

Feminist researchers are empowering themselves within qualitative and quantitative fields of data collection by exploring questions in inventive ways. A subject area or question that deals with adolescent girls' sexuality, for example, is so multifaceted, multidimensional, and complex that just to describe a small fraction of it might require both an interdisciplinary and mixed-methods approach. Mixed-methods designs, then, can enable the researcher to tackle complex issues that occur at multiple levels—the individual as well as the societal.

In addition, mixed methods can also enhance the validity of both qualitative and quantitative research projects. By using both methods, the researcher brings synergy to his or her research project (e.g., by enhancing validity through triangulation), while compensating for the deficits of the other. There is the idea that by using mixed methods "the whole is greater than the sum of its parts." There are caveats to consider, however, when using mixed-methods designs that span from the conceptual to the practical. Mixed methods obscure the divide between research paradigms, and it is unclear how much researchers should be concerned about this. As we have observed, "pragmatists" advocate for whatever methods work, with little regard for issues of epistemology and methodology. "Purists," on the other hand, see crossing the divide between qualitative and quantitative as disturbing the very foundations of scientific thought. Others take positions along a continuum between these two opposite positions on knowledge building.

Mixed methods are not a cure-all, magic potion that one adds to a research study to ensure a successful project. Mixed methods are a set of tools for getting at knowledge building. *More is not necessarily better.* In fact, in the Behind-the-Scenes piece featuring Janice Morse, a leading qualitative researcher, Morse notes that mixing methods is no substitute for the hard work of conceptual thinking and data analysis.

There are also economic constraints to consider because the costs of carrying out a mixed-methods project and the training required to do so may raise the overall budget of your research project. There are also issues of how well versed any given researcher can be in both methods. Can more harm than good be done in conducting a mixed-methods project, when researchers are not adequately trained in both methods? In addition, Janice Morse raises issues stemming from the expectations of funding agencies that may place pressures on researchers to carry out a mixed-methods design whether or not the research problem calls for it.

What Morse is emphatic about is that we as researchers do not forget the contribution that qualitative methods in their *pure* form make to our understanding of the nature of social reality.

Mixing methods may be risky business—feminist researchers are risking the effort, risking the difficult epistemological gaps, and risking the possibility of inconsistent results in an effort to break out of the dichotomy of qualitative and quantitative research methods. They are risking the possibility that their work will be subordinated by feminist purists who argue for qualitative methods. They are risking the possibility that the epistemological concerns remain that might preclude any feminist from engaging in a dialectical epistemological approach that may include violations of good research from the perspective of the purists. They risk the possibility that inconsistent findings will lead to pressure to take the quantitative findings over the qualitative. And yet these risks are sometimes outweighed by the emotional, creative, and exhilarating border work that can be achieved.

NOTES

1. Leonore Tiefer (2000) notes that "questionnaire, survey, and experimental studies, for example, which make up the bulk of psychological sex research can be seen as traditions that developed as psychologists differentiated themselves from philosophers around the turn of the century in Europe, England, and the United States" (pp. 84–85).

2. Quantitative survey research gathers data that can be reduced to numerical values. Quantitative researchers then use these data to mathematically and statistically analyze patterns and relationships among the data. Research psychology has a long tradition of use and development of quantitative research methods, although this is not to

the exclusion of qualitative methods. For a general overview, see Glynis M. Breakwell, Sean Hammond, and Chris Fife-Schaw (2000).

3. When speaking in terms of *methodology,* we are referring to a set of ideas and practices that help inform how researchers go about articulating their research questions and decide which tools, or methods, to use.

4. By *epistemology,* we refer to the set of theories that inform how a researcher thinks about the nature of knowledge and truth.

5. These categories of "good" and "bad" cause concern for feminist researchers in two ways. First, from an ethical, epistemological, and political perspective, feminist researchers are particularly concerned with the ways that girls are represented in research and knowledge building procedures, as described throughout earlier chapters. The reduction of girls' and women's actions and behaviors into uncompromisingly dichotomous "good" and "bad" categories neglect the context of girls' and women's experiences. Second, "good" and "bad" compose what are known as nominal variables. In other words, these are the sorts of quantitative variable that represent a categorical judgment but do not represent anything in a quantitative or numerical way. Statistically, good and bad cannot represent numerical values in the same way that height or years of education can in a quantitative analysis.

6. Similarly on this topic, Reid and Bing (2000) remark that in psychological research contexts as well as in popular culture, "the classic archetypes represent women in terms of both biological and psychological characteristics. They are either good or evil. The good woman will be represented biologically as virginal (i.e., pure, innocent, and naive) and psychologically as the self-effacing, self-denying earth mother. The evil woman is seen as a whore; she is scheming, ambitious, and a clever seductress" (p. 144). They move on to comment that these assumptions and stereotypes are particularly imbued with race and class stereotypes.

7. Welsh et al. (2000) label this as a "problem-oriented approach" where "popular notions of adolescent pregnancy, and therefore sexuality, as an epidemic, sweeping the country, and endangering future generations, have sparked an avalanche of studies and programs designed to illuminate and eradicate the 'problem'" (p. 112). They further note that in fact, this "problem" oriented approach to examining adolescent sexuality actually departs from psychological theories about development. Developmental theorists "have consistently defined sexuality as a fundamental aspect of personal identity, the formation of which is posited to be one of the most important developmental tasks of adolescence" (p. 112).

8. For example, Lackey and Moberg (1998) sought to look at adolescent sexual meanings and practices that are "embedded in cultural practices" (p. 491). They conducted 13 focus groups and a cross-sectional survey of 593 youth and 95 of their parents to look at the ways in which sexual activity is glamorized in American popular culture. Lackey and Moberg's research argued that "individual, family, peer, and structural constructs are important influences on adolescent sexuality, but would be better addressed in an integrated cultural model" (pp. 491–492). Lackey and Moberg's

research concludes with suggestions and recommendations for youth social and educational programs, as well as community groups for addressing risky sexual activity among young people. They argue that their mixed-methods approach to their research question better equipped them to make such statements and recommendations. This research will be addressed later on in this chapter.

9. Barbara J. Risman, Joey Sprague, and Judy Howard (1993) comment,

> The question must determine the methodology and that no one method is a priori more feminist than another. Quantitative feminists are not necessarily too elitist, careerist, or oppressed to use more radical techniques. These techniques may simply be inappropriate to the question being asked. Some feminist questions demand quantitative answers. (p. 608)

10. Tolman and Szalacha (1999) note that the field of psychology has addressed female sexual *behavior* (e.g., DeLameter & MacCorquodale, 1979; Lees, 1986; Levinson, 1986; Scott-Jones & Turner, 1988) and a history of theorizing sexuality development (e.g., Benjamin, 1988; Freud, 1905; Jordan, 1987), but they note that "there have been no studies that include the question of girls' sexual desire" (p. 8).

11. This is articulated well by Creswell (2003), "to better understand a research problem by converging (or triangulating) both broad numeric trends from quantitative research and the detail of qualitative research" (p. 100).

12. For a useful discussion of knowledge claims, research approach, and various strategies of inquiry, see John W. Creswell (2003, chap. 1).

13. By detachment, I am referring to the subordinate position that epistemological questions take when a pragmatic approach is taken by researchers. Rather than worrying about the political and epistemological implications of choices of method, pragmatists detach these questions from the work at hand. Dialectical positions tend to attach their research question with their method, always cycling back through issues of epistemology, methodology, and method.

14. We must note that the epistemological stance of the researcher is very likely to shape the reasons behind his or her choice of using mixed methods.

15. Feminist researchers who choose to mix their methods ask a wide range of questions about our social realities. They seek ways of accessing subjugated knowledge across race, class, and gender divides, and their questions often aim for social change. We also must note that mixed-methods research that is dedicated to creating social change often seeks institutional funding. Some feminist researchers are employing mixed methods in an effort to traverse the boundaries that have often left women-centered qualitative research unfunded and unsupported (Spalter-Roth & Hartman, 1999).

16. Triangulation can refer to methodological triangulation whereby multiple methods are used to study a single research question. Triangulation can also refer to data triangulation whereby multiple data sets are used to answer a particular question. Integrating multiple theories into a single research design might require that a researcher posit multiple explanations and multitheoretical perspectives that grapple

with a single question. Finally, triangulation can also refer to theory triangulation, whereby multiple perspectives are used or tested in a single set of data (Janesick, 2000, p. 391). For a nuanced discussion of the debates and implications of triangulation on social science research, see Udo Kelle (2001).

17. Creswell (2003) also identifies the reverse purpose for engaging in mixed methods, namely that of obtaining "statistical, quantitative results from a sample and then follow up with a few individuals to probe or explore those results in more depth" (p. 100).

18. Mixed methods might begin to serve as spaces where multidisciplinary and interdisciplinary research can be undertaken, building further bridges and further conversations amongst feminist researchers who otherwise might not collaborate.

19. This is articulated well by Creswell (2003) "to better understand a research problem by converging (or triangulating) both broad numeric trends from quantitative research and the detail of qualitative research" (p. 100).

20. John H. McKendrick (1999) describes multimethod research approaches to population geography, drawing in a perspective and a question to our understanding of mixed methods described in this chapter. He provides us with a nuance that, for the purpose of this chapter, must be relegated to our footnotes. He states,

> It could be argued that to use more than one method in a single research project is to pursue multimethod research. However, it could be argued that while such projects may involve more than one method, this is not sufficient to warrant categorization as multimethod. Tactical deployment follows the practice but not the principles or spirit, of multimethod research; the expansive model of research may be more appropriately conceived as a series of discrete projects of different methods, rather than a coherent multimethod agenda; and the pragmatic response, whilst drawing from different methods, is multimethod by chance, rather than by design. It is argued here that tactical deployment and the pragmatic response are examples of multimethod research as they involve situations *where one method is applied with reference to another to address a research agenda.* (p. 42)

Similarly, research that studies women's lives may not necessarily be feminist in its purpose, spirit, or design; multimethods or mixed methods may technically mix methods, but may not be mixed methods in their spirit or design. McKendrick's article does delve deeply into some of the more nuanced epistemological and methodological approaches to multimethods or mixed methods. See particularly his table regarding how epistemology informs methodological strategy.

21. Sprague and Zimmerman (2004) mark out spaces where feminists can grapple with the inconsistencies. They argue that we can entertain the possibility that, given that each involves selection and interpretation, "the outcomes are each 'partial truths,' which need to be woven together for a more complete representation" (pp. 53–54).

22. Although Westmarland does not discuss any subsequent considerations she might make in the future research endeavors, we might expect her to undertake a revision of her questionnaire. Improvement of survey measures is one reason or outcome of mixing methods as described above. Seemingly she might have used her qualitative data to improve on the measures she is using in her survey questionnaire to better measure and speak about violence with her respondents.

23. Parts of this conclusion are adapted from Hesse-Biber and Leavy (2006).

REFERENCES

Benjamin, Jessica. (1988). *The bonds of love.* New York: Pantheon Books.

Brannen, Julia. (1992). *Mixing methods: Qualitative and quantitative research.* Aldershot, UK: Avebury.

Breakwell, Glynis M., Hammond, Sean, & Fife-Schaw, Chris. (2000). *Research methods in psychology* (2nd ed.). London: Sage.

Cisneros-Puebla, César A. (2004). "Let's do more theoretical work . . .": Janice Morse in conversation with César A. Cisneros-Puebla. *Forum Qualitative Sozialforschung/Forum: Qualitative Social Research, 5*(3), Art. 33. Retrieved February 26, 2006, from www.qualitative-research.net/fqs-texte/3-04/04-3-33-e.htm

Creswell, John W. (2003). *Research design: Qualitative, quantitative, and mixed methods approaches.* Thousand Oaks, CA: Sage.

Creswell, John W., Fetters, Michael D., & Ivankova, Nataliya V. (2004). Designing a mixed methods study in primary care. *Annals of Family Medicine, 2*(1), 7–12.

Creswell, John W., Plano Clark, Vicki L., Gutmann, Michelle L., & Hanson, William E. (2003). Advanced mixed methods research designs. In Abras Tashakkori & Charles Teddlie (Eds.), *Handbook of mixed methods in social and behavioral research* (pp. 209–240). Thousand Oaks, CA: Sage.

Cuyvers, Rob, Wets, Geert, Zuallaert, Jos, & Van Gils, Jan. (2003). *Transportation dependence and transportation autonomy of children (aged 10 to 13).* Research Project CP/61. Belgian Federal Science Policy Office (FEDRA). Retrieved February 26, 2006, from www.belspo.be/belspo/fedra/proj.asp?1=en&COD= CP/61

Deem, Rosemary. (2002). Talking to manager-academics: Methodological dilemmas and feminist research strategies. *Sociology, 36,* 835–855.

DeLameter, John, & MacCorquodale, Patricia. (1979). *Premarital sexuality: Attitudes, relationships, behaviors.* Madison: University of Wisconsin Press.

Devine, Fiona, & Heath, Sue J. (1999). *Sociological research methods in context.* London: Macmillan.

DuBois, Barbara. (1983). Passionate scholarship: Notes on values, knowing and method in feminist social science. In Gloria Bowles & Renate D. Klein (Eds.), *Theories of women's studies* (pp. 105–117). London: Routledge & Kegan Paul.

England, Kim. (1993). Suburban pink collar ghettos: The spatial entrapment of women? *Annals of the Association of American Geographers, 83*(2), 225–242.

Fine, Michelle. (1988). Sexuality, schooling, and adolescent females: The missing discourse of desire. *Harvard Educational Review, 58*(1), 29–53.

Fine, Michelle. (1994). Working the hyphens: Reinventing self and other in qualitative research. In Norman Denzin & Yvonna Lincoln (Eds.), *Handbook of qualitative research* (pp. 70–82). Thousand Oaks, CA: Sage.

Freud, Sigmund. (1905). The transformations of puberty. In Sigmund Freud, *Three essays on the theory of sexuality* (pp. 73–96). New York: Basic Books.

Greene, Jennifer C., & Caracelli, Valerie J. (Eds.). (1997). *Advances in mixed-method evaluation: The challenges and benefits of integrating diverse paradigms.* San Francisco: Jossey-Bass.

Hesse-Biber, Sharlene Nagy, & Leavy, Patricia. (2006). *The practice of qualitative research.* Thousand Oaks, CA: Sage.

Janesick, Valerie J. (2000). The choreography of qualitative research design: Minuets, improvisations, and crystallization. In Norman K. Denzin & Yvonna S. Lincoln (Eds.), *Handbook of qualitative research* (pp. 379–400). Thousand Oaks, CA: Sage.

Jordan, Judith. (1987). Clarity in connection: Empathic knowing, desire and sexuality. *Work in progress/Stone Center for Developmental Services and Studies* 29. Wellesley, MA: Wellesley College, Stone Center for Developmental Services and Studies.

Kelle, Udo. (2001). Sociological explanations between micro and macro and the integration of qualitative and quantitative methods. *Forum Qualitative Sozialforschung/Forum: Qualitative Social Research, 2*(1). Retrieved July 8, 2004, from www.qualitative-research.net/fqs-texte/1–01/1–01kelle-e.htm

Lackey, Jill F., & Moberg, D. Paul. (1998). Understanding the onset of intercourse among urban American adolescents: A cultural process framework using qualitative and quantitative data. *Human Organization, 57,* 491–501.

Ladner, Joyce A. (1971). *Tomorrow's tomorrow: The black woman.* Garden City, NY: Anchor Books.

Lees, Sue. (1986). *Losing out: Sexuality and adolescent girls.* London: Dover.

Levinson, Ruth. (1986). Contraceptive self-efficacy: A perspective on teenage girls' contraceptive behavior. *Journal of Sex Research, 22,* 345–369.

Lincoln, Yvonna S., & Guba, Egon G. (2000). Paradigmatic controversies, contradictions, and emerging confluences. In Norman K. Denzin & Yvonna S. Lincoln (Eds.), *Handbook of qualitative research* (pp. 163–188). Thousand Oaks, CA: Sage.

Manfredi, Clara., Lacey, Loretta, Warnecke, Richard, & Balch, George. (1997). Method effects in survey and focus group findings: Understanding smoking cessation in low-SES African American women. *Health Education and Behavior, 24,* 786–800.

Maynard, Mary, & Purvis, June. (Eds.). (1994). *Researching women's lives from a feminist perspective.* London: Taylor & Francis.

McKendrick, John H. (1999). Multi-method research: An introduction to its application in population geography. *Professional Geographer, 51,* 40–50.

Morgan, David. (1998). Practical strategies for combining qualitative and quantitative methods: Applications to health research. *Qualitative Health Research, 8,* 362–376.

Nicolson, Paula. (2004). Taking quality seriously: The case for qualitative feminist psychology in the context of quantitative clinical research on postnatal depression. In Zazie Todd, Brigitte Nerlich, Suzanne McDeown, & David D. Clarke (Eds.), *Mixing methods in psychology: The integration of qualitative and quantitative methods in theory and practice* (pp. 207–23). New York: Psychology Press.

Reid, Pamela T., & Bing, Vanessa M. (2000). Sexual roles of girls and women: An ethnocultural lifespan perspective. In Cheryl B Travis & Jacquelyn W. White (Eds.), *Sexuality, society and feminism* (pp. 141–166). Washington, DC: American Psychological Association.

Reinharz, Shulamit. (1992). *Feminist methods in social research.* Oxford, UK: Oxford University Press.

Risman, Barbara J., Sprague, Joey, & Howard, Judith. (1993). Comment on Francesca M. Cancian's "Feminist Science." *Gender & Society, 7,* 608–609.

Scott-Jones, Diane., & Turner, Sherry L. (1988). Sex education, contraceptive and reproductive knowledge and contraceptive use among black adolescent females. *Journal of Adolescent Research, 3,* 171–187.

Spalter-Roth, Roberta, & Hartmann, Heidi. (1999). Small happinesses: The feminist struggle to integrate social research with social activism. In Sharlene N. Hesse-Biber, Christina Gilmartin, & Robin Lyndenberg (Eds.), *Feminist approaches to theory and methodology: An interdisciplinary reader* (pp. 333–347). New York: Oxford University Press.

Sprague, Joey, & Zimmerman, Mary K. (2004). Overcoming dualisms: A feminist agenda for sociological methodology. In Sharlene Nagy Hesse-Biber & Patricia Leavy (Eds.), *Approaches to qualitative research: A reader on theory and practice* (pp. 39–61). New York: Oxford University Press.

Tiefer, Leonore. (2000). The social construction and social effects of sex research: The sexological model of sexuality. In Cheryl B. Travis & Jacquelyn W. White (Eds.), *Sexuality, society and feminism* (pp. 79–107). Washington, DC: American Psychological Association.

Tolman, Deborah L., & Szalacha, Laura A. (1999). Dimensions of desire: Bridging qualitative and quantitative methods in a study of female adolescent sexuality. *Psychology of Women Quarterly, 23,* 7–39.

Weinholtz, Donn, Kacer, Barbara, & Rocklin, Thomas. (1995). Salvaging qualitative research with qualitative data. *Qualitative Health Research, 5,* 388–397.

Welsh, Deborah P., Rostosky, Sharon S., & Kawaguchi, Myra C. (2000). A normative perspective of adolescent girls' developing sexuality. In Cheryl B. Travis & Jacquelyn W. White (Eds.), *Sexuality, society and feminism* (pp. 111–140). Washington, DC: American Psychological Association.

Westmarland, Nicole. (2001). The quantitative/qualitative debate and feminist research: A subjective view of objectivity. *Forum for Qualitative Social Research, 2*(1). Retrieved June 19, 2006, from www.qualitative-research.net/fqs-texte/1-01/1-01 westmarland-e.htm

White, Jacquelyn W., Bondurant, Barrie, & Travis, Cheryl B. (2000). Social construction of sexuality: Unpacking hidden meanings. In Cheryl B. Travis & Jacquelyn W. White (Eds.), *Sexuality, society, and feminism* (pp. 11–34). Washington, DC: American Psychological Association.

TEN

FEMINIST SURVEY RESEARCH

Kathi Miner-Rubino

Toby Epstein Jayaratne

—◆•◆•◆—

Behind-the-Scenes With
Kathi Miner-Rubino and Toby Epstein Jayaratne

We are feminist psychologists who center our research programs on quantified data, primarily using survey methods, to explore issues of importance to women and to those with a social justice orientation. As such, we are well aware that some feminist criticism has been directed toward survey research and quantitative research in general. Much of this criticism claims that such research is antithetical to feminist aims. We take an opposite view and instead consider quantitative research as one method of investigation that can make a significant contribution toward advancing the feminist goal of improving the lives of women. What led both of us to hold this perspective and to merge our feminist values and our training as quantitative researchers?

For me, Kathi, they did not exactly coincide initially. I was actually a feminist long before I began conducting quantitative research. During adolescence I started becoming aware of the inequities women faced and I was incredibly angered by this realization. I was angry that my mother did the

(Continued)

(Continued)

cooking and laundry while my father sat in his big comfortable chair and watched television. I was angry that my sister received less pay in her position as a staff reporter at the local newspaper than the similarly qualified male in the next office. I was angry when men whistled at me when I walked by and then called me a bitch when I ordered them to stop. I was angry that I focused so much on what and how much I ate rather than doing well in school or learning about world events. It was not until I arrived at college that I realized that there was a name to what I was feeling: feminism. Feminism made sense to me and it became a part of my identity.

In college I also realized that people systematically studied these injustices. I was floored when I became aware that researchers could provide "hard data" to document what I was observing. What I observed back then still resonates: Women do significantly more housework and child care than men in heterosexual relationships (Bianchi, Milkie, & Sayer, 2000); white women make only 76% of what white men make in the same position, and this number is even lower for women of color (National Committee on Pay Equity, 2005); 54% of college women have experienced some form of sexual victimization (e.g., rape, attempted rape; Koss, Gidycz, & Wisniewski, 1987); 56% of adolescent girls have disordered eating patterns (Croll, Neumark-Sztainer, & Story, 2002); and 55% of girls 8 to 10 years old complain that they are too fat (Wood, Becker, & Thompson, 1996). These statistics moved me, and they move whomever I report them to. There is something powerful in quantification. When most people hear these statistics, they are in some way affected. And more often than not, these numbers convey in stark terms the social injustices that describe women's role in society.

As I became more proficient in statistics, I further understood the powerful story numbers could tell about women's lives—not simply the proportion of women affected by this or that, but the consequences of those experiences. For example, in my current research program I focus on the consequences for employees who observe rude, condescending, harassing behavior targeted at women in their workplace. When I talk about this research, I report not only the frequency of these behaviors but also the consequences of these observations (such as significantly lowered job satisfaction and psychological well-being for observers). I quickly recognized that people who would not call themselves feminists (and in fact would vehemently resist the label) listened when I explained these findings in quantified terms. They actually listened. Whether we like it or not, people respond to quantitative data. Numbers can inspire people to become social activists and they can influence those involved in public policy so that they enact legislation to improve the lives of women. With this in mind, a feminist quantitative survey researcher was born. My passion for social justice for women and my realization that numbers stirred people led me to want to conduct quantitative research on behalf of women.

I, Toby, grew up during the civil rights era in a family that was active in advancing a progressive political agenda. I learned from an early age the importance of understanding the factors that support policies of injustice, in order to challenge such practices. When I was in college, I had the opportunity to assist on studies of various social issues at a research institute at my university. The people with whom I worked, as well as many other scholars at the institute, conducted their research specifically for the purpose of documenting inequalities and determining the most effective ways to promote social justice. It was inspiring being surrounded by those who had committed their entire careers to such work. For the most part, these researchers employed survey methods. Due to the high quality of their research and the respect that it garnered from others, findings from their studies were powerful in advocating for social change.

Given my activist upbringing, my identity as a feminist came easily in the 1960s. With my training in survey research, I decided that I could employ the quantitative skills I learned in college to investigate how sexism operated in our society and to explore the most productive means for achieving feminist goals. Once I started doing my own survey research, I found it to be an effective technique for convincing others of the need to support various feminist causes. A few years later, however, when I was attending a women's studies conference, someone challenged the quantitative research methods I used, and suggested that such methods were not appropriate tools for feminist researchers. In response, I developed a critical eye with which to judge the methods I used, and I became aware of the value of various alternative, qualitative research strategies. However, rather than rejecting quantitative methods altogether, I came to believe that it was important for feminist researchers to remain open to using either (or both) of these methods, because they answer different types of research questions. As a social scientist whose main research topic focuses on the social

(Continued)

(Continued)

and political implications of the public's genetic explanations for perceived gender, class, and race differences, I attempt to follow this dictum. I use qualitative methods when I am attempting to gather initial information about an issue or to develop a more in-depth understanding of a topic. However, when I examine complex conceptual models or test theories, I use statistical (quantitative) methods, because they are best suited for that purpose. My professional experience has helped me realize that no one research technique works best in answering every question, but rather, each new exploration requires a thoughtful, critical assessment in selecting an investigative strategy.

Although we have had different routes to a similar location, we both acknowledge the influence of our training on the development of our research perspectives. The guidance we received during that training taught us to observe how the context of the research affects all aspects of the work we do and to maintain an awareness of the ethical and political issues associated with and implied by the research we undertake. Most important, however, we were educated to think about the research endeavor as a quest for knowledge in the service of social progress, a theme that we have carried with us as feminists and as survey researchers.

The purposes of this chapter are to describe the survey research process, show how it can be applied in the exploration of feminist issues, and explain why it is an important, valuable resource for feminist researchers. Both historically and more recently, there are innumerable examples of how the results of survey research have made a difference in women's and other marginalized people's lives. We will describe some of these examples throughout the chapter and point out the unique and influential effects survey research can have in understanding and alleviating gender oppression.

We come to this chapter schooled in the standards of mainstream social science research and with an appreciation for the utility of quantitative survey research. However, as feminists, we are also aware of feminist criticisms of quantitative research, and these inform our work in promoting social justice for women. Thus, bridging the disciplines of women's studies and psychology, we see ourselves as social justice scholars who come from a feminist perspective, striving to use survey research as a vehicle for advancing the feminist agenda.

The first section of this chapter focuses on several of the overarching issues regarding the use of quantitative methods generally, and survey research specifically, in feminist exploration, including (1) the historical development of survey research, (2) the major feminist criticisms of quantitative methods, (3) the difference between quantitative and qualitative research, and (4) the unique benefits of quantitative survey research for feminist aims. In the second section, we introduce the major components of survey research, highlighting significant issues that should be addressed in conducting quality, feminist survey research.[1]

HISTORY OF SURVEY RESEARCH

Perhaps the earliest and most well-known type of survey is the census, which began in the United States in 1790 and is conducted each decade by the federal government (U.S. Census Bureau, 1989). The census seeks to describe the characteristics (e.g., gender, average number of people per household) of an entire population (e.g., in the United States). The most recent census was conducted in 2000, and more than 281 million Americans were surveyed (U.S. Census Bureau, 2005). This most recent look at Americans provided important information regarding a number of feminist concerns, such as the number of women in poverty, the number of employed women, and the number of single mothers—this information is invaluable to feminists because it tells us the current state of affairs for women.

Another purpose of surveys in their early development was to gain an understanding of social problems, and indeed, even feminists employed such methods at that time. For example, during the late 1800s and early 1900s, feminists at the University of Chicago designed surveys and developed statistical techniques to assist social reform efforts (Deegan, cited in Spalter-Roth & Hartmann, 1996). This first generation of feminist survey researchers used the results of their surveys to educate the public and influence legislation supporting a host of progressive causes, such as reducing poverty, unemployment, and child labor.

A significant impetus for mainstream survey research development was World War II, as the federal government was interested in assessing

Americans' opinions and attitudes regarding the war and other social issues (Groves et al., 2004). This was a critical period in the evolution of such methods, because survey researchers began to learn the importance of question wording, data collection techniques, interviewer training, and sampling procedures (Converse, 1987; Groves et al., 2004), and how these factors might affect the results of studies. Specifically, researchers found that certain methods were better than others for collecting and analyzing data so that they more accurately reflected public opinions and attitudes. This led to the establishment of accepted standards for conducting survey research.

During the 1960s and 1970s, a second generation of feminist survey researchers was trained. Like earlier feminist researchers, they had an interest in advancing social policy and were passionate activists in the quest for social change for women (Spalter-Roth & Hartmann, 1996). However, this generation was generally critical of traditional science because science assumed that "truth" can be verified by observation and experimentation. These feminist scholars played an important role in pointing out how subtle (and sometimes not so subtle) factors continued to bias research in favor of the "male perspective." Many of their concerns were addressed by mainstream survey researchers and survey research methods improved in response. However, some of these critiques still resonate today, and the dialogue about the best way to do survey research continues, because it is an ever evolving process. Feminist survey researchers, then, have been influential in the broader effort to develop standards for conducting survey research that help to minimize bias and produce results that reflect social phenomena as accurately as possible.

FEMINIST CRITICISMS OF QUANTITATIVE RESEARCH AND THE SURVEY RESEARCH METHOD

While there has been rapid growth in the use and sophistication of surveys, the survey research method, as a form of quantitative research, has been criticized by some feminist scholars. These epistemological and methodological criticisms have been addressed in Chapter 2 and therefore we do not explain them in depth here. However, we do point out several issues that have particular relevance for feminist survey researchers. For example, as discussed previously, the major epistemological criticism of survey research has been that it is rooted in the tradition of *positivism*, which is a perspective that values objective and value-free science. Some of the problems with the positivist tradition were outlined in earlier chapters.

Interestingly, some feminist researchers have actually advocated stronger objectivity as a way of incorporating feminist principles into their research. This strategy has been labeled *feminist empiricism* (Harding, 1987, 1998). Feminist empiricists actually promote conventional objectivity and argue that male-centered bias can be eliminated from the research process *only if* the positivist principle of objectivity is rigorously upheld. They argue that adhering to the notion of objectivity will actually lead to data that are more, rather than less, representative of women's experiences because the research process is not influenced by a particular perspective.

Feminist quantitative researchers are often assumed to be stanch feminist empiricists who embrace this specific epistemological position (i.e., positivism). However, in truth, feminist quantitative researches actually have many different viewpoints regarding epistemology. In our view, to assume that all feminist quantitative researchers share the same philosophical perspective is as erroneous as assuming that all qualitative researchers share a specific perspective. Although we both conduct quantitative research, which stems from the positivist tradition, we also distinguish ourselves from this tradition in that we do not agree with positivism's philosophical underpinning that there is an objective truth "out there" that is truly accessible. Nor do we believe that scientific research can or should be completely impartial. At the same time, we also recognize the importance of conducting research in such a way as to reduce bias (error) as much as possible, whether that bias emanates from a sexist or a feminist perspective (or any other ideology). In other words, if we are to understand clearly how the social structure is maintained (which will allow us to identify the best ways to alter it for purposes of social justice), we must attempt to remove bias in our research. This approach was recently termed *strong objectivity* by Harding (2004) and earlier was called *feminist objectivity* by Haraway (1988). Hesse-Biber, Leavy, and Yaiser (2004) summarized feminist objectivity as

> knowledge and truth that is partial, situated, subjective, power imbued, and relational. [It] combines the goal of conventional objectivity—to conduct research completely free of social influence and or personal beliefs—with the reality that no one can achieve this goal . . . and recognizes that objectivity can only operate within the limitations of the scientists' personal beliefs and experiences. (p. 13)

In this view, by recognizing that knowledge is situated, objectivity is actually maximized. Thus, although we conduct our research within a more traditional paradigm, we do so using feminist objectivity, with the ultimate goal of making a real difference in women's lives.

In addition to epistemological issues, feminists also have expressed methodological concerns about quantitative survey research. For example, feminists have sometimes claimed that in using quantitative methods, researchers reduce people simply to numbers while ignoring the contextualized lives in which they live. This often leads feminists to conclude that qualitative research methods are "better" and "more feminist" than quantitative research methods. In fact, the debate over qualitative and quantitative research methods has been one of the most vigorous in feminist studies and some scholars have argued that conducting feminist research may *necessitate* the use of qualitative methods (e.g., Condor, 1986; Landrine, Klonoff, & Brown-Collins, 1992; Marecek, Fine, & Kidder, 1997; Sherif, 1979; Smith, 1987). We contend that both qualitative and quantitative methods are useful in feminist research and that researchers should choose a research method that most effectively answers their research questions rather than the method considered to be the "most feminist." To make that choice, it is important to know the major differences between quantitative and qualitative research methods.

DIFFERENCES BETWEEN QUALITATIVE AND QUANTITATIVE METHODS

When a researcher collects quantitative data, characteristics and experiences of the research participants are put into numerical categories, usually predefined by the researcher, and then evaluated using statistical analyses. For example, if a researcher is interested in the ethnicity of the study participants, she or he might include a number of categories which respondents can assign for themselves, such as Euro-American, African American, Hispanic American, or Asian American. It is also common for researchers to use categories when assessing sexual orientation, such as heterosexual and LGBT (lesbian, gay, bisexual, transgendered). These categories are then assigned an arbitrary number (e.g., white = 1, African American = 2) to be used in the analyses. Researchers might also ask participants how strongly they disagree or agree with some statement such as "Women should be able to make decisions about their own body," "Women are better at parenting than men," or "I often feel anxious" on a scale, say, from 1 (strongly disagree) to 5 (strongly agree). In these cases, the number on the scale the respondent chooses would be used in the statistical analysis.

Notice that in these later examples, research participants would need to make a general assessment of their attitudes or beliefs and would not be able to include more nuanced information (such as when or with whom they feel most anxious). It might also be difficult for those participants responding to the ethnicity and sexual orientation questions to include more specific information, such as being multi-ethnic or feeling that their sexual orientation is more fluid and changing over time. Thus, sometimes the categories are narrowly defined, with researchers deciding beforehand how detailed the responses can be. These decisions, however, are not arbitrary but based on many practical factors, such as the respondent's age and education level and the need to limit the time it takes someone to complete the survey. With the use of predefined categories, research participants have little influence on what information is analyzed (Jayaratne & Stewart, 1991). Moreover, because the categories are defined beforehand, researchers should know enough about the phenomena to construct inclusive categories (which most researchers strive to do). It is important to note, however, that not all quantitative research proceeds in this way. Sometimes researchers collect data without confining them to predetermined categories (e.g., asking race as a free-response, fill-in-the-blank question), and they later transform these responses into quantitative categories to be used in statistical analyses (e.g., collapsing responses from different categories).

In contrast to quantification, qualitative data (i.e., information in the form of words rather than numbers) are generally evaluated through the use of themes or categories that emerge *after* data collection (although this practice is not universal in all qualitative methods). This process can increase the likelihood that the researcher will take into account all of the details and nuances of the respondents' answers and allows the researcher to explore a number of different interpretations of them. Thus, because the themes or categories are not defined beforehand by the researcher, participants often have the freedom to respond to research questions in ways that make sense to them. As a result, these data typically include information that participants themselves think is important. Proponents of qualitative research methods argue that this aspect of qualitative research is important; participants should be able to describe their experiences as they perceive them, not through the researcher's ideas about what their worlds are like (Landrine et al., 1992; Marecek et al., 1997; Wallston & Grady, 1992). This does not mean that qualitative data are somehow more accurate, however. Indeed, qualitative research is also subject to the researcher's interpretation, as Gorelick (1996) points out:

> After all, it is I who asked the questions, I who read the transcript, I who selected the materials to be placed in the text. . . . It is when I am trying to be most faithful to their meaning . . . that I am most painfully aware that simply "giving voice" is not so simple after all. . . . It is fraught with interpretation. (p. 38)

Thus, as you can see, both quantitative and qualitative research methods have disadvantages in terms of the potential for altering the intended meaning of an individual's responses. However, such distortion might occur less frequently with qualitative methods and this is the major advantage of using such techniques.

ADVANTAGES OF QUANTITATIVE METHODS

Even though some feminists have raised concerns about quantitative survey research, this method can serve as an effective tool for supporting feminist goals and philosophies and can offer a number of advantages not found in qualitative work. First, quantitative survey research can provide a vehicle for feminists to introduce sexism, racism, classism, heterosexism, and other social justice issues into mainstream discussions (e.g., public policy and legislation). This is perhaps the biggest benefit of quantitative research methods. Because social science research is built on the ideal of objectivity, mainstream researchers and the general public may be uncomfortable with research methods they tend to perceive as less objective (such as qualitative research). In addition, those who are not strong supporters of feminist values might be particularly likely to distrust qualitative data that convey a feminist message, claiming that such data are biased toward a particular political agenda (even though *all* research has some agenda). Quantitative research may have more appeal for these groups of individuals, and thus they may be more apt to listen and consider quantitative research legitimate (Spalter-Roth & Hartmann, 1996). The importance of this benefit cannot be overemphasized—for real social change for women to occur we must be able to report our research findings in a way that will attract people's attention and convince them of the need for social change. Numbers and statistics talk, and they talk loudly and persuasively. Indeed, we want our research findings to be so influential that they cannot be ignored by nonfeminists and the lay public. Quantitative survey research can help us do that.

Second, the brevity of statistics makes them easy to remember and comprehend, and thus easy to communicate to others (Reinharz, 1992). One of the most compelling examples of this took place in the 1960s when the media reported that women earned 59 cents to every dollar that men made. This was a simple statistic, but it worked to inform the public about gender inequality in the workplace and, in some respects, became a rallying cry for feminists (e.g., bumper stickers and buttons were frequently seen with nothing but the words "59 cents"). Thus, quantitative data can effectively communicate important feminist ideas to the public in a simple, but powerful, way.

Third, quantitative methods are helpful for determining the best course of action in implementing social change for women because such techniques help us to identify patterns of gender oppression and reveal how oppression operates. For example, survey research can document the psychological, physical health, and economic consequences associated with domestic violence, pay inequity, eating disorders, and so on in large groups of women. If the results of quantitative survey research show that thousands (or millions) of women are similarly negatively affected by such experiences, it is more likely to result in legislation or policy advanced on women's behalf.

Finally, survey methods allow the researcher to assess the experiences or opinions of large numbers of individuals (rather than much smaller numbers, as is often the case in qualitative research). Thus, such methods have the potential to generate data that can represent a wide variety of perspectives and viewpoints, resulting in a more inclusive approach and widespread social change, important in feminist research.

As we hope is clear, there are undeniable benefits to using survey research and quantitative methods to advocate for feminist social change. You might now be wondering how to actually *do* survey research. We will spend the remainder of this chapter explaining how we go about conducting survey research on feminist issues. We will explain the overarching framework for doing such research, describe the major components and decisions involved in each stage, and highlight how being a feminist affects the process.

HOW DO YOU BEGIN A SURVEY RESEARCH PROJECT?

Framework for Doing Survey Research

Before we begin, it is important for you to know that doing survey research generally involves the same components and general decisions whether or not the researcher comes from a feminist or nonfeminist perspective. In other words, feminist survey researchers and those who conduct mainstream survey research, for the most part, engage in similar research activities. What distinguishes feminist survey research from other survey research is that in the former (1) the initial research questions that are explored (i.e., the main questions the survey will seek to answer), by definition, focus on an issue of interest to feminists and (2) the interpretation and application of the results are done in a way that attempts to advance feminist values. In line with Kelly (1978), this means that the feminist perspective is most applicable during two specific points in the research process: the development of research questions and the interpretation of findings. These two points occur at the beginning and end stages of the survey research process, respectively. This applicability of the feminist perspective can best be conceptualized as the "bookends" of the survey research process; it holds the core of the research together (i.e., the "books") and gives individual components of the research process shape, structure, and meaning.

The components of the survey research method that come after the development of research questions and before the interpretation of findings (i.e., the middle stage or "books") involve decisions about choosing specific survey research techniques. For example, it is at this stage that the researcher must make a choice about the type of survey to use, whom to interview, the design of the survey, how to collect the data, and how to analyze the data. In general, survey researchers (feminist and nonfeminist alike) must grapple with decisions regarding these components *before* the survey research process actually begins. Thus, much of the work occurs even before the data are collected! We also want to emphasize that to ensure good-quality research, it is extremely important that the decisions regarding the components in the middle phase of the research process be based on general principles of survey research (which in many ways are also fully consistent with feminist principles, as you'll see). The middle stage of the survey research process, then, should be the least influenced by the feminist (or any other) perspective, because it is during this stage that accepted survey research protocol should be followed.

THE FIRST PHASE OF SURVEY RESEARCH: FORMULATING RESEARCH QUESTIONS AND HYPOTHESES

The first steps in the typical research process (not just survey research) are to formulate research questions and develop hypotheses. *Research questions* are simply the questions the research will attempt to answer. For feminists, research questions come from an interest in improving the lives of women and achieving social justice more broadly. For example, a feminist researcher might ask: "What is the best way to make academic environments more supportive for lesbian students?" "How does pay inequity between men and women in the workplace affect children?" or "Why do some men batter women?" Of course, these are just a few examples of the multitude of questions a researcher might be interested in examining.

Hypotheses are the predictions that a researcher makes about the results of the study; that is, what they think the answer to their research question will be. Hypotheses are developed from an analysis of previous research and theory. Considering the research questions posed above, for example, based on the results of previous studies, a researcher might hypothesize that implementing policies denouncing the harassment of lesbian students leads to more supportive school environments for them, that pay inequity in the workplace decreases children's scholastic achievement, or that some men are violent against women as a means of power and control. In some mainstream research, questions derive solely from an interest in advancing theory, without direct application to solving social problems. However, feminists are more likely to ask questions (such as those above) and develop hypotheses in a manner such that the research findings will have direct relevance to feminist social change. In this way, a feminist perspective affects the formulation of research questions as well as the way the hypotheses are articulated. The purpose of actually doing the research is to answer those research questions.

Questions that should be asked during the first phase of the survey research process include the following:

- What is my research question, and why is it important as a feminist issue?
- What is my hypothesis? Is it based on a careful evaluation of existing theory and empirical investigation?

THE SECOND PHASE OF SURVEY RESEARCH: DOING THE RESEARCH

Only after the research questions and hypotheses are formulated should one consider which specific research method to use. What factors influence the decision to employ the survey research method? In general, if the goal of the research is to apply the findings beyond the research participants, to influence policymakers and public opinion, or to test hypotheses or complex theoretical models, the survey method may be an appropriate choice. For example, Jayaratne, Thomas, and Trautmann (2003) employed the survey method to evaluate an intervention program designed to keep middle school girls involved in science. The specific goal of the research was to determine the effectiveness of various aspects of the program among minority and nonminority girls. The survey research method was chosen for this project because it allowed the researchers to (1) gather the opinions of a large number of girls, (2) generalize the findings to middle school girls in general, (3) influence policymakers on the importance of science interventions for girls, and (4) statistically test hypotheses about outcome differences between girls who participated in the intervention and those who did not. Although qualitative interviews were initially considered because they would have yielded more in-depth understanding of the girls' opinions of the program, the needs of the researchers, as listed above, were better addressed with the use of surveys than with other strategies. This use of survey research reflects a feminist perspective in that the ultimate goal was to generate information that would be used in the development of programs to increase both minority and nonminority girls' participation in science.

Types of Surveys

Surveys are typically categorized by how they are administered; that is, how the data are collected. Traditional methods include face-to-face interviews (questions asked by an interviewer in person), telephone interviews (questions asked by an interviewer over the phone), and paper-and-pencil or mailed questionnaires (typically, when respondents fill in answers on paper and return the questionnaire to the researcher). Newer methods of survey administration employ computers in the data collection process, including Web surveys, which many survey researchers are now using to replace traditional paper-and-pencil questionnaires (Groves et al., 2004).

Each of these survey techniques has various benefits and drawbacks. Face-to-face interviews tend to be very costly, but they allow more direct involvement of the interviewer. This method is most appropriate for surveys that require extensive probing and clarification of answers. However, when the topic of investigation is particularly sensitive, face-to-face interviews may yield data that are influenced by *social desirability*, such as when the presence of an interviewer causes respondents to answer questions in such a way as to make the respondent appear to be a "good" person to the interviewer (see Campbell, 1982; Rogers, 1971). Respondents might also answer questions in a way they believe the interviewer prefers (i.e., supports the study hypotheses). This is important to consider when conducting research on gender, race, or sexuality issues, which may involve sensitive and controversial matters. However, high-quality feminist research on very sensitive issues has been conducted using such interviewing techniques. For example, Stewart and Dottolo's (2005) research on issues of gender, race, and sexuality in academia provides a good example. In this work, diverse groups of university faculty were interviewed regarding their experiences of sexism, racism, and heterosexism at work and the researchers received quite thoughtful and honest responses. If done respectfully and ethically, face-to-face interviews can provide a wealth of information on sensitive topics.

Telephone interviewing has been shown to produce results generally similar to those found with face-to-face interviewing methods (Groves & Kahn, 1979). Although telephone interviews are considerably less expensive and seem less intrusive, findings can also be affected by the interview process, often by what the interviewer says (or does not say) during the interview. In recent years, the development of devices or services for screening telephone calls (i.e., caller ID) has resulted in lower rates of response for telephone surveys. Research shows that, in general, these lower rates have not affected the types of individuals overall who answer telephone surveys (Pew Research Center, 2004). However, researchers should be aware of this issue and how it might influence the data.

Paper-and-pencil or mailed surveys and Web surveys are typically less expensive than either telephone or face-to-face surveys, but there tends to be less influence over how they are administered because respondents often fill them out in unknown circumstances. For example, respondents might complete the survey in one setting or over several days, or while asking for input from friends or family members. In addition, these types of surveys may have lower total response rates because people can easily refuse to participate. Incentives can help enormously with this problem (as detailed in Dillman, 1978), and many survey researchers compensate respondents for their time and effort (for all types of surveys). An advantage of paper-and-pencil surveys is that they typically allow more privacy and anonymity, and thus are helpful when investigating sensitive issues. This can create an important advantage for feminist researchers because research participants may feel more comfortable with the research situation and give voice to their true opinions or experiences when in private. Obviously, the decision about which type of survey to employ is multifaceted, but it is significant in that it affects all other aspects of the research and has major implications for the quality of the data collected.

Selection of Respondents

After the type of survey has been chosen, the researcher must decide how she or he will select the people to participate in the survey. *Sampling* refers to the selection of people from a population to whom the survey will be administered (Stangor, 2004). A *population* is defined as the overall group of individuals the researcher wants to study. For example, a population might be all African American women more than 50 years old in the United States, all incarcerated women in New Mexico, or all women who have given birth while attending Yale University. In contrast, a *sample* is the smaller subset of individuals that actually participates in the research. For example, following from the above, a sample might include African American women more than 50 years old who live in the researcher's county and who answer an ad recruiting participants from the local newspaper, a small group of incarcerated women from each detention facility in New Mexico, or women who birthed a child while attending Yale University and whose current address was listed in the alumni directory. Researchers very often are interested in applying the findings based on the sample back to the larger group of interest—the population, a process called *generalizing*. This is particularly important because the findings of a study then have meaning for a larger group of individuals and not just those who participated in the study. Generalization is possible, however, only if the sample is *representative*, that is, has characteristics that are approximately the same as the population in all important respects. Here is where sampling comes in. How the research participants are selected determines if it is appropriate to generalize the research findings from a sample to a population.

The best way to ensure the generalizability of a sample is to select respondents from the population randomly, resulting in a *probability sample.* There are many different kinds of probability samples, but they all include some type of random selection of respondents (Czaja & Blair, 1996). For example, if a researcher was interested in the experiences of incarcerated women in New Mexico (the population), but could not conduct a survey using the entire population, she might instead obtain a probability sample of these women. One way to do this is to randomly select a small subset of women from each facility to participate in the survey. This technique would likely produce a probability sample that is representative of the larger population of incarcerated women. Because probability sampling has the distinct advantage of producing findings that can be generalized to the population of interest and are thus persuasive, this sampling strategy is particularly useful if the goal of the research is to inform public policy regarding women's issues.

Despite this distinct advantage of probability sampling, sometimes a researcher is unable to use this method of selecting respondents. This may occur because the population is small (e.g., women of color who are CEOs of companies) or difficult to contact (e.g., sex workers). It can also be difficult to employ probability sampling simply because of lack of funding, since the methods to derive a probability sample can be costly. Because of these difficulties, many researchers use nonprobability samples in their research.

Nonprobability samples are those in which the sample is not representative of the population. In this case, the researcher can only apply the findings of the study to the particular group of individuals who participated, although she or he might speculate about how the findings apply to the broader population. The primary benefit of nonprobability sampling is that it can be relatively inexpensive and can usually generate a large sample more quickly than probability sampling strategies (Biemer & Lyberg, 2003). To obtain a nonprobability sample, the researcher identifies the population of interest (e.g., all African American women over the age of 50) but then includes in the sample only individuals who satisfy some additional criteria—for example, those residing in Moscow, Idaho, because that is where the researcher lives. This type of sample would clearly not represent the entire population.

One common type of nonprobability sampling, and the one used above, is *convenience sampling*. Convenience sampling consists of recruiting participants from places where they are easily accessible. For instance, much research in feminist social psychology uses samples of college students who attend the researcher's university (e.g., Smith & Frieze, 2003) and many researchers use samples of participants from their immediate geographical area. While convenience sampling can provide insights into the sampled population, researchers need to be cautious about generalizing their findings beyond the characteristics of their sample. For example, if a researcher conducts a study about the experiences of college women who have had a child while in school and selects women to participate in the research who attend the university where the researcher is a faculty member, she or he could undoubtedly learn valuable information about those students' experiences. However, it would be invalid for the researcher to generalize the findings to all women who have birthed a child in college. The choice of whether to use probability or nonprobability sampling ultimately depends on the resources available to the researcher and importance of generalizing the results. Researchers should carefully choose the sampling method by weighing the advantages and disadvantages associated with various sampling techniques.

Constructing the Survey

In the beginning stage of survey construction, it can be beneficial to conduct in-depth discussions (*focus groups*) with individuals who are representative of the population of interest. This can help the researcher understand the way people talk about the issues the survey will address and choose the appropriate vocabulary and phrasing of questions. This can also suggest issues, concerns, and ways of looking at the topic that the researcher has not considered (Fowler, 1984). Thus, these discussions can be a valuable tool to gain knowledge, especially about a subordinated group. For example, in their study of AIDS-related behaviors and attitudes, Quina et al. (1999) conducted focus groups with two community samples of low-educated women who expressed their opinions on this topic. This allowed the population of interest (i.e., low-educated women) to participate in the research process and have a voice in the research; these aspects are central to feminist principles and values.

The next step is the actual development of the survey. The process of survey construction concerns first, decisions about what is important to *measure* (i.e., what questions will be asked) and then, *how* the questions will be asked (Fowler, 1984); these decisions should be based on what information is needed to evaluate the hypotheses. Determining what questions to include in a survey should be a fairly straightforward process. Suppose a researcher is interested in examining dating behavior in lesbian adolescents and her hypothesis is that girls who come from more accepting families will report more positive dating experiences compared with girls who come from less accepting families. It should be obvious that the researcher should include questions about the girls' dating experiences and their family members' level of acceptance of their sexual orientation (plus any other issues of importance). However, the researcher must also decide *exactly* how those questions will be asked, a much more difficult task. How does the researcher go about doing this?

Designing Questions

When established measures already exist in the relevant research literature it is preferable to use them, if they have been shown to be valid (Fowler, 1984). Valid measures are those that have been empirically evaluated and actually assess what they are supposed to access. For instance, a question about family income should make it clear to the participant that they report total income from all members of the family. If this is not made clear by the wording of the question, then the measure might actually be assessing the participant's own income and it would not be a valid measure of family income. The issue of question validity is important to consider, whether using established measures or designing new ones.

If established measures are not available, or their exact format is not practical, the researcher will need to design questions or adapt an existing measure suited to the population of interest. The major issues to address in designing questions are comprehension (the ease with which the respondent interprets and understands the question), retrieval (the degree to which the respondent can recall the information needed to answer the question), and reporting (the ability to formulate a response and put it in the format required by the questionnaire; Groves et al., 2004). Clearly, if questions are not understood by the respondent, retrieval and reporting will be inaccurate.

An excellent example of feminist research that adapted a survey for increased comprehension is Quina et al.'s (1999) previously discussed work on AIDS behavior and attitudes. In the process of adapting their survey to their population of interest, they brought the readability level of the survey from the 12th-grade level (for which it was originally designed) to a 6th-grade level. They accomplished this with comments and feedback from groups of women who were similar to those that would be completing the survey (women with low literacy skills). This strategy allowed women in the population of interest to incorporate their voice into research that was ultimately about and for them—an important feminist concern in conducting research.

Research shows that respondents can and do sometimes have different interpretations of the same questions, especially when those questions are vague or contain technical terms (Groves et al., 2004; Schwarz, Groves, & Schuman, 1998). As a result, it is important to write questions so that all respondents are likely to interpret them similarly (Fowler, 1984). To minimize the likelihood of different interpretations, it is helpful to use everyday, non-technical, unambiguous language when designing questions. Additionally, following the principles of feminist research, it is important to take into account differences between various social groups (e.g., different ethnicities, social classes, or cultures; Fowler, 1984) and to use nonoppressive (i.e., nonsexist, nonracist) language (Eichler, 1988). Landrine et al. (1992) examined black and white women's interpretations of gender-related words and phrases (e.g., "I am feminine," "I am passive," and "I am assertive") and found that different women associated very different meanings with the words that influenced their responses. For example, while black women defined the word *passive* as not saying what one really thinks, white women defined it as laid-back/easygoing, suggesting differences in question meaning and interpretation.

Types of Questions

There are generally two different types of questions used in survey research: *closed-ended* questions and *open-ended* questions. Closed-ended questions present participants with a list of specific response options, while open-ended questions allow participants to provide their own answers (similar to qualitative methods). In survey research, open-ended questions are similar to fill-in-the-blank or short-answer questions, and closed-ended questions are more like a multiple choice format (Groves et al., 2004). For example, if researchers were interested in assessing feelings about gay men and lesbians serving in the military, they might ask respondents to choose between two alternatives in describing their views on this issue (e.g., "they should not be allowed to serve" or "they should be allowed to serve"). The researcher could also ask this as an open-ended question (e.g.,"What are your views on gay men and lesbians in the military?").

One example that illustrates the use of both open- and closed-ended questions is research on violence against women conducted by Smith (1994). He found that including both types of questions when asking about the prevalence of violence over a woman's lifetime aided tremendously in interviewer-respondent rapport, and that this practice ultimately led to a more nuanced understanding of victims' experiences. He suggests that both closed- and open-ended questions should be employed when assessing sensitive experiences, such as violence, in a survey. Although closed-ended questions can limit richness and variety since they do not allow respondents to answer in their own words, they can also be beneficial because they are often quicker and easier to answer, making individuals more likely to respond (Fowler, 1984).

Pretesting

After the survey instrument is initially designed, it is helpful to pretest it; that is, to administer it to a small group of individuals (similar to those who will be included in the final sample) to determine if it requires further revision. In a pretest, the researcher typically asks individuals not only to respond to questions, but also to articulate their thoughts about the wording of questions themselves (e.g., if the questions were clear). This process can provide insights into interpretations of question meanings (Schwarz et al., 1998) and therefore may enhance the quality of the measures.

Data Collection

Data collection refers to the *process* of actually obtaining the information (i.e., attitudes, experiences, thoughts, feelings, etc.) that will help answer the research questions. It is important to understand how different factors related to data collection (e.g., the interviewer, the interview setting, the answer options, as well as unrelated circumstances) can unintentionally influence the data, and thus may ultimately affect the results of the study. Early survey research tended to ignore the effect of some of these elements, resulting in data that were often biased in favor of the researcher's viewpoint or the prevailing social discourse. This aspect of traditional survey research was a major focus of much feminist criticism, because it meant that a woman's viewpoint was sometimes distorted. Riessman (1987), for example, documented how both ethnicity and social class influence the interview process, and ultimately how the data are interpreted. In her research, an Anglo, middle-class woman conducted an interview with both a middle-class Anglo woman and a working-class Puerto Rican woman on the topic of marital separation and divorce. In describing their experiences, the narratives of the two women interviewees differed dramatically, representing their dissimilar backgrounds. From an evaluation of the transcripts of these interviews, Riessman found that the interviewer's comments (reflecting her own middle-class background) influenced the interview process. Riessman showed how being from a different social class (despite being the same gender) can alter the meaning of the respondents' narrative, thus potentially increasing errors in the data. Current survey techniques emphasize the value of minimizing error effects during data collection (see Groves et al., 2004). Thus, both mainstream and feminist survey researchers promote awareness of how respondent attributes and interviewer attributes affect the quality of the data.

Ethical Treatment of Participants

Ethical principles are relevant to many aspects of the research process (e.g., truthful reporting of data, giving credit to those contributing to the research). Most discussions of research ethics, however, have tended to focus on how the participants in research are treated by the researcher. This emphasis is likely a result of serious abuses of research participants that have occurred in the not too distant past. Perhaps the most notorious, well-known examples are Milgram's (1974) obedience studies and the Tuskegee syphilis study (Jones, 1981). Milgram led participants to believe they were administering shocks to another person for purposes of "teaching," a procedure that greatly distressed many of the participants. In the Tuskegee experiment, the government studied the progress of syphilis in African American males without informing these men of their disease and without treating them, despite the existence of penicillin as an effective remedy. Although these are not examples of survey research, per se, an awareness of such exploitation resulted in a broad effort to prevent mistreatment of participants in all research on human subjects.

Among the voices included in this movement to enact strict standards for the ethical treatment of research participants were those of feminist scholars. In fact, many initial feminist critiques of research targeted this particular aspect of the research process, since exploitation of research participants conflicts with basic humanistic values that are fundamental to feminists. These critiques often advocated decreasing or eliminating the power differential between the researcher and the researched (Du Bois, 1983; Fee, 1983). For example, Reinharz (1979) suggests that an equal relationship between the two would likely yield information that reflects the participant's reality rather than the researcher's reality. Other feminists called for the need to redefine the process as "research with" or "research for" rather than "research on" (Stanley & Wise, 1983). Thus, feminists sought to appreciate and value research participants, instead of considering them as "objects" of study. One result of the effort to ensure the ethical treatment of human subjects was the establishment of Institutional Review Boards (now commonplace in most research organizations), which set mandatory standards for the conduct of research. These standards generally specify: (1) respect for persons (informed consent and protection from the risk of harm), (2) beneficence (maximizing benefits and minimizing risks to subjects), and (3) justice (fairness in the distribution of the benefits of research and equal treatment). While these guidelines cannot guarantee that all research involving humans will be ethical, they do go a long way in promoting these goals.

Preparing and Analyzing the Data and Evaluating the Hypotheses

Preparing the Data for Analysis

Once the data are collected, a series of procedures are frequently required before they can be analyzed. These involve data entry (entering the raw numeric data into computer files) and codebook construction (creating a guide that documents all questions and answer options). These procedures are routine and serve to minimize errors in the data while increasing the efficiency of the data analysis. One task that is more challenging during data preparation is the coding of open-ended questions. Because open-ended questions are often favored among feminist survey researchers, we briefly discuss coding this type of data below.

The goal when coding open-ended questions is to interpret and classify responses so that they can be assigned a numerical value in preparation for statistical data analysis. Open-ended questions with relatively few answer options or with short, simple answers that are easily interpreted (e.g., employment status) can be coded in a straightforward manner by assigning a number code to each category. For more complex open-ended answers, such as political opinions expressed in participants' own words, it is necessary to be more cautious about the coding process. On the one hand, because the interpretive process can be highly subjective, applying a feminist perspective (or any other perspective) when coding can distort the *intended* meaning of the response. On the other hand, such interpretation may be seen as using a feminist lens through which to view the data and articulating a feminist viewpoint (which may otherwise be suppressed). This dialectical aspect of feminist survey research is an important issue in feminist scholarship, as the researcher attempts to maintain conventional objectivity, while at the same time giving voice to women or any subjugated group. Various methods are used by feminist survey researchers to balance these goals. No method can guarantee, however, the accurate interpretation of the intended meaning, and therefore feminist survey researchers (as all researchers) need to be particularly careful when they code open-ended questions.

Data Analysis

Statistical analysis is a technique used to summarize and explain the information that participants report in a survey (e.g., a percentage or an average value). It is a necessary part of survey research because the information that is collected cannot be easily understood or reported in its raw form, because it represents the multiple diverse opinions or beliefs of many individuals. Without statistical analysis, determining the meaning of this information would be unwieldy and subject to a wide range of interpretations. Additionally, because statistics allow us to determine the probability or likelihood of certain outcomes based on the information we have gathered, they offer a way to judge various hypotheses (Jayaratne, 1983). For example, if two different but equally plausible strategies are proposed by feminists for persuading voters to support legislation upholding a women's right to choose, a statistical analysis of data on voter attitudes can demonstrate which method is likely to be the most effective in accomplishing this goal.

Some feminists criticize the use of statistics and claim that the quantification of subjective personal experiences does not adequately convey the richness of women's lives (e.g., Marecek et al., 1997; Wallston & Grady, 1992) and therefore seems antithetical to feminist traditions. While we agree that the use of statistics, as summaries of information, does involve the loss of some in-depth meaning, we also argue that such use does not violate any feminist principles. Moreover, as mentioned previously, statistics can be used to effectively promote feminist goals. Consistent with our viewpoint, some feminist scholars point out that it is not statistics, per se, that are objectionable, but rather how they are used within the broader context of research that determines whether they violate feminist ideals (e.g., Jayaratne & Stewart, 1991; Maynard, 1994; Peplau & Conrad, 1989). Certainly, statistics have been used to support sexist or racist theories (e.g., Buss, 1989; Herrnstein & Murray, 1994), but they have also documented the benefits of affirmative action and have been effective in shaping progressive social policies (e.g., Gurin, Dey, & Hurtado, 2002). We contend, therefore, that statistics are useful for feminist research.

Knowing which statistical techniques should be used to answer a specific research question is a significant issue, since using inappropriate statistics can not only distort the findings of a study but, in the worst-case scenario, can actually produce results that are opposite from those that accurately reflect the collected data. We therefore emphasize the importance of understanding statistics when doing (or evaluating) survey research. Although we cannot explain these techniques here (large volumes have been written on the appropriate use of statistics), one illustration might help make our point. Suppose a feminist survey researcher wants to document and publicize the pervasiveness of poverty among women in a particular country where the large majority of the women earn less than $1,000 a year but a small percentage earn more than $50,000 a year. If the researcher used a mean value (a statistic that is the average among all women) to describe women's incomes, it would appear that the average woman earns about $10,000 a year. This statistic might be correct, but is misleading.

An alternative statistic, the median (which represents the income level that divides the distribution of women's incomes in half, so that half the women are above that level and the other half below), might suggest that women's income is around $1,500. The mode (a statistic that represents the most common income level) could also be used and would suggest that most women earn less than $1,000. The median and mode would present a much clearer picture of women's earnings in this country than the mean. But an even better way to report the information is to simply give the percent distribution (a statistic) in various income categories. This example illustrates the value of having at least a basic knowledge of statistics, particularly in light of their frequent use in research that has feminist relevance.

Evaluating the Hypotheses

When statistical analyses are complete, researchers use the results to evaluate the hypotheses and determine if they are supported. Although this seems like a simple process, it rarely is straightforward. For example, it is not uncommon for statistical analyses to produce equivocal findings. Sometimes, one set of results appear to contradict other results. It might also be the case that the research findings seem to conflict with feminist ideals and interests. In this situation, it may be worthwhile to reevaluate the research to explore the possibility that such findings result from a deviation in accepted research protocol (e.g., misinterpretations of question wording). It may additionally be helpful to ask why a particular finding appears to conflict with feminist principles. This might lead to alternative understandings of the phenomena of interest that were previously not considered. Although it can seem frustrating not having a clear cut evaluation of a hypothesis, for many investigators studying complex phenomena without definitive answers is a valuable and rich part of the research process and often generates additional research questions that need to be explored.

Questions that must be asked at the beginning of the second phase of the survey research process include the following:

- Which survey research method is best suited to answer my research question?
- How should I select people to participate in my study?
- What questions should I ask in my survey and how should I ask them?

- How can I ensure that the people who participate in my study are treated ethically?
- What statistical technique would best test my research hypothesis?

THE THIRD PHASE OF SURVEY RESEARCH: INTERPRETING THE OVERALL RESULTS AND REPORTING THEM

In the final phase of survey research (the other "bookend"), the results are interpreted and reported. We consider the feminist perspective to be especially applicable and necessary in this phase because it is at this point that the research is applied to the real world and can be used to improve women's lives.

Interpreting the Results From a Feminist Perspective

How a researcher interprets the overall results is the culmination of the investigation in the sense that it answers the research question, put forth in the initial steps of the research process. For feminists, however, the answer to the research question is also usually given feminist meaning. That is, unlike the evaluation of the hypotheses using statistical information (a process that should follow accepted survey research practices), interpreting the overall research results should be subject to a feminist perspective. To illustrate this significance, suppose a researcher conducted a study exploring differences between American women and men in mathematical performance and the overall results of the study indicated that men performed significantly better than women. There are myriad interpretations of what that means. One could see this finding as indicating support for the "deficit hypothesis"; that is, women are naturally inferior to men—an orientation seen frequently in earlier (and sometimes current) psychological and social research and much criticized by feminist scholars (Eichler, 1988; Jayaratne & Kaczala, 1983). Alternatively, one could interpret this difference as reflecting the effects of gender stereotypes on women's math performance (thereby increasing performance anxiety), the educational system that puts limits on women's educational opportunities in math, or how parents encourage math achievement more in their sons than their daughters. These latter interpretations all point to the need for social change (improving the conditions that support and enhance women's math performance) rather than the acceptance of women's inferiority in this area. They also suggest some possibilities for bringing about this change and would be much more likely to be put forth by a feminist than by someone without an awareness of women's oppression or who does not support feminist goals. We should also note that in general, good research also often suggests new ideas and additional research questions rather than simply answering the question at hand. In sum, the feminist meanings we give our results are what mark the research endeavor as a significant feminist enterprise that works to improve women's lives.

The Dissemination of Research Findings

The final step of the entire research process can be an exceptionally gratifying part of the research journey because it addresses the most fundamental goal of feminist research—to enact real-world social change for women. This step is the dissemination of findings, which refers to the reporting of results to scholars, the public, the media, or policymakers, by linking the results back to women's lives with a clear understanding of how they can benefit women. As such, the research acts as a catalyst for social change. As we have argued, feminist survey research can be particularly amenable to advocating for women, because it uses many mainstream research methods that are likely more acceptable to individuals who might distrust findings derived from alternative methods.

One excellent example of how survey research can be applied to real-world social change for women is the Supreme Court's rulings on affirmative action at the University of Michigan. In 2003, the American Psychological Association submitted an Amicus Curiae brief to the Supreme Court, which supported the University of Michigan's policy of race- and gender-aware admissions in higher education in two court cases (*Gratz v. Bollinger*, 2003; *Grutter v. Bollinger*, 2003). This brief drew heavily on social psychologist Patricia Gurin's survey research on the benefits of diversity in academia (as summarized in Gurin et al., 2002). The Court's decision to uphold the principle of considering race and gender in college admissions is just one illustration of how survey results can be an important part of the effort to change social policy.

Questions that should be asked during the third phase of the survey research process include the following:

- How do I interpret the results in such a way that they can be used to advance feminist goals?
- How should I disseminate my findings to make those goals a reality?

CONCLUSION

Feminist research includes a multitude of methods, each of which can uniquely, or in combination, influence the social change effort to improve the lives of women. In this chapter, we focused on the survey research method and the important role it can play in this endeavor. We hope that this chapter provides budding feminist researchers with an understanding of why this method can be a powerful tool in their work on behalf of women and other socially marginalized groups. We also hope that we have adequately stressed the importance of attending to those aspects of the survey research process that will yield information able to withstand critical scrutiny. Such research can most effectively advance feminist goals. Certainly, there are an immeasurable number of feminist issues that need investigating, many of which could be effectively addressed using survey research methods or other methods described in this volume. Each of us has the potential to contribute to the research effort to ultimately benefit women or other groups of individuals who are disadvantaged under the current social system. As members of the feminist community, we invite you to join us in this quest.

NOTE

1. Although this chapter offers you a general introduction to survey research, we suggest that if you are interested in using these methods or learning more about them, there are several excellent sources of additional information (e.g., Alreck & Settle, 1995; Czaja & Blair, 1996; Dillman, 1978, 2000; Groves, 1989; Groves et al., 2004; Tourangeau, Rips, & Rasinski, 2000).

REFERENCES

Alreck, P. L., & Settle, R. B. (1995). *The survey research handbook: Guidelines and strategies for conducting a survey.* Burr Ridge, IL: Irwin.

Bianchi, S. M., Milkie, M. A., & Sayer, L. C. (2000). Is anyone doing the housework? Trends in the gender division of household labor. *Social Forces, 79,* 191–228.

Biemer, P. P., & Lyberg, L. E. (2003). *Introduction to survey quality*. Hoboken, NJ: Wiley.

Buss, D. M. (1989). Sex differences in human mate preferences: Evolutionary hypotheses tested in 37 cultures. *Behavioral and Brain Sciences, 12,* 1–49.

Campbell, P. B. (1982). Racism and sexism in research. In H. Mitzel (Ed.), *Encyclopedia of educational research* (5th ed., pp. 1515–1520). New York: Free Press.

Condor, S. (1986). Sex role beliefs and "traditional" women: Feminist and intergroup perspectives. In S. Wilkinson (Ed.), *Feminist social psychology: Developing theory and practice* (pp. 97–118). Philadelphia: Open University Press.

Converse, J. (1987). *Survey research in the United States.* Berkeley: University of California Press.

Croll, J. K., Neumark-Sztainer, D., & Story, M. (2002). Prevalence and risk and protective factors related to disordered eating behaviors among adolescents: Relationship to gender and ethnicity. *Journal of Adolescent Health, 31,* 166–175.

Czaja, R., & Blair, J. (1996). *Designing surveys: A guide to decisions and procedures.* Thousand Oaks, CA: Pine Forge Press.

Dillman, D. A. (1978). *Mail and telephone surveys: The total design method.* New York: Wiley-Interscience.

Dillman, D. A. (2000). *Mail and Internet surveys: The tailored design method.* New York: Wiley.

Du Bois, B. (1983). Passionate scholarship: Notes on values, knowing and method in feminist social science. In G. Bowles & R. Duelli Klein (Eds.), *Theories of women's studies* (pp. 105–116). Boston: Routledge & Kegan Paul.

Eichler, M. (1988). *Nonsexist research methods: A practical guide.* New York: Routledge.

Fee, E. (1983). Women's nature and scientific objectivity. In M. Lowe & R. Hubbard (Eds.), *Woman's nature: Rationalizations of inequality* (pp. 9–27). New York: Pergamon Press.

Fowler, F. J. (1984). *Survey research methods.* Beverly Hills, CA: Sage.

Gorelick, S. (1996). Contradictions of feminist methodology. In H. Gottfried (Ed.), *Feminism and social change: Bridging theory and practice* (pp. 23–45). Urbana: University of Illinois Press.

Gratz v. Bollinger, 539 U.S. 244 (2003).

Groves, R. (1989). *Survey errors and survey costs.* New York: Wiley.

Groves, R., Fowler, F. J., Couper, M. P., Lepkowski, J. M., Singer, E., & Tourangeau, R. (2004). *Survey methodology.* Hoboken, NJ: Wiley.

Groves, R., & Kahn, R. (1979). *Surveys by telephone: A national comparison with personal interviews.* New York: Academic Press.

Grutter v. Bollinger, 539 U.S. 306 (2003).

Gurin, P., Dey, E. L., & Hurtado, S. (2002). Diversity and higher education: Theory and impact on educational outcomes. *Harvard Educational Review, 72,* 330–366.

Haraway, D. (1988). Situated knowledges: The science question in feminism and the privilege of partial perspective. *Feminist Studies, 14,* 575–599.

Harding, S. (1987). Introduction. Is there a feminist method? In S. Harding (Ed.), *Feminism and methodology* (pp. 1–14). Bloomington: Indiana University Press.

Harding, S. (1998). *Is science multicultural? Postcolonialisms, feminisms, and epistemologies*. Bloomington: Indiana University Press.

Harding, S. (2004). Rethinking standpoint epistemology: What is "strong objectivity"? In S. N. Hesse-Biber and M. L. Yaiser (Eds.), *Feminist perspectives on social research* (pp. 39–64). New York: Oxford University Press.

Herrnstein, R. J., & Murray, C. (1994). *The bell curve: Intelligence and class structure in American life*. New York: Simon & Schuster.

Hesse-Biber, S. N., Leavy, P., and Yaiser, M. L. (2004). Feminist approaches to research as a process: Reconceptualizing epistemology, methodology, and method. In S. N. Hesse-Biber and M. L. Yaiser (Eds.), *Feminist perspectives on social research* (pp. 3–26). New York: Oxford University Press.

Jayaratne, T. E. (1983). The value of quantitative methodology for feminist research. In G. Bowles & R. Duelli Klein (Eds.), *Theories of women's studies* (pp. 140–161). Boston: Routledge & Kegan Paul.

Jayaratne, T. E., & Kaczala, C. M. (1983). Social responsibility in sex difference research. *Journal of Educational Equity and Leadership, 3,* 305–316.

Jayaratne, T. E., & Stewart, A. J. (1991). Quantitative and qualitative methods in the social sciences: Current feminist issues and practical strategies. In M. M. Fonow & J. A. Cook (Eds.), *Beyond methodology: Feminist scholarship as lived research* (pp. 85–106). Bloomington: Indiana University Press.

Jayaratne, T. E., Thomas, N. G., & Trautmann, M. T. (2003). An intervention program to keep girls in the science pipeline: Outcome differences by ethnic status. *Journal of Research in Science Teaching, 40,* 393–414.

Jones, J. (1981). *Bad blood: The Tuskegee syphilis experiment*. New York: Free Press.

Kelly, A. (1978). Feminism and research. *Women's Studies International Quarterly, 1,* 225–232.

Koss, M. P., Gidycz, C. A., & Wisniewski, N. (1987). The scope of rape: Incidence and prevalence of sexual aggression and victimization in a national sample of higher education students. *Journal of Consulting and Clinical Psychology, 55,* 162–170.

Landrine, H., Klonoff, E. A., & Brown-Collins, A. (1992). Cultural diversity and methodology in feminist psychology. *Psychology of Women Quarterly, 16,* 145–163.

Marecek, J., Fine, M., & Kidder, L. (1997). Working between worlds: Qualitative methods and social psychology. *Journal of Social Issues, 53,* 631–644.

Maynard, M. (1994). Methods, practice and epistemology: The debate about feminism and research. In M. Maynard & J. Purvis (Eds.), *Researching women's lives from a feminist perspective* (pp. 10–26). Bristol, PA: Taylor & Francis.

Milgram, S. (1974). *Obedience to authority*. New York: Harper & Row.

National Committee on Pay Equity. (2005). Retrieved December 7, 2005, from www.pay-equity.org/

Peplau, L. A., & Conrad, E. (1989). Beyond nonsexist research: The perils of feminist methods in psychology. *Psychology on Women Quarterly, 13,* 379–400.

Pew Research Center. (2004). *Polls face growing resistance, but still representative survey experiment shows.* Retrieved April 14, 2005, from http://people-press.org/reports

Quina, K., Rose, J. S., Harlow, L. L., Morokoff, P. J., Deiter, P. J., Whitmire, L. E., et al. (1999). Focusing on participants: Feminist process model for survey modification. *Psychology of Women Quarterly, 23,* 459–493.

Reinharz, S. (1979). *On becoming a social scientist.* San Francisco: Jossey-Bass.

Reinharz, S. (1992). *Feminist methods in social research.* New York: Oxford University Press.

Riessman, C. K. (1987). When gender is not enough: Women interviewing women. *Gender & Society, 1,* 172–207.

Rogers, T. F. (1971). Interviews by telephone and in person: Quality of responses and field performance. In E. Singer & S. Presser (Eds.), *Survey research methods: Scheduling telephone interviews.* Chicago: University of Chicago Press.

Schwarz, N., Groves, R. M., & Schuman, H. (1998). Survey methods. In D. T. Gilbert, S. T. Fiske, & G. Lindzey (Eds.), *The handbook of social psychology* (Vol. 1, pp. 143–179). New York: McGraw-Hill.

Sherif, C. W. (1979). Bias in psychology. In J. Sherman & E. T. Back (Eds.), *The prism of sex: Essays in the sociology of knowledge* (pp. 93–133). Madison: University of Wisconsin Press.

Smith, C. A., & Frieze, I. H. (2003). Examining rape empathy from the perspective of the victim and the assailant. *Journal of Applied Social Psychology, 33,* 476–498.

Smith, D. E. (1987). *The everyday world as problematic: A sociology for women.* Boston: Northeastern University Press.

Smith, M. D. (1994). Enhancing the quality of survey data on violence against women: A feminist approach. *Gender & Society, 8,* 109–127.

Spalter-Roth, R., & Hartmann, H. (1996). Small happinesses: The feminist struggle to integrate social research and social activism. In H. Gottfried (Ed.), *Feminism and social change: Bridging theory and practice* (pp. 206–224). Urbana: University of Illinois Press.

Stangor, C. (2004). *Research methods for the behavioral sciences.* Boston: Houghton Mifflin.

Stanley, L., & Wise, S. (1983). *Breaking out: Feminist consciousness and feminist research.* London: Routledge & Kegan Paul.

Stewart, A. J., & Dottolo, A. L. (2005). Socialization to the academy: Coping with competing social identities. In G. Downey, J. Eccles, & C. Chatman (Eds.), *Navigating the future: Social identity, coping and life tasks* (pp.167–187). New York: Russell Sage.

Tourangeau, R., Rips, L., & Rasinski, K. (2000). *The psychology of survey response.* Cambridge, UK: Cambridge University Press.

U.S. Census Bureau. (1989). *A century of population growth, from the first census of the United States to the twelfth, 1790–1900.* Baltimore: Genealogical Publishing.

U.S. Census Bureau. (2005). *Census 2000 demographic profile highlights.* Retrieved December 8, 2005, from http://factfinder.census.gov/servlet/SAFFFacts?_sse=on

Wallston, B. S., & Grady, K. E. (1992). Integrating the feminist critique and the crisis in social psychology: Another look at research methods. In J. S. Bohan (Ed.), *Seldom seen, rarely heard: Women's place in psychology* (pp. 307–336). Boulder, CO: Westview Press.

Wood, K. C., Becker, J. A., & Thompson, J. K. (1996). Body image dissatisfaction in preadolescent children. *Journal of Applied Developmental Psychology, 17,* 85–100.

PART III

FEMINIST PRAXIS

ELEVEN

PUTTING IT TOGETHER

Feminist Research Praxis

Sharlene Nagy Hesse-Biber

———◈———

The basic premise of this entire book has been to provide you with a hands-on experience in conducting research from a feminist perspective. My coauthors and I have discussed a range of methods that feminists have employed in their research projects, from survey research, ethnography, in-depth interviewing, focus groups, oral history to mixed-methods research. I leave you with an example of putting your own research ideas into practice, and I provide you with an example that illustrates the genesis and analysis of a feminist research project. While I cannot tackle all the methods we have learned in this final chapter, I will select one method and follow it from the research questions to how you might begin to think about the analysis of your data. I discuss the use of computer software programs as an option for con-templating the analysis of your data. I also address some general issues you might consider when you're interpreting and writing up your research results. Last, I provide you with a general checklist of things to consider once your project is complete.

Note: Portions of this chapter are reprinted with permission from Hesse-Biber and Leavy (2006), *The Practice of Qualitative Interviewing,* Sage Publications, Inc.

PUTTING IT INTO PRACTICE:
CONDUCTING A RESEARCH PROJECT

Setting the Scene of the Research Project

The following excerpts are the voices of college women who were interviewed about their body image during their freshman year of college, and more specifically on their feelings about the infamous "Freshman 15," the 15 pounds that college age women frequently report gaining during their first-year experience at college. Before we consider the research process, let's listen to some of their comments.

Pam: I remember when I was in freshman year I came to school and gained that weight, and when I went home for Christmas I remember my dad remarked that I was getting a little chubbier, especially in my butt. And I think that was one of the main reasons when I came back to school I started excessively losing weight.

Emily: I gained it quick. When I went home for Christmas I had gained 15 pounds!

And somebody noticed it?

Emily: Yeah, my whole family.

So what happened then?

Emily: After that, I came back from my semester break, I noticed that my friends who had gone to school hadn't really gained weight. My parents had noticed, and my brothers. And so when I came back, I stopped eating between meals and I rarely ate breakfast. I ran 2 miles a day. . . . I wanted to lose weight. To avoid eating at night I would go to the library and study. That's what I did. Studying in the library, I'm not in my room. When I came back, I would say I have to go to bed because I had been sick and so I was conscious about going to bed early.

Judy: You know, when I overate it was my freshman year. The most I ever ate in my life. I never vomited it out. I wouldn't know how to do that. I did do it sort of secretly you could say. My freshman year roommate, you know, she was thin and fine and she could eat what she wanted. She didn't overeat. She could eat a hamburger and French fries for lunch.

She just wouldn't go out and have a sundae and everything on top of it. She was just that type of metabolism. And freshman year when you have the points, and you got the store, and you got the cookies and the candy bars. My mother never really bought that stuff, which is great. We never had any kind of junk food like that around. Once in a while, my mother would buy it and we'd gobble it up. We'd have ice cream, plenty of that, so I wasn't like a hog over that. I didn't need that. When I went to college, I did buy like cookies and candy, and when she wasn't there I was eating them. I was eating alone.

The Research Project

What is the lived experience of college freshmen women regarding their perceptions of their body image in college?

My goal for this project is exploratory in nature. I am interested in understanding the specific body image issues college freshman women may be experiencing. I have read some literature on this topic, but I want to better understand women's subjective experiences. I have some general agenda items I am particularly interested in, such as whether or not college freshman women experience what has been termed the "Freshman 15," the 15 pounds that many college women are alleged to gain during their first year at college.

I decide to conduct a *convenience sample* of college freshman women who attend the university at which I am also a professor. I will recruit women by putting up signs around the campus, including the local women's resource center. I want to obtain a *purposive convenience sample* of college freshman women with diverse backgrounds, so I am interested in a fair representation of freshman women by race, ethnic background, and social class wherever possible. I am interested in obtaining 25 interviews in order to make some statements about differences among women by race and ethnicity and, where possible, by class status. I obtain approval to conduct this study from my college's institutional review board (IRB) by following some simple steps. After writing up a short proposal that follows the IRB guidelines and creating a set of open-ended questions I will ask my respondents, I submit these materials to the IRB along with a detailed consent form for their approval. A consent form must be signed by my respondent and agreed to before the interview process begins.

I choose to start out my interview with a set of general, open-ended interview questions with the goal of gaining insight and understanding into the lives of freshman women. I follow the guidelines on interviewing discussed in the in-depth interviewing chapter. I am mindful that I am an "outsider" as well as an "insider" in the college community. As a white, middle-class, female college professor, I am interviewing college students, and there is an inherent power dynamic in my relationship with them. In my interviews with women of color, there will be differences to consider in terms of my race, ethnicity and, possibly, class status. It is important at this point for me to reflect in a research memo on these differences and how they might affect the research situation. How do my unique differences bump up against those I interview? What biases do I bring to the interview situation?

I gather my data by using a digital recorder with the permission of my respondent. I am careful at the end of each interview to ask each respondent if there is something she would like to talk about that we have not touched upon. I am also aware of the valuable data that can emerge when I turn off the recorder and continue to talk with my respondent, and I do my best to recall what transpired without the recorder running right after I leave the interview. I am careful to follow what I have learned about the importance of establishing rapport with my respondent and being careful to listen intently to what they are telling me, mindful of any muted language contained within their dialogue.

After each interview, I immerse myself in the data I have collected by playing back the recording with my respondent. As I begin to transcribe the interview, I am also beginning to analyze and interpret my data. That is, I am writing down any ideas that come to mind (memoing), and noting the themes that I find particularly important. After a few interviews, I especially look for the common pathways or patterns of behavior whereby individuals experience their bodies within a college culture. I am particularly mindful to write down my ideas as a set of data memos.

Data Analysis*

The key to data analysis is to search for meanings within the data. *Memoing* and *coding* are two important ways to find these messages and

---

*Parts of this section are adapted in whole or part from Hesse-Biber, Sharlene Nagy, & Leavy, Patricia. (2004). Analysis, interpretation, and the writing of qualitative data. In Sharlene Nagy Hesse-Biber and Patricia Leavy (Eds.), *Approaches to qualitative research: A reader on theory and practice* (pp. 409–425). New York: Oxford University Press.

Coding an Interview: Pam, College Freshman Interview Excerpt

(Text/Segment/Chunk)		*Code*
I always wanted to be the thinnest, the	→	Thinnest, prettiest
prettiest. I wanted to look like the girls	→	Look like girls in magazines
in the magazines. I'm going to have so	→	Boys will love me
many boyfriends, and boys are going	→	Positive body image
to be so in love with me, I won't have to	→	Provides economic resources
work, and I'll be taken care of for the	→	Thin rationale
rest of my life	→	Thin as a means of security
	→	Media creates standards

SOURCE: Adapted from Hesse-Biber and Leavy (2004, p. 412). Reprinted with permission of Oxford University Press.

meaning within the data. In the following table, I have excerpted one of my interviews with college freshmen women concerning their eating patterns and disordered eating habits.

As you can see from this excerpt, I have "coded" the first few lines of text from one interview using a "literal" coding procedure that uses the respondent's own words. These are descriptive code categories. If we proceed down the code list, we will see that the codes become more "analytical"; the term *positive body image* is an excellent illustration of this shift. Nowhere does the respondent directly say this, but the researcher is able to generate the more conceptual code of "body image" by building from the respondent's work. This appears to fit what the respondent is saying when she notes, "I'm going to have so many boyfriends, and boys are going to be so in love with me." As we continue down the code list, the codes become much more interpretative.

We should remember that to "code" means to take a segment of text and give it a "name" or sometimes a number. There are many ways to code a given text. I began by doing some "literal" coding and moved quickly to a more "focused" coding procedure. Sociologist Kathy Charmaz (1995) uses the term *focused coding* and suggests that the researchers look at all the data they have coded from the interview. In our example, the researcher would look at "positive body image" and consider each piece of text associated with that code for each interview. The researcher could then compare each segment with the other to come up with a clearly delineated working idea of what the concept *positive body image* means (Charmaz, 1983, p. 117).

Focused coding differs from "literal" coding in that you are not placing a "label" on something to describe what it is, but rather you are looking for a code description that allows you to develop an understanding or interpretation of what your respondents are saying about their body image. To engage in focused coding means to sort your literal codes into more abstract categories. This modification of code categories is a process that moves your analysis from a literal to more abstract level. This method is important to generate theoretical ideas.

You might begin this process in earnest after coding a number of interviews with the college freshman and retrieving the texts associated with specific codes. Let's refer to the preceding table. Suppose I retrieved all the text associated with the code "thin." When I read through all the text segments associated with this code, I am able to see that respondents are in fact talking about thinness in a variety of ways. For example, in the text segment above, I note at the bottom of the segment, "thinness as a means of security" and "media creates standards." "Thinness as a means of security" is capturing what my respondent is voicing when she says that she wants to have a boyfriend, love, and money and to be taken care of, but this definition is quite different from "media creates standards of thinness." Each idea of thinness has its own voice and idea, and I quickly found that other interviews uncovered a range of reasons respondents wanted to be thin. Some respondents saw "thin as healthy," but others might see "thin as empowering," and the reasons continued to unfold in the interviews. This eventually led me to develop an even larger code category that I termed "thin rationales," of which the code category "thinness as a means of security" was a subset. A second, larger category, "media creates standards" of behavior, was developed in a similar manner. I eventually came up with a whole series of codes that I modified, and these evolved into more abstract codes. For example, in the freshman body image study, we can see that the code "clothing made for thin people" evolved into the code category "clothing that fits." Eventually, this category morphed into part of a still larger code titled "body surveillance," which represents the idea that women are constantly watching and monitoring their bodies. This can include checking to see whether or not their clothing fits them, watching their image in the mirror, weighing themselves several times during the day, and even comparing their bodies with those of super thin models in the media. With this example, we can see how the initial codes then became part of a larger conceptual category that overall captures the importance of surveillance as a "control" mechanism used to coax women's bodies toward the thin ideal initiated by the self and society. You can see how we are moving our analysis from the literal plane to a more abstract and theoretical understanding of women's body image concerns, and we are beginning to see what might be some of the factors that help us better understand their need to be thin. We might then begin to look at differences among the sample in terms of whether or not women differ on these issues by race and ethnicity and, where possible, by class.

Initial Codes in the Body Image Study Were Changed as Follows

From	To
Clothing made for thin people	Clothing that fits
Minimal diet	Control over body and eating
Magazines	Media creates standards
Will always want to be thin	Values thinness
1. Thin as a means of security	All four characterized
2. Thin and healthy	"Thin rationales"
3. Thin as part of identity	
4. Thin/beauty is empowering	

SOURCE: Hesse-Biber and Leavy (2004, p. 412). Reprinted with permission of Oxford University Press.

Grounded theory provides a window into understanding meaning in your data, and it is both a method as well as a theory. As a method of analysis, it provides a way to develop "progressively more abstract conceptual categories to synthesize, to explain and to understand" data (Charmaz, 1995, p. 28). If we recap the analysis example I just took you through, we can discern the outlines of an analytical method. A grounded theory analysis begins with a close reading of the interview data. Charmaz (1995) suggests that one begins with "open coding." This consists of literally reading the data "line by line" and coding each line of the text. The questions one might consider during this process are as follows (Charmaz, 1995, p. 38):

- "What is going on?"
- "What are people doing?"
- "What is the person doing?"
- "What do these actions and statements take for granted?"
- "How do structure and context serve to support, maintain, impede, or change these actions and statements?"

There is a dynamic interaction between memoing and coding. I derive my ideas directly from my data, not some overarching theory that I start out with about women's body image. Memoing allows the researcher to "elaborate processes, assumptions and actions" that are often embedded in codes (Charmaz, 1995, pp. 42–43). Writing memos also elevates a literal code to a "category." The interaction between coding and memoing is truly at the heart of a grounded analysis, for I literally ground my ideas in the data through this process. Ideally, the memo-writing process should occur throughout the many steps of analysis, for well-developed memos can be helpful in guiding research. Just as one reviews the interview transcripts, one should also read and sort through memos. It is crucial to read and review these memos, for these steps help us develop and elaborate ideas and theories. Memos are particularly helpful because they allow me to see the relationships between code categories and my hunches about what might be hidden in my data. The memos are most important, though, because they are a roadmap to discerning what the research codes truly mean, and the ideas that are jotted down might even bring up new ideas and relationships within the data. This is why it is so important to review and reread research memos and field notes.

When we discuss a grounded theory approach, it is important to remember that there are many other ways to dissect and develop your data. You might decide to do a narrative analysis whereby you would not begin with line-by-line coding, but instead you would be interested in the ways in which respondents frame meaning in terms of the stories they relate to you in their interview. You would be interested in examining the structure of the narrative and considering probing questions about the story being told. Is it episodic or chronological? What are the meanings of specific stories contained within the interview? How does the respondent represent their lived reality in a story form? These are all pivotal questions and there are infinitely more that can unveil new depths of your interview. The unit of analysis of your interview is not the line but the beginning and ending of the stories contained within the interview.

In the following Behind-the-Scenes piece, the feminist scholar Dana Crowley Jack lets us behind the curtain of her analytical process, touching on issues such as coding, grounded theory, and computer-assisted data analysis.

Behind-the-Scenes With Dana Crowley Jack

On Moments of Rapid Refocusing and What Leads to Them

One cold, November afternoon, two undergraduate assistants and I poured over lengthy interviews, focusing on women's accounts of what makes them angry and how they express anger. It was getting late; we were all half brain-dead from the painstaking detail of creating and checking a coding manual using the grounded theory method (Strauss & Corbin, 1990). For feminist researchers, this method facilitates our commitment to hear participants in their own terms rather than appropriating women's words to existing theories. I had conducted the interviews using a voice-centered relational approach that follows the interviewee's lead and inquires about women's histories, thoughts, and fears about their anger (Jack, 1999).

According to grounded theory, the researcher is led by data—that is, categories and theories emerge from the data. Even though it is impossible to approach interviews without any preexisting paradigms, this method works well to correct a researcher's misconceptions, particularly when the data force us to notice any implicit frameworks we may unconsciously hold. In addition, feminists have made it clear that women often silence their own feelings and perspectives, which operates as a means of oppression (Jack, 1991; Lorde, 1984; Rich, 1979). To overcome silences about women's experiences, we need to read and reread narratives, recognizing that there are different aspects of experience being spoken to, hearing different aspects of the woman's "voice." The Listening Guide, a feminist interpretive method, can help hear silences through focusing the researcher's attention on both the narrator's voice and the coder's (listener's) responses (Brown & Gilligan, 1992; Brown, Tappan, Gilligan, Miller, & Argyris, 1989). In this short account, I will attempt to describe the misconceptions I had about women's anger and how method and data corrected them.

For the anger study, I had imported the interviews into Ethnograph, a computer-guided software program. Interviews were stripped of all identifying information about the participant, with lines numbered and ready for coding.

The student assistants (Samya Clumpner and Athena Stevens) and I were following a process: (1) read over interviews separately to see what themes emerged; (2) compare themes together, using examples from interview data, and decide on categories that encompass the themes; and (3) check

(Continued)

(Continued)

our categories against the remaining interviews to see if new categories/ themes challenge those previously developed. We were at Step 3 of the process on that dark, rainy afternoon.

Here's what happened. We had fallen into coding women's anger expression using the prevailing terms of internalization and externalization that dominate psychology and ordinary language. These metaphors conjure a picture of anger as contained inside a person (where it may seethe, sizzle, or burn) or as exploding out of that container/person with greater or lesser force and consequences. Charles Spielberger et al. (1985) base their widely used Anger Expression Scale on these anger-in, anger-out dimensions. As a feminist, I knew that women and men face very different responses for directly expressing their anger, with women incurring more extreme interpersonal, economic, and legal consequences than men. In these interviews, women filled their accounts with stories of expected negative reactions to their anger, even when conveyed with a mild voice tone. Or they detailed how they used anger as a protective shield in a dangerous world. I had not yet found a way to represent the complex ways that women expressed their anger and for what purposes they did so, but I was relying on the existing, well-worn categories of externalization and internalization that were present in theory, language, and my own mind.

We were in the middle of examining a woman's account of being furious with her husband over, guess what? Housework! She left the house, got into the car, and drove off in a rage but did not show any anger to her husband. Two blocks away, she pulled over to pound the steering wheel, yell, and cry. The coders said, "externalization," but this left out too many of her thoughts; it did not fit. As we discussed why not, bingo, the picture shifted to the woman's concerns. What mattered to her were the consequences of her anger on the relationship. My attention quickly refocused, following the traces of her words, moving away from the woman as the container of anger to land on the *relationship* as the context that mattered. What mattered was whether or not she was willing to bring her anger into dialogue in the relationship or tried to keep it in by, for example, pounding the steering wheel away from her husband's awareness.

One of the anger items on the Spielberger anger expression scale is "I often slam doors." This context-free item does not capture women's concerns about interpersonal consequences: It makes a big difference whether or not that door is slammed in someone's face or in an empty house. Rather than the person as the unit of analysis (a container from which anger moves in or out), the relationship became the new unit of our analysis: whether or not a woman tried to keep her anger out of or brought it into her relationship, with what goals or purposes, using what behaviors. With this new focus, it became easy for us to categorize the ways that women dealt with their anger vis-à-vis their relationships (Jack, 2001).

We celebrated the breakthrough with coffee and laughter. This process of documenting women's words through their own perspectives—which is at the heart of a feminist inquiry—requires being well versed in psychological theory. But it also requires that we hold accepted ways of seeing and hearing in check and listen to what is not being captured by existing categories or theories. Also, we can listen to the concerns, the silences, the inner arguments and dialogues of our study participants and to our own discomfort with existing explanations.

Now that I have offered an example of the coding process, let's turn to interpretation and writing, which have been discussed in part throughout this book.

INTERPRETATION AND WRITING UP OF YOUR RESEARCH PROJECT

In the next sections, I will provide you with a general overview regarding issues of interpretation and writing up of your research project. Norman K. Denzin (2000) suggests that there is an "art of interpretation":

> This may also be described as moving from the field to the text to the reader. The practice of this art allows the field-worker-as-bricoleur . . . to translate what has been learned into a body of textual work that communicates these understandings to the reader. (pp. 313–314)

There is no specific path to interpreting your data. In fact, the researcher goes back and forth from data analysis to data interpretation. This journey ultimately leads to the collection of more appropriate data. These are not separate phases of the research endeavor; the process is depicted in Figure 11.1.

This diagram illustrates the fluidity of the research process, for the researcher is constantly engaged in data collection, data analysis, and the

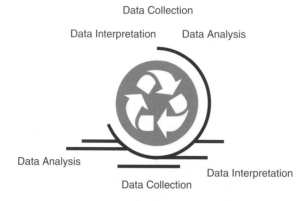

Data Collection

Data Interpretation   Data Analysis

Data Analysis

Data Interpretation

Data Collection

Figure 11.1   Diagram of the "Iterative" Process
in the Analysis and Interpretation of Data

SOURCE: Adapted with permission from Hesse-Biber and Leavy (2006). *The Practice of Qualitative Interviewing.* Sage Publications, Inc.

interpretation of research findings in dynamic ways. Memo writing is the link between analysis (what did I find?) and interpretation (what does it mean?). Researchers should use early notes and memos to develop and enrich the analytic process. Think back to the questions that you initially asked: "What does it mean? Which of my ideas are supported by the data? What additional questions do I need to ask that I haven't asked? Who else should I interview? What have I not followed up on? What new data do I need to collect?" These early memos can be helpful and might guide your research in a new direction. David Karp notes the following concerning early memo writing:

> Especially at the beginning, you will hear people say things that you just hadn't thought about. Look carefully for major directions that it had just not occurred to you to take. The pace of short memo writing ought to be especially great toward the beginning of your work. We advocate "idea" or "concept" memos that introduce an emerging idea. Such memos typically run 2 to 3 pages. (quoted in Hesse-Biber & Leavy, 2006, p. 142)

After sorting through your memos and doing some substantial coding, Karp suggests that you are in a good position to "grab onto a theme." It is at this time now that one should begin what he terms a "data memo." By this, I mean a memo that integrates the theme with data and any available literature that fits. A data memo begins to look like a paper, but it contains more data on a point than you would actually use in a research paper. If you make a broad point and feel that you have 10 good pieces of data that support it, lay them all out for inspection and later use. David Karp emphasizes that a good researcher must "make sure to lay out the words of people who do not fit the pattern" (quoted in Hesse-Biber & Leavy, 2006, p. 143).

More questions come to the surface as we begin to put together the story of what we have found. We begin to see specific issues and perspectives of our respondents' stories that show us how to go about representing our respondent's subjective understandings of their lived experiences. At the center of this phase of the research process is the question of whose story we are in fact representing: the respondent's or our own.

Feminist researchers are particularly aware of the power and authority that is invested in the researchers in terms of how they deal with representing their research findings and interpretations. We have seen many of these issues grappled with throughout the book—for example, when we were thinking about the editing of oral history transcripts, the collaborative nature of feminist qualitative research, and the postmodern perspective on using categories such as "woman" or "women's experience."

> "What role does the researcher play in the process of interpreting his or her data?"

> "To what extent does the researcher allow his or her feelings to enter into the interpretation process?"

> "Whose point of view is the ethnographer really representing with his or her data?" (Van Maanen, 1995, pp. 16–17).

Feminist researchers recognize the general power dilemmas in the research process as a whole, and they specifically address issues of power and authority in the interpretation of women's voices, especially those who have experienced oppression in terms of their gender, race, class, age, and so on. Feminist researchers can use these experiences to explore and grasp the issues they are studying, and the researcher's personal understanding of the issues can be a great advantage. In fact, Dorothy Smith (cited in Lemert, 1999), a feminist sociologist, argues that sociology for women is a study that embraces the perspective of the "other."

USING A COMPUTER SOFTWARE PROGRAM TO ANALYZE AND INTERPRET YOUR DATA: COMPUTER-ASSISTED SOFTWARE AND FEMINIST RESEARCH

- Should I employ computer software, and what will this software do for the analysis and interpretation of my data?

A researcher's analysis can be enhanced by the use of computer software packages. Recent decades have yielded developments in computerized software programs that have transformed the work of sociologists and researchers (Fielding & Lee, 1998). These software programs can be categorized into two main types. The first consists of "generic software" that was not specifically designed for qualitative research. There are three types of software in this category. The first, word processors, can be used to type and organize interviews and field notes as well as develop an organizing scheme for these data. The second, text retrievers, can be used to sort through various data to find a specific pattern or "string" of characters that might enable the researcher to identify themes and topics within a large body of data. The last generic software type are the "textbase" managers. These large database systems allow for the retrieval of semistructured information, which is entered into "records" and "fields" (Fielding & Lee, 1998).

The second type of software that has been specifically designed for qualitative data analysis are the "dedicated qualitative analysis packages." There are four types of software in this category. The first is the "code and retrieve" program, which allows codes to be assigned to particular segments of text. This facilitates easy retrieval of new code categories when the researcher uses sophisticated "Boolean search functions." The second package consists of "code-based theory building programs." These allow the researcher to analyze the systematic relationships among data, codes, and code categories. Some programs provide a rule-based systematic approach that facilitates the testing of a hypothesis, and others allow for a visual representation of the data. "Conceptual network buildings" and "textual mapping software" are the last two packages of this specialized software type. These programs allow the researcher to draw links between code categories in his or her data. This feature could be considered an "add-on" to code-based theory building programs (Fielding & Lee, 1998, pp. 9–11). The field of qualitative software development has grown significantly over time, and these products have generally been well received. Fielding and Lee (1998) note that there is a growing and extensive national and international community of software users.

Computers promise to revolutionize the way researchers conduct their analysis, but they also have a set of caveats for the qualitative analyst. Researchers should experiment with these programs to assess their strengths and weaknesses while considering the implications of using computer software programs to analyze qualitative data. We recommend that you try these programs when appropriate and see how they work for you and your research.

WRITING IT UP*

Norman Denzin (2000) notes that "writing is not an innocent practice," but rather, it is a tool that helps change the world (p. 898). Language is a powerfully influential cultural force, and writing becomes a researcher's means of communicating and passing on valuable information and interpretations to a greater public audience. Researchers become engaged and immersed in the craft; consequently, their personal intentions significantly shape their writing style and process. It is virtually impossible to separate the spheres of writing and interpretation from each other. Writing is a powerful interpretative form of discourse that has a "material presence in the world" and can be "central to the workings of a free democratic society" (pp. 898–899).

When beginning the writing phase of a research project, researchers should be mindful of the intimate connection between their writing and the process of interpretation that has guided their research studies. The connection between writing and interpretation is important, but these elements can also be considered one and the same process. Issues of interpretation and representation are particularly salient in feminist research, where in addition to the routine ethical and pragmatic considerations researchers confront, the feminist researcher must also think about negotiating her political project, her activist intentions, her epistemological commitments, her desire to unearth and make available subjugated knowledge, and her obligation to empower and not oppress.

A researcher should remember that while there are multiple tales from the field, he or she is charged with writing just one of them. This does not mean that he or she should lose sight of the notion that other representational possibilities exist. Van Maanen (1995) critiqued traditional ethnography and

---

*Parts of this section are adapted in whole or part from Hesse-Biber, Sharlene Nagy, & Leavy, Patricia. (2004). Analysis, interpretation, and the writing of qualitative data. In Sharlene Nagy Hesse-Biber and Patricia Leavy (Eds.), *Approaches to qualitative research: A reader on theory and practice* (pp. 409–425). New York: Oxford University Press.

introduced modern researchers to the idea that singular tales of field studies are limited at best. He argues that several stories can be told from a field experience. Many voices can be heard, but inevitably, some are left out. In this regard, Van Maanen makes "a strong argument to counter any faith in a simple or transparent world that can be known with any certainty" (p. 18).

In this refutation of one reality, Denzin (2000) argues that a new genre of writing is emerging in the postmodern era. Some of these styles were addressed in Chapter 4 on postmodern feminism. Different styles are being tested by researchers and journalists alike, and they emphasize that facts need to be considered as social constructions (p. 899).

While the traditional "logico-scientific mode" of social research once yearned for empirical proof and a collection of "universal truth conditions," the test is now to deconstruct this type of pervasive rationality (Richardson, 1995, p. 201). We are not suggesting that there is one truth out there, one experience, one beginning, middle, and end to a story. The lines of reality are being blurred and reshaped by researchers who are struggling to find the best way to write up their research. Many questions challenge and direct their writing processes. Do these look familiar?

- What should a researcher's standards be? In this fluid world of interpretative writing, how can a researcher represent the other without somehow representing herself?

Knowing that writing is not a "'true' representation of an objective 'reality,'" such postmodern researchers are working to identify and redefine their audiences and research goals (Richardson, 1995, p. 199). Writing involves ethical, moral, and personal decisions. A writer's language and stylistic choices can create value, bestow meaning, and constitute the form of the subjects and objects that emerge from a study (Shapiro, 1985–1986, as cited in Richardson, 1995, p. 199).

In this way, writing also gives the audience the chance to develop what C. Wright Mills (1959, quoted in Richardson, 1995, p. 216) calls the "sociological imagination" by considering the social context around which personal experiences have been framed. Indeed, "people everywhere experience and interpret their lives in relation to time," and they are better able to "gauge their 'own fates'" when writing helps them to understand the sociohistorical context of their lives (Richardson, 1995, pp. 207, 215). Mills considers this to be the promise of sociology and illustrates how writing can take on different meanings for different people.

Researchers like Laurel Richardson (1995), who advocates the use of the narrative as a means of sociological communication, also contribute to the so-called blurring of social reality. In her discussion of the narrative as a useful mode of "reasoning and representation," Richardson argues that we should consider alternative forms of writing (p. 200). To dismiss the narrative as a channel of expressing social experiences is to do a great disservice to all of society. Writing in the social sciences influences public discussions of politics, policy, identity, and transformation, and the narrative can be influential and helpful in guiding these debates.

According to Richardson (1995), the narrative form tells a story that "reflect[s] the universal human experience of time and link[s] the past, present, and future" (p. 218). By combining literature with history and the individual with the communal, the narrative makes "individuals, cultures, societies, and historical epochs comprehensible as wholes" (p. 200) while helping people to see themselves as part of a larger system. In this way, the narrative can stimulate liberating civic discussions about important social concerns because it encourages readers to use their "sociological imaginations" to "reveal personal problems as public issues, to make possible collective identity and collective solutions" (p. 216).

Narrative accounts are becoming increasingly popular with researchers, and experimental methods of interpreting society through writing have created new styles of sociological accounts. Researchers are using narrative accounts of everyday life, real-life dialogue, multiple points of view, and a plain, sparse style to convey the interpretive voice of the writer (Harrington, 1997, as cited in Denzin, 2000, p. 899; see also Denzin, 2000, p. 902). Writers may be present as either narrator or participant or invisible in the text, but at all moments, their perspective is being communicated. They are producing a "symbolic tale, a parable that is not just a record of human experience" (Denzin, 2000, p. 902). This tale is an important key to the research process, for it helps the reader and the researcher discover ethical truths and multiple points of view on a particular issue.

These new writing practices have also made great strides in capturing the essence of some of society's lost voices. Women, for instance, have long been silenced in ethnographic studies, and partiality has often been given to male studies (Clough, as cited in Van Maanen, 1995, p. 2). Recent attention to feminist issues has only begun to recognize the presence of women in society and the problems they continue to face today. It is only through research that action can now be taken to remedy such plights, and it is important that such writing on this kind of subject matter be continually forthcoming. The language and experiences of marginalized groups must be actualized and discussed in words so that an increased level of social consciousness can be raised.

As Denzin (2000) notes, such writing demonstrates an "affectionate concern for the lives of people" (p. 899), and it is through this type of writing that social change can be propelled. The language of the author can produce it, but the experiences of "the other" can guide this process. Both voices will undoubtedly be interwoven into the script, and they will ultimately work together to empower those who need to break the piercing silence of the past.

CONCLUSION

As I end this chapter, I provide you with a checklist you might consult as you begin to undertake your research project. This list of questions is not exhaustive but is meant to highlight some of the important factors you might consider in undertaking your own evaluation of your research project as a whole.

Evaluation Checklist of Questions to Consider as You Evaluate Your Research Project (Hesse-Biber & Leavy, 2006)

Overall Research Question

Ask: Why should anyone "buy" your story? Trust your story?

Issues of Credibility

Ask: What are some of the criteria for assessing the validity of your research study? Do participants recognize their own experiences in your analysis and interpretation of the data? Why or why not? Do you provide an "audit trail" of your work? Can the reader follow the analytical steps you provide as evidence of credibility?

Data Collection

Ask: Do the data fit the research question?

Method

Ask: Is method compatible with purpose (research question)? How thoroughly and well are your data collection strategies described?

Sample

How were respondents chosen? Are these respondents a valid choice for this research?

Ethics

Ask: How are human subjects issues dealt with?

Analysis

Ask: How did you arrive at your specific findings? Are specific analysis strategies talked about? Have you done what you said you would do? Are data analysis approaches compatible with your research question?

Interpretation

Ask: Can the reader get a sense (gestalt) of the meaning of your data from your written findings? Are your research findings placed in context of the literature on the topic? Does the evidence fit your data? Are the data congruent with your research question?

Conclusions/Recommendations

Ask: Do the conclusions reflect your research findings? Do you provide some recommendations for future research?

Significance of Your Work

Ask: What is the significance of your research?

This chapter has illustrated how the iterative, or "back and forth," process of research is somewhat like fitting together the pieces of a puzzle. A few bits of data can go a long way in gathering meaning, but one should not be tempted to gather too much data while failing to reflect on the information bit by bit. A creative spirit and a set of analytical and interpretative skills are imperative to this process. Coding and memoing are two powerful techniques you might employ to the process of understanding and interpreting your data. You may encounter false starts as well as moments of great discovery and generation of theoretical insights into the analysis and interpretation of your data. This type of work is not for the "fainthearted," and it often requires attention to detail, perseverance in the face of chaos, and a knack for tolerating ambiguity. The writing up of your research also requires that you, the researcher, be reflective of your own positionality—the set of social and economic attributes you bring to bear in analyzing and interpreting your data. It is a journey well worth taking, for it ultimately leads to our better understanding and capturing of the lived reality of those whom we research.

For feminists, this journey is always bound to and guided by a set of principles, commitments, and concerns that extend beyond their own particular research projects. For feminist researchers, the knowledge-building process is necessarily linked to a commitment to unearthing the knowledge of women and others who have historically been marginalized. For us, the journey is a site where the personal and political merge and multiple truths are discovered and voiced where there had once been silence.

As our journey comes to an end, Patricia Leavy and I hope that your ride has been insightful, and we believe that the perspectives and tools we have provided you with will come in handy as you begin your journey down life's pathways, back roads, and uncharted terrain.

REFERENCES

Brown, Lyn M., & Gilligan, Carol. (1992). *Meeting at the crossroads.* Cambridge, MA: Harvard University Press.

Brown, Lyn M., Tappan, Mark, Gilligan, Carol, Miller, Barbara, & Argyris, Dianne. (1989). Reading for self and moral voice: A method for interpreting narratives of real-life moral conflict and choice. In Martin Packer & Richard Addison (Eds.), *Entering the circle: Hermeneutic investigation in psychology* (pp. 141–164). Albany: State University of New York Press.

Charmaz, Kathy. (1983). The grounded theory method: An explication and interpretation. In Robert M. Emerson (Ed.), *Contemporary field research: A collection of readings* (pp. 109–126). Prospect Heights, IL: Waveland Press.

Charmaz, Kathy. (1995). Grounded theory. In Jonathan Smith, Rom Harre, & Luk Van Langenhove (Eds.), *Rethinking methods in psychology* (pp. 27–49). London: Sage.

Denzin, Norman K. (2000). The practices and politics of interpretation. In Norman Denzin & Yvonna Lincoln (Eds.), *Handbook of qualitative research* (pp. 897–922). Thousand Oaks, CA: Sage.

Fielding, Nigel, & Lee, Raymond. (1998). Introduction: Computer analysis and qualitative research. In *Computer analysis and qualitative research*. London: Sage.

Hesse-Biber, Sharlene Nagy, & Leavy, Patricia. (2004). *Approaches to qualitative research: A reader on theory and practice.* New York: Oxford University Press.

Hesse-Biber, Sharlene Nagy, & Leavy, Patricia. (2006). *The practice of qualitative research.* Thousand Oaks, CA: Sage.

Jack, Dana C. (1991). *Silencing the self: Women and depression.* Cambridge, MA: Harvard University Press.

Jack, Dana C. (1999). *Behind the mask: Destruction and creativity in women's aggression.* Cambridge, MA: Harvard University Press.

Jack, Dana C. (2001). Understanding women's anger: A description of relational patterns. *Health Care for Women International, 22*(Special issue), 385–400.

Lemert, Charles. (Ed.). (1999). *Social theory: The multicultural and classic readings* (2nd ed.). Boulder: Westview Press.

Lorde, Audre. (1984). *Sister outsider: Essays and speeches* (The Crossing Press Feminist Series). Trumansburg, NY: Crossing Press.

Rich, Adrienne C. (1979). *On lies, secrets, and silence: Selected prose, 1966–1978.* New York: Norton.

Richardson, Laurel. (1995). Narrative and sociology. In John Van Maanen (Ed.), *Representation in ethnography* (pp. 198–221). Thousand Oaks, CA: Sage.

Spielberger, Charles D., Johnson, E. H., Russell, S. F., Crane, R. J., Jacobs, G. A., & Worden, T. I. (1985). The experience and expression of anger: Construction and validation of an anger expression scale. In Margaret A. Chesney & Ray H. Rosenman (Eds.), *Anger and hostility in cardiovascular and behavioral disorders* (pp. 5–30). New York: Hemisphere/McGraw-Hill.

Strauss, Anselm, & Corbin, Juliet. (1990). *Basics of qualitative research: Grounded theory procedures and techniques.* Newbury Park, CA: Sage.

Van Maanen, John. (1995). An end to innocence: The ethnography of ethnography. In John Van Maanen (Ed.), *Representation in ethnography* (pp. 1–35). Thousand Oaks, CA: Sage.

INDEX